American Jewish Political Culture
and the Liberal Persuasion

Modern Jewish History
Henry Feingold, *Series Editor*

American Jewish Political Culture

AND THE Liberal
Persuasion

HENRY L. FEINGOLD

SYRACUSE UNIVERSITY PRESS

For a listing of books published and distributed by Syracuse University Press,
visit our website at www.SyracuseUniversityPress.syr.edu.

ISBN: 978-0-8156-1025-0 (cloth)   978-0-8156-5244-1 (e-book)

Library of Congress Cataloging-in-Publicaton Data
Feingold, Henry L., 1931– author.
American Jewish political culture and the liberal persuasion /
Henry L. Feingold. — First Edition.
pages cm. — (Modern Jewish history)
Includes bibliographical references and index.
ISBN 978-0-8156-1025-0 (cloth : alk. paper) — ISBN 978-0-8156-5244-1 (e-book)
1. Jews—United States—History—20th century.   2. Jews—United States—
History—21st century.   3. Jews—United States—Identity.   4. Jews—United
States—Attitudes toward Israel.   5. Jews—United States—Politics and government.
6. United States—Ethnic relations.   I. Title.
E184.354.F45 2014
973'.04924—dc23   2013035776

Manufactured in the United States of America

This study is dedicated to Clio,
who, like her namesake, the muse of history,
inspired its writing with her joyful presence.

Henry L. Feingold is Professor of History Emeritus, formerly of Baruch College and the Graduate Center of the City University of New York. Among other works, he is the author of *Silent No More: Saving the Jews of Russia, The American Effort, 1967–1989*; *Bearing Witness: How America and Its Jews Responded to the Holocaust*; and *A Time for Searching: Entering the Mainstream, 1920–1945*, a volume in his highly acclaimed five-volume series, *The Jewish People In America*.

Contents

Preface

Another election season has passed and again Republican political leaders raised high hopes that this time the Democratic hold on the Jewish electorate would be broken, and again they were disappointed. Unlike the descendants of the immigrants with whom his forebearers entered the country, the contemporary Jewish voter remains consistently loyal to the Democratic Party whose left wing has given shelter to his liberalism since the heady years of the New Deal. It was Franklin Roosevelt who, more than any other president, brought Jewry into the American political arena and transformed the Jewish immigrant voter to one of the most politically engaged citizens of the republic. Searching for the sources of that engagement in the political culture of American Jewry is the subject of this book.

To succeed in that endeavor some knowledge of the historical context of Jewish political development is required. The reader will find such historical episodes throughout this book and especially in the first chapter. But the reader is cautioned that this discussion is not intended as a history of American Jewish political culture. Rather, it is focused on how a major factor in that culture, its liberalism, gave it its distinct place in national politics. It situated the Jewish electorate astride the principle axis of American politics, what role government should play in the management of the economy and beyond that in the larger society. It is the issue that holds the major place in the American political dialogue since the New Deal. That quest places it at some distance from the way a political scientist, armed with statistics and polls predicting voting patterns, presents a picture of how Jewish voters behaved collectively but can tell us little about the American Jewish political psyche, where the secrets of political behavior are buried. The hope is that we will find a clue to the prominent role

American Jewry continues to play in American politics while the ethnic voting blocs with whom it entered the political arena in numbers at the turn of the twentieth century have grown virtually silent. The findings of the political scientist concerning such matters as determining the weight of the Jewish vote in five "pivotal states" or the role of Jewish "fat cats" in campaign financing and even the tradition of political activism are not discounted in this study. While writing, I sometimes wished that there existed a discipline that does for the politics of ethnic communities what the psychoanalyst does for his clients. I speak not of a cure for troubled behavior but an explanation of it. The reader will undoubtedly become aware that at some rare moments in this discussion I found myself, with some trepidation, assuming such a position. I emerged a little worse for wear but with an image of an incredibly complex yet also resilient political persona.

To gain insight into that persona I have utilized three major concerns that in different ways help drive American Jewish political culture. The first is its broadly defined liberalism composed of several historic layers superimposed on one another, and viewed here as being more than merely a point slightly left of center on the political spectrum. It encompasses so many sometimes contradictory principles that it goes beyond being a political ideology to resemble a deeply held secular faith. At its heart is the conviction of the majority of Jewish voters that the role of government is to improve the lot of its citizenry. Those who are perplexed by the refusal of American Jewish voters to abandon it seem unaware of its deep roots in exilic history that requires governance to be especially protective of the strangers who live among them. It is as if Jews in America cannot forget what it means to be "strangers in the land."

The second concern involves the Jewish homeland, Israel, which represents at once their assurance of survival as a people and the hope for renewal. The American Jewish tie to Israel places it in the middle of one of the most intractable and threatening problems in international relations that has required the most sustained deployment of American Jewish political influence. Surprisingly the polls inform us of a deepening gulf between liberal American Jews and the Likud-controlled government of Israel. The universalistic element in Jewish liberalism increasingly places it in conflict with the nationalism generated by a beleaguered Israel. Wilsonian liberals who favored fulfilling the hopes of people, especially their right of national self-determination, only vaguely foresaw the possibility that two related people, Jews and Palestinians, would lay claim to the same land, nor could leaders of the newborn Zionist movement foresee that the liberalism that prevailed during the post–World War I years would be at odds with the liberalism of the post–World War II decade, which focused on ending colonial empires.

Third is American Jewry's obsession with the Holocaust. It is the only voting bloc that witnessed directly and indirectly the radical losses of its kin mandated by public policy of a modern nation-state. The Jewish voter has living evidence in the survivors that have settled among them that the European world conspired against their presence. More than most voting constituencies, Jews are exquisitely aware of what can go awry even in the most civilized of societies. They carry that catastrophe perspective into the political arena.

Each element of this triad has its own historical resonance and weight. They are not always in harmony, so that the historical voice of the American Jewish electorate sometimes sounds like a cacophony emanating from the different centers of community politics. We witness that in its response to the Holocaust and today in its response to the Middle East crises. Liberalism, which boasts the most sustained shaping influence on the Jewish political mindset, often puts Holocaust consciousness and concern about the security of Israel to the test. The advantage of this triple focus is that it allows for the inclusion of virtually all the issues and interactions that today form the substance of American Jewish political culture. It not only opens a path that allows us to probe the context in which the conflicts confronting the Jewish voter are imbedded but also deals with the crucial broad-ranging issues that drive the Jewish political dialogue forward.

The issues considered here include the entire political dialogue confronting the American electorate. For the Jewish voter they vary considerably in importance. Included may be issues as seemingly insignificant as a scandal in the national game of baseball to the contretemps over same-sex marriage. Even if such mundane matters do not necessarily come to a vote there is usually a tangible Jewish political presence on most issues in the political arena. The ballot is far from the only finger-print of a group's political persona. Political pundits, for example, cannot remain unaware that the Jewish voter was overwhelmingly in favor of government-supported stem cell research but has mixed feelings about same-sex marriage. The Orthodox minority is joined by many other Jew-ish voters in its opposition to *Roe v. Wade*. Liberal Jewish voters who are passionate about the separation of church and state can be nevertheless attracted to "faith-based" government-sponsored entitlement programs. The most telling evidence of the varied composition of the Jewish politi-cal voice is its frequent lack of internal consistency.

A word on the organization of this study. Though hundreds of surveys and polls on Jewish political behavior are available on the Internet, I have where possible paraphrased the findings and mostly confined the frequently uncertain and contradictory numbers and percentages to foot-notes. There is some doubt about their accuracy and the reality that such statistics can reveal about the Jewish political persona. Records of voting behavior are in any case not terribly reliable until the years immediately preceding World War II, and often the announcement of how a voting bloc will cast its ballots are based on prior records that have themselves become an instrument of campaign politics. For example, the Jewish vote is said to have played a crucial role in the much-touted Truman victory in the election of 1948. The 75 percent of the Jewish vote that was supposedly given to Harry Truman was in appreciation of his early diplomatic recog-nition of Israel. Truman did narrowly win the election, but not necessarily with the help of the Jewish vote, 14 percent of which went to Henry Wal-lace in New York state. Yet any study that purports to deal with Jewish political culture is compelled to refer to voting statistics, though one soon realizes that the emerging picture of Jewish political culture gathered from them is incomplete and often misleading. As a historian I prefer a time exposure offered by history to the statistical snapshot presented by political scientists.

The study itself is presented in seven chapters. We begin with an introductory chapter in which the broad outline and content of Jewish political culture is explored. Chapters follow that deal with liberalism, Zionism/Israel, sometimes called Israelism after 1948, and the Holocaust. Each chapter is further divided into numerous subsections to probe the various aspects these visions have assumed over time and the complex interaction between them. The tapestry that emerges shows a culture of great complexity and a political voice that often lacks coherence. The weakening of Jewish communal ties makes it seem like the political arena is filled with many Jewish voices. In years to come it may no longer be possible to determine what precisely is Jewish and what is American about Jewish political behavior. For the moment its defining core is embodied in liberalism and its interaction with Zionism and Holocaust consciousness. Historians-to-be may need to find new prisms through which to view the changing political behavior of American Jewry.

The final chapter includes a projection of the dilemmas, fears, and hopes the politically highly engaged Jewish electorate may face in the fast-changing world of the twenty-first century. Indeed, I dare contemplate whether there will be a role to play and an American Jewish community sufficiently cohesive and coherent to play it. I realize that it is the riskiest aspect of this study and offer these thoughts with some trepidation. I hope the detached spirit I have tried but not always succeeded to muster will somehow conceal my personal political passions. Those readers who are familiar with my work are aware that these are issues about which I care deeply. I am uncertain about the political future of American Jewry. Indeed, if I were a poet this study might take the form of a lament.

I do not intend this work to be a chronological study of Jewish political behavior, nor is it intended to be an all-inclusive scholarly monograph. Unlike my prior work, it is based primarily on relevant secondary monographs. Relevant sources and surveys are deployed where they are needed, but a good part of the discussion is drawn from my personal notes gleaned from prior writings and lectures over the course of thirty-five years of teaching and lecturing about the American Jewish experience. The narrative assumes the form of a sustained discussion in essay form, as one might find in political magazines such as *Commentary* and *The New York Review of Books*. The research apparatus is kept to a minimum. There are three types of footnotes. The first and most important are notes that add additional information and argumentation that would impede the flow of the narrative but may be of interest to the reader, as they were to me. The second type of note is used in those rare instances when I quote or closely paraphrase a source. Such notes end with a page reference. The third type of note is bibliographical. I cite studies and articles that may take the reader further into the subject if desired or indicate what others have said on a particular point. In order to allow the reader to pick and choose and avoid complications, chapters are divided into titled subsections, and if that is not sufficient to kill the reader with kindness, two additional subdivisions follow. A series of three asterisk signals a transition to a new aspect of the theme and double spacing of a section tells readers that they are being transmitted to yet a smaller part of the whole.

Organizing the discussion on the basis of a triad of influences inevitably creates a threesome when the Jewish political persona, much like a braid of hair, is in fact one. It is an organizational device that gives the discussion a certain shape and focus but also risks some repetition. In the hope that it helps make things clearer I have occasionally allowed such repetition and reminded the reader that this point was touched on earlier in another context. Sometimes it helps the author too.

This study deals with American Jewish political culture, viewed here as the political persona emanating from an identifiable community. It goes beyond the normal telltale signs of political behavior reflected in its voting on political issues or candidates for office. I assume that what tells us most about why a community votes one way and not another can best be found by mining its communal history. The reason why Jewish voters demonstrate an extra sensitivity to genocide or why they display a special affinity for certain liberal candidates for office lies buried in a communal history waiting to be dug up. Nor are Jewish voters exempt from favorable and unfavorable public images of officeholders. Their normal voting patterns were turned almost upside down when it came to the candidacy of "Ike" Eisenhower in 1952 or Ronald Reagan in 1980. I believe that *chochma*, a Hebrew/Yiddish term denoting intelligence and beyond, has an especially deep impact on Jewish voters. I am aware that going beyond statistics to probe communal historic experience and even the communal psyche is not an exact science. I deal here with what the computer cannot do. It cannot tell us or even speculate about the reason why the statistics fall the way they do. Yet it is in that speculation that we come nearer to understanding the soul or psyche of the group. Such searching to find and explain American Jewry's political soul is not an easy task and there are many pitfalls. A group's political culture is like a fingerprint, it is infinitely variable. I would be satisfied if this study reveals at least some of what makes the American Jewish voter tick. The unexplained responses, and there are many, I leave to future researchers. I believe that there is an element in Jewish communalism from which its political culture springs that remains forever a mystery, but that is a subject for rabbis and theologians who have the comfort of believing that they possess a total explanation of why the Jews are the way they are. Students of American Jewish political culture can muster no such confidence.

American Jewish Political Culture and the Liberal Persuasion

1

Jewish Political Culture

The American Wrinkle

It does not take long to discover that while pundits ponder the importance of the Jewish vote in practice it is difficult to identify a collective Jewish political identity other than the fact that there are ballots cast by voters whose names and voting districts indicate that they may be Jewish. Moreover, while researchers may agree that politics focuses on the relationship of power to governance, there is little agreement on what might be included within the definition of the term "political culture."[1] Voting surveys do not deal with the fact that deep economic, cultural, and religious fissures characterize Jewish communal politics. Only for the researcher is the Jewish voter simply another ethnic vote for the statistical tables. A Jewish member of a Hassidic sect in Williamsburg, Brooklyn, casts his ballot far differently than a voter residing in the Park Slope section of the same borough. Yet, that American Jewry has a specific political presence in the polity is undeniable. Ask any political campaign manager.

Defining Political Culture

Our task is to identify it and find the role it plays in American politics. To do that we must first define what we mean by political culture. As suggested in the preface, political culture generally is shaped by historically derived collective values and assumptions about the nature and value of human society. Others may prefer to define it as a communal or tribal political personality. As used in this discussion the term refers to those things of habit and style developed by historical circumstance that shape

1

the aspirations, goals, and political strategies of a particular political collectivity. In a word, the community carries into the political arena habits
and values developed over time through a kind of collective reaction formation to its historical experience.

In the case of Jews, or for that matter any political collectivity, there
are recognizable habits and customs that account for behavior in the
political arena. That may come as a surprise to the highly individuated,
independent-minded Jewish voter who enters the voting booth to pull the
levers favoring his or her choices only to be informed by exit polls that
these choices were the same for the majority of other Jewish voters, as if
commanded by some tribal chieftain. Despite enormous communal variations pollsters have been able to identify a specific Jewish political profile.
The broader the voting electorate, the more distinct becomes the Jewish
political voice. In relation to a domestic issue like government support of
stem-cell research the Jewish political identity is unmistakable, as it is in
its support of Israel.

Conditioned by different historical experiences, the political cultures
of national communities are as varied as fingerprints. Our assumption
about other groups attests to that. For example, there exists an assumption
that Russia can never develop a democracy in the Western sense. It must
first be ruled in order to be governed, so that whatever governing system
prevails Russians will always prefer an authoritarian government.[2] On
the other hand, wherever Britain has imposed her control the rule of law
prevails. America sees itself as a singular bearer of the mission of democracy, which views overweening government authority as threatening. In
contrast, prewar Germany favored the direct intrusion of government
power so that a much-desired "order" might prevail. The Japanese think
of themselves as a small, beleaguered island nation, which prefers to
attack on the Christian Sunday without declaring war in order to assure
an even playing field.[3]

Of course such observations skew the image of a political culture
because they give too much weight to seeming truths that have come
down through history sometimes in the form of myths. Not all Germans
preferred to command and be commanded and there are many Russians who yearned to be self-ruling. Similarly, not all Americans consider

unchecked government power to be demonic and rue the failure to regulate Wall Street. English imperial governance was often tyrannical and few would accuse the Japanese of lacking martial courage. But while such caricatures can give the reader an idea of the wide variation between particular political cultures, they tell us little about the binding actual values and visions shared within communities that actually define why a political community feels the need for an independent existence. We shall note later that these special conditions and the values they bring to the fore are particularly evident in American Jewish political culture, which is generated by a community that does not exercise political power directly. American Jewry has had to develop a political personality to deal with the duality of belonging to two separate historical streams and not being fully empowered in either. It makes the recent attention given to the discovery of inordinate Jewish power exercised in the making of American foreign policy so difficult to reconcile to the reality of its condition. At the same time we will have opportunity to note that duality goes far to explain the popularity of liberal humanistic ideals that continue to prevail in the community.

More problematic still is how to determine who speaks for the collectivity, who controls its voice. We can never know precisely who speaks for Jewish or for Italian Americans or any ethnic voting bloc. Its most revealing signs are reflected in a group's general voting behavior rather than in the fiat of some interest group like AIPAC (American Israel Political Action Committee) that wants to speak for it on a particular issue. No matter how highly ethnic or other than ethnic political communities are organized, none possesses the legal authority to speak for the entire community. The instances when a communal voice has been preempted are so numerous as to appear almost to be the norm. For example, the Jewish support for environmental programs or its passion for federally sponsored stem-cell research is well known. But it is only an anecdotal consensus not legitimatized by democratically elected communal governance. The Jewish voter did not directly vote for stem-cell research, though he or she might have supported candidates who did. We have no instrument to determine ethnic interests and agendas. German Americans did not necessarily agree with the activities of Fritz Kuhn's Bund during the thirties and Italian

Americans may not have been offended by Roosevelt's "hand that held the dagger speech" after Mussolini's invasion of France in June 1940. Even American Catholics who came closer to having formal governance through the church did not necessarily fully comply with the mandate of the church hierarchy. Given the turbulence of Jewish communal politics and their historically contested governance threshold, the case for the delivery of a Jewish vote is even less imaginable.

Historical Roots of American Jewish Political Culture

Before its American experience, Jewish communities had survived for millennia in hostile host nations by fulfilling certain essential roles ranging from the production of spermaceti oil, an offshoot of the Jewish role in the whaling industry in colonial America, to finishing furs and leather for clothing. A reputation for astuteness in business preceded the arrival of Jews in New Amsterdam. Sometimes knowledge of Hebrew, still in use for prayer, created a special wonder, if not an affinity, for Jews as "the people of the book." From its place names, which read like a biblical atlas, to its religious beliefs modeled on those believed to have prevailed in ancient Israel, early colonial American society envisaged itself as Hebraic. Their belief that the general colonial community-building experience was based on a reenactment of the biblical model created the sense that there existed an ancient link between the two faiths. To be sure, it was a Hebraism projected through a Christian lens that sometimes also proffered slanderous calumny, making Jewish immigrants feel unwelcome. The Christian piety of Peter Stuyvesant, who received the first contingent of Sephardic Jewish immigrants from Recife in September 1654, found little that was worthy about these members of a "deceitful race," the appellative for Jews he used in his complaining correspondence with his company headquarters in Amsterdam about the arrival of Jewish settlers.

Like most strangers in a strange land, Jews were resilient and developed a survival strategy that sought sufficient space to preserve their own distinctive culture while at the same time complying with the requirements of a religiously prescribed host culture. Aside from becoming taxpayers and insisting on serving the "watch and ward" duty that provided security in New Amsterdam, they became merchants and traders who provided a commercial link to the outside world, especially the preexisting Jewish settlements in the Caribbean. Colonial Jewry did not only argue that the full rights of citizenship ought to be granted to them as a matter of natural rights. They also traded on the prevailing anti-Semitic caricature that acceptance of the Jews would stimulate commercial development.[4] Jews became prominently involved in the twentieth century with the fight for civil rights, but certain peculiarities might already have been noted during the colonial period. Jews first aligned themselves with the Federalist Party and after the French Revolution initiated a wave of democratic reforms; the majority became adherents of Jefferson's Democratic Republican Party despite the fact that the party was basically oriented toward agriculture rather than the commercial sector with which Jews had cast their lot and that self-interest would have dictated.

Despite the prevalence anti-Semitism found in all Christian societies, conditions in the colonies were superior compared with the Christian states of Europe from which they came. In the late twentieth century it would be the openness of the American host culture rather than intolerance that posed the greater threat to Jewish communal survival. During the colonial and early national periods religious observance had not yet felt the full impact generated by the free spirit of secularism. Communal cohesion was partly rooted in the need to comply with the myriad religious laws, such as the requirement of a separate cemetery plot and a place for the religious congregation to meet for religious services. The need for a Torah scroll could serve as the source of a connection with a distant, more established Jewish community. But some rules, such as the requirement for kosher food and ritual slaughter supervision (kashrut and shechita), and religious marriages and circumcision, were more difficult to observe and often had to be modified to meet the special conditions in the New World.

The interaction that took place in commerce and increasingly in social life was not easily controlled in a society that was relatively open. Since large seaboard towns like New Amsterdam were from the outset remarkably ethnically and racially diverse, colonial Jewry was comparatively successful in retaining its separate culture space while sharing much they had in common with the already highly variegated population of the five larger seaboard towns that composed the core of colonial life. In the potentially divisive political arena differences were not so easily reconciled, since standard anti-Semitic barbs were used by both parties. Difficulty in adhering to the myriad religious regulations combined with a comparative openness, especially in the commercial sphere, became major forces deepening early Jewish cultural and political interaction with their Christian neighbors. By the time of the arrival of the rustic, young, mostly Bavarian Jewish settlers during the second decade of the nineteenth century, the dominant Sephardic Jewish community was already involved in the consuming political issue concerning the vexing question of whether slavery should be allowed to gain a foothold in the new West.

The projection of a distinctly Jewish political voice can be detected in the earliest days of the Jewish settlement. It suggested an early willingness to share in the communal obligations for security. Peter Stuyvesant, who included Jews together with Catholics and Quakers as undesirable settlers whom he preferred to exclude from burgher rights, exempted Jews from "watch and ward" guard duty. Instead of the obligation to perform such duty a tax would be levied against them. After considerable petitioning, Jews wrested the right to fulfill the "watch and ward" obligation. They seemed to have understood that belonging to the polity of New Amsterdam meant allowing no onerous distinctions to be drawn. Endenization, to which they aspired, required fulfilling all communal obligations as well as sharing the privileges of the community. It is mentioned here to show that Jews were not slow to insist on equality of status. Such victories did not imply that Jews would thenceforth be free from discrimination. As late as December 1862 a special order was issued by the Union army high command ordering Jews to be evacuated in mass from the Tennessee department that straddled the border between the Union and the Confederacy. The charge was that Jews were involved in trading with the enemy.[5] Lincoln rescinded General Order no. 11 on March 3, 1863, after a personal appeal by Cesar Kaskel, the Jewish president of Paducah's Union League. It is the only incident of collective punishment of Jews in American history. Kaskel's visit to the Oval Office to plead a special Jewish case established a pattern of going directly to top national political leaders. The path

to the Oval Office would become well known among later Jewish petition-
ers, but Kaskel's success in getting the order rescinded was not repeated at
the time. The law limiting military chaplains to Christian denominations
was not amended until July 1862 and no rabbis ever succeeded to the post
during the war years.

By the 1840s Jews had mastered many of the political skills required
for advocacy. It occurred most frequently over the perennial need for aiding Jewish communities abroad. The Damascus blood libel (1840) was one
of the earliest documented cases where Jewish communal leaders turned
to the administration for diplomatic intercession. Thereafter virtually
every crisis faced by Jewish communities abroad brought pleas for such
intercession from communal leaders. American political leaders were
willing to pen such diplomatic notes of concern provided there was no
political price to be paid. There rarely was, so that requests for diplomatic
intercession in the Mortara kidnapping case (1858) and the depredations
in Romania and tsarist Russia were granted as a matter of course and
today compose a sizeable portion of the archival evidence researchers use
to trace the outlines of American Jewish political concerns abroad.[6] Petitioning government authorities for redress, as in the General Order no.
11 case, or more likely for diplomatic intercession, as in the Damascus
case, developed into the major instrument of Jewish advocacy. The archival record of such requests allows the researcher to learn what concerned
Jewish leaders and to estimate the strength of the ties to world Jewry,
which was a primary interest in Jewish communal politics.

The years during which the precedent for seeking government intercession and otherwise involvement in domestic politics was established
correspond roughly to the Sephardic and German periods of the eighteenth and nineteenth centuries. During the Sephardic settlement, which
dominated Jewish life in the colonial through the Jacksonian period, Jewish political activity remained fairly low-key. Though numerically much
larger than the earlier Sephardic immigration, the young Jews of Bavaria
and Posen who began to arrive after 1820 took some of their political cues
from the larger non-Jewish German migration whose '48ers became known
for their liberalism.[7] Preoccupied with establishing themselves, the quarter-million German Jews who settled after 1820 did not project a distinct

political voice. The question of the expansion of slavery at the center of antebellum politics was predictably framed in an Old Testament context, which meant that willy-nilly the people of the book were assumed to have a special guiding insight. But eschewing such an elevated position, Jewish voters preferred to adopt the protective political coloration of the local regions in which they lived. To be sure there were Jewish abolitionists like Rabbi David Einhorn of Baltimore and August Bondi, who marched with John Brown in "Bloody" Kansas. Jews fought on both sides during the Civil War and suffered the customary canards regarding their valor on the battlefield. Some might argue that with names like Judah P. Benjamin and Senator Yulee of Florida holding high decision-making positions in the Confederacy, Jews were better represented in the Confederacy. In a sense that was true, since Jews were proportionately a much smaller part of the community in the South.

It is difficult to determine the reason for the easier accommodation of German Jews to the new land compared to the later mass arrival of the Eastern Jews in the final decades of the nineteenth century. Letters and diaries of Jewish peddlers attest to the reality that anti-Semitism was alive and well, especially in the rural areas of the country. The rapid increase of the general population and their comparative political quietude may have made these German Jews a difficult target for a special animus. Their youth and poor religious training may also have made them more flexible and willing to fraternize with non-Jews. In any case, with the exception of the heavy German accent that was the source of constant teasing the gulf between Jews and non-Jews seems to have been more negotiable for the German Jews of the nineteenth century compared with later arrivals from Eastern Europe. They also came in smaller numbers, did not concentrate in the larger cities of the eastern seaboard, and were not easily distinguished from the larger non-Jewish German immigration of which they were part.

During the Sephardic and German Jewish phase, the small Jewish community shared an interest in the major domestic political interests of the day, which ranged from the question of the Louisiana Purchase to the War of 1812, to the various issues involving the expansion of the plantation system. But even after the Mexican War (1846) and the Civil War (1860-1865), the United States remained a minor power primarily concerned with its internal development and, unlike the case in the twentieth century, welcoming to most immigrants, including Jews. Events abroad played a minor role until the Spanish-American War (1898) awakened an interest in empire. As citizens Jews took an active interest in these issues. They were as torn on the prime issue of slavery and the Civil War to which it gave birth as any other voting block in the polity, perhaps more so since, as suggested earlier, for an uncommonly religious electorate the moral validity of the slave system was in some measure determined by what scripture had to say. That context gave the Jewish electorate an uncommon prominence. But for the most part, with the exception of the immigration issue, the American Jewish interest in American politics tilted toward foreign policy issues that were not yet of prime concern in the young republic. That orientation was understandable. Jews were an immigrant community with an abiding concern for their often-beleaguered kin abroad. Unlike other immigrant groups they were impacted by two streams of history, the preexisting Jewish stream and the American stream of their adopted land. That duality became a threat when their opponents later used it to level the charge of dual loyalty against them.

This necessarily cursory outline of eighteenth-century Jewish political behavior should not be taken as a reflection of passivity on the part of the Jewish electorate. That would have been highly uncharacteristic. Jews were active in the colonial and antebellum polity. They favored the Whig pro-independence position during the revolutionary period, though there were prominent loyalists like the David Franks family of Philadelphia and the Harts and Pollocks of Newport. Generally they mostly favored the movement to sever ties with Britain and, in case of Boston and New York, the communities chose resettlement rather than live under British occupation. Despite their involvement in commerce and despite Jefferson's broad deism, which generated distaste for Judaism as a medieval tribal superstition, Jews, if they were aware of Jefferson's distaste, did not make much of it. The preference for Jefferson serves as early evidence that the liberal disposition that led the Jewish electorate to vote against their pocketbook interests, furthered by Hamilton's financial program in favor of a federal program supporting an economy based on agriculture, preceded the arrival of the later eastern Jewish immigration. The practice of not "voting their pocketbooks," thought to be characteristic of contemporary Jewish political culture, preceded the arrival of the Socialist-oriented Jews of eastern Europe.[8]

During the Jacksonian period (1828-1836), to the extent that their preferences were discernable, Jews were both for and against the Bank of the United States. Gradually there developed from the disparate elements a sense of communal interest requisite to petition government to intercede for their religious brethren abroad and, as we note below, they produced several remarkable political personalities to do so. But by dint of numbers, which are crucial in measuring political weight in a democracy, Jews were concerned primarily with establishing themselves economically. One rarely heard apprehensiveness about the "Jewish vote" before the turn of the century. The eastern immigration that began in earnest in the final decades of the nineteenth century completed the shaping of the American Jewish political persona. It gave the Jewish electorate numbers and a kind of political engagement that made its influence felt on the local as well as the national level.

While it is difficult to trace Jewish political voting patterns that might indicate the existence of a communal political culture before the arrival of the mass migrations from Eastern Europe, there existed prominent Jews who can serve as a prism through which to view the challenges Jews faced in entering politics. As the first high-ranking Jewish naval officer, Commodore Uriah P. Levi (1792-1862) holds a special place in the scroll of heroes in American Jewish history. He did not easily come by the rank of commodore, the equivalent of today's rank of admiral. Levi's Jewish faith, which he wore proudly, and his activities in trying to bring disciplinary flogging to a halt, culminating in the pathbreaking antiflogging bill of 1850, did not earn him medals for popularity among the officer class. He was court-martialed six times and twice dismissed from the service, only to be reinstated by a court of inquiry in 1855. Near the end of his career he was finally awarded the rank of commodore, then the highest rank in the United States Navy. His achievement was not limited to his naval career. He found sufficient time and energy to garner a personal fortune from speculating in New York City real estate. Some of his fortune was invested in purchasing Jefferson's neglected estate in Monticello. His feistiness and willingness to pit himself against existing authority is reminiscent of a later Jewish admiral, Hyman Rickover, who spearheaded the introduction of atomic power as the energy source for large naval vessels on a reluctant naval establishment in the 1960s. In the early writings of American Jewish history he is projected as at once an American patriot and a committed Jew, a combination of traits reflecting the aspirations of pre-twentieth-century American Jewry.[9]

Levi's distant cousin Mordecai Noah (1785-1851), whose career was more varied and closer to the centers of political power, displayed a similar fearlessness, which brought him to the highest political prominence of any American Jew in the nineteenth century.[10] He was offered and declined the post of American consul in Riga, and finally accepted a post as consul in Tunis, where he was purported to have helped break up the thriving trade in slaves. Like Levi, his career was plagued by anti-Semitism, which led to his removal as consul by James Madison, then secretary of state. These minor diplomatic positions were an early sign of his hyperactivity in the public arena. He became in fact an early prototype of the twentieth-century Jewish public-relations types, newspaper editors, publicists, and *fueilletonists*, and thereby wielders of political influence that sometimes extended to becoming holders of local political office. From 1817 to 1828 Noah was a Tammany Hall Sachem, the political machine that dominated New York City politics.[11] His remarkable public career was not limited to politics; he became a well-know playwright and author of fiction as well as a noted political pundit. Like Levi, Noah carried his religion proudly, but there is an added wrinkle in his remarkable venture in proto-Zionism. In 1825 he began to implement his plan for a Jewish settlement on Grand Island in the Niagara River near Buffalo. His plans for the settlement he called Ararat, after the biblical story of Noah's ark, were grandiose. Noah dreamed of a Zion in America. Perhaps the settlement would attract American Indians, whom he believed were remnants of the ten lost tribes. But Noah's enthusiasm for the well-publicized project waned almost before it started. He never attended the elaborate inaugural ceremonies and never set foot on the island itself. Whether the Ararat scheme reflected a general concern of the Jewish community or was merely evidence of Noah's overheated theatrical imagination is difficult to determine. Proto-Zionist schemes that viewed America as Zion were not uncommon in nineteenth-century America, nor was Noah the first American to conceive of bringing Jews to settle in America.[12]

But the primary interest in Levi and Noah and several other politically prominent Jews is that these early Jews who gained prominence in American politics were types not much in evidence in the Jewish community. They were fearless in their advocacy, whether it was prohibition of flogging or bringing Jews to the New World. There is little evidence of self-imposed limitations to professional careers, such as might have been found in other communities of the Jewish diaspora. They foreshadow a new Jewish independent political type who openly advocated a commonality between American and Jewish interests, a type that became prominent in the second half of the twentieth century, especially after the June war of 1967 when Jewish seekers of office became more able to win elected office on their own steam and less dependent on political appointment.[13]

The Genesis of Jewish Political Activism and the Immigration of East European Jews

The more intense political engagement of the Eastern Jewish immigrants grew out the eastern European soil from which they stemmed. It found its roots in the revolutionary atmosphere of eastern Europe, which in a strange way offered an ethnic identity associated with modernity to supplement and ultimately replace the diminishing religious one. The most active Zionists and Bundist thinkers and leaders were nourished by the revolutionary ferment of tsarist Russia and the Austro-Hungarian Empire. Preoccupied with establishing themselves economically in America, Jews of the eastern immigration first turned inward to their own communities to practice their distinct style of politics. Its best sons did not consider the machine politics of the American city a fitting career. The interest in the "who gets what" of local politics could not compete with the grand issues of revolution and reform involved in building a new society. The characteristic high voting volume in Jewish election districts is of comparatively recent vintage. In the early years of the twentieth century the almost all-Jewish election districts of the Lower East Side of New York and other Jewish ethnic enclaves had a comparatively low voter turnout or at least no higher then their immigrant neighbors from Italy or Poland. The deeper engagement of Jews with politics begins in earnest with the gradual conversion of the Jewish vote to the Democratic Party, which was completed in the election of 1928 when the Jewish vote went heavily for Al Smith. The high democratic voter turnout, which has remained a prime characteristic of Jewish political culture, became linked to the left wing of the Democrat Party with the election of Franklin Roosevelt in 1932.[14]

The revolutionary ferment that contributed to the politicization and in many cases radicalization of the Jews of western and central Russia was related to the turmoil that followed upon Russia's defeat in the Russo-Japanese War. The revolution of 1905 forever ended tsarist Russia's political stasis in favor of a period of often violent change. The American Jewish world, reeling from the impact of the Kishinev pogrom two years earlier, had already entered upon a period of political activism that fed into the public agitation of the October revolution. Still, living with a foot in the political world they had abandoned, the radicalization of American Jewry was deepened by the developments that exposed the internal weakness of Russia. The Russian masses massacred in the streets on Bloody Sunday in a vain attempt to overthrow the tsarist regime was perhaps felt almost as deeply in the Jewish political class developing in America as was the loss of Jewish life in Kishinev. The mistreatment of the Jews of Russia became a major plank in the communal agenda of American Jewry, whose major organizations were still dominated by German Jewish funding and leadership. Jacob Schiff, the German-born president of Kuhn Loeb, among the richest banking houses in the economy, was so passionately opposed to tsarist Russia joining the Allied side that he openly favored Germany even after April 1917, when the United States joined the Allied side.

The focus on the travail of Russian Jewry was a portent of change to come in Jewish communal politics. What was different about Jewish political culture was its remarkable strata of native American Jews, descendants of the earlier wave of German-speaking Jews, who were able to pass on their knowledge of how the American political process worked and where the levers of power were. Louis Marshall, president of the newly established American Jewish Committee, managed through the use of the law and a skillful deployment of public relations to develop a distinct Jewish voice in American politics. His use of the passport question to demonstrate how Russian demands were compromising the American concept of citizenship and equality before the law, and the threat of economic retaliation by the American government, became the model of how Jews could project political influence in the foreign policy arena.[15] Notable too was the development of a new group of opinion leaders composed of radical intellectuals, mostly of the Eastern Jewish Socialist persuasion, whose style and rhetoric diverged from the moderate model of liberalism of the Protestant majority that was followed by Americanized German Jews.

Making their interests known and voices heard went hand in hand with acceptance of Jews as full citizens in the parliamentary democracies of Western Europe in the early decades of the twentieth century. The emancipation process granting Jews citizenship rights was completed in defeated Germany in 1919 with the approval of the Weimar constitution.[16] Not surprisingly the emerging voting patterns of the American Jewish electorate were similar to those of the post-Enlightenment Jewish communities of the transatlantic world. In America the domestic reform of the progressive movement, some based on the model of the advances in Europe, tended to give evermore access to the newly emerging immigrant leadership that spoke to a literate electorate. Made aware of the need for reform by avid reading of their own press and the native press, the Jewish voter gave strong support to the progressive reform program at the polls. Lincoln Steffens, the muckraker journalist, in turn appreciated the reform sprit displayed by Abraham Cahan, the editor of the Yiddish daily *Forward*. American Jewish would-be change agents were less burdened than their European counterparts by a need first to undo preemancipation restrictions and habits. Since even during the antebellum period Jews were not considered outside the broadened general enfranchisement process, the movement of inclusion of Jewish citizens in the *pais legal* was more complete and achieved with fewer roadblocks standing in the way.

The earliest evidence of the American Jewish affinity for politics is found on the communal level. The penchant for establishing evermore organizations, each with its own newspaper or weekly journal, was common in the early decades of the twentieth century. Almost every shade of Jewish public opinion was represented in the long, often fiery discussions that preceded the negotiations at Versailles. In preparation for these negotiations the Congress movement, composed largely of Eastern Jews, challenged what they called the "diktat" imposed by "court" Jews. They continually raised the issue of the democratization of Jewish communal life, which was viewed as a direct challenge to the leadership of the "uptown" established German Jews. For the growing number of Zionists something more concrete was at stake. The breaking up of the Ottoman Empire opened an opportunity to realize the promise of the Balfour Declaration supported by President Wilson in 1917, which raised the hope of establishing a Jewish national home in Palestine.

Paradoxically that opportunity polarized American Jewry. On one side were those like Louis Marshall, president of the American Jewish Committee, who hoped to assure the security of the Jewish minorities in the diaspora through minority rights clauses to be inserted in the founding charters or constitutions of the new nations created by the Treaty of Versailles. On the other were leaders like Louis Brandeis, attracted to the Zionist movement in 1914, and Louis Lipsky, who became its leader in the twenties, who dreamed of a Jewish homeland in Palestine where there would never again be a threat of denial of civil rights for Jews. The two survival strategies were at loggerheads, as was the delegation Marshall led to Versailles. The delegation had been brought together only after a national election legitimized the Congress movement.[17] Predictably the delegation was unified in name only, so that few were surprised when in 1921 Rabbi Stephen Wise broke his pledge to disband a Jewish Congress delegation to Versailles by adjourning it and instead called a new successor organization, the American Jewish Congress, into being. Thereafter the American Jewish Committee headed by Marshall and the American Jewish Congress headed by Wise represented two opposing approaches to communal governance. The minority rights clause of the Versailles Treaty became an additional source of debate within the Jewish community. Lacking confidence that nations would comply with notions of separate language instruction and schools in reconstituted nations like

Poland, nationalistic-minded Zionists proposed a solution to the Jewish security question through the establishment of a reconstituted Jewish commonwealth in Palestine, a territory of poorly defined borders that had been part of the dissolved Ottoman Empire. Zionists arguing that such an investment would be better made in rebuilding the historic Jewish homeland again remained staunchly opposed when Agro-Joint, the resettlement agency of the Joint Distribution Committee, invested millions in establishing agricultural settlements in the Crimea. So unbridgeable did the division between Zionist and non-Zionists become that not even the threatening danger in Europe could bring the two sides together. American Jewry entered the decade of the thirties a riven community.

The search for communal unity was not confined to the foreign policy area. The quest for some form of governance began in earnest with the establishment of the American Jewish Committee in 1906. In the immediate post–World War I years an effort to create a local communal polity was attempted in New York and Chicago. The New York Kehillah (1919-1921) led by Rabbi Judah Magnes is perhaps the most remarkable example of Jewish political values and strategies at the grassroots level in the twentieth century. In name and policies it conjured the image of the preemancipation governing *Kahals* responsible for the immediate needs of the community. There exists no similar example of an effort to establish voluntary local communal self-governance on such a scale among the several immigrant groups. The proliferation of organizations including the American Jewish Committee (1906) and the American Jewish Joint Distribution Committee (1914), as well as national defense and welfare and religious organizations, gave American Jewry the richest communal infrastructure among the immigrant voting blocs. Yet the over one hundred national Jewish organizations found little in common and often overreached themselves. The unsuccessful attempt by the Kehillah to control such things as standards of morality and education was ultimately not successful, but it did contain a lesson on the limits of ethnic governance in a free society.[18]

Signs of failure hardly put a crimp in the organizational impulse and the intense Eastern Jewish interest in social and political change. The social democratic origins of American Jewish liberalism in which these ideals for social justice found their roots is examined in chapter 2. For the moment, the reader needs to be aware that from the outset the social democratic element in Jewish political culture was more focused on implementing social justice programs then on sophisticated economic theories concerning class struggle and surplus value.

In the early years of the eastern immigration the impulse for better communal organization and regulation also concerned the need to overcome the social chaos linked to mass transplantation. Issues like price gouging for kosher meat and open prostitution and the dependency created by family desertion claimed much communal attention and resources. The comparative early passivity to issues of national politics may conceivably be traced to the urgency of these local problems. If the maxim that all politics is local is true, then it is even truer of political activism. It was in the ghetto neighborhoods of the eastern seaboard cities where it first became possible for Jewish immigrants to recognize themselves as belonging to one people despite differences in language and cuisines and cultural habits. The consideration of a marriage between a Galitzianer and a Litwak or a Sephardic Jew from Aleppo and one from Damascus as a kind of intermarriage waned after the immigrant generation passed from the scene, but in their prime these cultural differences based on region of origin seemed insurmountable.[19] The Jewish immigrant community began as a divided tribe in which only the enthusiasm for progressive universalist ideology and a common religion transcended divisive regional differences.

Jewish politics everywhere was driven by activists and pundits obsessed with what they loosely called "democracy," which had little relation to the civics they learned in the night-school classes to which they flocked. They knew little of democracy as a "politics of process" but rather absorbed it as ideology in the eastern European sense. Whether Socialist or merely part of the religious code related to *Tikkun Olam* (repair of the world) incumbent on every Jew, the ideology contained a powerful reformist impulse unlike anything that prevailed in the land in which they had settled or among other immigrant communities. The Jewish electorate produced a disproportionate number of change agents determined to bring reform to American governance. Unable to fathom that the

American political system, albeit imperfect, offered avenues for change and improvement, they missed the grandiose ideas for systemic social change that held sway in the "old country." Seeing the imperfections of the American system, especially on the municipal machine politics level, some undoubtedly came to believe that revolution was the most effective way to eliminate the systemic inequities and corruption. When the creation of communal democratic institutions got underway its change agents would be the most Americanized of the immigrant generation that led the way. Its first manifestations was a movement to organize and govern the New York and Chicago Jewish communities from within, which meant challenging the German Jewish patriciate that exercised communal power. In its aspiration to control education and regulate morality, the aforementioned New York Kehillah went far beyond the normal boundaries of communal self-government. In its failure to understand the limits imposed by the national political culture, which adhered to a fundamental principle of limiting the role of government in human affairs, the Kehillah crossed established red lines. Its failure was not unexpected. But such confrontations with the majority political culture were not the rule. The most numerous and popular form of organization in the immigrant generation was the *Lansmanschaftn*, which were based on common old world regional ties. Practical in their outlook and little tinged by demanding political ideologies, they offered the immigrant services that extended from health insurance and care to burial plots.[20] There was great social, cultural, and political variety in Jewish organizational life in which Jewish political culture was incubated. When faced with the direct survival crises of the Holocaust years that variegation and disunity was not easily overcome and weakened the communal unity requisite for making the case in Washington for a liberal refugee policy.

Immigration: A Central Issue in Jewish Political Culture

The issue that preoccupied American Jewry in the first half of the twentieth century was immigration policy, which appears in various guises. We first note the restrictive sentiment faced by the founding Sephardic Jews of Recife after 1654, which is followed by not dissimilar problems faced by the German Jews who began to arrive after 1820. But it was the eastern European Jewish immigrants who settled after 1870 who faced a deepening public resistance to a liberal immigration policy. It became fully blown with the passage of the Johnson-Reed Immigration Law of 1924, which contained the national origins formula on which immigration quotas were based. The telling refugee crisis of the thirties forged American Jewry's most direct link to the Holocaust and became ultimately a major hinge on which Jewish history hangs in the first half of the twentieth century. Resistance to granting Jewish refugees haven extended well beyond the Holocaust to include the survivors in the Displaced Persons (DP) camps. It culminates in the communal advocacy for the admission of Jewish Displaced Persons after the Harrison Report (1946). The rejection of the Jewish refugees, which extended to their children, accounts for a facet in the American Jewish psyche that is rarely mentioned in historical accounts of those years, the feeling that they did not do enough to open the "golden gates" of America during those critical years. In measuring the impact of various hostile laws on Jewish well being, some historians place the Johnson-Reed law ahead of the May laws in tsarist Russia (1881), the Nuremberg laws of 1935 in Germany, as well as the 1492 order expelling Jews from Spain, as having the most lethal impact in Jewish history. The impact of immigration policy on Jewish well being can hardly be exaggerated.

Yet viewed from a historical perspective the immigration and acculturation of mass immigration had been a relatively successful experience. Some historians go as far as attributing the nation's startling industrial growth in the final decades of the nineteenth century to mass immigration. Even today while European nations reel under the impact of the absorption of Islamic immigrants, America boasts a record of a comparatively successful acculturation of dozens of immigrant groups. Political leaders often herald the fact that America is "a nation of immigrants" and cite their own immigrant background with pride. The slogan "e pluribus unum" stamped on its coinage evokes an image of unity within diversity. But in truth the current image of a rich human tapestry composed of different ethnic groups living in harmony is part of a sanitized version of immigration history. A feeling of unwelcome was often the reality at the grassroots level and unease within the immigrant communities was often high. Even without such concerns communal harmony was not a given. The reception of the Sephardic Jews who arrived in New Amsterdam in the spacious New Amsterdam harbor in September 1654, and were in a sense "present at the creation" of the New Amsterdam colony, was not a friendly one. It did not exempt them from the animus of Peter Stuyvesant, its governor. The image of a Polish immigrant as simply a Pole was frequently belied by the fact that within the immigrant group there existed wide cultural, language, and religious differences. How America came to terms with eastern European Jews who arrived after 1870 was different than its transaction with German Jews who began to arrive in numbers in 1820 when the frontier was still open. Though not reflected by a panoply of restrictive legislation and administrative orders until the final decades of the nineteenth century, and fully developed by the restrictive laws of the 1920s, the reception of the Eastern Jews we have noted was less welcoming compared with their German brethren. The growth of a sense of ethnic identity was undoubtedly strengthened in the face of a hostile host culture.

But like all Jewish settlement ventures, Jews arrived armed with certain useful historically learned practices based on their need to engage the governors of the various host cultures in which they resided. These practices proved crucial to assure their economic, social, and physical security, which required above all else a high level of communalism. Governed by Jewish law (Halacha), they not only had the need for a separate Jewish cemetery but also an understanding of their place, as transacted with the governors of the host community. Everywhere Jewish political leaders entered into written and unwritten contracts with such governing groups. How to fulfill the responsibilities assumed and the governance that followed from them became a source for the development of Jewish political culture. For example, after calling for support from their shareholding brethren in the governing council of the West India Company to counter Stuyvesant's threat of banishment, Jews contracted with him to care for their own, which they did until 1934.[21]

The acculturation process that began the day they landed did not always proceed smoothly. There were lumps in the "melting pot," rooted in different rates of acculturation within and between immigrant communities. In the early decades the core of the immigrant Jewish political

agenda concerned issues involving immigration policy, requests for intercession regarding the treatment of their brethren abroad, and occasionally church-state issues. When coupled with incidents triggered by the
often lukewarm treatment at home, the immigrant political agenda never
lacked for issues. Despite feeling compelled to leave their mother country, nostalgia for the cuisine, language, and music of the homeland made
preservation of the old culture a reason for remaining separate. Clearly
emigration did not end the relationship between the immigrant and the
mother country that sometimes seeks to enlist the political and financial
support of its brethren in America. There was a need for immigrant communities to transact political business with the host as well as their former governments, which concerned such things as treatment in passage,
estates, and conscription laws, and keeping America's gates open for relatives to follow. But ultimately the struggle to retain that culture in the face
of an accommodation that required in some measure the absorption of
the language and the lifestyle of the host culture was a loosing one. In
the case of non-Jewish immigrants a common religion could furnish a
meeting ground with the general population while religious aberrance,
as in the case of Jews, might serve to sort out those who would not fit.
The practice of bigamy customary among certain subcultures of native-
born Mormons would never be acceptable to the host culture. But Jews
were a relatively minor religious minority that at least shared an Abrahamic origin. Despite a deep-rooted tradition of anti-Semitism in Christian
countries, Jews were comparatively well situated for accommodation in a
heterogeneous, pluralistic America.

The first-generation immigrants form a hyphenate culture based
partly on nostalgia for their former home. Before World War I German-
Americans, then the largest hyphenate group in the nation, opposed
entering the war on the side of the Allies and thereby earned the anger
of the nation. Sauerkraut became "liberty cabbage," frankfurters became
"hot dogs," and the study of German was frequently dropped from the
school curriculum. The path of the nation's foreign policy could trigger enormous problems for an immigrant group. In the case of Japanese
Americans in 1942 it caused mass internment and denial of basic civil
rights. While Jewish immigrants were not winning popularity contests

compared with other immigrant groups, at least from southern and eastern Europe, the path to their acceptance by the majority host culture was comparatively smooth.

Yet given the delicate balance hyphenate communities must maintain between loyalty to the "old country" and the pull of the new, their internal politics was often tense and complex. There could be conflict about how the political agenda should be determined and presented to the host government. The terms and pace of acculturation within an immigrant community differed sharply. In the Jewish ghetto newly arrived Jewish immigrants were called "green," while those who assumed native cultural trappings, especially clothing styles, with sometimes unseemly haste, were referred to as "alrightniks." At the same time the immigrant community was not exempt from the conflict wracking the mother country. It was a compounding factor in an already complex political environment. Whether to support the German or Allied war effort during World War I was a divisive issue. Many eastern immigrants joined Jacob Schiff in their unwillingness to reconcile themselves to fighting on the same side of the hated tsarist government. When national socialism made its debut in Germany during the twenties it virtually split the German American community apart, as descendants of liberal approval '48ers, led by such men as Karl Schurz, fought with Nazi supporters whose numbers were enlarged by a new wave of German immigrants in the twenties, many of whom were disappointed German war veterans.[22] Similarly, we will note later that the advocacy of political Zionism was a bone of contention within American Jewry. Deep divisions developed in the Jewish community where the issues centered on how much of the philanthropic dollar should go to the *yishuv* and how much for domestic needs.[23] Today the support of Washington's trade embargo policy imposed against Cuba no longer earns unanimous approval among Cuban immigrants. Similarly, many Chinese Americans opposed extending diplomatic recognition to the People's Republic of China (PRC) while removing it from the nationalist government in Taiwan. We note later how the problem can be exacerbated when one faction preempts the voice of the community. Most American Jews take a softer position on the disposition of the "occupied territories" and the settlements than does AIPAC and the right-wing

Zionist Organization of America (ZOA). The problem of communal strife is exacerbated by the absence of a political mechanism to determine the will of the community and who speaks for it, which frequently leads to the co-option of the communal voice.

Having personally experienced the often heartless process of family uprooting and resettlement, immigrant voters keenly felt the need to keep the doors of America open as well as the need to humanize the process itself. Their interest in those left behind broadened their political interests beyond the ethnic enclaves where they settled. The need to extricate a relative often served as the first contact with the American political process. The hyphenate culture formed by the immigrant generation was based partly on nostalgia and ties of kinship and concern for those compelled to remain in their former home. What was happening in the "old country" naturally became a primary concern in all immigrant politics and could put them at odds with the prevailing opinion of the host culture. Fueled by their ethnic press and church, immigrant communities tend to develop a political culture peculiarly their own, especially in the first generation after resettlement. While the residual loyalty of the immigrant community for the mother country could be a formidable political influence in the communal politics of immigrant communities, for obvious reasons, the American Jewish immigrant voter could not muster such enthusiasm for the government from which he had emigrated. Israel, which might have been the object of such nostalgic longing, was not yet in existence. It was not the place where they had spent the carefree years of their youth.

The love for Palestine, the Jewish homeland to be, had to be created from scratch with stories and photos of a modern nation coming into being. Photos of the building of modern Tel Aviv and athletic young men and women were common in the public-relations brochures of the young Zionist movement. Paradoxically, the acceptance of a national homeland other than one's own could interfere with the Americanization process that all immigrants underwent. The opposition to the American Zionist movement that developed after World War I relied on the fear of dual loyalties, which was a persistent theme of the Reform movement in the pre-state period. Apprehensiveness regarding dual loyalties is not a notable aspect of American Jewish political culture today, but beneath the surface it continues to act as a factor in its political behavior. One Holocaust survivor who settled here in 1946 still observes that Jews are indeed at home in America but then adds an afterthought: "But how much 'at home' can a Jew be anywhere?" That became a favorite post-Holocaust rallying cry of Zionists who argued that Israel is the only place where Jews can really feel fully at home.

Achieving communal consensus on immigration policy was not a foregone conclusion. Zionist-minded Jews, of whom there were a growing number, did not necessarily rue the growth of restrictionism, and undoubtedly some more acculturated German-speaking Jews, convinced that the "green" immigrants would delay their ascendancy and full acceptance, did not bemoan the curtailment of immigration from eastern Europe. The primacy of immigration to Palestine, which the world Zionist movement championed after restriction became buttressed by law, was never a favorite goal of the eastern immigrants. Instead, as we will later note, American Jewry developed a Zionism without Zion.

The Refugee Crisis of the Thirties

Interest in keeping the doors of the *goldeneh medinah* open was the primary issue of grass roots Jewish politics during the early decades of the twentieth century.[24] We have noted that the movement to restrict immigration especially from eastern and southern Europe, which reached a new high point after World War I, fed that concern. The Emergency Immigration Law of 1921 and its permanent successor in 1924 were not focused exclusively on restricting Jews, but aimed generally to restore the nation's ethnic composition to what it had been before the closing of the frontier in 1890. Nevertheless, revoking the Johnson-Reed Immigration Law (1924) with its infamous national origins quota system became a rallying cry in Jewish communal politics. The national origins system, which was the basis for calculating the quota, used a complex formula based on the number of native sons already in the country to determine how many would be admitted. Since Jews had no "mother country" they had no specific quota but shared the quota of the sending country, so that the law bore down particularly heavily on potential Jewish immigrants who over-whelmingly stemmed from the countries of eastern Europe.

The catastrophic impact of the restrictive immigration laws of the twenties were fully felt after Berlin's extrusion policy, directed first against the Jews of Germany and quickly followed by the Jews of Austria, which fell under German control in March 1938. The refugee crises that occurred in the years before war broke out in September 1939 mark the beginning of the great tragedy of modern Jewish history. Despite the Reich's early agreement to a plan to peacefully resettle these unwanted Jews, receiving nations were reluctant to accept what would soon become a massive stream of humanity with no place to go.

The refugee crises of the thirties placed American Jewry in a precarious position. It was expected to assume the mantle of leadership ensconced for centuries in the communities of east and central Europe, which were suddenly cut off in preparation for the Final Solution. At the same time early efforts to speak to the Oval Office with one voice became hopelessly entangled in communal politics. Considering the availability of the Jewish homeland in Palestine and the enormous cost of resettling an ageing population of refugees, most Zionists were reluctant to support resettlement of European Jewry in places like British Guiana. The Bergson group composed of a delegation of the Irgun active in the United States, was alone in realizing that the *Yishuv* could not absorb all who required haven and that the power to convince London to revoke the white paper limiting immigration and the buying of land was politically unrealizable. Peter Bergson pointed out publicly that the goal of rescuing as many as possible and bringing settlers only to Palestine were at loggerheads. The highest priority should be to get the Jews out and settle them anywhere possible. Such questioning of the exclusivity most Zionist gave to *aliyah*, immigration to Palestine, did not earn the Bergson group great support among mainline Zionists who wielded considerable influence in the decision-making circles of American Jewry. Most Jews remained convinced that a Jewish homeland in Palestine was the most practical way to rescue the Jews of Europe. It was after all the only haven that cried out to receive the hapless Jewish refugees. The desperate need to make Palestine accessible may have led to an overestimation of the possibility of softening Britain's Jewish immigration restriction to Palestine by a public-relations campaign. London responded with offering resettlement in British Guiana, the scene of two prior resettlement failures.[25]

If Britain's will to deny a Palestinian haven to Jewish refugees was implacable, the restrictionist impulse in America, fueled by the Depression, seemed no less so. It developed that there was good reason for Jews to fear the restrictionism that came fully into bloom during the Harding administration. A nativist impulse had always existed in the American public mind, but in the twenties the major cities of America, inundated with the black immigration from the South and an enormous influx of immigrants from eastern and southern Europe, convinced American citizens that such alien types could never become Americans. It was not only their strange language or the false gods they worshiped, but they also preferred to live in cities, which even under the best of circumstances were somehow thought to be alien, perhaps even the spawning ground for sinfulness. The "real" America was the America of agriculture composed, with the exception of the Catholic Irish, of immigrants from Northern and Western Europe.

Pseudo-scientific studies of immigrant inferiority made their debut, which, when reinforced with images of congestion and the lower standard of living that developed in the ethnic enclaves, became evidence of the need to restrict immigration. The drive to return the nation to the imagined idyllic state that existed before the frontier was declared closed after the census of 1890 was a powerful one, especially when it merged with the farmer's last stand against the city. The great paradox was that, with the exception of the Jewish immigrants, the millions who composed the "new" immigrations were largely a displaced peasantry, as unfamiliar with and alienated by city life as was the American farmer.

For the Jewish citizen the restrictionist legislation that came to fruition with the Emergency Immigration Law of 1921 had a special impact. The turmoil in eastern Europe triggered by the Russian revolution created a more urgent need to find haven elsewhere. The antirevolutionary White military forces frequently joined by the Red forces signaled out unarmed Jewish civilians in the villages for slaughter without mercy. America as always was the preferred destination, but the willingness to receive Jews diminished quickly after World War I. The rationale behind immigration restriction, we have already noted, was based on the idea of Nordic supremacy, which resembled the pseudo-scientism of Aryanism later projected by Nazi ideology. It found the racial type associated with Northern and Western Europe preferable as human stock. The Jewish media laughingly called the concept "Nordomania," but the quota system based on the national origins formula that became part of the immigration law of 1924 proved to be no laughing matter. It effectively held Jewish immigration to a trickle and marked the end of the period of great demographic growth of American Jewry, which lasted from circa 1871 to 1924. The defenders of the Johnson-Reed Immigration Law insisted that there was no intention to signal out Jews, but later evidence pointed to the fact that rumors of an impending inundation by thousands of Polish Jews contained in diplomatic dispatches played a primary role in hastening the passage of the law. When a refinement was added to the law in 1929, few were able to foresee the lethal impact the law would have on the survival of Europe's Jews, especially when combined with its strict administration during the Depression. When the depredations broke out in Germany with the advent of Hitler in January 1933, finding haven in receiving nations became imperative. The decision for a Final Solution made emigration the only alternative to the gas chambers. That lethality of Nazi intent became evident in July 1939 when Cuban authorities prohibited a passenger ship of the Hamburg American line, the *Saint Louis*, from landing its almost one thousand passengers, mostly Jews seeking to escape the developing danger in Germany and Austria. The ship was forced to return to Europe with its hapless cargo. The centrality of the immigration issue was confirmed by events in the thirties. As Berlin implemented its policy of extrusion of its Jews, the situation became desperate. It was summed up in a plaintiff Yiddish ballad that became popular in the late thirties, "Where Oh Where Shall I Go."

Efforts by American Jewish leaders to alleviate the situation proved of little avail. The blocking activities of the Roosevelt administration were not confined to a strict interpretation of the law's "Likely to Become a Public Charge" (LPC) provision, so that even those who might have found haven within the quota system were denied by "administrative devices."[26] The effort to restrict immigration beyond the law actually began in 1930 with the State Department's instructions to its consuls that immigration should be limited to 10 percent of the quota. Predictably, only in 1939 were the relevant quotas fully utilized. For Jewish activists the rejection of the Wagner-Rogers bill, which would have sheltered twenty thousand Jewish refugee children stranded in France during 1939 and 1940, was particularly onerous. It demonstrated clearly that the administration's blocking activities was related to the Jewishness of the refugee children, since less than a year later, supported by a popular craze to admit British children, victims of the "Blitz," the administration with the support of Congress passed a law waving legal requirements for visas and affidavits for non-Jewish British children.

In response to the charge of anti-Semitism articulated at dozens of mass rallies, the hostile State Department claimed, with some truth, that it was carrying out the will of the American people. The strategy of liberalizing the immigration laws through public pressure had little chance of success. It was far beyond the power of American Jewry to realize. The failure to change immigration policy fueled a pervasive sense of failure and guilt that became manifest in the postwar years. That sense was compounded by the anger especially prevalent among the survivors who settled here in great numbers after the war.[27] For American Jews the witness posture of the Roosevelt administration was a particular paradox. Despite a disproportionate representation of Jews in Roosevelt's inner circle, a presence that served as fodder for the anti-Semitic imagination, and despite early strong Jewish voter support in favor for early intervention, Jewish leaders were unable to get the rescue of Jews and other victims of Berlin's racial policies to be included in the nation's war aims.

The Atlantic Charter spoke of "freedom from fear and want," but Allied information strategy was silent about the operation of the Final Solution lest the war become a war to save the Jews. None of the wartime conferences ever considered the Jewish question, which Berlin spoke about endlessly. Berlin's propaganda also spoke constantly of its imagined Jewish control of the Roosevelt administration, but in Washington Jewish leaders were unable to move the Roosevelt administration to a more active rescue effort until 1944, when Roosevelt finally responded affirmatively to the pressure to establish the War Refugee Board (WRB).

Strangely, the administration's indifference to the fate of its European brethren was not reflected in a Jewish voter decline of loyalty to Roosevelt and his New Deal. In contrast, the political support as reflected in the vote of hyphenate immigrant groups subsided after the election of 1936 at the political juncture when the Jewish love affair with Roosevelt grew in intensity. It was Jewish voter commitment to the New Deal welfare state rather than the administration's indifferent performance on the rescue front that serves as early evidence that support of a government role in the economy had become the core of American Jewish political culture. It remains so to this day. In the end the inability of American Jewish leaders to influence wartime policy to rescue the Jews of Europe is considered by many the greatest failure in the history of American Jewry. But as we note later, the question of failure goes far beyond an imagined indifference of American Jewry. It involves the question of political power, how much and what kind did American Jewry have, that might have been mobilized to fulfill its responsibility to its brethren in Europe. Anti-Semitic propaganda emanating from Berlin spoke constantly of Jewish control of the Roosevelt administration, but when a crucial need involving the very survival of European Jewry was at stake Jewish leaders found that they lacked the political leverage to extend the nation's wartime priorities to include the rescue of European Jewry. They had assigned themselves a responsibility that could not be fulfilled, almost as if they had become convinced that they actually possessed the required power that so agitated the growing number of professional anti-Semites. Endlessly pictured by indigenous anti-Semites as all-powerful, the Jewish community was in reality powerless and vulnerable. (Chapter 6, which deals with the Holocaust, contains a fuller discussion of this aspect of the story.)

Given Nazi fanaticism on the Jewish question, had it been possible to enlist the power of the American government, would it have made a difference? The Final Solution reached a high point in 1943, when many military experts had already concluded that Germany could no longer win the war. Yet Berlin remained so committed to the total war *vernichtungs* (annihilation) goal in which the Final Solution was embedded that the killing operation did not abate even after it was clear that the war was lost. The war against the Jews was the war that could still be won. The destruction of Hungarian Jewry had Berlin's highest priority when it was clear that the back of Nazi power had been broken. The family of Anne Frank was deported from the Amsterdam attic in which they had been hiding in September 1944, four months after the successful invasion of Europe.[28] The will to save Jewish lives never remotely matched Berlin's will to complete the Final Solution even when it was clear that the war was lost. Given Berlin's determination to liquidate European Jewry, to then assign responsibility to Jewish leadership without the existence of matching power, inevitably produces a lament, not history. The failure to convince the Oval Office at least to make the attempt at mitigating the slaughter left many American Jews with a sense that Jews were simply not considered part of the "universe of obligation" that makes organized civil life possible. That sense that more might have been done by the wartime Allies to at least mitigate the slaughter haunts American Jewry. The failure is deeply rooted in its political psyche.

The Perception of American Anti-Semitism in the Thirties

No discussion of American Jewish political culture can gain traction without understanding that the perception of anti-Semitism is a core element that shapes Jewish political opinion. The fear of it is always beneath the surface. For most immigrants even the heightened sense of threat following upon an incident like the Frank lynching in 1915 or the limited enrollment policy for Jewish students at Harvard and other Ivy League schools was still a far cry from a life-threatening pogrom in Ukraine. American society certainly offered few roadblocks for their headlong drive to achieve middle-class rank, which became fully evident during the prosperous twenties. But with tensions generated by the worldwide depression and the rise of national socialism in Germany, American Jewish equanimity regarding anti-Semitism was replaced by apprehension. The fear that what was happening in Germany, whose culture held a high place in Jewish estimation, was about to happen here gripped American Jewry.[29] Paradoxically, anti-Semitism reached its zenith during a war in which the nation was expending its treasure and the blood of its sons to defeat a state that had made the liquidation of the Jews its major war aim.

Despite its low profile, nineteenth-century American Jewish communal life was hardly exempt from the affect of anti-Semitism. It came into fuller bloom after 1890, when the census declared that the western frontier, an open cutting edge of settlement, was closed. Then, as if in the absence of open space where passions against native tribes could be vented, anti-Semitism came to the surface together with other nativist sentiments. Its occasional outbreaks became one of the major concerns around which Jewish "defense" organizations were established. B'nai B'rith's Anti-Defamation League (1914) focused its activities exclusively on fighting anti-Semitism, while organizations like the American Jewish Committee incorporated a "defense" element in their programs. Their activities were strengthened by the lynching of Leo Frank in 1915 and by the renewed activity of the Ku Klux Klan, which had added Jews and Catholics to their hate list in the early twenties.

There are many incidents that could be cited in this cursory description to offer a rationale of the enormous attention anti-Semitism received and the role it played in the postwar development of American Jewish political culture. Survey research shows that anti-Semitism reached a high point precisely at the historic juncture when victory against Germany, whose principle war aim was the total destruction of the Jews, seemed imminent. Though in sharp decline after 1944, Jewish defense agencies found sufficient evidence of its continued virulence in the prosperous postwar years. Yet there was little overt evidence of it during the years of McCarthyism, where its toxic effect might have been found. Many Jewish voters remained convinced that even the victory over nazism did not preclude the possibility that anti-Semitism could again become a viral force in the future. It was as if the loss of one out of three Jews had created a permanent trauma.

That fear was fed when merely six years after the war's end events conspired to convince even the most secure American Jew that anti-Semitism was deep and perennial. The Rosenberg espionage trial, which occurred almost at the same historic moment as the Doctor's Plot in the Soviet Union and the Rudolf Slansky spy trial in Czechoslovakia, convinced many that the threat of anti-Semitism could now come from both extremes of the political spectrum. Even as the polls showed that American anti-Semitism was at a low point Jewish concern about it climbed to new heights. It was there beneath the surface ready to strike. It was easy to imagine that Jews lived in a threatening world when drunken mobs attacked Jewish families in Ukraine at the turn of the century. But what sustained such a high level of apprehensiveness in the America of the twenties when Jews were achieving new heights of prosperity was puzzling.[30] It may be that many individual American Jews who had close ties to their extended family in Europe felt as if they experienced the depredations firsthand. These first-generation immigrant Jews might still have been able to recall the deprivation felt in the "old world." Time had not yet played its healing role.

The longer-range reason for sensing danger relates to modern Jewish history. The political values of modernizing Jews was rooted in the enlightenment that supported individual rights including freedom of movement. When combined with the immediate grassroots sentiment of the Eastern immigrants, driven by their concern for the security and welfare of those of their brethren who remained behind, the concern about the restrictive immigration laws became the most powerful political force in the early decades of the twentieth century. That the Jewish political agenda would call for a liberal immigration policy and diplomatic intercession regarding depredations particularly in Russia and Romania was predictable. On the family level that overriding concern is evidenced by the monetary remittances sent back to the poverty-ridden towns and villages where relatives depended on them. No estimate of the role played by these remittances on both sides of the Atlantic is available and their importance is generally neglected by historians of immigration. Conceivably it amounted to many millions of dollars and was so widespread that it could have been one of the sources of the dire poverty observed in the Jewish ghettoes of New York, Philadelphia, and Boston.[31] The financial support immigrants sent to their families in eastern Europe was more than matched the post–World War I activities of the "Joint" that involved the expenditure of millions of dollars in planned programs of rehabilitation and training. It is one of the unsung pages of Jewish philanthropy in Eastern Europe and was unstintingly given by "uptown" Jews, some of whom retained the negative image of the immigrants whom they blamed for lowering the national tolerance threshold. Like the progressive reformers they admired, they held their noses and helped.

Jewish Communal Concerns during the Cold War Years

Aside from the problem of the Jewish Displaced Persons, those fortunate enough to have survived the Holocaust, two processes that bracket the cold war between 1945 and 1989 permit us to see the emerging outlines of the American Jewish political persona more clearly. Both involve the deep abiding interest in the security and general welfare of Jewish communities abroad. American Jewry mobilized itself to use all its influence and newfound resources to support the establishing of the Jewish state at the beginning of the cold war and again to extricate those Soviet Jews who wanted to leave the Soviet Union at its end. Though pictured as similar crises that required the full resources of American Jewry, they were in fact quite different. There are in addition many events of a lesser valence that allow us to view that political culture in its maturity.

During these years the cold war was the context in international affairs against which specific Jewish problems were projected. The Jewish electorate recognized the threat posed by the Kremlin but for various reasons were not enthusiastic proponents of high military budgets. On the domestic scene early Jewish involvement in the civil rights movement and the leading role Jewish youth played in opposing the war in Vietnam distinguish it from other ethnic voting blocks.[32] These political processes existed side by side with matters of peculiar Jewish interest such as the treatment of the Jewish DPs, which in its early months following the war seemed to be a continuance of how Jewish refugees were treated during the thirties. The concern for Israel went on to become the very heart of Jewish political consciousness. Individual incidents during the cold war years, such as the Jewish response to the espionage trial of the Rosenbergs and their relationship to individual American political leaders like John F. Kennedy and Ronald Reagan, illustrate the wide variety of preferences and opinions held by the Jewish voter. The contours of Jewish political culture as it developed in the postwar years inform us at a glance about communal priorities that determine the investment of its power and influence. At the same time it poses enormous problems for the researcher since the question of Jewish power is at the heart of the anti-Semitic imagination. It is a risk worth taking since the role power and its absence plays, its nature and composition, and how and for what purpose it is deployed, can clarify the myriad of factors that together compose Jewish political culture. It deserves special attention.

American Jewish Political Power and Political Culture

At the heart of any examination of political culture or any ideology is the question of political power, how to gain it and keep it or, as in the case of the Jews, how to assure minimum security needs despite the limitation of its power. We begin by confirming the assumption that despite the absence of normal accoutrements of power embodied in national sovereignty Jews are not bereft of power of a certain kind. The political instruments through which American Jewry acts on power holders to transmit communal interests are comparatively well developed, particularly in the area of public relations. Aside from the power of its votes there are other power instruments, such as lobbying, through which influence can be projected on the possessors of formal power.

It warrants repeating at the outset that lobbying government agencies on behalf of clients, whether exercised by the pharmaceutical industry or by an ethnic organization, is a legal activity. Some maintain that in a society that seeks to empower its citizenry it is a necessary and desirable one. Jews have become proficient in wielding these informal instruments of power, especially in the foreign policy arena, which compels our search for its play to be focused largely on the federal level. American Jewry's organizational infrastructure is the largest of any ethnic group in America. The number of lay members who by dint of income and experience are able to assume leadership positions is also comparatively large. The rank and file of the community is increasingly formally educated and of comparatively high income. Some consider its Federation/UJC network as the highest level of communal governance achieved by any ethnic group in the United States.[33] Because of its special security needs it is also compelled to mount a more sustained effort to influence public policy.

While playing a prominent role on issues concerning the national welfare, the Jewish electorate is also hyperactive locally on specific issues involving such matters as zoning regulations, taxing policy, and the related management of the schools and police and sanitation issues. But with the exception of the perennial argument concerning the placing of religious symbols, such as Christmas crèches on public land, there are few issues that draw the overwhelmingly secular Jewish voters on the religious level. No pattern of Jewish dominance or overrepresentation in local issues is discernable, since Jewish citizens are not alone in favoring such things as better schools and roads. But contrary to popular belief, on the federal level their record of effectiveness has been far from consistent. Already noted is the failure of Jewish leaders to prevent restrictionist immigration laws during the twenties and thirties, a failure that was more costly in Jewish lives than the expulsion from Spain or the Russian May laws.

The two most direct examples of the successful use of power or political influence are the conversion of Harry Truman to support the diplomatic recognition of the Jewish state in May 1948 and the passage of the Jackson-Vanik amendment in December 1974. Even in these cases a closer perusal shows that the model of simple successful projection of Jewish influence to achieve desired goals is an oversimplification. Truman's overruling of his closest advisers on the recognition of Israel issue involved political as well as personal consideration and stands in sharp contrast to a better positioned Jewish leadership's failure to appreciably move the Roosevelt administration on the refugee rescue issue. Nineteen forty eight was an election year and Truman wanted to run for a second term. He also had developed a genuine feeling that some form of compensation to assure Jews security as a people should be granted after the radical losses they had suffered during the war. In sharp contrast, the steps taken to support the Soviet Jewry movement emanated from Congress and not the executive branch, which was committed to the détente policy advocated by Henry Kissinger, its Jewish secretary of state. Muting cold war conflict

in favor of disarmament and trade, the policy pushed by the Nixon administration required downgrading the release of Soviet Jewry lest its inherent anti-Soviet tone allows it to become a major cold war issue. Congress
nevertheless passed the Jackson-Vanik amendment. The lopsided vote in
the House for the amendment to the Trade Reform Act of 1974 (Jackson-
Vanik) was 325 in favor to 36 opposed, and in the Senate, 72 to 4. With the
help of Senator Jackson and his followers it proved possible to get around
the executive through preponderant support in Congress. The Jackson-
Vanik amendment marks a high point in the exercise of Jewish political
influence and a completion of a change in its locus from the Oval Office to
the halls of Congress.[34] The Jackson-Vanik amendment went far to generate the impression that Jewish power in America was supreme.

The Jewish Vote, Ethnic Power, and the National Interest

The problem of determining the limits of influence an ethnic or interest
group should exercise on the making of public policy, especially in foreign relations, is a long-standing one in American history. The unsuccessful role of Irish Americans in trying to prevent a general rapprochement
between Britain and the United States could not prevent the Anglo-American alliance of 1902. The role of the Cuban "junta" in bringing on the war
against Spain in 1898 was apparently more successful, but like the American Jewish effort to influence Middle East policy there is little evidence
that it was a decisive voice in shaping policy. The most successful effort
in recent memory was the role played by Cuban Americans in the Bay of
Pigs invasion in 1960. Before the establishment of Israel in 1948 there was
little evidence that might make the case for Jewish dominance of foreign
affairs, for the Middle East or elsewhere. But thereafter Jews in particular
have been plagued by the charge of having dual loyalties when they exert
influence to enhance the security of Israel. No such charges have been leveled against Irish Americans in their conflict with Britain or Greek Americans in their conflict with Turkey regarding Cyprus.

The strong interventionist position American Jewry took in the
pre–World War II years prompted Charles Lindbergh in his Des Moines
speech in September 1941 to accuse Anglophiles and Jews of trying to

bring the United States into the war against Germany. The charge did not resonate with the public and raised the ire of Franklin Roosevelt. But it caused apprehension among Jews. Lindbergh was after all an American national icon, so that when he raised the charge of an inherent conflict of loyalties coupled with an image of an all-powerful Jewry, it had an affect. A similar accusation in the recent work by Professors John Mearsheimer and Stephen Walt, which presented evidence purportedly showing that the "Jewish lobby" exerts an unwholesome influence on American Middle East policy, aroused less concern. It had become a familiar charge repeatedly articulated by the late Senator William Fulbright (Dem. Arkansas), chairman of the powerful Senate Foreign Relations Committee, who was convinced that rather than confluence between American Jewish and the national interest in the Middle East, the "Israel lobby" has a nefarious effect on the national interest. Such charges cannot be easily laid to rest since there is never absolute certainty about what best serves the national interest. It is precisely that question that is at the heart of the perennial debate over foreign policy issues. But as uncertain as the effect of projecting such influence may be, some would argue that it is necessary. The fact that it raises long-standing charges regarding a Jewish misuse of power is a perennial cause of concern for Jewish communal leaders.

The misperception of Jewish influence might normally have been based on the growing Jewish congressional representation, notwithstanding the fact that the variation of political positions within the Jewish community makes it nigh impossible to organize a monolithic group requisite for control of policy. There are a slightly disproportionate number of Jewish legislators in the 112th Congress, 2011–2013), thirteen in the Senate and twenty-seven in the House, six fewer than in the 111th and overwhelmingly Democrat.[35] But they are of strikingly different backgrounds, political positions, and degree of communal adherence. In a disputed race in Minnesota, claiming Jewish origin was viewed as an election asset. In the Al Franken versus Norm Coleman disputed Senate election in Minnesota in 2008, both candidates claimed Jewish bona fides they barely possessed. Few Jewish legislators can claim the Orthodox religious affiliation of Joe Lieberman, former Democratic senator from Connecticut and former Democratic vice presidential candidate, but his positions on medical insurance and the regulation of financial institutions is some distance from the typical Jewish voter. Senator Arlen Specter, formerly a Republican of Pennsylvania, had been involved with Jewish institutions when he was a Republican and continued to be so as a Democrat. Like Senator Lieberman, the former Republican House whip, now Speaker, Eric Cantor is a strongly affiliated Jew, but his position on major issues shows little affinity for the majority Jewish political position. In contrast, the well-known former Jewish Democratic senator Russ Feingold of Wisconsin was fiercely independent and rarely mentioned his Jewish origins, nor was he closely affiliated with Jewish congregational delegations or an active participant in Jewish organizational life, yet his voting record comes close to liberal Jewish affinities. The same pattern is true for the recently retired Barney Franks (Dem. Massachusetts). There is a Jewish congressional caucus whose agenda is focused primarily on Israel-Palestine issues.[36] The variety of Jewish legislators and the contrasting degrees of affiliation does not suggest that they adhere to a commanding voice stemming from Jewish communal leaders. It may well be that in the mysterious relationship between American Jewry and liberalism the latter precedes the former.

Jewish lawmakers taking similar positions on various issues suggests the existence of a Jewish voting bloc, yet identifying a single commanding voice or leadership group that determines tactics and positions is difficult. The most one can hope for is that such a caucus can supply an instrument whereby positions can be hammered out in those cases where representatives, an increasing number of whom do not stem from "Jewish election districts," are anxious to demonstrate their Jewish credentials. While there are certain commonalities such as level of education among Jewish members of Congress, it is hard to find a common cultural background that accounts for the near uniformity of the Jewish vote on certain issues such as healthcare. No matter what the party affiliation, few Jewish legislators support prayers or hymnals in the schools. Nevertheless, despite their diversity in politics and degree of communal affiliation, Jewish lawmakers continue to be viewed by some not as normal legislators exercising their rights but as members of a separate Jewish political nexus with its own interest in shaping public policy. That the vote of Jewish lawmakers usually corresponds to how most Jews have cast their ballots since the

New Deal should not come as a surprise. They are after all products of the American Jewish political environment, which is in fact very similar to how urban/urbane citizens of a certain type cast their ballots. But the proposition that Jewish legislators adhere to Jewish rather than national interests is increasingly being put to the test as more Jews are elected to office in districts with no sizeable Jewish population.

While we can speak of a liberal core in the Jewish vote, it is in fact quite variable. Clearly the old UJA slogan "We Are One" is more an aspiration than a reality. Within the communal tent there exists several subcommunities such as the ultra Orthodox and several Hassidic courts whose vote can be delivered, in contrast to the liberal/secular majority whose vote cannot be. That broadness of Jewish secular culture makes the idea of a cohesive Jewish vote based on a monolithic culture unrealizable. On the local level, especially on issues like support of education, the Jewish vote is fairly certain to be affirmative. Education is an overriding cultural value in the Jewish community. But not all groups within the community favor public education. Religious Jewish voters do not send their children to public schools and are likely to vote for charter schools with a religious bent where possible, or for outright government support of programs supporting school lunches and even student counseling. But when there is general agreement on a particular issue before the electorate, the Jewish vote can be decisive and gains leverage when it is a potential swing vote.

The constancy of the Jewish electorate on major liberal issues such as a tax-supported entitlement programs and civil rights is most apparent in federal elections. But while its location in the aforementioned five pivotal states can amplify Jewish influence, the Jewish vote is rarely decisive. It also has considerable flexibility. The Obama administration policy of extending aid to middle-sized businesses or start-up enterprises, based on the theory that most employment is generated by this middle sector, encountered little opposition among Jewish organizations despite its clear pro business Republican coloration. Jewish political influence extends beyond the delivery of an uncertain Jewish vote, but those who claim that it somehow has sufficient weight beyond the circa 2.2 percent of the Jewish population are in the throes of mythical thinking. It is not merely the Jewish vote that accounts for the important role Jews play in the American political arena. The number of ballots cast by Jews may in fact be the least of it.

More interesting are the reasons for the general increase in the Jewish congressional delegation and general officeholding on the state and local level and in the courts. The increase may be attributed to the fact that with the lessening of discrimination more Jews fit into the pool from which candidates for public office are drawn. They boast a comparatively high level of formal education and professionalization (disproportionately lawyers) and usually possess an above-average annual income and estate. Such candidates do not feel it necessary to play the Jewish card in order to garner a Jewish vote, which is in most cases insignificant on the local level. Michael Bloomberg, the second Jewish mayor of New York City, rarely touches on the fact that he is Jewish. One can find in his political career additional reasons why Jews have moved from a behind-the-scenes political role to a preference for wielding the direct power that comes from holding political office. Judging from their higher incomes and estates, Jewish politicos may have readier access to the heavy funding required for campaigning for office.[37] More important, Jews are comparatively well informed on major issues and more engaged in politics generally. Their deeper interest in political affairs makes them natural members of the political class. Why so many Jewish would-be officeholders possess such an interest and whether it is indeed inordinate is a discussion that would lead us far afield. I believe that it is almost as much correlated to a high level of formal education as it is to a political personality shaped by historical circumstance. A generational factor may also be involved to account for the increase in Jewish officeholding. In second- and third-generation Jews, talent and resources flowed into business, followed by the professions, especially medicine and law. In a sense, holding political office represents a remaining height to be scaled.

Ready access to a political career relates to the ability to raise money either from one's own estate or from friends, but that does not mean that such Jewish officeholders are beholden to Jewish moneyed interests. Financial independence may in fact make the Jewish aspirant for office refreshingly immune from pressure of any kind. Judging from the most exact measure of power in a democracy, the number of votes that can be directly mobilized and delivered for a favorite candidate or program, the answer clearly is that Jewish voters project slightly above their voting power as reflected in numbers. But, as noted, that voting pool is so small and fragmented that on most issues Jewish influence, when it can be identified at all, is peripheral. Even a communal interest such as a supportive policy toward Israel, is difficult to identify. There are considerable differences among Jewish voters regarding American policy toward West Bank settlements. Within communal politics the Reform and Conservative branches continually protest the Orthodox monopoly over such matters as marriage and conversion in Israel. The numerical proportion of the Jewish electorate is in fact declining. At its zenith in the 1940s and 1950s Jewish voters composed approximately 3.5 percent of the electorate, or 1.2 million strategically located votes. Today it is estimated at being anywhere from a low of 2.2 to a high of 2.5 percent, probably numerically closer to 2 million votes but a proportionate decline of a full percentage point. Two new fast-growing ethnic/racial voting blocks, blacks and Latinos, already far outweigh the Jewish vote in numbers without any special effort to get out their vote. When African American voters can form a coalition with elements of the white Protestant leadership, as they did during the Ocean Hill–Brownsville conflict under the administration of New York Mayor Lindsay, hard-won social gains like the merit civil-service system, which assured Jewish candidates employment as teachers and in the municipal civil service, were quickly swept aside in the name of community control of the schools.

In the long run, of the factors that balance the grand image of Jewish political power the growing disaffiliation of Jewish voters from their organizational network is most significant. It foretells a point in the future where the communal instruments that shape and turn out the vote are no longer effective, so that despite its strategic location in pivotal states and its high voting volume that maintains its weight at 4 percent of the electorate beyond its actual percentage of perhaps 2.5 percent, the actual Jewish weight at the voting booth may be diminished in years to come. As noted, other instruments in its political arsenal such as campaign fundraising, skills associated with communications and public relations, and the traditional activism and engagement of the Jewish voter fill the vacuum. Most important in compensating for its declining numbers is a penchant for drawing on values embedded in Jewish culture that are consonant with American values. We have noted shared values embedded in common Hebraic roots in the Old Testament that allow Evangelic Protestants to become fierce protectors of Israel. Civil rights fully protected by an independent judiciary coupled with high regard for the parliamentary process of democracy are shared by Israel and the United States. They are crucial factors in the protective mantle Washington has thrown over Israel that makes America's relations with Israel resemble those of an ally like wartime Britain rather than an ordinary client state.

Ethnic Politics and Political Life

Whether the principles embodied in American Jewish political culture can find a full expression in American political life depends on the context of ethnic politics that still plays a role in American politics. In practice office seekers seek votes where they can find them. The so-called Jewish vote continues to be important in national elections where its collective weight is most felt. Other older ethnic groups anchored in the new immigration, such as Polish Americans or Italian Americans, are no longer a voluble presence on the American political scene as are the Jews. But new hyphenates from the Caribbean and the Moslem world will undoubtedly find their political voice in coming years. The importance of the ethnic vote was recognized early in American politics and catering to it was the bases of the big city machine that dominated urban politics in the last quarter of the nineteenth century.[38] A full realization of the importance of the ethnic vote awaited the restrictive immigration laws that were implemented during the twenties. Al Smith, who became governor of New York in 1924, was among the earliest political leaders to fully utilize its potential to gain political leverage, and Roosevelt followed suit in the election of 1932 by establishing an ethnic division in his campaign for the presidency. Both welcomed Jewish talent into their inner circles. By Roosevelt's third term much of the business of mobilizing the Jewish vote fell to David Niles, who advised Roosevelt directly from his official position on the War Production Board. Niles continued in that role under Truman.

Some attribute Truman's decision to disregard the advice of Secretary of State George Marshall to withhold diplomatic recognition from the newly established Jewish state to David Niles.[39] To garner the Jewish vote in the presidential campaign of 1972 the Democratic candidate George McGovern established a Jewish section with its own staff and budget. Neither the Republican nor Democratic Party had such sections to garner the Italian or Irish vote as they once might have.[40] Aside from an ethnic division in the presidential campaign, the presidents often chooses their own "ethnic" for consultation in the Oval Office.[41]

Accelerated by the rapid Americanization process, with the exception of the Jewish vote, the influence of ethnic voting blocks diminished after World War II, especially among those ethnics stemming from the "new" immigration that began roughly in 1870.[42] As the influence of older ethnic immigrant voting blocs wanes a new Asian and Latino immigrant presence is making its political weight felt on the municipal levels of government in New York City. It is composed of Russian, Korean, and Chinese immigrants, and Muslim immigrants stemming from the South Asian countries of India, Pakistan, and Bangladesh. In New York City 110,000 of such potential new voters were added to the registration roles between 2004 and 2007. Of these, 38,000 stemmed from South Asia and an additional 29,000 joined the Hispanic bloc. By 2007 there were a total of 676,000 such new immigrants in the metropolitan New York area, mostly in the outlying boroughs of Brooklyn and Queens. While these new voting blocs are not monolithic and have not yet fully plugged into the system by forming political clubs and civic associations to forward their specific agenda, the potential for overshadowing the older ethnic voting blocs of Irish, Italian, and Jewish Americans is already manifest. The Jewish vote in the New York metropolitan area now stands at 489,100, a decline of about 2,000 votes since the election of 2006.[43]

We have noted that votes are not the only instrument an interest group can muster to affect public policy. What gives American Jewry the ability to exercise what appears to be disproportionate power is the fact that Jews are politically engaged and use the system well, especially when compared with other existing and emerging immigrant voting blocs. Despite its declining numerical proportion of the vote, the Jewish communal interests continue to hold their own. Partly this is attributed to the high voting volume that brings the circa 2.2 percent of the vote they would normally cast to near 4 percent. More important is the location of the Jewish vote in pivotal states where even a small Jewish vote becomes critical in a tight race. A decisive Jewish preference in California (55 electoral votes), New York (31 electoral votes), Florida (27 electoral votes), and New Jersey (15 electoral votes) would give a hopeful presidential candidate 128 of the 270 electoral votes needed to gain the presidency. If the next four pivotal states are added, Illinois (21 electoral votes), Pennsylvania (21 electoral votes), Ohio (20 electoral votes), Massachusetts (12 electoral votes), and Maryland (10 electoral votes), it would bring 84 additional electoral votes, raising the potential Jewish influence by 212 electoral votes, or 78 percent of the total needed to win the presidency. The Jewish vote is important and its amplification by dint of high voting volume is especially noticeable in Pennsylvania, where Jews compose 2.5 percent of the population but cast 4.5 percent of the vote; California, where they are 2.9 percent of the population but cast 6 percent of the vote; and Florida, where they are 4.2 percent of the voting population but cast 5 percent of the vote. There are researchers who note that without a decisive majority in the Jewish electorate the impact of the Jewish vote in national elections would be marginal, partly because of its predictability.[44]

Though Jewish voters increasingly identify themselves as independent, their customary allegiance to the Democratic candidate gives them a voice in the party leadership that is made more audible because of the willingness of Jewish funders to contribute to the costly campaigning process. Jews in America also generally have more to give and have not been reluctant to use money and other forms of largess such as opening their homes for fundraising events during campaigns, which amplifies their political voice. Over 60 percent of the funds raised for political campaigns of the Democratic Party and an increasing percentage of Republican campaign funds stem from Jewish sources. There was concern among campaign strategists that the McCain-Feingold legal strictures against soft money, direct unlimited giving to the campaign would have a negative impact on Jewish funders. But after the campaign of 2004 it became clear that there are more Jewish givers who make small contributions, below the $2,000 limit, and that much of Jewish giving is focused on issue advocacy through advertising and other marketing techniques, which is not restricted by the McCain-Feingold law. Also, Jewish givers are more prone to utilize bundling, that allows a major donor to act as a collector for a collective grant to the campaign. The possibility of soliciting huge sums of money, compensating for smaller donations by skillful use of Internet networking that was so effectively used by the Obama campaign in 2008, was earlier noted as characteristic of Jewish giving. In Jewish political fundraising the donations of the "big giver" were nearly matched by smaller givers. In short, Jewish givers are at once issue focused and altruistic. The money given to campaigns usually has no quid pro quo. It is given to a candidate who supports the "right" causes, which does not necessarily mean that it is confined to Jewish causes. Using their foundations rather than organizations or interest groups such as trade unions, individual Jewish funders can give campaign money that in most cases supports liberal causes.[45]

Against these political assets must be weighed the growing possibility of fragmentation of the Jewish vote as assimilation and its accompanying decline in affiliation with religious congregations and secular organizations increases. Survey research, for example, indicates that Orthodox Jews, the fastest-growing segment but still less than 10 percent of the American Jewish vote, deviate from the prevailing liberal voting pattern, especially on the crucial separation of church and state issue. In local elections that deviation from the Jewish norm can make a big difference. In New York City's municipal election for mayor in 1988 Mayor Dinkins won over half of the large liberal Jewish vote in Manhattan, but the more conservative and frequently more religious Jewish voters in the outer boroughs gave Giuliani over 70 percent of their vote. Dinkins won by a narrow margin, but in the next election Giuliani, running on a Republican and liberal line, easily won the election.

The primacy of the security of Israel issue also continues across the board, but there are considerable variations among Jewish political subcultures concerning the definition of security and its relation to an enduring Arab-Israeli peace. Orthodox Jews of all stripes stated that they feel "very close" to Israel (74 percent) and supported the invasion of Gaza in 2008, compared with Jews who identified themselves as "just Jewish" (31 percent), who usually did not.[46] In decades to come American Jewry may no longer be able to bring a unified voting block to the polls on crucial issues. Yet certain red lines that the majority of Jewish voters will not cross continue to exist. The Republican aspiration to win a majority of the Jewish vote or at least a higher percentage seems more futile than ever after the election of 2008, which gave Obama 78 percent of the Jewish vote. It is possible that moderate liberal Jewish voters may give up all hopes of consistency by voting affirmatively for Israel's military action against Iranian proxies like Hezbollah and Hamas while opposing the war in Afghanistan. That would be reminiscent of Lyndon Johnson's dilemma concerning Jewish opposition to North Vietnamese aggression against South Vietnam while strongly supporting military aid to Israel to defend against the aggression of its Arab neighbors. For the Jewish voter it sometimes depends on whose ox is being gored.

American Jewry is one of several ethnic communities that, more by seduction than coercion, obey the call to meld into the majority culture. Other ethnic voting blocs, like German or Irish Americans, heeded that call more rapidly. Some groups find some comfortable middle ground that they may hold for generations. American Jewry follows the latter model only to discover that the middle ground of slow immersion into the majority culture creates problems of group coherence based on generational fissures. Questions also arise about whether there can be a definable political identity for a community whose governance is based on voluntary compliance of a free citizenry. Politics after all deals with power, and when it seeks compliance through persuasion rather than command, political coherence is often lost.

Within the open pluralistic arena of American politics the maintenance of a separate and sometimes aberrant political culture can also be problematic. Commitment to an issue is given for the moment but there is little assurance of constancy. It is not inconceivable, for example, that we may some time in the future awaken to find American Jewry will lessen its financial support of Holocaust museums and memorials and perhaps even pull down a conservative voting lever. That becomes more probable when the organizational and religio-cultural communal ties that bind Jews together loosen so that, like other ethnic cultures, it is no longer speaks with one distinct voice that is easily heard in the American political arena. Even today the identification of Jews as liberal or conservative, or recently neoconservative, can hardly represent the total picture of where Jews stand politically. The very freedom to advocate its communal political agenda also acts as a stimulant to highly individualized rather than communal views regarding public policy. In any Jewish group one can find autonomous, sometimes aberrant views, insisting to be heard. When sufficiently compelling such charismatic voices sometimes speak louder and more compellingly than the communal one.

Jewish Communalism as a Factor in Its Political Culture

It is tempting to probe what lies behind the communalism or "groupiness" in which Jewish political culture is incubated. As used here the term "groupiness" serves as a synonym for the communal bonding and identity without which a distinct political culture cannot develop. There are a variety of views regarding the sources of the elaborate communal organizational network that shaped exilic Jewish political culture. It has led to challenging the view of Jewish life in its diaspora as a chronicle of powerlessness and victimization. In its place there is a more complex reality that notes that Jewish communities were often able to develop virtually autonomous institutions within the host cultures. In some cases, as during the Jagiellonian dynasty in Poland (1386-1582), they became almost completely self-governing. That is to say, even before the reestablishment of the Jewish state in 1948, many of the requisite political habits and instruments for nationhood were already in place in some nascent form. The rich organizational network joined with the religious congregation kept Judaism alive. "Without some modicum of political strength and the ability to use it," observes one historian, "the Jewish people would certainly have vanished."[47]

It may be that the Jewish tradition of self-governance accounts for the conjured fear that there is an inordinate Jewish political power at play in the American political arena. The vision contains a peculiar twist since it is leveled against a community that historically has been very vulnerable.

A rational approach would have to come to grips with the fact that if such control were a reality it would say much more about the weakness of the American policymaking process than about Jewish power. One rarely mentioned consequence of the charge of excessive Jewish political power is that it feeds a catastrophic perspective in the Jewish political persona, which, fueled by the memory of the Holocaust, has deepened in recent years. American Jews, especially those who have lived through the years of the Holocaust, rarely feel that they are totally secure. Sensing a continuous threat, they react with a greater need to develop and possess power or to call for protection from those who already have it. There is a constant need to generate support of government, which in turn creates a greater need to master the skills required to play the game of politics.

That urgency, rooted in fear, has placed a premium on using the political system effectively. American Jewish political agencies and leaders deploy resources to inform Jews and all citizens of their advocacy. They have a good knowledge of the location of the national power centers and how to gain access to them. We have no measure of how Jewish political influence or power compares with other ethnic voting blocs, but it is safe to assume that American Jewry can bring power into play beyond its voting volume, especially on the Israel issue. They have in their arsenal some of America's most astute and knowledgeable students of politics who understand the rules, written and unwritten, that govern the wheeling and dealing characteristic of the American political process. Jews are a comparatively small constituency, yet they are disproportionately the fundraisers, the campaign organizers, the speechwriters, and the pundits involved in the practice of professional politics. We have already noted the change that has occurred in the involvement of Jewish candidates in elective politics. Where once such potential candidates for office kept themselves in the background, today they are more likely to seek office. The result has been that Jewish citizens proportionately are more likely to run for political offices and to some unknown degree win office beyond their proportion of the electorate on all levels of government.[48] Jewish representation in Congress is more than three times its proportion of the electorate.

That does not mean that Jewish officeholders always stand ready to do the bidding of Jewish communal advocates. They first and foremost belong to the growing group of Jewish citizens who list themselves as "just Jewish," meaning that religious faith shares commitment with other shaping influences, which may be secular and even antireligious. They may belong to a religious congregation for political reasons but are in fact only nominally Jewish. Such nuances remain unknown to those who are apprehensive about Jewish political power. The image of disproportionate power in the hands of Jews persists despite the fact that the play of Jewish power has remained well within the customary and legal limitations imposed on special interest pleading. When combined with another mainstay of anti-Semitic rhetoric that pictures Jews as disloyal or of divided loyalty, the charge that Jews exercise too much power can be threatening because it enables the building of a caricature of a disloyal minority with foreign ideas and culture that seeks to undermine the nation, an image that is a centerpiece of the anti-Semitic imagination.

Under normal circumstances politics is related to the control of the instruments of state power, embodied in its purest form in its taxing and police powers.[49] The power to collect taxes, for example, belongs everywhere to government, but political power or influence can also be exercised privately by the individual citizen and by ethnic, religious, or business interests that seek help from government to further their goals. There is an unspoken quid pro quo whereby such special-interest groups are assured security and access in turn for loyalty to the national government. In a mature polity governance is enabled by interlocking power arrangements formalized by law. All elements of society play the power game to find their place in the polity that represents society. What we observe in the American polity is that the Jewish electorate is an accepted participant in these power arrangements. The complaint that Jews exercise too much power is sounded by those not yet reconciled to the fact that Jews are an integral part of the polity. The assumption that Jews are somehow separate converts a normal concern about the security of Israel to evidence that their loyalties serve communal rather than the national interest. For such a mindset that the two interests may be confluent is not considered.

American Foreign Policy and the Ethnic Interest

In the case of the Jews and other ethnics like Greek or Irish Americans, the play of power is best observed in the foreign policy arena. Jews may strongly favor government support for abortion rights, but that does not distinguish them from other groups who feel strongly one way or the other about this issue. Jewish voters demonstrate keen interest in politics on all levels, from local zoning regulations to environmental issues, but it is in the area of foreign policy that the American Jewish interests can best be observed. The wielding of its communal power, real and imagined, occurs on the national rather than the local level of politics. Such a projection of ethnic power is not unusual. At the turn of the century Irish Americans loved to "twist the lion's tail," and political leaders gladly complied to gain the Irish vote.[50] After the Yalta Conference in February 1945, Polish Americans made reversing the "Crime of Crimea" the centerpiece of their foreign policy position. The immigrant community of Cuban Americans passionately opposed the Castro regime, and during the sixties its role in the Bay of Pigs invasion and the missile crisis that was its sequel nearly plunged the world into darkness. Greek Americans placed the State Department in a quandary when they pushed hard to regain their Turkish-occupied territory of north Cyprus. Turkey was an important NATO partner. In the same vein, Jews possess a special need to support Israel, so much so that during the fifties and sixties communal needs for facilities for the ageing and for education of the young had a lower claim on the Jewish philanthropic dollar than financial support of Israel. In short, such ethnic advocacy poses special problems for the making of foreign policy, and nowhere more so than in issues of special concern for American Jewry that involve the strategic oil-rich region of the Middle East.

There is a direct relationship between American Jewry's concern about Israel's security and the sustained high level of hostility maintained by her Arab neighbors for over seven decades. A sizable portion of Jewish political activism is generated by that sustained threat. The end of the cold war might have signaled an end to the Arab-Israeli conflict, but all attempts, including the noteworthy Oslo Accords (1995), proved to be fruitless. It is the very intractability of the conflict that serves as fuel for the continued high level of Jewish voter interest.

Yet as deep as is the American Jewish concern about Israel, is it is not the only concern that turns the interest of the American Jewish voter to foreign policy. Jewish voters also harbor a broad interest in international peace and comity among nations as part of their liberal world outlook. That high interest in world affairs may also be related to the comparatively high Jewish educational level, where such interests are more pronounced. More difficult to describe is a certain urban/urbane *mentalité* linked to city living that seeks to go beyond the local and provincial. That posture, which is disproportionately found among Jews, is not confined to the United States. During the cold war Jews were condemned in the Communist world as "rootless cosmopolitans" to indicate that their loyalty was questionable. They were seen as somehow less patriotic. Cosmopolitan Jews seemed immune from the nationalistic jingoism and totalistic ideologies that prevailed in the societies in which they lived.

Their universalistic worldview was also embodied in democratic socialism, some version of which had a strong drawing power among European Jews. It was that orientation, which assumed various forms, that became the hallmark of the derivative political culture of American Jewry. It finds its place in the statism favored by Jewish voters who found a home in the left wing of the Democratic Party. Of course, it no longer answers to the social democratic label, and many Jewish voters would blanch if they realized the social democratic roots of their ideological orientation. Yet the Jewish "love affair" with Roosevelt's New Deal was in fact within striking distance of the idea that government must regulate and monitor to insure an equitable humane social order. We will have more to say on the relation between urbanity and the Jewish political persona in our discussion on Jewish liberalism in the following chapter.

The attraction for the universal rather than the national can also be observed in the Jewish passion for international law and their attraction to a transnational planned language like Esperanto, which became particularly popular among Jews at the turn of the century.[51] It has been deepened by a heightened interest of the Jewish voter in the moral aspects of the use of power and its relation to war. There are no statistics available on how individual Jews express their abhorrence of war by becoming conscientious objectors, but, like Quakers, American Jews have been prominent in the peace and disarmament movements of the twenties. Noteworthy in the quest for peace as a response to the bloodletting of World War I in the decade of the twenties were the activities of Salmon O. Levinson, a Chicago Jewish lawyer whose willingness to commit his wealth allowed him to play an important role in the formulation of the Pact of Paris in 1928.[52] At the height of his fame Albert Einstein became deeply involved in the peace movement and attracted many Jewish thinkers to follow his lead.

In the year before Wilson declared war in April 1917, some Jewish voters were torn by the inconsistency of belonging to an alliance to "make the world safe for democracy" that included the tyrannical tsarist regime. The Eastern Jewish immigrant welcomed the first Kerensky phase of Russian revolution, which held out the promise of equal rights for Russian Jewry. Encouraged by Lenin's open denunciation of anti-Semitism and the rapid advancement of the younger educated strata of Jews into the highest echelons of the civil service and the Communist Party itself, American Jews hoped that the Soviet regime would put an end to the age-old Russian plague of anti-Semitism. The commitment by Agro-Joint, a subdivision of the Joint Distribution Committee, of $16 million for resettlement of hard-pressed Ukrainian Jews in the Crimea, was partly a reflection of that early optimism. But it was not destined to last long. The regime's persecution of the Bundist leaders of a separate Jewish branch of the world Socialist movement, as well as Zionists, dampened enthusiasm among the divided American Jews, who had in addition to carry the onus of supporting a regime that demonstrated increasing evidence of its totalitarian impulse.

After the Jewish labor movement barely survived the attempt by the Comintern to infiltrate and redirect its energies in the late twenties, Jewish support for the Communist Party waned. Compared with the support for the revolution sixteen years earlier, Roosevelt's diplomatic recognition of the Soviet regime in 1933 was not well received by the Jewish press. By the 1930s enthusiasm for the Soviet system, once fairly widespread among Socialists, became largely limited to the small Communist wing of the Jewish polity. The inconstancy of the party's foreign policy position and the purge trials of the thirties further dampened Jewish support. Yet it was the only regime that seemed willing to resist Berlin's onslaught, which contained an open genocidal threat against Jews. When the Kremlin entered into a nonaggression pact with the Nazi regime in August 1939, which cleared the way for the dual occupation of Poland and the war that inevitably followed, much of the remaining support for the Soviet regime was dissipated.

American Jewry and the International Crises of the Thirties

It is not surprising that American Jews were among the first of the ethnics to warn of the threat emanating from Berlin. In the "great debate" of the thirties concerning the direction of American foreign policy, Jews were predictably strongly interventionist. The left wing of the community contributed notably in volunteers and finances to support the Loyalist cause in Spain. Even after the failure of the Evian Conference (July 1938) to find a haven for the thousands of Jews being extruded from the Reich, Roosevelt could rely on Jewish support to counteract the isolationist block in Congress. Among the ethnic voting blocks in the unprecedented third-term election of 1940, Roosevelt won the largest majority from the Jewish electorate. Jewish voters were concerned about the limitations of the "cash and carry" policy and supported Roosevelt's controversial implementation of the Destroyer Bases Deal (September 1940) by executive order and Lend Lease (February 1941), including shipping supplies to the Soviet Union after June 1941 when the Nazi juggernaut turned eastward. The principles of the Atlantic Charter that came out of Roosevelt's meeting with Churchill in Argentia, Newfoundland (August 1941), spoke of "freedom from fear and want" as well as "freedom of religion," precisely what Jewish community-relations organizations had been heralding.

But it would require more than the rhetoric of liberal democracy to convince Berlin to abandon its genocidal campaign. Roosevelt had shown political courage in bringing a reluctant nation to accept the necessity of at least saving Britain. But the Rublee Schacht Wohlthat negotiations that produced a "Statement of Agreement" designed to bring order into the refugee chaos was soon outpaced by events. A move to allow a "one-time" exception so that thousands of stranded German Jewish children in

France could be admitted outside the quota system, the Wagner-Rogers Act, was rejected by Roosevelt and died in committee. As noted, a year later during the London "Blitz" a bill admitting non-Jewish British children was passed in record-breaking time. The meaning of the rejection of the Wagner-Rogers bill did not escape Jewish leadership. Roosevelt would not risk the image that the war was a Jewish war, which would have been strengthened by the rescue of twenty thousand Jewish children. The assumption was that the American people were not ready to mobilize for a war to rescue European Jewry.

The Roosevelt administration's reluctance to directly intervene with Berlin concerning the Jewish question went beyond indifference to the fate of the Jews. It involved a critical need to mobilize American public opinion still mired in the immediate problem of the Depression. Not until 1944 would Roosevelt feel it politically feasible to circumvent the restrictive immigration laws. Wartime American information strategy was based on the principle of playing down the Jewish aspect of the catastrophe lest Nazi propaganda based on the accusation that the United States was waging a war to save the Jews was reinforced. Yet American Jewry's support for waging a "just" war was drawn from the deepest recesses of its political culture and went beyond the rescue of its kin. But during the period of American neutrality between September 1939 and December 1941, when isolationism remained strong, such a strongly interventionist sentiment posed political problems for the administration. Roosevelt's political instincts told him that even a hint that he was embarking on a "Jewish war" would place his administration in jeopardy. But as the war in Europe raged and it became clear that Berlin's intent was to destroy the North Atlantic community, which strengthened the nation commercially and buttressed its democratic ideology, the strength of isolationism waned. By the time of the bombing of Pearl Harbor on December 7, 1941, it had become a far less significant force in the nation's politics. But the need to prevent the war from being imaged as a Jewish war, the primary thrust of Berlin's propaganda, remained even after the successful invasion of Europe in June 1944 when it became possible to envisage victory. As the full horrific details of the Final Solution became known, the administration's information strategy that played down the Jewish aspect of the war in an effort to avoid Berlin's "Jewish war" label proved to be effective. There was virtual silence regarding the deportations and the death camps. Only with victory was the "curtain of silence" concerning the "Final Solution" partially lifted.

As noted, it was Roosevelt's Jewish secretary of the treasury Henry Morgenthau Jr. who brought evidence of the State Department's subverting of rescue activity that convinced the president to establish the War Refugee Board in January 1944, eleven months before his campaign for a fourth term. A few months later in June, the successful invasion of Europe helped remove most doubts Roosevelt might still have had regarding an ultimate Allied victory. That certainty, which was momentarily undermined by the surprise German winter offensive in the Ardennes in December 1944, was followed by his circumvention of the immigration laws by executive order to establish a "Freeport" in Oswego, New York, which reenters our discussion in chapter 6. Despite urgent pleading by Jewish leaders, little could be done to convince the president to abandon the policy that the best way to rescue European Jewry was to win the war as quickly as possible. When it was most critically needed, Jewish political influence proved insufficient to gain the inclusion of the rescue of European Jewry in American war aims. The creation of the War Refugee Board and the circumvention of the immigration laws with the creation of a Freeport in Oswego, New York, came too late to save the millions who perished.

Organization and Leadership

While the independent-minded Jewish voter determines his or her own position on the political issues of the day, the communal stance on any particular issue, if indeed one can be determined, is transmitted to Congress or the Oval Office by communal leaders who hold their position by dint of their positions in the myriad Jewish communal organizations and religious congregations. That relation between Jewish voters and their organizations is anomalous, since the question of who legally speaks to government authority for American Jewry in the absence of a formalized legal procedure does not exist. No formal way, such as binding elections, to determine the leader can be imposed, since ethnic organizations do not possess legal sanction over their constituents, whose status as free American citizens is immutable. But the absence of legal authority hardly discourages those who claim to speak for the community. Organizational leaders are compelled to rely on persuasion rather than coercion. Would-be leaders proliferate even while few Jews see themselves as followers. Yet leaders would not long hold their elevated place if they flew in the face of the positions that prevail among their constituents. How Jacob Schiff felt about entering the war on the side of the Allies in April 1917 (he opposed it) or how Stephen Wise felt about lend lease can tell us a great deal about how American Jewry viewed itself and the assumptions it brought into the political arena. Their positions resonated with what many Jews felt. A flaunting of the popular will was less possible after 1914, when the Congress movement called for the democratization of Jewish organizational life.

The role of Nahum Goldmann is especially interesting. For years the founder and president of the World Jewish Congress wanted to play the role of world diplomat for the Jews, and he occasionally convinced others that he held that imperious position. The reparations agreement that Goldmann was instrumental in negotiating with Konrad Adenauer, the chancellor of the German Federal Republic, brought desperately needed capital to Israel. But in a community increasingly concerned about democracy, in which every faction jealously guarded its prerogative, Goldmann, who was sometimes out of step with the communal consensus, was made painfully aware that he was a leader without followers. Nor did he possess the sizeable estate that helped bypass the need to find popular consensus. Israel's right-wing parties opposed the reparations agreement, and other conduits for leadership such as the willingness to give to Jewish causes were not available to him. In the end he was dependent on his position in the World Jewish Congress, a Zionist-oriented agency founded by Rabbi Stephen Wise in 1934. Goldmann never found an independent base in the American Jewish community to play his leadership role.

In the case of Mayor Michael Bloomberg of New York City, who humorously calls himself "a short Jewish billionaire," the requisite capital was available but the Jewish connection was missing. Unlike Jacob Schiff, who was immersed in Jewish causes, Bloomberg is almost disconnected from them and displays no special ease or familiarity before Jewish audiences. Also unlike Schiff, who was a staunch Republican, Bloomberg's loyalty to party is vague. He is nominally a Republican, but depending on political circumstance, his position often falls closer to the Democratic Party. He participates in some Jewish agencies like the Board of Trustees of the Jewish Museum, but his favorite charity is his alma mater, Johns Hopkins University. Those familiar with this new leadership type have a special acronym for them. They are called WASH, White Anglo Saxon Hebrews.[53] George Soros also qualifies as a WASH but differs markedly from Bloomberg, whose political attraction is based on his hardheaded managerial skill transferred to the administration of municipal government, while Soros retains an attachment to a familiar universalized Jewish liberalism. Neither is focused on a Jewish need or agenda. They rather are members of the political class who happen to be Jewish. The age when communal leaders like Rabbi Steven Wise had access to the Oval Office during the Roosevelt administration has passed. Almost as a kind of compensation, the number of Jews holding appointed and elected office has increased notably. Yet these Jewish officeholders would face considerable political risk if they projected an image of exclusive representation of a Jewish communal interest. They serve the commonweal. In a sense, the Jewish connection to national political leadership has become more nebulous. It is difficult to know who speaks for American Jewry and about what.

Is an empowered Jewish citizenry governable when the organizations that want to speak for it do not have governing authority? A good window to view the play of Jewish political power is in the area where the political priorities of an interest group are transmitted to officeholders. It is in that transaction that the vexing question of who speaks for the community and what message should be transmitted arises. From Mahjong clubs to the American Jewish Committee, which boasts special ties to the State Department, Jews seem to have given birth to every type of organization humankind is heir to.[54] *The American Jewish Yearbook*, which gives a yearly statistical breakdown of these organizations, lists only a portion of the approximately 17,500 organizations divided into forty-nine categories. The United Jewish Appeal (UJA), which reaches into virtually every Jewish community, acts like a voluntary internal revenue service, and together with the local federations joined nationally in the Council of Jewish Federations (CJF), are at the very heart of Jewish communal governance.[55]

The best known of these organizations, like the Hebrew Immigrant Aid Society (HIAS) or the American Jewish Joint Distribution Committee (JDC or "Joint"), are in the community service area. Eighteen percent are religious organizations that expanded in the twenties to serve the growing need in areas of second settlement. Most conspicuous are the Jewish defense organizations such as the American Jewish Committee (AJC), the American Jewish Congress (AJCong) (now defunct), and the Anti Defamation League (ADL), which was spun off by B'nai B'rith in 1914. This fraternal order was the first American Jewish agency to establish branches abroad. The claimants of those who seek to represent the Jewish political voice are multiple and, as we shall note, often irreconcilable.

Aside from the fact that Jews, like most Americans, are "joiners," the multiplicity of organizations finds its roots in the Jewish condition. With the rise of the Zionist movement in the thirties, the number and type of organizations were duplicated across the board so that Hadassah, a Zionist women's fraternal order also involved in philanthropy abroad, duplicated the program of the National Jewish Women's Organization. When the centrist Zionist organization no longer met the needs of Jewish women involved with labor Zionism, they established their own Pioneer Jewish Women (Na'amat). Religious congregations and agencies are triplicated, one for each major branch, and since the growth of branches (or twigs) continues with the establishment of the Reconstructionists and the secular humanists, the sheer number of organizations seemed to grow even as the number of Jews attracted to them diminished.

Proliferation of Jewish organizations grew out of the historical circumstances of Jewish communal life in the diaspora. In some countries where there was no recourse to the authority of the state, Jews developed organizations to meet the need for courts, healthcare, and social services. Sometimes these functions were combined in one body or *Kahal*. As late as the first decade of the twentieth century, some communities retained virtual autonomy for such matters as marriage and burial and their right to assess and collect taxes, which were often recognized in secular public law.[56] With the rise of the modern state much of the sanction of Jewish communal law fell into disuse. Where it persisted in the area of religion, as in the need for a "get" (divorce) among observant Jews, it often generates endless problems. In recent years long-standing organizations like Hadassah, while still able to generate great acts of devotion and generosity from its membership, could no longer claim official communal status. While Jewish secular mass-membership organizations were able to build hospitals and implement massive philanthropic projects, they could not create communities of faith. The religious congregation proved far more able to sustain itself than did secular mass-membership organizations, an unexpected reality for a highly secularized community.[57] They were generational phenomena that primarily met the social and economic needs of first- and second-generation Jewish families. Their proliferation was also a reflection of the growing variegation of Jewish life and the fact that the social networks of the host society remained closed to them. A country club that was restricted could lead to the establishment of a Jewish country club. Every restricted professional or social organization served as a launching pad for a duplicate Jewish organization.

As Jews professionalized, the habit of establishing separate organizations, from the country club to Jewish dentists' associations, continued, fueled partly by a policy of restriction in gentile clubs and residential neighborhoods. Upscale Jewish neighborhoods like the Grand Concourse in the Bronx and Eastern Parkway in Brooklyn, and many of the newly established golf clubs of the suburbs, trace their origins to gentile membership restriction. There are Jewish lawyer groups and organizations for Jewish doctors, scientists, and engineers that would not have been established had membership in gentile clubs been open. The increasing openness of American professional and social organizations after World War II may partially account for the decline in membership in exclusively Jewish organizations. Survivalists note hopefully that despite the loss of drawing power of exclusively Jewish organizations, the primary association of Jews continues to be with other Jews, but Jewish "groupiness" is a less apparent phenomenon today when a separate Jewish mobility ladder is less necessary. The rising level of intermarriage reflects the fact that in the colleges and social institutions were young people meet and court, Jewish separateness is no longer a noteworthy phenomenon.

The turn-of-the-century proliferation of Jewish organizations, especially in the political realm, also reflected the fact that there was great diversity in the immigrant Jewish community. When added to the seriousness Jews assigned to political ideology, the conflicts that followed made it appear that the sense of common ground that shores up the idea of community was far from the minds of the Jewish immigrant. The cultural, religious, political, and regional divisions within the community did not remain an innocent fact. Communal fragmentation became a source of weakness in the 1930s when American Jewish leaders found themselves unable to speak to the Roosevelt administration with one voice to advocate a more active rescue effort. The three attempts to unify American Jewry in the face of the Holocaust failed.[58] Despite the establishment of the National Jewish Community Relations Advisory Council in 1944 to create better coherence, the Holocaust experience did not provide a lesson on the price of ever-increasing fragmentation and individuation. It may well be that organizational pluralism may be inherent in modernity, which most Jews cherish.

Three decades after Auschwitz when the opportunity to "rescue" Soviet Jewry materialized, Jews again proved unable to agree regarding the crucial question of resettlement of the Soviet emigrants, many of whom "dropped out" in an effort to settle in the United States rather than the destination stated on their Israeli visas.[59] In domestic politics the absence of a common vision was again observable in the varying attitudes toward George Bush's "faith-based" social welfare programs, which challenged the basic church-state separation principle held dear by most American Jews but today welcomed by many Orthodox Jews. More recently a division has developed on the central question of the strategy for Palestinian-Israeli peace. The more conciliatory approach proposed by the recently formed "J Street" organization is at odds with the harder view of AIPAC, which generally takes its cues from the Likud Party in Israel. Clearly the spectrum of positions held by the American Jewish voter on crucial issues is broad. But even if a common position unity was achievable in a free democratic environment, some would question its desirability. It is precisely because the Jewish vote is not monolithic on most issues that keeps the hope that positions can be changed alive. Without that plasticity American Jewry would not long remain a player in the game of politics, which is based on compromise.

Some view the proliferation of organizations supporting widely varying positions positively. They reason that it is organizations rather than individual Jews speaking to power holders that transmit the needs and desires of the Jewish voter, and that it is an indication of a vital polity where many flowers bloom. But while this may have been true in earlier periods, in the free atmosphere of America today the abundance of organizations of all kinds is more a reflection of the broad variety of often conflicting interests in the community. Unanswered is the question of what happens when the inability to achieve unity becomes a matter of life and death, as it did during the Holocaust years. Then we see that the very signs of political vitality as reflected in diverse opinion makes for loss of communal coherence. We shall return to this dilemma in chapter 4, which deals with American Jewry and the Holocaust.

Not only is the development of a coherent communal position difficult, but how such an agreed position is then transmitted to government policy makers is also unclear. There is little agreement on who should speak for American Jewry. The model that shows leaders of Jewish communal organizations transmitting their respective positions to waiting lawmakers, where they are then considered by policymakers and merged or rejected into proposed legislation, is vastly oversimplified. The policymaking process is multileveled and enormously complex. Many of the proposals of the agenda of any special interest group cannot be accommodated. They are destined for the legislative wastebasket to be raised again at some more favorable moment. The development of the agenda of proposals or wishes to be considered by decision makers is still more complex at the communal end. Opinions are ostensibly developed through dialogue and, as in the case of American Jewry, they often reflect irresolvable conflict rather than consensus. In some rare instances, such as advocating change in an anti-Semitic Catholic liturgy, a unified position can be achieved, but organizational turf considerations interfere with the delivery of the message. Usually the decision maker or power holder hears only a cacophony of voices rather than a focused message.

All ethnic communities face the challenge of how to balance their communal culture and politics in order to meld into the majority culture. The challenge in Jewish communal politics has been to find the political juncture where the need to act jointly with the majority political culture can be reconciled with the need for communal survival. In most cases the tensions between survival and belonging can be resolved over time. But there are a few examples, such as the communal position on the admission of Jewish refugees in the thirties, that could not be reconciled with the restrictive immigration sentiment that held sway in the American electorate. The consequence was one of the deepest tragedies in Jewish history. The majority culture was able to view the Jewish need as only a sectarian demand that, if realized, would interfere with their welfare. There is no assurance that the democratic process will always yield a humane response.

On the level of national politics, finding a way to attract and hold the ethnic vote is a major party concern. By the midtwenties ethnic voting blocs were recognized as important elements in achieving electoral success. Often the administration in power would assign their "house" Jew to communicate with communal leaders, thereby preempting community choice. David Niles played such a role for Roosevelt and Truman, as did Leonard Garment for Richard Nixon. Both men were only nominally involved in Jewish affairs but had impeccable party credentials. Jews chosen to speak for the Oval Office did not represent a communal interest. They spoke for the administration in power. Like other Jews in Roosevelt's inner circle, Sam Rosenman, whom Roosevelt retained from Governor Smith's administration, considered himself an American who happened to be born to Jewish parents. He had great reservations about pressing a Jewish interest in the Oval Office.[60] Rabbi Stephen Wise and Louis Marshall, on the other hand, considered themselves Jewish communal leaders first and foremost. It would be Jewish members of Roosevelt's inner circle, derisively called the "Jew Deal" by Roosevelt haters, who could furnish access to the Oval Office during the war years. With the exception of Henry Morgenthau Jr., they were usually unwilling or unable to do so.

Theoretically the contours of Jewish political culture can be studied by viewing the positions taken by Jewish leaders and the organizations they represent vis-à-vis government officeholders. But since the community has never produced one political leader or political grouping accepted by all factions while remaining acceptable to the administration in power, American Jewry has many voices, none of which can claim sole legitimacy. There have been Jews like Albert Einstein or Rabbi Joshua Heschel, whose popularity calmed the normal communal tensions, but no single charismatic leader that embodies the communal voice has yet developed.[61] We are left with the problem of determining who actually speaks for American Jewry to whom and about what.

The reason for the absence of such leaders is that the road to communal power is difficult to negotiate, requiring the rare combination of political savvy and spiritual depth. The comparatively high level of education of the Jewish electorate and its growing secularization works against the drawing power of the charismatic leader.[62] It is not a simple matter of projecting political stardom on a prospective leader like Elie Wiesel, the well-known survivor and writer on Holocaust themes. It requires dozens of steps until a communal consensus can be achieved. More often than not it is never fully reached. The image of a monolithic community is mostly a figment of the anti-Semitic imagination. To reach consensus a shared platform has first to be built and then a policy hammered out even while the political ground is shifting. Presidential administrations change, ideologies like Zionism that might furnish common grounds become fragmented, new political leaders come to the fore, so that, except for its abiding liberalism that is itself ever changing, there is little constancy in the Jewish political world. What was true yesterday is often no longer true today. Frequently the moment common ground is reached the delicate structure collapses and the parties are forced to begin over. Yet few Jewish names are found on the rosters of gun clubs and the permissibility of same-sex marriages is almost taken for granted.

The Jewish Voter: Forever Maverick?

Finally, our quest for finding out what makes American Jewry tick politically would not be complete without addressing the most salient characteristics of the American Jewish political persona, the individual Jewish voter. That is not an easy task, since determining the personality of a group comes to more than learning about the collective proclivity of its voters. If there is an element of truth in the observation that contentiousness is the most constant element in the Jewish political personality, we may test thousands of Jewish voters only to discover that group consensus cannot be precisely determined. Jewish voters are generally in agreement on certain issues but differ on the meaning of the agreement and on its details. We can safely dismiss the indictment at the center of anti-Semitic rhetoric, which ranges from the inability of Jews to fit into the polity to their conspiratorial hunger for power. There are dozens of other characteristics, positive and negative, that can be cited to describe the Jewish political personality. We here confine ourselves to a few.

We leave the discussion of one of the most frequently cited characteristics, Jewish radicals and radical Jews, to the following chapter, where it is viewed in the context of Jewish liberalism. The disproportionate Jewish attraction to various kinds of political radicalism turns out not to be a primary trait that distinguishes the Jewish voter, who under normal circumstances is actually conservative though also liberal. American Jewish political behavior departs from the norm of other ethnic voting blocs in other respects, like its commitment to the Democratic Party. The temptation is to dismiss these distinctive characteristics on the assumption that every voting bloc has something distinct, an eccentricity or aberration that departs from the majority norm. That is the reason why they form separate voting blocs in the first place. But Jewish maverick political behavior, whether it concerns political hyperactivity or a penchant for organizing and voting for third parties, can yield important clues to the historically rooted forces that shape its political behavior. Most interesting is the tendency for Jewish voters to veer off to third parties in proportionately higher numbers than other ethnic voting blocs, especially if the candidates are on the left side of the political spectrum. Accurate figures are difficult to come by. Eugene V. Debs may have tolled as high as 38 percent of the Jewish vote in the election of 1920 and Bob La Follette as high as 22 percent in 1924. We have noted that the vote for Henry Wallace in 1948 was 14 to 15 percent. In New York State the American Labor Party, sponsored by Jewish labor leaders, won 15 percent in 1936. John Anderson won 14 percent in 1980, but Ross Perot's Reform Party, emerging out of the "cranky" political right, received only 9 percent in 1996, suggesting that the maverick Jewish voter is still more comfortable on the center left of the political spectrum.[63]

Viewed in the context of ethnic or immigrant politics, the most interesting departure is their penchant for going off on their political own to form parties like the American Labor Party (1935) and Liberal Party (1944) in New York State, where Jewish voters were concentrated. Though local phenomenon, these parties addressed national rather than Jewish issues but were organized by Jews and funded by secular agencies that were part of the Jewish labor movement, such as the International Ladies Garment Workers Union (ILGWU). They were not packaged as Jewish parties. With the possible exception of Finnish Americans no American ethnic group has served as the home of a political party, though some like the Wobblies or the Communist Party have been dependent on immigrant support. Generating a third party from within an ethnic voting bloc has been relatively rare in all Western democracies.[64] Withal, of all ethnic voting blocs, the Jewish vote on the national level for the Democrat ticket has been the most sustained. We have noted that in contrast to other ethnic voters after the election of 1936, Jews increased their support for Roosevelt. The Jewish voter's constancy was not always so. After the election of Warren Harding, the Republican candidate in 1920, Jews began to change their party allegiance to the Democrats. The conversion was fairly complete by the election of 1928.[65] Thereafter the Jewish vote has remained consistently in the Democratic fold.

In recent years the uniqueness of Jewish political culture is evidenced not only by its penchant for creating and supporting third parties and its loyalty to the liberal wing of the Democratic Party, but also by serving as the seedbed for new political movements rooted in unattended grievances or an unpopular war. The best-known of these developed during the later cold war years and was concerned primarily with strategic planning to stave off Soviet expansionism. The Neoconservative movement traces its roots back to the thirties, where the integrity of the world Socialist movement after the depredations of the Stalinist regime became a serious issue for disaffected Marxist intellectuals. Most were Trotskyists, who claimed to be the earliest savants of the Left. The "Neocons" early recognized that under the Kremlin's control, the dream of a Socialist movement for a just and equitable social order had gone awry. Thereafter they spared no effort to alert others regarding the Communist threat. Theirs was a movement composed of public intellectuals, journalists, academicians, disproportionately of Jewish origin, who provided the American conservative movement, formally reestablished by William Buckley in the fifties, with intellectual muscle. The ongoing debate within the Jewish community between Right and Left was in a sense extended to the American polity.

Yet the Neoconservatives had almost no internal impact in the Jewish polity. Had they been obliged to garner votes in the Jewish community during the seventies they would have had a very poor showing. But their goal, if indeed there was a collective goal, was not to impact Jewish political culture but rather the larger national one. Most Jewish voters were not yet ready to accept the idea that truth and enlightenment could emanate from the Right.[66] Nor could a group of Jewish intellectuals and publicists bound by family relations and school ties shaped at CCNY and the University of Chicago win easy acceptance of paleoconservatives, the indigenous conservatives who attracted few Jewish adherents. From the perspective of American Jewish political culture the Neoconservatives were reminiscent of the seriousness with which ideas and ideologies were held in the Jewish community. But there was something new here as well. An amorphous movement of a handful of primarily Jewish public intellectuals, speaking and writing in English but otherwise bearing no resemblance to an organized political movement, was able to project a strong influence on American foreign policy during the final phase of the cold war (1967–1989). It is the first time we witness such a cluster stemming from the right side of the political spectrum rather than the left. Even here its conservative position was focused on foreign policy, where it assumed a hard anti-Soviet stance. There exists no survey research that examines their position on domestic issues, but it is difficult to imagine that Norman Podhoretz or Irving Kristol abhorred stem-cell research or favored privatizing social security. Jewish "Rockefeller" Republicans like the late Senator Jacob Javits (Rep. New York) retained some element of their Jewish liberalism. In the presidential campaign of 2011 there were few Jewish politicos visible among the Tea Party caucuses.

The rhetoric of a new presidential political campaign fills the media. Which party and candidate will win the "Jewish vote" is anxiously analyzed. Strangely, the political pundits seem far less concerned with the vote of the descendants of the immigrant groups with whom Eastern Jews came to America, the Italian or Polish or Greek American vote. They have mostly melded into the general political atmosphere, so that identifying them as a separate voting bloc has become problematic.[67] The Eastern Jews whose political stamp is on American Jewry were part of the post-1881 "new immigration," but their political impact has been more sustained than other ethnics. That opens the door to two mysteries. Jews after all have also melded into the general society. Today they are strongly identified with the left wing of the Democratic Party, but so are holders of the doctorate in the liberal arts. Why the special attention? The mystery deepens when we consider what our search reveals about the Jewish political persona. The community is politically often deeply riven, which makes it difficult to identify a single tribal political identity. Jews have been radical but also deeply conservative. They retain a collective support on certain issues like civil rights but are generally fragmented and divided on others. Not only is the highly individuated Jewish vote not deliverable, but it is also often maverick. With the exception of the ultra Orthodox and Hassidic communities that form a tiny fraction of the voting population, there is no tribal chieftain who can deliver a Jewish vote. No one commands this riven tribe. In short, the Jewish political voice lacks coherence and cohesiveness. Yet somehow there is a Jewish voice in American politics. Some hold out the hope that Jewish liberalism, the subject of the next chapter, will help locate the mysterious force that somehow creates a workable "unity in diversity." They may discover that only a very broad humanitarian universalistic definition of that political persuasion can sometimes provide a fragile bridge between contending groups. The ethos that can conceivably act as such a bridge comes down to a belief that government should, in the words of a Jewish Florida snowbird, "do the right thing." She does not reveal what that might be.

2

American Jewish Liberalism

How Deep the Roots?

Whatever else we can observe about Jewish political culture few will take issue with the fact that, of the triad of shaping forces examined here, its abiding liberalism exerts the strongest continuous impact. Jewish voters proudly identify themselves as liberal.[1] Explanations for its persistence range from certainty that it is the continuing impact of humanistic values deeply embedded in scripture (Torah) to theories proffered by social psychologists related to Jewish social marginality. On closer examination such explanations seem wanting. Religious observance is a poor predictor of liberal enthusiasm. Nonobservant Jews, for example, are not only more liberal than their observant counterparts but they are also more liberal than nonreligious Christians. With intermarriage estimated as high as 37 percent, it is difficult to imagine a special apartness or marginality that may feed into the political behavior of the contemporary American Jew.

Similarly, those who find that the challenge to overweening authority, considered by some as the mainstays of liberal behavior, is learned in the Jewish family are compelled to contend with studies indicating that Jewish children have little cause to question parental authority, since the Jewish family is less authoritarian than its Christian counterpart. Usually these theories are variations on the familiar theme that adult political posture is determined by early childhood experience. Jewish children are raised permissively to be autonomous, expressive, thoughtful, and tolerant of deviation, while contrasting non-Jewish child-raising styles are authoritarian, rigid, and inhibited. The former produces an open liberal personality while the latter produces a smug conservative. Caricatures aside, whether permissive Jewish homes, or at least homes of uncertain authority, prevail in the Jewish middle class and whether the fact that Jewish children don't get spanked feeds into a liberal gestalt is difficult to prove. While upbringing may contribute to political preferences in adulthood, we are a long way away from determining with any precision that a certain type of upbringing results in a specific type of political profile.[2] In reality the urban/urbane configuration of contemporary Jewish liberals is not notably different from their gentile counterparts.[3]

A more plausible view of the origins of Jewish liberalism becomes possible when viewed from the perspective of history, which sees the roots of Jewish liberalism as stemming from the dependent condition of living as virtual guests in often hostile host societies for much of their exilic history. It compelled the development of communal responsibility for the bereft and dependent, a basic tenet of liberalism that became rooted in Jewish law (*Halacha*). The assumption of communal responsibility for those in need is imagined to have become an intrinsic part of a survival strategy for Jewish life in the diaspora. There was no one else to turn to. The most important condition that Peter Stuyvesant, governor of New Amsterdam, imposed on the hapless Jewish arrivals in September 1654 was that the passengers of the *St. Catherine* take care of their own. But that could not have come as a surprise to the contingent of Jews who had arrived from Recife in September 1654. Jewish community leaders automatically assumed that responsibility. American Jewry maintained its pledge to do so until 1934, when the Great Depression forced communal leaders to apply for federal relief along with millions of other Americans.

From "Strangers in the Land" to Liberal Universalists

Jews are not wired to be liberal, but the inclination to be so is deeply rooted in their history and culture. American Jewry's political position slightly left of center corresponds roughly to that of other Jewries in parliamentary democracies like France, England, and pre–World War II Germany. Like its counterpart in other Jewish diaspora communities, it is the persistence of the sense of living as guests in the host society that still prevails among a few that sometimes lends a peculiar twist to the Jewish liberal mindset. That outsider posture goes far to explain Jewish voters' support for a liberal immigration policy in the first half of the twentieth century. American Jewish liberalism is rooted in the Jewish diasporic experience of belonging nowhere and thereby everywhere. That sense is at the heart of the universalistic liberal mindset. Such Jewish thinkers can at once view themselves as tribal and at the same time as a world people that live in time rather than space. We shall note later that its sense of being joined by memory rather than territory has made Zionism, with its historic quest to return to the ancient Jewish homeland, so anomalous. Zionism challenges the requisite homelessness of the liberal intellectual.

The penchant for favoring the victims of society, the underdogs, so characteristic of Jewish political behavior, may also stem as much from the accommodations required by dint of not belonging to the majority culture as from their Torah, which counsels the importance of kindness to the strangers who live among them. They view their history as one of victimization and are reminded that they were once "strangers in the land of Egypt." Yet Jewish liberalism goes beyond an exercise in political altruism. There are practical reasons for individual Jewish citizens making a generous political donation to candidates for office that are no different from the campaign contributions of non-Jews. There is always an element of self–interest in such giving. The donation is made and becomes thereby a bridge to the majority culture through one who holds power in it or hopes to do so. That is what is transpiring when AIPAC enlists congressmen on organized VIP trips to Israel, all expenses paid. There is no apparent transaction, no votes are bought, but somehow "goodwill" is created.

Similarly, when in the give-and-take of the political dialogue Jews ask the opposition to live up to the nation's founding creed, noted previously to be basically liberal, it assumes the existence of an ideological link between themselves and the host nation. It is in the American Jewish interest to support basic general liberal principles like tolerance, racial harmony, and the empowerment of suppressed groups and those who are different and even radically other, as Jews were once imagined to be. The memory of their own historic experience and the occasional contemporary reminder of lingering anti-Semitism fuel Jewish voter support of racial, economic, and religious minorities. Jewish liberals imagine that communal concern for the needy outsider will hasten that person's acculturation and normalize the painful situation posed by being "strangers in the land." Behind its altruism Jewish liberalism may embody a well-honed survival wisdom. Fueled by historic vulnerability, Jews everywhere have developed an early warning system regarding societal stability, which tells them that, left unaddressed, inequity and victimization have the potential to destabilize the host community and with it their lives. One hears less of the rhetoric of humanitarianism and moral obligation in Israel. A sovereign Jewish community is less dependent on the good behavior of the host society. Zionism has liberated Israel's Jews from the need to be better and kinder. It has normalized its Jews.

History may counsel the Jewish voter to be kinder or at least more careful than his fellow citizen, but that is difficult in a democracy where there are many choices and many ways to conceal one's real intentions. Preferences vary considerably from candidate to candidate even within the liberal fold. Much depends on the internal sense of communal empowerment that prevails at a given historical moment. When a modicum of recognition and reward is granted from an administration, as it was during the Roosevelt period, Jewish voters moved overwhelmingly to support it. But when the liberal position clashed with communal interest most Jewish voters abandoned the "progressive" position, as in the case of community control of the schools in New York City. The majority supported Al Shanker, then head of the heavily Jewish United Federation of Teachers, to oppose the wholesale abandonment of the merit system that had served Jews well. Though the trajectory of Jewish economic success was faster and steeper than other ethnics, that rapid rise in the postwar decade did not diminish the Jewish sense of insecurity.

The portrait that emerges from the later Jewish involvement in the civil rights struggle presents a far more complex portrait of Jewish liberalism. On the one hand it is committed in local districts to defending hard-earned communal self-interest in the name of equal access to civil service position based on the merit system, a cardinal plank of former municipal reform liberalism. On the other hand, on the national level Jewish voters support a broad civil rights program that includes affirmative action programs and early education enrichment.[4]

Historically, regional accommodation can make a big difference in Jewish commitment to the liberal position. During the Civil War, for example, Jews in the Confederacy remained loyal to the slave system. They were silent regarding the internment of the Japanese in 1942. Apprehensive about the reaction of their neighbors, the Jews of Birmingham and other southern communities spoke out against the freedom riders, many of whom were Jewish. While generally supporting steps to integrate schools and housing on the national level, on the neighborhood level, where a Jewish interest was directly challenged, Jews often opposed affirmative action and busing to assure school integration. When neighborhoods tipped, Jews were among the first city dwellers to opt for "white flight" to the suburbs. Opposition often balances their contribution to liberal causes, especially when communal interest in security and social mobility are affected. All of which is to say that Jewish liberalism at the grassroots level is often conditional when balanced against an immediate communal interest. When their communal security is involved, positions can change overnight. Yet such conditionality is true of all groups and brings us no closer to explaining why generally Jews are more deeply committed to the liberal position.

The singularity of Jewish political behavior comes into better focus when it is compared with that of other ethnic groups. Altruistic behavior such as demonstrated by Jews in the civil rights struggle is barely discernable among other immigrant groups. Anti–Catholicism did not produce liberalism among Irish or Polish Americans, and Mexican Americans are not notably liberal when considering the entire liberal agenda. The persistence of liberalism among Jews into the more economically secure second and third generation has been explained by their continuing sense of social marginality. Combined with their normal search for accommodation and belonging, first and second descendants of Eastern Jewish immigrants seemed to retain an exaggerated sense of their otherness. Few groups were more ethnically and religiously self-conscious than American Jewry.

Care must be taken to limit generalizations on the mystery of Jewish identity. Explanations based on alienation or marginalization, if it is a factor at all, would apply more to later-arriving Ashkenazic Jews than the Sephardic Jews of colonial New Amsterdam. Having a history of close relationship to Islamic culture, the early Sephardic settlers harbored less of the sense of separateness compared with the Ashkenazic German-speaking Jews who arrived after 1820. For the early Jewish settlers who insisted on their full citizenship rights in political and economic activity of New Netherlands, there existed the possibility of calling for support on the West India Company, a proportion of whose shares were owned by their Sephardic brethren in Amsterdam. Such audacity was not possible among the unconnected rustic Bavarian immigrants of the later German Jewish migration. From the outset the early largely Sephardic settlers possessed a greater degree of assimilability and knowledge of the Christian world, whose religious dogma some, like its leading merchant Aaron Lopez, had been compelled to learn firsthand by forced conversion during the Inquisition. It gave them a greater desire and potential for inclusion.[5] They did so despite Stuyvesant's initial attempt to rid the colony of these "blasphemers of the name of Christ." Papists and Quakers were held in similar contempt and deflected actions that might have targeted Jews exclusively. Embedded in the spirit of commercial enterprise of the Netherlands, the liberal spirit, linked to the rise of commerce, undoubtedly contributed to the acceptance of the Jews. That the initial practice of inclusion was established by Sephardic Jews, and New Amsterdam itself was in fact intended as a commercial enterprise, went far to establish a precedent different from the separateness of the later Ashkenazi experience. That does not mean that the inclusion of Sephardic Jews in the emerging polity went unchallenged, merely that from the outset the American model was less resistant to Jewish desire to be part of society and commerce. It was as much a common meeting ground in commerce as the ideal principles of democracy that account for the more porous boundaries that led ultimately to the full inclusion of Jews in the polity. It was not always a straightforward acceptance, but that early willingness, albeit often hesitant, to absorb the Jewish settlers reinforced their liberal proclivities.

We have noted that the location of the American Jewish political center of gravity slightly left of center was similar to the pattern in the prewar Western democracies, Germany, France, and England. That preference originated primarily from a common historical circumstance. The granting of full rights of citizenship triggered by the French Revolution set the stage for the emancipation movement for European Jewry. The rights of citizenship, granted partially through the endenization process in the colonial period, did not occur all at once. But by World War I Jewish citizens in the Western democracies had achieved equal rights and the security that already existed in the New World. Within certain limits European governments gradually moved to extend to Jews the rights of citizenship and formal inclusion in the polity.

The process of emancipation was slower in Europe, which in the German principalities had earlier imposed onerous population control measures on their Jews. It was often these restrictions on marriage that triggered the immigration process. The nineteenth-century liberalism carried to the New World by the Jews of central Europe blended well with the comparative openness of American society. Young and rustic and busily establishing themselves, these young Jewish settlers took some of their political cues from the liberal German '48ers among whom they lived and later from the Republican Party of Abraham Lincoln. They developed what one researcher has called a "consensus liberalism" institutionalized in the Reform movement, which became the mainstay of nineteenth-century American Jewish liberalism.[6] Based on a religious ideology of the teachings of the biblical prophets and pushed forward by such bridging figures as Felix Adler, the founder of ethical culture, and Rabbi Stephen Wise, who built such liberalizing institutions as the Free Synagogue and the American Jewish Congress, Jewish liberalism moved considerably beyond its roots in American Protestantism.[7]

But it remained a movement of ideas with little power at the polls. That awaited the arrival of the "Jewish Jews" of Eastern Europe who brought in their cultural baggage their own version of liberalism based on socialism. We have noted in chapter 1 that the hyperpolitical activism of the Eastern Jewish immigrants did not begin all at once. As late as the election of 1906 "der ate," the almost all-Jewish eighth election district on the

Lower East Side of New York had a low voter turnout. With the exception of Socialist-oriented candidates like Morris Hillquit, who won 22 percent of the Jewish vote in New York City's mayoralty campaign in 1917, and Meyer London, who was elected to Congress in the heavily Jewish East Side twelfth election district in 1914, 1916, and 1920, Jews did not customarily direct their best sons into politics.[8] Unlike the Irish Americans, Jews were not strong claimants for municipal employment until the initiation of the merit examination during the Great Depression of the thirties. The rapid build-up of the Jewish ethnic economy, especially in the garment trades and small retail businesses, enabled Jews to better withstand the blandishments of the corrupt political machine. They were less dependent on its largess.[9]

Ideological Roots

Jewish liberalism is a composite of several streams of influence rooted in the collective Jewish response to its dispersion in Europe primarily. The European element was carried in the cultural baggage of the first Jewish settlers, especially the nineteenth-century German Jewish immigrants who eventually embedded it in the religious Reform movement.[10] It presented the notion of *Rechtstaat*, which viewed government as bound by law and seeking above all to do justice. That meshed well with Hebrew scriptures and the Lockean ideas of the English Enlightenment that recognized the threat of overweening government power to individual liberty. A later strand carried by immigrants from Eastern Europe had at its core various forms of socialism as well as the later development of Socialist Zionism that produced the kibbutz movement.

Jewish liberalism as an active political force is a comparatively recent phenomenon. Confining our search for roots to the Enlightenment omits the millennia of prior Jewish historical experience that feeds into the Jewish liberal spirit. In the pre-emancipation years the Jewish experience of being "resident aliens" everywhere but fully belonging nowhere generated a conservative political position. Since their security and well being depended on the authority of those in power, Jews supported the existing authority. They prayed for the good health and longevity of a good king and retained their detachment and separateness from the polity of the host nation. The tradition of compliance counseled by the rabbis, "the law of the kingdom is the law" (*Dina dimalkhuta dina*), was adhered to. To some degree among the Ashkenazim that detachment endured for generations after being granted the rights of the "citoyen."[11] It is conceivable that had full emancipation been realizable earlier in Europe Jewish liberalism might have muted its emphasis on social justice and egalitarianism, since the link to communal self-interest was less direct.

Common roots in the Enlightenment also served to link Jews to their new homeland. The emancipation process that sought to grant Jews the rights of citizenship stemmed from the Enlightenment, as did the core political ideology of America. Small wonder that compared to the Jews of Europe, American Jews encountered less resistance to being granted full and equal citizenship rights. The result was that there was little of the apartness from the polity often noted among the Jewish communities of Europe. In colonial America Jews would not remain a people apart. Rather, almost from the outset American Jews took advantage of the inclusiveness of the new nation and responded with a greater sense of belonging and involvement.[12] That benevolent version of Jewish political belonging is a far cry from the thinking of the late Charles Lieberman, who, while not discounting the impact of the religio-ethnic tradition embedded in the Jewish historical experience, nevertheless viewed Jewish liberalism as growing out of its marginality and the confusion of an incomplete emancipation that required living in two cultures. For Lieberman Jewish liberalism became a resonance of a psychological malaise.[13]

In practice, at the grassroots Jewish communal governance was compelled to come to grips with a conflict embedded in the slogan that fueled the French Revolution: "Liberty, Equality, Fraternity," since left to its own devices "liberty" is bound to make shambles of "equality" and threatens "fraternity" as well. In their *Kehillot*, Jewish leaders recognized that "liberty" needed to be contained by necessity, growing out of their actual political condition in the diaspora. A sense of responsibility had to be carefully matched with its limited power of governance. Those that endangered the Jewish community from within by aberrant behavior could be severely punished. But freeness from governance also allowed free play for Jewish entrepreneurial energy that could develop into great differences in wealth. This small class of wealthy Jews was rewarded with leadership and an extra burden of responsibility. The result was often remarkably stable communal governance based on the matching of available power with responsibility.

While the proportion of the Jewish electorate attracted to some version of liberalism remains high, there is considerable generational variation. An immigrant coming out of the Jewish labor movement produces a liberal coloration quite different from a postwar baby boomer influenced by the civil rights movement. It was Roosevelt's New Deal welfare state that welded the separate strands of Jewish liberalism into the powerful force it became in the post–World War II period. The strands of Jewish liberalism are also linked to the phases of its historical development and to generational changes. Generally 55 percent of the so called baby boomers born in the years between 1946 and 1964 and the generation of boomers born between 1965 and 1983 actually displayed a lower allegiance to the Democratic Party (43 percent) and are increasingly more likely to identify themselves as independent voters, albeit of a liberal bent.[14] By 1970 it was possible to identify three age cohorts of Jewish liberalism. The older survivors were associated with the prewar Jewish labor movement and other liberally oriented communal agencies such as the Reform movement and the American Jewish Congress. They are followed and sometimes overlap with a group of slightly younger citizens that became identified with the New Deal. Finally there are new liberals composed of middle-class, formally educated secular citizens, many mobilized during the civil rights struggle of the sixties, who are reenergized by the systemic economic crisis that began in 2008. Having little experience with the labor movement or the New Deal and a weaker affiliation with organized Jewry, this last-mentioned group opens an entirely new page in Jewish liberalism.

American Sources of Jewish Liberalism

The comparative ease Jews experienced in gaining full access to the American political arena was based to some degree on the liberalism it shared with the political culture of its American host.[15] From its support for the war for independence from Britain to its staunch support for civil rights, liberalism has acted as a principal connecting bridge for Jews to cross into the general American polity. By seeking out the regnant inequity and placing it on the political agenda, liberal Jews provide the fuel to move the political dialogue forward. The founding principles of the republic that rationalized the overthrow of the legitimate monarchy and spoke passionately of equality were liberal. These principles left little room for an authentic conservative ideology to flower in the new republic. Early American Jewish liberalism was partly a resonance of that indigenous liberalism. Jews favored the Whigs, who ultimately came to favor independence from Britain and were the winning side. Jewish liberalism in America borrowed heavily from the regnant Protestant establishment, whose ethos dominated governance and whose tolerance had allowed Jews to prosper. Liberalism was inherent in the American society and polity. Anchored in a Whig anticolonial rebellion, having no corporate feudal past, and born in revolution, colonial political culture could not support a genuine conservative spirit. Instead it imbibed the notion, which remains vaguely recognizable in the core ideology of the Republican Party, that for the spirit of individual liberty to thrive government power must be bridled.

There was little attempt to formalize an indigenous conservative ideology until the late William Buckley founded the conservative journal *National Review* in 1955. Buckley set the stage for a conservative movement in the United States, albeit one that remains bereft of a consistent legitimizing ideology. There existed no party in the American political arena that risked naming itself conservative until 1974.[16] Conservatives faced the problem that in American political history the very principles to be conserved were an integral part of the founding liberal doctrine embodied in the constitution and the Declaration of Independence. Traditional conservatives, sometimes called "paleoconservatives," speak of getting the government off the backs of citizens, which would lead naturally to lower taxes and spending. Their underlying assumption is that liberty would be expanded when the power of government is limited. The core of American politics is located between the libertarian and egalitarian axis of the Enlightenment. The incompatibility between *liberté* and *égalité* is the source of the constant tension in the American political dialogue. It is, however, a truism learned from experience that, allowed full sway, liberty will make shambles of any movement that seeks to equalize a citizenry born with unequal talents. The American Jewish vote is weighted heavily on the egalitarian side of the axis. That is yet another way of identifying its liberalism.

Yet liberty is also a building block of liberalism. It meant freeing citizens from the social, economic, and political fetters that bound them. Jews would devote themselves to the struggle for the liberation of the unfree, whether slaves, women, or gays. During the colonial period that meant supporting those who were disfranchised by property and religious qualifications. In the second half of the twentieth century it would be racial inequities in American society that for a time became liberalism's center of gravity. That led ultimately to desegregation of public facilities including schools and the election of an African American candidate, Barack Obama, to the highest office in the land in 2008. There are, of course, many other factors that account for the high percentage of Jewish ballots cast for Obama, and there is no certainty that his election marks the end of the centrality of the race issue in American politics. What it does tell us is that the liberalism with which Jewish political culture is linked continues to be the most powerful force for change in American politics. It could be argued with some validity that the notion that American Jewry has inordinate influence in national politics is a resonance of its liberalism, which acts as the nation's principle ideology for change.

A measure of the depth of American Jewry's liberalism is the fact that Jewish voters were staunch supporters of virtually every issue on the liberal agenda in the twentieth century, with the possible exception of the strategy of quotas linked to affirmative action. Most Jews supported liberal issues with only their vote, but a comparatively small group of Jewish activists could usually be found in the forefront of these "liberation struggles." That is as true for the campaign to "save the whales" and other environmental issues as it is for civil and women's rights. But there is a perceptible difference in the kind of Jewish activists drawn to primarily Jewish issues such as the campaign to undo the fetters of anti-Semitism or the defense of Israel and those issues more distant, from communal self-interest involving healthcare to abortion rights. As in the case of Jewish radicalism, there are Jewish liberals and liberal Jews. The former are incidentally Jewish and usually more universalistic in approach; the latter are more sectarian, their liberalism is related to their Jewishness. That division between the two Jewish upholders of liberalism was hardly in evidence during the colonial period when a Jew was simply a Jew. It came into its own when Jews became part of the American business community. Colonial Jews were part of a polyglot commercial class that demanded equal citizenship rights with others in the economy as a matter of right.[17] It was a normal transaction partly sweetened by their purported ability to enhance commerce. For contemporary Jewish universalistic liberals, a transaction that bargained for rights that rightfully belonged to all citizens would have been anathema.

For the freeing of enslaved or encumbered groups, liberalism was joined at the hip by libertarianism, which sought to free the citizenry from the dangers of tyrannical government. In the former, government is the agent of liberalism; in the latter, its object. In the colonial period many Jews opposed the monarchy based on what would be considered liberal principles. Democracy itself became a liberal aspiration. After being attacked in a Federalist newspaper, Benjamin Nones, a Jewish veteran of the war, declared simply that he was a "Republican" on religious grounds, since kingly government proved a curse and a "punishment" for ancient Israel.[18] During the colonial and national periods, for example, one would naturally have assumed that a community linked to the commercial sector would have favored the financial program contained in Alexander Hamilton's *Report on Manufacturers*, which was designed to place the economy on a firm economic foundation. But the small Jewish community composed of merchants and artisans that originally favored the Federalists gradually made their way to Jefferson's physiocratic position that idealized the agrarian way of life. Jefferson himself was not immune to the negative stereotype of Jews prevalent in his day, but together with James Madison he was a staunch advocate of the separation of church and state, whose fiercest defenders became the nation's Jews.

Though a small inconspicuous minority, there was some Jewish representation in all the liberal crusades of the nineteenth and early twentieth century. Researchers find little organized Jewish political advocacy during the Jacksonian period, but undoubtedly Jewish citizens supported the further liberalization of the franchise and breaking up the Bank of the United States., citadel of government-supported privilege for the few. Similarly, some Jews joined the abolitionist campaign to end slavery, and several including August Bondi joined John Brown in Kansas. Others, like Rabbi David Einhorn of Baltimore, were forced to flee; in Einhorn's case because his congregation did not approve his abolitionist sentiments. Undoubtedly liberal Jews also supported the civil rights amendments of the Reconstruction period. Yet others like Mordecai Noah and Judah Benjamin, who was himself a slave owner, were not known for their opposition to the slave system that surely was at the center of what might have passed for antebellum liberalism. When trusts and other forms of business consolidation threatened to corrupt the political process while narrowing the opportunity for enterprise, reform forces headed by the Progressives and a group of "muckraking" crusading journalists advocated checking private power accumulated by "robber barons." One might take issue with classifying the opposition of the Socialist-minded Jewish immigrant masses to "big business" as liberal phenomenon, but there were prominent Jews like Louis Brandeis, appointed to the Supreme Court in 1914, who led the legal movement to regulate the trusts in the courts. His legal briefs explaining the threat of consolidation to democratic governance could serve as a textbook for turn-of-the century liberalism. Yet Brandeis would not fully fathom the Jewish source of his reform impulse until Jacob de Haas, a Zionist activist, broke through his austere personality to awaken his interest in the Zionist movement in 1912.[19]

The Democratic Socialist roots of Jewish liberalism were enriched by the reformist impulse of the Progressive movement, which it absorbed as part of the general Americanization process. It took time for the revolutionary thrust of radical socialism to be muted so that the progressive idea—of amalgamating the classical liberal spirit of laissez-faire with the idea of a mixed economy in which business would be regulated and management principles—would be applied to governance. That amalgamation, it was hoped, would harness the unbridled free enterprise spirit that threatened the republic, according to Herbert Croly (1869–1930), author of the *Promise of American Life* (1909) and founder of *The New Republic*. That amalgam of an efficient but regulated capitalist system was within acceptable striking distance of Socialist-oriented Jewish liberalism of the interwar period. The American progressive reform spirit joined to Jewish democratic socialism to form the ideological base of Jewish liberalism.[20] The first communal fruit of that amalgamation was the Congress movement, which was organized on a temporary basis to form a broad representation of American Jewry at the forthcoming peace negotiations at Versailles. It was followed by the New York Kehillah, a broad-ranging effort to reform local Jewish communal governance. The two organization builders, Rabbi Stephen Wise for the Congress movement and Rabbi Judah Magnes for the New York Kehillah, embodied the essence of Jewish liberalism. Both organizations remained for a time the pillars of Jewish liberalism, but neither was able to sustain itself over the years.

Periods of reform somehow often end in wars, as if the spirit aroused by the reform program is compelled to seek new worlds to conquer.[21] Lest the link between Jewish liberalism with progressive reform is overstated, it should be noted that the outbreak of World War I in August 1914 marked a decisive turn of events that deeply affected Jewish internal politics. It compelled the reform impulse of the progressive period, imbibed by many immigrant Jews, to share the historical stage with the possibility the war opened for establishing a Jewish homeland in Palestine. For Jewish immigrants the war and the Russian revolution that followed, marking a sharp decline in the fortunes of Eastern European Jewry, served as a reminder of how precarious was the Jewish condition in their former homeland. In the election of 1916 Wilson's slogan "he kept us out of war" proved peculiarly attractive to Jewish voters, many of whom were unable to tolerate the Allied acceptance of the tyrannical tsarist regime in a war touted as one "to make the world safe for democracy." But Wilson's record as a progressive reformer and, more important, his status as a professor and expert in the science of government gained him great favor with Jewish voters.

The trek of Jewish voters from the Republican to the Democratic Party was accelerated by the Wilson administration and was complete by 1928, when Jews voted overwhelmingly for the Catholic candidate, Al Smith.

Wilson appointed Henry Morgenthau Sr. to the Jewish post of ambassador to Turkey and approved of the Balfour Declaration supporting the establishment of a Jewish state in Palestine, then the southernmost province of the moribund Ottoman Empire. The stage was set for the American Jewish electorate to evolve into the most loyal ethnic voting bloc of the Democratic Party. That American Jewry and liberalism found a home in the Democratic Party at virtually the same moment in history was no coincidence.

By the turn of the twentieth century American Jewry had sufficient critical mass to assure its continuity at least for the moment, and even an aspiration to generate its own culture. It was the "new" post-1870 immigration that lent American Jewish political culture a distinct eastern European flavor. They were finally combined in a social democratic container joined by a common historic experience of immigration restriction, which in a decade became the source of one of Jewish history's most catastrophic experience—the closing of the access to the American haven during the refugee crises of the thirties.

The preexisting Judaic stream, the Lockean stream and the European German stream, were recombined in American Jewish political culture where they were joined by a Jewish immigrant version of eastern European socialism. There were lumps in this ideological stew manifested in deep divisions between the extreme Left, which often shared a reformist agenda, and the center Left, which was heavily influenced by social democrats. American Jewish liberalism did not come fully into its own until these political passions were banked in the years following World War II. In historic terms the deep division in the non-communist Jewish Left was a resonance of the division between the American libertarianism and Socialist egalitarianism elements. The Lockean libertarian element that speaks of the rights of property and seeks to expand the sphere of personal liberty stems primarily from the Scottish Enlightenment. The egalitarian balancer, previously noted, held sway in the German Enlightenment, embodied in the concept of *Rechtstaat*, that envisaged the state as seeking to mediate the injustice growing out of the unequal distribution property and therefore of power. Both were joined in American liberalism, but clearly Jews who found their political voice shortly before World War I were more drawn to the latter.[22]

This description of a complex historical process is not intended to render the full story of a complex historical amalgam. There are hidden ingredients in Jewish political culture that may also feed into a description that might explain the reason why a beleaguered guest people advocate concern for the weak and vulnerable as a key element in its political ideals. It may be that in some subconscious way Jews have discovered that it is in their long-range interest to develop a political community that cares for the vulnerable and powerless. That is, after all, how they used to see themselves. All that can safely be said is that the nation's Jewish citizens produced a more robust liberalism whose longevity outlasted that of other immigrant groups as well as the reform-minded Progressives and other indigenous carriers.

Despite the oft-predicted demise of Jewish liberalism, once reinforced by Roosevelt's New Deal welfare statism, it has proven to be an enduring reality on the American political scene. In 1932 immigrant Jews and their descendants, many retaining a Socialist orientation, could vote for a high-born Episcopalian because the concept of government playing a direct role in stabilizing and stimulating the economy was within striking distance of its own political sensibility. If nothing else, socialism counsels the need for strong government, needed to implement the restructuring of society and general amelioration. It is statist. Over the years the Democratic Socialist proclivity at the core of Jewish liberalism moved to the political center of the political scene until the divide between Jewish social democrats and the New Deal was finally spanned. Reeling under the impact of the crash and the Depression, American mainstream voters moved to the Left, where Jewish voters were already concentrated. The Jewish response to the crises came from the American Labor Party, founded in New York in 1935 and funded by the Jewish labor movement to attract the Socialist-oriented Jewish working-class voter to the New Deal.

That the immigrant Jewish voter would develop a "hotter" political style was predictable. Unforeseen was that the new sizeable Jewish voting bloc would be strangely averse to sending its sons into practical politics.

During the interwar period most Jewish representatives in Congress were undistinguished types. Representatives from Jewish districts in New York and Philadelphia like Sol Bloom and Samuel Dickstein were hardly the most outstanding types that could be found among their immigrant constituents. The exception was Meyer London, elected to Congress from the Lower East Side, whose politics was driven by his affiliation with the Socialist Party and who was one of the few who voted against entering World War I. The reason for the aversion to practical politics may relate to the fact that in the early decades of the twentieth century Jews were preoccupied primarily with establishing themselves economically. Politics was considered the provenance of the Irish, who dominated the city political machine. The morally austere, liberal Jewish types released their reformist passions within the community by a largely failing attempt through the aforementioned New York Kehillah to regulate morality and education as well as *kashrut* (dietary laws).

From Democratic Socialists to Liberals

The Jewish transition from socialism to liberalism was not an easy one. Native American liberalism was fashioned for the American polity and had little of the universalistic thrust of socialism or the conviction that when all else failed the best corrective for unbearable conditions was revolution. In pre–World War II decades the fierce ideological conflicts between Jewish radicals and radical Jews was in some cases deeper and more intense than the gulf between Republicans and Democrats.[23] Not until Roosevelt's New Deal was the bridge between the democratic socialism of the immigrant generation and American reform liberalism fully in place. It then became possible for a Jewish Socialist voter to cast his ballot for a highborn patrician like Franklin Roosevelt without feeling that he had betrayed his principles or supported the corrupt Tammany sachems.

The presence of a comparatively politically intense Jewish electorate in American politics after 1905 is based in some degree on the influence of the Yiddish press that articulated the message of a radical intellectual leadership stratum. The radicalism of the Jewish immigrant masses was partly a "trickle down" affair. The press played an important role in "educating" and orienting the immigrant community politically. Highly esteemed intellectuals like Abraham Cahan, publisher of the Yiddish daily *Forward*, which became the ethnic daily with the widest circulation in the nation, possessed enormous power. Projecting socialism as simply a secular or modern version of Judaism helped convert its Jewish readers to the cause. The press not only served as an instrument of political indoctrination but it also educated the Jewish immigrant in the details of American politics and citizenship education. Its popularity rested on the fact that it spoke the Yiddish language in which, whether they stemmed from Warsaw, Moscow, or Bucharest, Jews were literate. The drawing power of the press was strengthened by its willingness to address the abysmal working condition in the sweatshops and other areas of the Jewish ethnic economy. It spoke directly to the conditions that concerned its readership.

The new immigrants harbored distaste for the German Jewish stewards who dominated the Jewish polity by dint of their wealth and familiarity with American governance and governors. The predictable challenge to their communal leadership began in earnest with the rise of the Congress movement and its cry for democratization of communal governance and the need for full representation at the forthcoming negotiations at Versailles at the close of World War I.[24] Behind specific political and class differences there was a cultural gap that resembled nothing so much as the gap between Slavs and Teutons. By the time of the death of Louis Marshall in 1929, Eastern Jewish leadership and organizations were making their weight felt. Their Socialist-oriented leadership was based on a triad of institutions consisting of the Jewish labor movement, represented by United Hebrew Trades, the Workman's Circle fraternal order, and other labor-oriented *landsmanschaftn* and the *Forward*. Eventually a smaller group of labor Zionists, also socialistically inclined, joined the loosely organized coalition. In the post-Holocaust years the labor Zionists would become supreme in community governance, as over 80 percent of American Jewry favored strong support of Israel, where labor Zionism led by Ben-Gurion ruled supreme. We will have the opportunity later to observe how American Jewry was zionized more by the refugee crisis of the thirties than by abstruse ideological dialectics. It was the Zionist movement, especially its dominant labor Zionist wing, that helped build a bridge between Jewish liberalism and Israel.[25] Its success in the interwar period contributed to forcing the extreme Jewish Left, led by the Communist Party, which rejected Zionism, to the margins of the Jewish political arena. The Berlin-Moscow Non-Aggression Treaty of August 1939 did the rest. In the early decades after the founding of Israel, American Jewish support was based as much on the conviction that the Jewish state realizes the major attributes of liberalism as it did Herzelian liberal nationalism. We will note later in this discussion that the association of liberal democracy with the parliamentary democracy of Israel remains a crucial pillar of liberal Jewish support for the state.

The Zionist element in the development of Jewish political culture was personified by the American Jewish Congress, which integrated liberalism and Zionism. Its appeal for communal democracy helped the Labor Zionist wing of the American Zionist movement to add yet another ingredient to Jewish American liberalism, its attachment to Israel. That attachment became the principle differentiator between Jewish liberals and the more radical Jewish Left anchored at its extreme in communism. The priority the Congress movement gave to ethnic peoplehood, which did not require religious adherence or congregational affiliation, corresponded to the position that postimmigration Jewry was assuming. Zionist leaders like Rabbi Stephen Wise, by emphasizing the ethnic Jewish element in Judaism, opened a door for the increasing number of nonobservant but committed Jews to advocate for secular reform issues such as the corruption of the city political machine, an issue at the heart of the early liberal agenda, while at the same time boasting about the modernity of Tel Aviv, the newly built Jewish city on the Mediterranean.

In summary, at the close of World War I the American Jewish polity was composed of several factions living in an uneasy relationship with one another. Its political center of gravity was its social democratic approach to issues of the day. It was a fragile communalism; German Jews were not anxious to surrender their leadership and the new Eastern Jews were bedeviled by left-wing extremism on the one side and religious conservatism on the other. Superimposed on all was a growing Zionist movement with its own solution to the perennial Jewish problem of continuity. Soon to be called on to rescue its beleaguered European brethren, a riven American Jewry was poorly equipped to play the role history had assigned it.

Religious Sources of Jewish Liberalism

It remains for us to probe the religious stream that fed into contemporary Jewish liberalism, based on the solemn calls for justice and charity embodied in values that stem from the biblical prophets and from Jewish law. We have previously taken note of the Reform and Reconstructionist branches' sustained advocacy of liberal causes motivated by their special heed to the prophetic aspect of Judaism. They are not alone in doing so. In the Orthodox branch adherence to *Halacha* (Jewish law) that views Jews as a commanded people, there is also a strong adherence to basically liberal principles of *mitzvoth*, the specific deeds of goodness and righteous behavior incumbent upon every Jew. These laws or regulations are often similar to the principles of the contemporary liberal persuasion ranging from the need to seek justice to the imperative of collective and individual giving. The commandment of *Tsedakah* in Jewish law is different from charity in Canon law. It generates a distinct resonance in the political arena because it is not confined to giving only for those in need.[26] Unlike Christianity, Judaism mandates concern for the poor but does not idealize poverty. Jews give, not necessarily out of love as among Catholics (caritas), but because it is the law and because there is human concern. We need also to add that Jews are comparatively generous in their political giving because it is a residual cultural habit emanating from the religious tradition. Strangely, secular Jews who are not bound by Jewish law are frequently seen to be more generous in their giving and give more broadly than observant Jews who are so bound.

The "habit" or tradition of giving has considerable impact on the power aspect of Jewish political culture. Funding and fundraising is a crucial aspect of American politics, which, in the Jewish case, can sometimes be traced to giving to a candidate that identifies with the liberal position. It is a kind of religious act performed by nonobservant Jews. Yet religious faith is an important but not an exclusive source of Jewish philanthropy, and need not necessarily be related to liberal causes. There are Jewish philanthropists who give exclusively to conservative causes. Jewish givers are also driven by less noble motivations. There is a status reward for those who comply with the communal imperative to give and there is in addition the fact that Jews often have more to give.[27] Like "philanthrapoids" generally, Jewish givers may be driven as much by the federal tax code as by the religious commandment. Philanthropic giving becomes a matter of individual motivation, and while it can be influenced by the fundraising drives of communal agencies it cannot be commanded. Living in modern democratic societies where the *kahal* has no legal sanction, Jews are free to select the degree of adherence to religious law in which the commandment for giving is embedded.[28] That accounts for the fact that more "Jewish money" goes to secular non-Jewish institutions and causes than to Jewish communal needs. The giving is far from anonymous as prescribed by Maimonides' code as the highest order of philanthropy. Nevertheless, the habit of giving is deeply imbedded in Jewish culture. It allows Jewish liberals to "put their money where their mouth is." Together with the principle of *Tikkun Olam*, the obligation to repair the world, which one hears more and more frequently among secularized liberal Jews, it is an identifiable cause for Jewish political behavior, especially in the area of campaign funding. Giving to a liberal cause or candidate is in some magical way considered a good deed, with the result that Jewish money has a measurable impact on American politics as well as on cultural and educational institutions like universities and museums. The Jewish penchant for giving is an important factor in Jewish political culture because in a direct way it is an enhancer of political influence.[29]

Living in a modern democratic secular society where the church has no legal sanction, Jews are free to determine for themselves the degree of adherence to religious law in which the commandment for giving is embedded. Most Jews do not confine their giving to Jewish causes. More "Jewish money" is given to non-Jewish institutions than to Jewish communal needs. Nevertheless, the habit of giving is deeply rooted in Jewish tradition and part of what makes Jewish liberalism distinctive. Its activism goes beyond rhetoric to the performance of deeds. The giving of money is an acceptable substitute for other forms of activism. Judaism is a religion of deeds; in the best of circumstances so too is its liberalism.

The structure that has been developed to collect contributions reaches into every Jewish community. United Jewish Communities, formerly the United Jewish Appeal, is so omnipresent in Jewish communal life that it can be likened to a voluntary internal revenue department. Virtually all affiliated Jews are solicited. The communal politics closest to communal giving concerns the perennial question of all politics, who gets what? Jewish communal politics is budget politics and the great political and economic decisions are made by the closest thing resembling communal governance on a national level in America, a yearly General Assembly of large and small federations. In a sense Jewish communal politics are serious and fractious because there is pork or spoils in the form of millions of philanthropic dollars at stake. That accounts for a remarkable tension in Jewish communal politics. It is at once highly ideological but also firmly bound to practical reality.

The principle of *Tikkun Olam* is today most frequently heard in the world of fundraising. Giving to a liberal cause or candidate is in some magical way considered a good deed. Yet the liberal principles embedded in Jewish law can come into conflict with a central principle of contemporary Jewish liberalism, the separation of church and state. Few things are more disturbing to modern secular liberal Jews than to observe Orthodox Jewish agencies break ranks and abandon this central principle by requesting federal aid for their school programs. But the penchant for philanthropic giving remains and is an important factor researchers must consider in studying Jewish influence in American politics.

We cannot leave the question of religious sources of Jewish liberalism without again addressing the issue of altruism, which is, at least in theory, related to principles embedded in Judaism itself. Their reluctance to "vote their pocketbooks" is often given as an example of Jewish political altruism. One assumes that an element of altruism exists in all religions, but questions arise on whether the transition to acts of concern for others plays a central role as it does in Jewish liberalism. In the final analysis the liberal entitlement programs are based on the notion that people in need should be taken care of at least on a minimal level, a view supported by most Jewish voters. We have already noted that communal aid for the needy was a practice of long standing in the Jewish community. The high development of contemporary Jewish organized philanthropy can serve as a certain sign that this facet of Jewish communalism has survived the years.

Withal, the contention that it is religious principles that contribute to the funding of Jewish political lobbies like AIPAC or liberal candidates for office is only partly true. Religious Jews are usually more committed to Israel, but they also form less than one-tenth of the Jewish community with only a small proportion of Jewish voters who are financially able and willing to make such political contributions. More important, Orthodox givers are least likely to support liberal causes that are usually secular or aimed at achieving a universal good. A local issue aimed at prohibiting smoking in a local court building because of the dangers of "secondary smoke" would arouse little concern of most observant Jewish citizens, but prohibiting the wearing of head covers would. Similarly, the principle of using government power to assure an even playing field so that justice and fair play could prevail cannot be found in Judaic historic sources, where in the pre-exilic period what might be classified as benevolent theocracy was favored. A law to supply the local school with computer laptops would not win the support of the Orthodox community, which doesn't send its children to local public schools, but the community does stake a claim for such tools of educational enhancement by arguing that it is in the national interest that the education level of all students, public and private, is raised if the religious school were included in such government largess, separation of church and state notwithstanding.

A kind of private welfare system is deeply embedded in the religious tenets of Judaism. It includes such laws as forbidding farmers to harvest the corners of the field so that the poor may be fed. Jewish laws required the just and prompt payment of wages, honest weights and measures, and in certain cases called for the regulation of working conditions and even laws for the protection of the powerless and vulnerable. Jewish law concerning social justice could alone fill the pages of this book. But how the concept of *Tzedakah* (religious obligation for charity and righteousness) that undergirds the social justice laws generated a political culture impassioned with the need for social justice cannot be easily discerned. Jewish political culture is after all primarily secular and universalistic.

The exception to this rule may be found in the Reform branch, which views the core of its Judaic belief system to be centered in the biblical prophets from which is distilled the aforementioned idea of *Tikkun Olam*. Yet such a quick transition from the religious ethos to practical politics often runs into difficulties. Jews who base their liberalism on their Reform affiliation encounter a problem in reconciling Judaic notions of choseness or election with the inclusiveness and egalitarianism that form the bedrock of contemporary liberalism. Reconstructionism, the most liberal branch of Judaism, felt compelled to strike such expressions of gratefulness for choosing Jews "from all the nations" from their prayer books and otherwise changing the specialness implied in the term "chosen." Moreover the need to "repair the world," often cited by liberal Jews, may account for some portion of the deep engagement, but it is picked out of a multiplicity of commandments concerning observance and ritual that are otherwise differentiating and discriminating, especially as concerns gender. A liberal Jewish man would ostensibly find it difficult to thank the divine powers for not having made him a woman. Donning phylacteries every morning or demanding that a quorum for prayer be confined exclusively to ten adult Jewish men is not acceptable to those secular Jews who claim that they seek primarily to "repair the world" and who muster little interest in Jewish law. The difficulty in seeking a source of Jewish liberalism in religious text or practice is that when it is found it is usually concealed in a tribal cover. It speaks primarily to Jewish man rather than the universal brotherhood of man.

The weight assigned to "Torah-based values" as a source of contemporary Jewish political behavior stems from the use of the religious metaphor by secularists to gain support for their programs. Passover became a holiday of liberation, the blowing of the Shofar on the Jewish New Year (Rosh Hashanah) became a sounding for all oppressed people, and a third Passover Seder is dedicated to a current "progressive" cause, the liberation of the oppressed the world over. "Religification" becomes a means of supporting the universalistic values inherent in secular liberalism. The religious culture is transmogrified until it is barely recognizable.[30] Yet for American Jewry the benefits of acknowledging an imagined religious affinity with a host culture that viewed itself as the "New Zion"

and was obsessed with its biblical roots improved the possibility of muting the inherent anti-Semitism of a Christian culture whose Messiah was
believed to be Jewish.

However manifold roots of Jewish liberalism and however changing
its contents there is one principle, the separation of church and state, that
is almost ethnic specific. Whether it is the inclusion of the "under God"
phrase in the Pledge of Allegiance or a Christmas crèche on municipal
property, Jewish defense organizations are quick to take umbrage at a
seeming breech of the constitutional legal wall separating church and
state. The historic reason for that response needs no elaboration. Less
apparent is the philosophical rationale on which separation of church and
state is based. In granting the individual citizen, including Jews, individual rights, the separation of the private realm of activity from the public
was requisite. The rights of the citizen were at one stroke made primary
over the rights of religion and its institutions. In the modern liberal society
faith itself is privatized and becomes a matter of the individual citizen's
soul. In a pluralistic society of many faiths, the division between private
and public makes religion merely a particular perspective or culture with
no particular claims on the state. The church was no longer the single
bearer of an eternal truth.[31] Yet even within a highly secularized Jewish
community, religion, or better, observance, has had remarkable staying
power and has even experienced a renewal of influence. While national
secular organizations are on the wane, the Jewish religious congregation
has largely held its own. In some local cases the church-state tension has
been replaced by an internal conflict between observant and secular Jews
over such matters as the location of a ritual bath (*mikveh*) required for
women. The tension between secular and religious Jews, which accompanies the majority's acceptance of a liberal lifestyle as part of being modern,
is ongoing.

Disarming the Communist Left:
From Social Democrats to Liberals

If the several branches of the Jewish religious establishment influenced the
development of Jewish liberalism it was, as we have noted, the influence

of the various strands of European socialism, as rerooted in American ethnic soil, that more than balanced their influence. But the socialism advocated by the American Jewish Communist movement was separate and distinct from other forms of democratic socialism. That difference went beyond the passion of its commitment and its organizational discipline. The pervasive influence of the party and its fellow travelers on Jewish communal life, an oft-repeated canard of the anti-Semitic Right, is belied by its comparatively small membership. Factors outside the Jewish community, including pervasive anti-Semitism, have led to a considerable overrating of its actual communal influence on Jewish affairs.

Jewish Communists were above all else superb organizers and activists. The party's influence was also related to Marxist doctrine that value stemmed from labor; that doctrine was seductive to an immigrant cohort drawn from the sweatshop. It was reinforced by the fact that the garment industry, where Jewish labor was concentrated, was perhaps the most poorly organized industrial system in the nation. There is then no mystery to explain why Jewish immigrants, more than other immigrants, were drawn to socialism of all stripes. If socialism could improve their miserable working conditions then surely it deserved attention. Other pulls may have been equally important. Marxism, after all, held out the promise of liberating the industrial worker and not only Jews per se. Spokesmen for socialism like Abraham Cahan, the editor of the *Forward*, presented the ideology as an ethnicized version of Judaism, thereby making their ancient faith pertinent to their daily lives. That linkage helped Jews steeped in their religious tradition cross a bridge into modernity. But while such rationales could be effective in the short run when thousands toiled in sweatshops, it was not relevant for a second and third generation who were seeking to rise, not with their class but above it.

Another reason for the amplified influence of the party had little to do with ideology. Socialist parties of all stripes offered lonely immigrants a full social life with people of similar immigrant background. Socialism preached a doctrine that explained their deplorable condition and spoke of the possibility of improvement by becoming an actor in history. What could have been more seductive? Party activists were often recognized by their commitment and passion for the broader goals shared by the general Left. They displayed a special passion for the need to make progress on the race question. But their inability to separate their Jewish agenda from the organizational goals of the party, especially when they differed on the question of Israel, which was to become the primary commitment of Jewish voters, eventually made party activists unacceptable in the shops. The resultant weakening of party influence enabled liberal organizations like the American Jewish Congress to purge Communist infiltrators set on converting it to a "front" organization. The fifties set the stage for the majority of Jews who accepted a social democrat position to define the legitimate boundaries of their liberalism.

Jewish Socialists had a separate place in the Socialist Party of America, headed by one of their own, Morris Hillquit. In 1908 it claimed about 42,000 members, 70 percent of whom were native born. German Americans composed 8 percent of its membership. By 1920 Jews predominated in the Socialist Party and the several anarchist factions that composed the left side of the political spectrum. There were not as well represented in the radical wing of the American Left, the Industrial Workers of the World (IWW), known fondly as the "Wobblies," whose rank and file stemmed from the industrial centers of the Midwest.[32] The period of industrial turmoil between 1881 and 1905 brought violence as the attempt to organize labor unions grew. There were approximately 37,000 strikes called to organize and raise the standards of working conditions. The violence experienced during these strikes was often triggered by strife between Social Democrats and Communist-led workers. The latter group was known to be the most militant of union organizers, but they also held an instrumentalist view of the role of labor. The improvement of working conditions that unionization would bring was ameliorative, but it was the revolution with its promise of a "new day" that offered the ultimate solution for workers. Jews fought their own bitter battles to improve conditions in the garment industry, but in scale and level of violence they were tamer than the bloody Homestead Steel (1892) and Pullman (1894) strikes.[33]

The untimely and unforeseen destruction of European Jewry does not permit a projection of how long the Socialist-oriented Bund, the largest and most successful of the Socialist organizations in eastern Europe, might have endured.[34] What is clear is that its democratic socialism, transplanted to America, retained the east European orientation of its incubation. It began as a foreign import that sought to address the problems Jews faced in eastern Europe. In contrast, the highly developed political instinct of Jewish Communists was manifested in the fact that they were able to adjust a dogma addressing the Jewish condition in eastern Europe to the American urban scene in one generation. By the second and following generations it was clear that the Jewish sojourn in the working class would be temporary. The Jewish worker was not the son of a worker, nor would he produce a son who was. The Jewish liberalism that found its roots in the Left sought its anchorage in an American Jewry that was becoming part of the middle class. The wellsprings of Jewish politics would be less in the sweatshops and more in small business and the university classroom.

One could speculate that it was precisely the otherness of Socialist dogma, its concern for the underdog, that attracted Jews whose abandoned faith had altruism at its foundation. It enabled Socialist spokesmen to market socialism and later liberalism as merely a modern version of their ancient Jewish faith. That strategy was not totally based on fraud. Socialism offered the immigrants full membership in an alternate moral community. There were Socialist rules for daily living and behavior not remarkably different from the governing acts of kindness and repairing the world found in Jewish law.[35] Socialists talked to Jewish workers in their language about their condition. Their success in converting thousands who had been raised in pious homes should also be attributed in some measure to the fact that the faith, which had already weakened in Europe, underwent further thinning in the urban secular environment of America's cities. The reluctance of rabbis to immigrate to the *tref medinah* (unobservant society), and the difficulties of organizing themselves in a way suitable to the openness of the new social environment once here, gave the radical Socialist-minded little competition to win the minds of the Jewish masses, especially the young.[36]

The development of Jewish liberalism is marked as much by an internal struggle against the "demons of the Left" as it was in the search for a just social order. The primary demon was the small but highly effective Jewish wing of the aforementioned American Communist Party (CPUSA), which felt little compunction about exploiting contemporary issues that ranged from anti-Semitism to gouging landlords and "bosses." After considerable turmoil the party received the Comintern's imprimatur of legitimacy in 1922 and rapidly drew to its ranks the Socialist Party clubs, whose membership was predominantly Jewish.[37] What often attracted Jews of all stripes was the party's activism. Frequently the party was the first to recognize a festering social or economic injustice and to mobilize action for amelioration. That was especially common when calling for action on the nation's unresolved racial problem. As in the case of the penetration of the Jewish labor movement, the Communist activists and organizers proved to be the most devoted. Committed party activists successfully tapped into the deep wells of idealism in the Jewish community. The party's concern for racial justice went beyond a strategy to attract members. Jews involved in the earliest years of the civil rights struggle sincerely believed that they were fighting for justice. Aside from being a powerful ideological presence in the Jewish community, the party demonstrated great resilience as the party line went through its many changes and the party itself split into contending factions. Its Jewish membership rose during its United Front period in the thirties, which culminated in Soviet support for the loyalists during the Spanish Civil War and declined sharply after the signing of the Nonaggression Pact in August 1939, only to regain favor after the Red Army's victory in battle of Stalingrad in February 1943. For the Jewish voter the Red Army stood alone in withstanding the Nazi onslaught. During its United Front period about 15 percent of the party's 75,000 members were of "Jewish background."

In the immediate years following World War II the sense that it was the Red Army that had finally bled the *Wehrmacht* to death brought with it a more positive view of the Soviet Union generally, which momentarily strengthened the Communist movement. For Jews of a social democratic persuasion, the fact, cited endlessly by Soviet propagandists, that the Soviet Union had played a critical role in rescuing over a million Polish Jews, coupled with the early recognition of Israel and the crucial military aid extended by its new satellite Czechoslovakia, restored some confidence that the "wave of the future" would come from the East. The war itself served as a great divide in the development of Jewish political culture. For a few years it seemed that the extreme Left had made its much sought-for breakthrough to the Jewish electorate. In New York state, where the strength of the party was concentrated, Communist-sponsored candidates did well in Jewish districts in the by-election of 1946.

The high of influence by the extreme Left was reached in the presidential campaign of 1948. The candidacy of Henry Wallace, Roosevelt's visionary secretary of agriculture, on the Progressive Party ticket received 14 percent of the Jewish vote despite some indications that the CPUS controlled his campaign. In heavily Jewish election districts Wallace often received over half of the Jewish vote. The enlistment of Jewish youth in the Wallace campaign by the organization of chapters of the Young Progressives of America (YPA) on college campuses could be taken as a sign that the left-wing torch had been passed on to a new generation of young Jews.[38] The Wallace campaign also marked a high point for those voters, most non-Communist, who saw in the developing cold war the seedbed of a possible third world war. It was the Communist-led Left that early capitalized on that fear by attracting Jewish liberals with the cry of "peaceful coexistence." Peace became a major talking point of the extreme Left and neither the invasion of South Korea in June 1950 nor the uprising in Berlin in 1953 could easily dissipate the image of a peace-seeking Socialist camp. It took time for Jewish liberals to delineate the real from fantasy.

The Jewish wing of the Communist Party never became an integral part of the American Jewish polity. Rather, it sought to address the American working class through the Jewish community, especially its labor movement. Its primary loyalty was to the international Communist movement represented after 1919 by the Communist International (Comintern), a powerful Kremlin-sponsored agency designed to advance the interest of the Socialist revolution as developed in the Soviet Union. With few exceptions immigrant Jews belonged to their own unions and Socialist clubs. The strategy of the Communist Left that aimed to bring the Jewish polity into the international Communist orbit was a divisive factor in Jewish communal politics, especially in its labor movement. Within the Jewish Socialist movement during this early period a split between left and right wings developed in the two major labor unions, the International Ladies Garment Workers (ILGWU) and the Amalgamated Clothing

Workers (ACW) and their affiliated unions. From there it expanded to the supportive affiliated membership organizations like the Workman's Circle, the International Workers Order, and the Jewish People's Fraternal Order (JPFO). In the case of the Workman's Circle, the more radical Left split off twenty-six of its schools and summer camps, including the well-known Kinderland. The conflict between the Social Democratic and Communist Left for control of the Jewish labor movement was marked by uncommon violence. The comparative civil calm and stability in the Jewish polity seemed forever broken as Jews were given their first taste of the political passions that lay just beneath the surface. Some signs of that tension between moderate social democrats and impassioned Communists can still be observed today.

After several disastrous schisms in the twenties, the party, aided by the breakdown of the economic system in 1929, succeeded in rebuilding its membership. Though proportionately small in numbers the party's hyperactivity generated the impression that the Communist-led Left had gained a decisive voice in the Jewish polity. That image was somehow enhanced by the fact that while Jewish party cardholders were a small minority within the Jewish polity, they formed the largest ethnic group within the general party. The 22,000 readers of the Yiddish-language *Morning Freiheit*, the Yiddish daily established in 1925, outnumbered the English-speaking readership of the *Daily Worker*, the general organ of the party established in 1927. Indeed, the party-led left faction proved to be effective in its organizations like the Young People's Socialist League (YPSL), followed in the fifties by the Labor Youth League and Young Progressives of America (YPA). The party's influence was expanded by establishing schools like the Rand School of Social Science and later the Jefferson School. The party's role in these endeavors was concealed by the use of "front" organizations, so that the various journals and unions seemed autonomous but in fact took their cues from the party.

The ability of the party to recoup its disaffected Jewish support during its United Front period of the thirties could be attributed in part to a change in tactics in relation to Jewish communal politics. The party not only dropped its dogmatic discussions regarding the true path of Marxist-Leninism, which caused endless schisms, but it also raised its voice regarding anti-Semitism and endlessly pointed out that the party had after all predicted the crisis in capitalism that led to the Depression. Such rhetoric proved particularly attractive to the radicalized Jewish younger generations whose enrollment in colleges had raised high hope of rising to middle-class status. A comparatively small group of devoted party members were also able to project an influence on Jewish political consciousness far beyond its number by infiltrating and then working from within Socialist and liberal Jewish organizations. Jewish defense agencies like the American Jewish Congress devoted much of their energy to maintaining autonomy from the onslaught of the Communist-led Left. Shortly before the Nonaggression Pact of 1939, which again caused a plunge in Jewish membership, the party could boast over 72,000 Jewish members, more than three times as many as the Socialist Party of America.

But the extreme Left's moment in the sun would not long endure. Withal, actual party membership and related "progressive" organization was a minority phenomenon among Jews whose primary energy was expended in rising above their class rather than with it as mandated by Marxist doctrine. The postwar years offered ample opportunity to do so and extreme left-wing impulse among Jewish voters underwent a sharp downward trajectory in membership and influence.

We have previously noted that the campaign for the Progressive Party candidate Henry Wallace in 1948 was a demonstration of the influence the Left could generate in the Jewish electorate. In a brilliantly organized campaign the Communist Party made the election of Wallace a crusade, especially among Jewish youth. But with the advent of the cold war the mood of Jewish voters became less susceptible to the alarms raised by the Communist-led Left. Jewish support waned further when the Kremlin projected the Jewish state as a vestige of Western imperialism and the expansionist thrust of the Kremlin became clear on the Korean peninsula. America's Jews never became enthusiastic cold warriors but the influence of the extreme Left was broken by the midfifties, allowing liberalism to develop free of Stalinist fetters.

The movement of some Jewish leaders away from the extreme Left to its normal position slightly left of center may also have been part of a long-term movement toward Americanization and a sense that Jews would share in the postwar prosperity. Jewish urban neighborhoods, which served as incubators for the party organization, began to thin out with the movement to suburbia. One could not call a rent strike in the privately owned homes of Levittown. The generation of the fifties, dubbed the "silent generation," seemed less interested in politics and more in "catching up" for time lost in military service. The sons of the immigrants that had nurtured the Socialist ideal during the twenties and thirties were attending college on the GI Bill. The general rise to middle-class status led to the diminution of the working-class base from which the party preferred to recruit its membership. As in the prosperity of the twenties, which recurred in the fifties, most Jews preferred a rise in station rather than casting their lot as workers as suggested by party directives. They carried their heightened political consciousness, incubated in the Jewish politics of the Left, into the political mainstream, where it reemerged as the vibrant form of Jewish liberalism of the sixties and seventies.

Yet the campaign against communism posed a dilemma for liberal-minded Jews. Half of the Communist Party leaders indicted under the Smith Act were of Jewish origin, but the Communist Party had after all once been a legal party. Should a communal protective mantel be extended to nominal Jews claiming persecution for being Jewish, who may in fact have been in the service of a foreign power? The trial of the Rosenbergs for espionage crystallized the liberal dilemma. Many Jewish voters still viewed the Soviet Union as an ally in the great war against the Nazi Reich and some questioned whether there was such a thing as an atomic secret. If they were not spies, how far could dissent be extended?

The dilemma posed by the Rosenberg case was projected against McCarthyism, which prevailed simultaneously with the disenchantment with the Communist Left after the Soviet Union had embarked on a campaign to destroy Jewish culture and communalism. The so-called black years between 1948 and 1953, the year of Stalin's death, dissipated the belief of even the most loyal Jewish party members that the Soviet constitution of 1936 had somehow banished anti-Semitism from the Soviet Union, as party propagandists were wont to argue. Anti-Semitism remained generic in the Russian people and was present in the party's highest echelons, who used it as a binding tie to the Russian people. The destruction of Jewish communal organizations, the open anti-Semitic ranting of the controlled press, and the following of the anti-Semitic Soviet lead in the satellite states, which culminated in the Slansky trial (1952) and finally the "Doctor's Plot" (1953), weakened what remained of appreciation of the wartime role in defeating the Nazi juggernaut.

The extreme Left did not leave the historical stage all at once. Some of the enthusiasm for social change was transplanted from children of now prosperous former left-wing Jewish activists who sent their children for higher education to universities like Chicago, Berkeley, and Wayne State, and to colleges like City College of New York and Brooklyn College, where a new generation of Jewish radicals could be spawned. In a sense the campus uprising of the New Left in the late sixties and early seventies drew much of its leadership from this strata of students, the children of former left-wing activists.[39] But by the end of the sixties little remained of the rich network of organizations, summer camps, student organizations, and informal groupings that formed a separate but related Jewish community that served as the basis of a culture of the extreme Left. By 1952 the two left-wing newspapers, the *PM* and its successor *The Compass*, heavily favored by Jewish readers, had ceased publication and the Communist daily *The Worker* and its Yiddish counterpart the *Morning Freiheit* had experienced considerable decline in circulation. *The National Guardian*, whose investigative journalism was on a higher level than the Communist daily tabloids, served the needs of the more educated younger generation of progressives. It would hang on for a few more years, but the movement of the Jewish electorate to the political center by the late fifties was clear. The more moderate liberal daily *The New York Post*, whose circulation was 266,784 in 1949, had risen to 408,150 eight years later.

For Jewish veterans on the GI Bill the growing prosperity of the fifties, juxtaposed with the fear generated by the McCarthy "witch hunts," led to a more cautious attitude. Unlike the thirties the postwar years offered a vision of prosperity not lightly discarded. The cold war deepened with the testing of an A-bomb by the Soviet Union in September 1949, years earlier than expected. The spy trial of the Rosenbergs possessed all the earmarks to generate apprehensiveness among Jews who just experienced the decimation of the Jews of Europe. This time it would be American Jewry's sense of security that was threatened. For many Jews the Rosenberg trial, which began a year prior to the Slansky trial of Jewish spies in Czechoslovakia, marked the juncture in which they were ready to abandon the idealism of the Left that had drawn them. The tandem Slansky and Rosenberg spy trials were disheartening for middle-of-the-road Jewish voters who made their political home in the liberal wing of the Democratic Party. Less than ten years after World War II it seemed like nothing had changed—there was no security for Jews at either end of the political spectrum. Yet the party-sponsored government trials of Jewish conspirators in Prague, so reminiscent of Moscow's purge trials of the thirties, was no more palatable than the random anti-Semitic incident that continued to plague Jewish life in America.

The overwhelming majority of Jews in the postwar era opted for the promise of America. In 1945 membership in the Communist Party had hit its peek of about eighty thousand, four years later it was less than four thousand. Whether in their organizations or local politics, liberal proponents of democratic governance proved no match for would-be professional revolutionists and party activists. Yet in the long run Jewish social democracy, which contributed notably to the development of Jewish liberalism, was able to sustain itself. The fifties mark the end of the powerful pull of the extreme Left on Jewish liberalism. The end of that sometime bitter conflict set the stage for the full development of Jewish liberalism.

From Republicans to Democrats

So beset was the newly organized Communist Party with its raucous internal politics and the attraction of high-profile issues like the Sacco and Vanzetti case that it failed to recognize the outward tilt of the of the politics of Jewish immigrant generation. The early role Jews would come to play in American politics derived mostly from their primary interest in immigration policy fueled by concern for their brethren abroad. The change in party affiliation from Republican to Democrat, which began in earnest with the administration of Al Smith in New York state, was particularly badly timed, since Warren Harding, Calvin Coolidge, and Herbert Hoover were Republican stalwarts, reluctant to acknowledge the political needs of the new ethnic constituencies, particularly on immigration policy.[40] Only Wilson's timely veto of the literacy Test Act in 1915, which Jewish leaders like Louis Marshall believed was promulgated to hold off a pending Jewish immigrant inundation, held off an earlier restrictionist onslaught. By 1920 the dam was broken by a flood of anti-alien and anti-immigrant legislation.

The Jewish conversion to the Democratic fold during the twenties occurred simultaneously with another development, a growing interest in domestic reform coupled with an interest in the peace and disarmament movements that became prominent among the intellectual elite after the carnage of World War I. There were as yet few signs of the later virulent anti-Semitism in the Soviet Union in the twenties, which was generally a hopeful period for Soviet Jewry. Generally, American Jews shared the prosperity of the twenties, making much progress in improving their educational level and in small business. But events in Europe, where it was already possible to observe the growth of a new type of anti-Semitism in Germany, aroused apprehension. The change in American Jewry's political focus would be sudden and involuntary. It was related to a new threat emanating from Berlin, where authority was assumed by the National Socialists in January 1933, and whose führer spoke of ridding Germany of its Jews in his writings. His was an anti-Semitism that went far beyond the normative type seen in Poland or France and pre-Nazi Germany. But when the Nazis seized power few recognized the full danger posed by the lethal combination of racial anti-Semitism and social Darwinism. An extremist aberrant form of a well-known phenomenon had come to power in Europe's most powerful state. Few political leaders were prepared to cope with it, least of all American Jewry's leadership.

The opposition to mass immigration from southern and eastern Europe was ostensibly favored to restore the ethnic composition before 1890. Preoccupied with finding their way in the new culture, the immigrant generation focused their political energy on providing relief and advocating a more liberal immigration policy that would facilitate the entry of their brethren. The linking of immigration policy to the liberal agenda followed naturally from Louis Marshall's efforts to ameliorate Russian anti-Jewish depredations during the early years of the twentieth century. There was little that could be done to halt government-sponsored pogroms, but the Kremlin's efforts to impose its anti-Semitic strictures abroad, related to the rights of American Jewish citizens who returned to Russia for business or family visits, offered Louis Marshall a target to gain the intercession of the American government. The so-called passport question was handled by the established Jewish political class led by Marshall and Schiff, who had reconciled their differences regarding support of the Allies to focus on the pending flood of anti-immigration legislation.

Informed that millions of Polish Jews were about to inundate the United States, the congressional hearings on immigration legislation revealed a specific intent to limit Jewish immigration. Spurred by the signals of unwelcome generated by the emerging restrictionist immigration policy, restoring access to America became the political issue that most concerned the newly enfranchised eastern European Jewish citizen. Few could foresee the devastating impact these restrictive laws would have in the thirties when, unable to find a haven, Europe's Jews confronted state-sponsored extrusion and mass murder. The new quota restrictions on Jewish immigration from eastern and southern Europe were imposed first by the Immigration Emergency Law of 1921 and then formally established by the Johnson-Reed Law of 1924.

The quota system based on the national origins formula hastened a change in Jewish political concern to the critical condition of Jews in Soviet Russia and Poland. The relief efforts of the newly organized American Jewish Joint Distribution Committee (1914) that included retraining as well as food distribution and kitchens to feed the hungry complemented the relief efforts of Herbert Hoover. Though the "Joint" was composed of three separate fundraising agencies, the postwar relief effort in eastern Europe was primary and demonstrated the funding capacity of the moneyed "uptown" Jews. But as in the case of the aroused response to the Kishinev pogrom, the dire situation in eastern Europe acted as an accelerator to bring the newly minted voters from eastern Europe into communal politics. A new energy and organization came to the fore. That change would inevitably be reflected in the changed power arrangements governing American Jewry. After the death of Louis Marshall in 1929, it was "downtown" Jewry that dominated the grassroots of the American Jewish polity and infused a less self-consciousness and a more activist spirit into Jewish communal politics.

The Congress movement and the campaign to keep immigration policy liberal dealt primarily with the security and impoverishment of east European Jewry in the post–World War I years. Zionists and many non-Zionists could agree that immigration to the United States or Palestine held out greater hope for the amelioration of the Jews of eastern Europe. But we have noted that a sizeable portion of the "uptown" leadership, led by Louis Marshall, placed greater stock in the proposed national minority rights clauses to be included in the founding charters of new nations created by the League of Nations. In the end neither could prevent the deterioration of the security of European Jewry, the issue that became the major concern of American Jewry in the thirties.

In communal politics the fragmentation within the strife-ridden Communist Party, formally organized in 1921, set the stage for the turmoil of Jewish leftist politics of the twenties. At the same time, the political maturation of "downtown" Jews carried forward by Zionist organizations, coupled with the comparatively rapid ability to raise money that developed during World War I, altered the internal political balance of American Jewry. German Jewish dominance in communal affairs waned while the Eastern Jewish immigrants came into their political own. The introduction of democracy into communal governance, which was the war cry of the Congress movement, formally reestablished by Rabbi Wise as the American Jewish Congress in 1921, also had a downside. It became more difficult to determine who spoke for American Jewry. The German Jewish leadership was no longer able to provide that unifying voice. We have noted that the effects of that fragmentation were especially notable in the fundraising arena, where Zionists and other "downtown" elements were in continual conflict with the JDC/AJC group concerning the distribution formula for the proceeds of the annual campaign. The sizeable Democratic Socialist group centered in the Jewish labor movement, the *Forward*, and the Workmen's Circle were so riven with internal divisions that they proved unable to withstand the machinations of the Communist Party, which became the Comintern's instrument to infiltrate the Jewish labor movement. An ill-conceived garment industry strike in 1926 proved disastrous for the democratically oriented Jewish Left and hampered the effort to develop an independent Jewish liberal politics able to resist the blandishments of the extreme Left.

We have already noted the shift in Jewish party preferences from the Republican to Democrat that began during the Wilson administration and was largely completed by the time of Al Smith's Brown Derby campaign in 1928. Smith lost to Herbert Hoover, but he won 72 percent of the Jewish vote, a marked change in American Jewish politics. The change in party affiliation marked a crucial turning point in the growth of Jewish liberalism. Jews became the ethnic voting bloc most committed to the liberal wing of the Democratic Party, where they remain to this day. That rapid change in party preference also had a profound shaping effect on American political culture.

Yet sharing in the prosperity of the twenties and evidence of considerable entrepreneurial energy, especially in merchandizing and in developing new specialized industries such as film, garment, and scrap iron, brought little change in Jewish liberal proclivities. In the twenties there were already signs of Jewry's growing attachment to an independent form of liberalism with a separate list of issues that required attention. One could oppose Ford's anti-Semitic ranting in his *Dearborn Independent* and passionately proclaim the innocence of Sacco and Vanzetti, while at the same time take full advantage of the promise of America by accumulating ever more degrees attesting to completion of formal education and professional certification, or by possessing material signs of prosperity such as a new apartment with a sunken living room on Bronx's Grand Concourse. Why should not such well being be available to their beleaguered brethren in Europe? The campaign against immigration restriction remained a basic long-range issue on the political agenda that all Jewish voters could agree on and that could serve as a bridge to other ethnic voting blocs. But after the advent of Hitler it became a life and death issue for the Jewish electorate.

But in the forefront of Jewish political consciousness were immediate threats such as the lynching of Leo Frank in 1915; the Palmer raids, which rounded up radicals, among whom were many Jews; the activities of the Ku Klux Klan, which had added Jews and Catholics to its hit list; and the Harvard *numerus clausus* case, which sought to limit Jewish enrollment. These were the immediate issues that attracted Jewish voters and their defenders like Louis Marshall. Signs of unwelcome were distressing, but anti-Semitism in America was mild compared with what Jews had experienced in Europe. Before the crash of 1929 Jews had fully partaken in the prosperity of the twenties. Why storm the closed gates of Harvard when public state and city colleges welcomed Jewish enrollment? Aside from the failure of the Kehillah by mid-decade and the conflict between Zionists and non-Zionists over the formula for distribution of funds garnered from the annual campaign, little was allowed to interfere with the climb to achieve middle-class status.

To fathom the development of the Jewish political spirit of the twenties it is necessary to understand the passionate Jewish reaction to the trial of two Italian anarchists, Sacco and Vanzetti, who were accused of killing two payroll clerks during an armed bank robbery attempt in Braintree, Massachusetts. The controversy of the case continued for seven years and through two trials before their execution on August 23, 1927. The case attracted worldwide attention and Jews were hardly alone in sensing that there had been a miscarriage of justice. The intense Jewish reaction to the case was difficult to explain. Though often sharing urban enclaves, relations between Italian and Jewish immigrants were not particularly close, and while Jews raised their own radicals, bomb-throwing anarchists were alien to them. But there was the feeling that the men had been railroaded and were innocent. Two of their public intellectuals, Felix Frankfurter, who taught law at the prestigious Harvard Law School, and Walter Lippmann, who was on the road to becoming a premier journalist and public intellectual, wrote learnedly about the innocence of Sacco and Vanzetti. Amplified by the widely read Yiddish press, which shared their judgment of both intellectuals, outrage about the injustice of the trial filtered down to the Yiddish-reading public through the Yiddish-speaking intelligentsia that argued politics endlessly over tea in the cafés of the Jewish neighborhoods. The interest of the Jewish masses in the trials was aroused by memories of their own crucible regarding their political radicalism and questionable loyalty. Strident nativism symbolized by the movement to restrict immigration and actualized by the Palmer raids, which witnessed the attorney general's office crowding hundreds of radicals aboard the "Red Arc" to be shipped to Europe without due process, sensitized the Jewish voter. For many Jews the raids served as evidence that American justice was often miscarried, especially in the case of radicals. Not far beneath was the fact that the Socialist-oriented Jewish voter did not share the native hysteria about radicals. The Jewish passion about the innocence of Sacco and Vanzetti tells us a great deal about the political emotions of the immigrant Jewish generation. The agitation over the arrest of idealistic anarchist radicals was still present during the Rosenberg trial in 1952. For many Jews they were not dangerous spies but misguided idealists.

Summing Up

The full development of American Jewish liberalism occurred primarily during the interwar years after the Jewish electorate found a home in the liberal wing of the Democratic Party. It has remained that party's most loyal ethnic constituency ever since. Shaped by its vulnerability of being an alien yet self-conscious presence in other lands, the roots of its liberalism extend deeply into Jewish exilic history. Communal commitment to ethical principles derived from the biblical prophets and embodied in Jewish law hardly mitigated an almost universal anti-Jewish animus. It may be that normative sense of being outside the political process that above all else accounts for the special feeling many Jews developed of being at home in America. To be sure, America was not exempt from the plague of anti-Semitism, but it was overshadowed by the fact that both the American and Jewish polities were children of the European Enlightenment in which the principles of liberalism were embedded. The Jewish liberalism that emerged fully in the twentieth century went beyond being a political ideology. In its commitment to human betterment it possesses many of the earmarks of a secular faith. There is a liberal position on virtually every issue on the domestic political calendar from *Row v. Wade* to the myriad of "green" environmental issues. Above all Jewish liberals believe that government is the best agency for societal improvement. That commitment places the Jewish constituency astride the major axis of national politics, which concerns the role of government in the economy and the lives of the citizenry. In the tension between liberty and the unending search for a just social order based on equality, Jewish liberals place egalitarianism above libertarianism. They favor government regulation and entitlement programs to level the playing field. One might say that in some measure it is the Jewish voters' liberalism that makes them among the most politically engaged voters in the American electorate. The Jewish liberal proposes while the Republican conservative disposes, or at least tries to do so.

In its American historical odyssey Jewish liberalism faced challenges from the Left as well as the Right. It shared the Socialist label with the Communist Party, whose influence was enhanced by the collapse of the economy in the thirties. Yet Communist influence, which seemed so pervasive in the twenties and thirties, virtually disappeared from the Jewish political stage during the fifties. The prosperity of the fifties, in which American Jewry fully shared, deprived the party of a working-class constituency that might have generated the radicalized cadres ready to do the party's bidding. Their remarkable social mobility suggests that Jews preferred to rise above their class rather than with it. The growing revelations that the Soviet version of socialism had produced a tyranny convinced many Jewish intellectuals, traditionally held in high esteem, that their hope for a just society stemming from the Kremlin was forlorn. The Kremlin's staunch opposition to Israel, coupled with evidence of official anti-Semitism in the Doctor's Plot and Slansky trial in Prague, convinced even the truest believer that the Soviet experiment with socialism had gone awry. Once the influence of the Communist Party on the Jewish Left was broken, Jewish liberalism emerged as an integral part of the national electorate. Yet only in New York was a liberal party established.

Liberalism among Jews remained primarily a matter of individual preference exercised in the voting booth. That vote was an important factor in strengthening Jewish influence in the American political dialogue even while its proportion was declining compared with the Latino and African American vote.

Jewish liberal voters help give the American political dialogue a certain stability. Despite the perennial hope by Republican stalwarts that liberal Jewish voters would finally be detached from their moorings in the Democratic Party, it has never been realized. Since the election of Woodrow Wilson in 1912, no Republican presidential candidate has ever received a majority of the Jewish vote. Yet some like "Ike" Eisenhower in 1952 and Ronald Reagan in 1980 have done far better than others, which convinces some pundits that Jewish voters might someday become "swing" voters. More likely, Jewish voters are as subject to the charisma of the Roosevelts, Kennedys, and Reagans as are other American voters. Jewish votes for a candidate with a normal Republican preference for limited government and opposition to entitlement programs, like John McCain in the election of 2008 or Mitt Romney in 2012, yields a more realistic picture. It ranges between 25 and 35 percent and has gone as low as 19 percent. Liberalism seems to be in the political DNA of American Jewry.

3

The New Deal Jewish
Liberal Amalgam

Just as the prosperous twenties had been dominated by the libertarian notion of "the less government the better," so the New Deal decade that followed promised to be one fueled by the idea that government must play a role in the economy. The liberal ascendancy of the thirties pulled Jewish liberalism with it. To some extent, it was also pushed by Jewish liberalism. Programs in public housing, medical care, unemployment insurance, and social security were pioneered in the Jewish labor movement and often first conceived by professional Jewish social-work agencies. Preexisting proclivities in Jewish political culture were reinforced by the government's presence in major areas of the economy during the thirties. Since a role for government was already a mainstay of Socialist-oriented assumptions of the Jewish immigrant electorate, the role of the Roosevelt administration in guiding the nation's recovery was accepted as a matter of course. The assumption of the primacy of government is one of the factors that accounts for the almost proprietary interest that Jews had regarding the Roosevelt administration. The Jewish love affair with the New Deal went beyond the fact that some of its welfare programs found their experimental roots in the Jewish labor movement and social-worker agencies. The notion that government had a role to play in social amelioration and economic regulation was a basic assumption of Jewish political culture. During the thirties it seemed, at least for the moment, that the American polity had come to share these convictions.

Jewish relations with the New Deal should not be limited to its reform and recovery program, which fit so neatly into its psyche. The troubling events in Europe also compelled Jews to turn desperately to the Roosevelt administration. Their overriding commitment to Roosevelt was complete when the patrician president unhesitatingly appointed Jews to administer the new regulatory agencies. What anti-Semitic rhetoric labeled the "Jew Deal" was, for Jewish voters, seen as liberalism in action. It meant that they too were included. When that enormous faith in Roosevelt was not fully realized by his failure to open the door for Jewish refugees seeking to flee the charnel house of Europe, some Jewish voters undoubtedly felt betrayed. But that occurred after the massive scale of the genocide was revealed and it never became the general Jewish consensus. Roosevelt consistently rates as the first or second most popular president in polls among Jewish voters. That is politically possible because there is a separation in Jewish political thinking between the Roosevelt administration's failing witness role to the Holocaust and its domestic role in fighting the Depression. (We will note in chapter 6 that the question of the response of the Roosevelt administration to the Holocaust remains unresolved.)

Six decades after the Holocaust, the Republican Party's hope that Jews would abandon their liberalism remains unfulfilled because it fails to come to grips with how deeply the New Deal reinforced the preexisting statist orientation in Jewish political culture. There is no uncertainty regarding the New Deal domestic economic program. Most Jewish voters continue to believe in the words of that Jewish "snowbird" who, upon being interviewed, pronounced simply that in the case of a crises like the Depression, "government needs to do the right thing." That statement contains the basic assumption of Jewish liberalism—"government ought to do." Government should play a role. Yet it leaves unanswered the question what the "right thing" might be, leaving an area of uncertainty in the very center of Jewish political culture. For the liberal Jewish voter it meant programs to assure the welfare of citizens. That would include medical care and social security as well as physical security. Without saying so directly, in order to do the "right" thing government would be required to redistribute property and income through the tax instrument. It is that sequence that is at the heart of the contemporary great debate between conservatives and liberals in the national political dialogue. Conservatives want low taxes and limited government. Liberals want government to uplift those least favored by using the taxing instrument, among others, to assure a level playing field. We have previously taken note of the oddity that today Jews rank comparatively high in per capita income yet generally strongly support a "progressive" graduated taxing formula. In years to come the maintenance of a graduated income tax will join the testy issue of regulation of Wall Street as the surest measure of whether the nation remains liberal. Despite their high per capita income there is little doubt on which side most of the Jewish electorate will stand.

It was not until the Roosevelt era that it was possible to fully see how the democratic socialism of the immigrant generation with its strong statist element could be joined to the welfare element of a government confronted with the Depression. The economic crises set the stage for the amalgamation of the social democracy of immigrant Jewish political culture to the improvised welfare state policies of the New Deal. The immigrant generation's attraction to socialism established the requisite ideology for the organization of the Jewish labor movement. Socialists believed that labor was the source of all value. It was the ILGWU and the ACW that pioneered much of the New Deal's labor legislation that became the essence of the New Deal. The Jewish labor movement demonstrated how liberal ideology could be transmitted from mere words to programs at the grassroots level. At the same time it gave the Jewish worker a bridge to enter practical American politics. That was the role played by the American Labor Party (ALP), which was established in New York State in 1935. It allowed Socialist-oriented Jewish voters to cast their ballots for the patrician, wellborn Franklin Roosevelt rather than a corrupt Tammany Sachem without needing to compromise their Socialist principles.

American Jewry was the only immigrant group to create its own political party and the only one to formally carry the term "liberal" into the political arena. The ALP soon dubbed itself "the party of the permanent New Deal." But it could not escape the shoals of Jewish politics. After an eight-year effort to resist Communist infiltration, David Dubinsky, head of the ILGWU, and Alex Rose, head of the Hat Makers Union, left the ALP in 1944 and with the help of such public intellectuals as John Dewey and Reinhold Niebuhr established the Liberal Party. Officially it was a secular rather than a Jewish political party and the union leaders took care to run non-Jewish candidates for office, but in fact the funding and the rank and file was overwhelmingly Jewish. In its time the Liberal Party successfully amplified its power by playing the role of balancer in the fragmented politics of New York State. But after the death of the original founders in the midseventies and the decline of the Jewish unions that supported it financially, the party lost its place on the New York State voting ballot in 2002. Raymond Harding, Alex Rose's successor in 1976, was indicted for corruption.

It was the New Deal's welfare-state legislation that became a crucial component of Jewish liberalism. Jewish voters became the most enthusiastic supporters of the Roosevelt administration and sustained their support after other ethnic voters began to abandon the New Deal following the election of 1936. Prominent Jews like Samuel Rosenman, Roosevelt's speechwriter, and Samuel Untermeyer, a well-known writer, are given credit for coining the term "New Deal," while Rabbi Stephen Wise took inordinate pride for having submitted the term "forgotten man" for Roosevelt's first inaugural address. The Jewish voter's relationship to the New Deal became so proprietary that the anti-Semitic pejorative "Jew Deal" almost lost its sting. Having gotten a taste of the rewards reserved for those who belong and participate, some Jewish voters may even have believed that it was so.[1]

From the perspective of history the New Deal welfare state represents an extension of the liberal idea of equality that now assumes that the less fortunate citizen has a right to be protected in some measure from the uncertainties of the business cycle. Behind the popular "relief, recovery, and reform" slogan was a political philosophy that sought to further the egalitarian aspect of democratic ideology from the libertarian free-for-all that was believed to have plunged the nation into economic chaos. The "reform" aspect of the New Deal sought to put in place what John Adams called "political architecture" to establish a balance between the private and public sectors of society. The precedent for such checks and balances could be found in the constitution. The result was a growth in the size of government, which became the bugaboo of the Republican Party. For the Jewish voter the supportive network of government welfare agencies and programs to draw a red line beyond which no citizen would be allowed to fall became the very essence of what government should be about. It required that Socialist revolutionary doctrine be purged of its instruments of violence to be replaced by the instruments of democracy and the parliamentary system that prevailed in America. New Deal conservation programs, regional planning like the Tennessee Valley Authority (TVA), and dozens of make-work programs became the glue that fastened the Jewish voter to the Roosevelt administration. It was not quite the socialism immigrant voters may have dreamed about but close enough for them to cross a bridge into the American political arena.

Yet in their political heart of hearts American Jews remained Social Democrats, but now dressed in American liberal clothing. The close relationship of Jewish liberalism to the social democracy that was carried in the cultural baggage of the east European immigrants gave American Jewry a vision, if not of "the city on a hill," then of something resembling it. Jewish liberalism developed into a political persuasion that had sufficient breadth to contain both aspiration for the release of entrepreneurial energy, which Jews also generated in disproportionate numbers, and recognition that unaddressed economic inequities could destabilize the system. We have noted that the narrowing distribution of power concerned Progressive reformers who proposed a regulatory government policeman to mediate between the "haves" and the "have nots" and to maintain a balance between freedom and the entrepreneurial energy that accompanied it and the basic security of the citizenry. The effort to control the growing inequity and insecurity led to the social security law at the heart of the New Deal.[2] The New Deal shaped Jewish liberalism into a powerful new political sensibility whose statist principles were almost unanimously accepted by the Jewish electorate. It would not long remain a solitary unifying force in the dynamic political atmosphere of American Jewry. Buoyed by the prosperity of the postwar decades, which promoted a rapid climb to the middle class, and liberated from the missionary clutch of its extreme Left, Jewish liberalism found its way to the position of the political spectrum it holds today, slightly left of center in the Democratic Party.[3]

The new Jewish liberalism allowed for considerable wiggle room but basic principles remained constant. Though belonging to the nation's most financially secure class, few American Jews can be found supporting the privatizing of social security and most remains staunch supporters of the graduated income tax. It is that view of government as enabler, as justice seeker, as arbitrator between conflicting interests, and, when necessary, as provider that distinguishes Jewish liberalism. Assigning government a major role in stabilizing the economy and insuring growth and security for the workforce was what democratic socialism became in America. Had statism not influenced the American system of governance, Jewish voters might in any case have come to the same position regarding the need for government to play a regulatory as well as planning role in the management of the economy. The political culture developed by the immigrant generation hastened that process and made it less wrenching. More than anything else that is what accounts for the Jewish "love affair" with the Roosevelt administration.

For the liberal Jewish voter the great attraction of the New Deal lay in the fact that it helped the Jewish Socialist-minded voter to gain entrée to the American polity whose fear of socialism of any stripe was dissipated by the ameliorative role government played during the Depression. Once purged of its alien class-conscious elements and the notion that the "means of production" must be owned by government, and replaced by the Keynesian ameliorative role assigned to government, the New Deal became a pillar of Jewish liberalism. Eight decades later it lingers in the soul of the Jewish voter who supports President Obama's quasi-Keynesian approach to staving off the near economic "meltdown" of 2008–2009.

The proliferation of Jewish officeholders on all levels of government is also rooted in the Roosevelt era. It was in the urban, ethnic, labor coalition that buttressed the New Deal that the Jewish voter found a new political home. The formation of that political alliance did not develop all at once, nor did Jews enter directly into politics as candidates for office on the local level. New York City, which boasted the largest aggregation of Jews in the world, did not produce its first Jewish mayor, Abe Beame, until 1974. But the Democratic Party, which now produced several local political clubs dominated by Jewish members in urban areas, was becoming the ascendant political force in the Jewish polity during the thirties. The liberal-urban-ethnic labor coalition at the heart of Roosevelt's New Deal remained intact until the election of the popular Republican Eisenhower in 1952, who gained a whopping 32 percent of the Jewish vote despite the popularity of Adlai Stevenson, who received 64 percent. Everyone, including the Jewish voter, liked "Ike." That preference marks a kind of turning point in Jewish political culture. That a popular Republican candidate could so affect Jewish voting would not have been predicted as late as the election of 1944. Was the Jewish electorate gaining a new ability to view a Republican candidate with equanimity, even with a modicum of support? What was so remarkable in the election of 1952 is that Adlai Stevenson, the Democratic candidate, fit the Jewish voter's liberal preference almost perfectly. He was patrician, well educated, a staunch proponent of the liberal program, and his speeches displayed an elevated use of language. The Jewish voter was indeed "madly for Adlai," but not at the rate one would have expected. The ranks of the postwar Jewish voters now filled with veterans had become more acculturated and had no problem voting for a military man who had been their commanding officer. There were of course many other factors at work, including a moderation of the New Deal influence during the prosperity of the fifties.

The Testing of Jewish Liberalism: War and the Holocaust

We have noted that during the war the signals of indifference from Washington and London to the threat of annihilation emanating from Berlin were devastating for all Jews. Liberal Jews had special reasons to grieve. How could the New Deal building block of Jewish liberalism be reconciled with Roosevelt's listless effort to offer haven to those fleeing the Reich? Until 1944 the Allies assumed virtually no risk in trying to stay Berlin's genocidal hand. London and Washington, the former in Palestine and the latter in its own vast interior, withheld resettlement possibilities for refugees that had succeeded in escaping the Nazi deportations. Yet the ideological aims of the war, the "four freedoms," two of which, freedom from fear and freedom from want, were mentioned in the Atlantic Charter (August 14, 1941) and might have served as a founding document for New Deal liberalism, never became part of the American information strategy.[4] Berlin spoke endlessly of the Jewish question and converted Roosevelt to the Jewish faith, but the Roosevelt administration, perhaps fearing that Berlin would succeed in turning the war into one to save the Jews, remained silent about the death camps.

The Holocaust went far to sensitize the Jewish voter to the danger posed by modern societies going awry and threatening the humanitarian principles of liberalism. From a Jewish perspective, the weakness of the democracies in facing the Nazi threat and the indifference of the Allied witnesses was disheartening. It was difficult to overlook the fact that a totalitarian power, the Soviet Union, was bleeding the Nazi war machine to death and incidentally provided a haven for 1.5 million Polish Jews while Roosevelt personally rejected the admission of twenty thousand Jewish refugee children stranded in France in 1940. We noted that there was no such hesitation by the administration when public support grew to bring non-Jewish British children, victims of the Blitz, to the United States, outside the quota system. When the war began in September 1939 the courage of the British in the face of the Nazi onslaught was a major theme in the American media, but for Jews it was London's White Paper that closed the door to Palestine, the only settlement that cried out to receive the Jews in the teeth of the refugee crisis. In maters of rescue, Jewish interests focused on the rescue of their brethren but strongly supported the national consensus that was slowly turning away from isolationism. We have noted that Jews were strongly interventionist-minded, offering strong support in their press for such programs as the Destroyer Bases Deal and sending lend-lease supplies, even to the Soviet Union after June 1941. But Jewish support for lowering the barriers for the admittance of refugees, if only on a temporary basis, departed too sharply from majority opinion.

Such negative signals would have a long-range impact on Jewish voters, but in the short run their support for the New Deal liberal agenda remained intact. In 1940 there was no other choice. Wendell Wilkie, the Republican candidate, sometimes pejoratively labeled as "a simple barefoot Wall Street lawyer," and Thomas Dewey, the Republican candidate in the election of 1944, gave little evidence of concern about the plight of the Jews and were far removed from the New Deal liberal sensibility that so enthralled the Jewish electorate. The Holocaust should have once and for all undermined the basic humanitarian assumptions on which liberalism is based and served as a great turning point in Jewish political culture. Yet, in contrast to other ethnic voting blocs, Jews raised their percentage of votes for Roosevelt in the election of 1940, and despite Roosevelt's indifferent rescue policy, they supported a fourth term in 1944. That should give the reader an idea how strong was the Jewish electorate's bond to the New Deal and the Roosevelt administration. What we witness in the postwar years are Jewish liberal-minded activists, some children of Holocaust survivors, anxious to do in Darfur and Bosnia what the nations of the world did not do for their kin during those bitter years.[5] In a sense, alerting the world to incidents of genocide, which has drawn a disproportionate number of Jewish activists, is a supreme example of a Jewish liberal sensibility.

From the New Deal to the Liberalism of Civil Rights

The civil rights movement that flowered in the postwar years sought to add the plight of the American Negro to the list of the New Deal's "forgotten men." Though Allied war aims as declared in the Atlantic Charter resonated classic liberal principles, the American armed forces remained segregated until the Korean conflict. But the defeat of Nazi Germany, whose governing principle was based on racialism, marked a victory for liberalism, especially its belief in racial tolerance and pluralism. Though America did not come to the conflict unburdened by its racist tradition, the victory would inevitably be reflected in a new openness on the race question in its domestic politics. The seeds of the postwar struggle for civil rights were planted during the war years.

It is possible to measure the depth of Jewish liberalism through the prism of the civil rights movement, which reached its apogee during the Lyndon Johnson administration. We have seen that Jews were at once strong supporters of the movement while opposing specific implementing steps like the abandonment of the merit system for hiring in the civil service, which had been a cardinal plank in the liberalism of the twenties and thirties. Predictably, Jewish voters were less concerned than Lyndon Johnson, who warned that the political price of his civil rights legislation would be the loss of the "solid South" and the weakening of the party that carried the liberal program. Jewish voters were by and large staunch supporters of Lyndon Johnson's civil rights initiative.[6] Like many other liberals, many Jewish voters were willing to abandon political realities and let the wayward southern sister go. Before Kennedy's tenure was cut short by assassination the implementation of the liberal program in the area of medical care and civil rights was overshadowed by an unforeseen intensification of the cold war, marked by the failed invasion of Cuba at the Bay of Pigs followed by the Cuban missile crisis. Lyndon Johnson's White House tenure, especially his successful steering through Congress of the two crucial civil rights acts in education and voting, marks at once the high point of liberalism and the end of the forward New Deal reformist thrust. The Democratic coalition that dominated the Johnson administration could not withstand the double blow of the loss of the "solid South" and the militant opposition to the war in Vietnam.

Richard Nixon's triumph over the liberal Hubert Humphrey in the election of 1968, exploiting the "southern strategy," marks the beginning of a new period in which Jewish liberals, their youth disaffected by the Vietnam War, find themselves out of step with the conservative wing of the Democratic Party. The liberal bridge built by Roosevelt that encouraged Jewish political integration had, at least for the moment, been broken. It would take several years before public opinion also concluded that the war was a mistake. The rupture between Jewish liberal activists and mainline Democratic Party members would not be fully healed until the election of Barack Obama in 2008. By that time liberalism had to confront economic collapse and the costly wars in Iraq and Afghanistan that left little energy or consensus for the implementation of a program of liberal reform. That much the struggle to get even a moderate medical-care program through Congress in 2010 demonstrated. The national political mood had turned in a conservative direction. Nixon's telling victory over the liberal George McGovern in the election of 1972 ushered in a new period of Republican ascendancy that, with the exception of the election of Carter in 1976, lasted until the election of Bill Clinton in 1988. Yet strangely, rather than the liberally oriented Jewish voting bloc loosing leverage, the Jewish vote, which experienced a proportional decline, seemed to increase in importance with each election.

Jewish voters changed their priorities but not their liberal passions. The 1972 election demonstrated the firmness of the Jewish commitment to liberal principles. We have noted previously that the Jewish voter stuck with Roosevelt in 1940 when the ardor of other ethnic voting blocs had cooled. By 1972 it was clear that in terms of per capita income and professionalization the Jews had risen higher on the socio-economic ladder than other immigrant blocs. But their loyalty to the Democratic Party, which Nixon sought to change, proved to be steadfast.[7] Given their large per capita income and the fact that in the urban enclaves of the large cities in which many still resided had been impacted by race-based urban violence, one might have expected a preference for security promised primarily by conservative candidates. But no such preference is discernable in Jewish voting patterns. In fact it is precisely the educated Jewish urban middle class that was most likely to support the liberal position favoring integration. A pattern already discernable in the twenties prevailed in the seventies. Jews remained issue oriented and the issues they favored were drawn from the liberal agenda. The 65 percent of their vote they gave to the liberal George McGovern was still substantial, but 16 percent below the vote given to Hubert Humphrey in the preceding election of 1968. Jewish voters continued to compose the most loyal, albeit no longer the most liberal, constituency of the Democrat Party.[8]

The advent of the Nixon administration in 1969 witnessed a politically stranded Jewish voter that, together with other liberally oriented voters, was searching for something to hold on to. The Republican aspiration to break the Democrat hold on the Jewish vote seemed at times almost within reach.[9] After the election of 1972, when Nixon garnered a surprising 35 percent of the Jewish vote after his dismal showing in the 1968 election (17 percent), he aspired to bring the Jewish vote into the Republican column even while he privately ranted about Jews before his secretary of state, Henry Kissinger. When the bombing of Cambodia indicated that a broadening of the war rather than the promise of peace was planned, support for the administration waned. Watergate, which most Americans considered a moral low point in American politics, also marked the return of liberal Jews to the national political consensus. Most Jewish voters had not supported the war, and even after

Nixon's more than doubling his Jewish support in the 1972 election and the opening to China, few could muster much enthusiasm for the president's public personality. By the campaign of 1975 the liberal Jewish voter, while hardly enthusiastic about the candidacy of "Jimmy" Carter, nevertheless cast their ballots for him and returned unhappily to their home in the left wing of the Democratic Party wondering if being a "decent Christian" would suffice to negotiate the shoals that were ahead. Through the decade of the seventies and eighties when the Republicans reigned supreme, Jewish liberalism remained in a kind of political limbo even as a new development, the influence of the neoconservatives and the New Left, set the stage for a new challenge to Jewish liberalism. Both would have a profound effect in shaping American politics and both in different ways found their roots in the internecine conflict within the Jewish Left.

The Liberal Jewish Amalgam of the Sixties and Seventies

To fathom the change in postwar Jewish political culture we need first to understand how the new fears and sensibilities emanating from the cold war gradually unshackled liberals from their remaining Socialist moorings. That ideological reshaping was abetted by the aggressive posture the Kremlin assumed in its struggle for world dominance. The sharper liberal identity that set Jewish liberalism on a new track in the fifties rested on two historical processes. The first involved the separation of Jewish liberalism from the remnants of Socialist theories of political economy, leaving only the notion that government should play a role in regulating and if necessary stimulating a free-enterprise economy, including creating a favorable climate for the growth of labor unions. It was the moderate social democratic wing that positioned American Jews to be within striking distance of a more indigenous form of liberalism. That waited the decade of the fifties, when the influence of the radical Jewish Left was contained if not broken.

The second factor, to be more fully examined in the following chapters, concerned the desire of an Americanized second and third generation, whose young men were war veterans, to enter fully into the majority

American society and culture. For some it was not an easy passage. The fear of loosing one's own culture and yet not fully belonging to that of the host nation was first carried into the twentieth century by the scions of the nineteenth-century German Jews who were informed in the nation's schools and the celebration of its holidays that they lived in a "Christian nation." The challenge of having to balance secular and religious life was also more problematic for the observant portion among the Eastern immigrants. In the new country the norms and practices of the religious culture that for many acted as a protective shield in a strange new world would be difficult to maintain. Observing their children reaching out for the new lifestyle, the older religious generation may have felt a sense of failure, since they were commanded to raise God-fearing children. But the American secular culture, the Depression, and then the war released forces that were too powerful to contain.

Jewish Communists were early to perceive the problem of living in two worlds. Despite strenuous efforts to appear indigenous, which included a passion for American folk music and the wearing of jeans and rural dress, the party was unable to shake off its foreignness. That was anathema for Jews who were becoming so secure in their Americanism that they were not remiss in altering some native customs to better fit their still-distinctive ethnic, urban subculture. Some became great interpreters of native folk songs and masters of the guitar and banjo. For others that insecurity led to placing political causes on a low-flame back burner while allowing the "bourgeois values" condemned by the ascetic party code to be replaced by the enjoyment of material comfort. The extreme Left was hardly alone in sensing displacement.

There were some instances in the civil rights struggle when liberals often served as the instrument used by the more militant party members to push the social reform agenda forward. But in their passion for social justice, Jewish Social Democrats and Jewish Communists had different ends in mind. For the Party it was a kind of packaging that worked well with Jewish audiences. In the end Jewish liberalism became the centerpiece of American Jewish political culture, but that could not be fully realized until the grip of the Communist-led Left was finally loosened. During the sixties political circumstances on the national level created an opportunity for Jewish liberalism to come into its own. The decisive defeat of Goldwater by Lyndon Johnson in the election of 1964 could serve as a clear mandate by the American electorate regarding the direction the nation should take. The deluge of social reform legislation between the last year of the Kennedy administration and the first three years of Lyndon Johnson's (1963–1966) had not been witnessed since the "one hundred days" of the New Deal.[10] But the liberal wing of the Democratic Party proved too weak to seat Mississippi's Freedom Democratic Party and at the same time witnessed the fracturing of the budding civil rights movement into separatist Black Power and integrationist factions, the latter mostly favored by Jewish liberals. The result was the purging of Jewish activists from organizations like the Congress of Racial Equality (CORE) and other organizations involved in the struggle for civil rights.

The affect was reflected in the overwhelming victory of Richard Nixon in the election of 1968, which some interpreted as a popular rejection of the steps that had been taken during the Johnson administration. The Civil Rights Act (1964) and the Voting Rights Act (1965), which came to dominate the liberal agenda, were eventually pushed to the margins of the political canvas by the bitter opposition to the war in Vietnam. The mediating middle seemed to have dropped out of politics after the election of 1968. As if previewed by the violence that occurred at the Democratic convention in Chicago and fueled by the endless war in Vietnam, American cities erupted in violence in the final years of the sixties, which many saw as a sign of American decline. Lyndon Johnson became convinced that his "Great Society" had overreached on the civil rights issue, leading to a loss of the South for the Democratic Party.[11] After the defeat of Hubert Humphrey in the election of 1968, the only winning Democratic candidate for the presidency until the election of Bill Clinton in 1992 was Jimmy Carter.[12] The heady period of experimentation and change was over. With the decline of the Democratic Party liberalism lost some of its influence in national politics.

The Nixon victory in 1972 was especially gloomy for liberally oriented Jewish voters. Israel's remarkable victory in 1967 had raised great hope that the vexing problem of achieving stability in the Middle East could now be pushed forward. But the 1968 election one year later indicated a defeat for the liberal position with which many Jewish voters identified. It was evidenced by the slowness with which Nixon moved on the Vietnam peace issue and the reluctance to move directly on the Soviet Jewry issue that was becoming a Jewish communal concern. What few foresaw was that the problems that grew out of the Jewish victory in the June War, which placed the West Bank in Israel's hands, would so divide the Jewish polity that the liberalism at its heart would barely be able to play a bridging role.

During the Nixon seventies, followed by Ronald Reagan's startling popularity in the eighties, and abetted by the unpopular war in Vietnam, liberalism lost the élan achieved with the election of John Kennedy in 1960 and was compelled to assume a more defensive posture.[13] There were the old staunchly anti-Soviet paleoliberals like Lyndon Johnson, Jack Kennedy, Hubert Humphrey, and "Scoop" Jackson, who in different degrees feared the prospect of defeat in Vietnam. These were matched by the Nixon administration that was no less anxious to preserve America's status as a world power but convinced the prospect of a nuclear encounter was the greater danger. The policy of détente that sought to scale down armaments and stimulate trade was based on the assumption that in a fair competition the American free-enterprise system could beat anything the Soviet system had to offer. It was a theme that Richard Nixon, then vice president, sounded in the well-publicized "kitchen debate" with Nikita Khrushchev at the American National Exhibition in Moscow in July 1959. In a strange way the pre-Watergate Nixon carried the liberal agenda forward, nowhere more so than in foreign affairs. He pushed for arms-limitation talks, he established the first environmental protection agency on the federal level, and, most important, he made it possible to bring the cold war to an end by his opening to China. It was that move on the diplomatic chessboard more than anything else that took the expansionist wind out of the Soviet sails. In addition, he favored affirmative action, going as far as favoring quotas, which many Jewish voters still considered a mixed blessing.

From a political perspective the post-Watergate years were hardly a boon for liberals. During the Ford and Carter administrations that followed, the liberal position, so dominant during the Kennedy and Johnson years, seemed to have lost momentum. Liberal lawmakers that normally made their home in the left wing of the Democratic Party welcomed the greater political coherence that developed as a result of the "solid South" leaving the party. But coherence was no match for the stronger Republican Party that emerged from the rearrangement. A weakened Democratic Party would inevitably resonate in liberal circles. Moreover, the civil rights movement, which might have served as the mainstay of liberalism, especially its Jewish element, had become fragmented after the assassination of Martin Luther King Jr. in April 1968 and also encountered serious rearguard political opposition in fulfilling its goals. After the election of 1968, halting the war in Vietnam had taken on such urgency that it overshadowed other issues on the liberal agenda, including civil rights. It never recaptured its full momentum as the war was finally brought to an end in 1975. The year of liberalism's low point can be precisely pinpointed to the election of 1972, in which George McGovern was massively defeated.[14] Thereafter the political spectrum shifted to the Right. With the election of Ronald Reagan in 1980, a decade of lambasting liberalism reached its apogee. The very name could not be used in polite company. Instead the "L" word took hold. The election of Ronald Reagan in 1980 marks the juncture when the Republican Party began its sharp swing to the Right, radically altering the political character of American party politics.

Saving Soviet Jewry

From a Jewish political perspective the security of Israel seemed assured by its decisive victory in June 1967. The victory also made room for a new issue concerning the emigration of Soviet Jewry to move toward the center of the Jewish political stage. The idea of saving Soviet Jewry, faced with the threat of communal and cultural liquidation, became the ideological motivation of a worldwide Soviet Jewry movement. Its mission was strengthened among Jews by marketing the "rescue" of Soviet Jewry as a replay of the Holocaust that must "never again" be allowed to happen. American Jewry would be able to redeem itself for the failing witness role it imagined it played during those years.

But events rarely follow the scenario set out for them. The strategic considerations concerned Israel's increasing population deficit in comparison with the burgeoning birth rate of the Palestinians. Israel leaders viewed the estimated three million Jews in the Soviet Union as one of the keys to solve their pending demographic crises. Both sets of reasons were put forth to justify the expenditures and danger faced in awakening Soviet Jews to their identity as Jews. Predictably, the conflict between these strategic and ideological motivations opened a division between the movement in Israel and America concerning the liberal principle of freedom of movement, which arose after thousands of Soviet Jews, furnished with Israeli visas, were able to leave only to "drop out" in Vienna or Rome.[15] Liberal-minded Jews would not abide compelling the Soviet refugees to settle in a place other than where they wanted to go. The "drop outs" were after all following in the very footsteps of the masses of Russian Jews who also chose America for their Zion at the turn of the twentieth century. Moreover, freedom to move from place to place was a right assured in the Universal Declaration of Human Rights, which served as a major founding charter of the liberal persuasion.

The resultant tension between the American Soviet Jewry movement and the Jewish Agency in Israel (JAFI) serves as an early sign that the core principles of American Jewish political culture, especially the liberalism at its heart, could come into conflict with its Zionism. On the one hand, liberal-minded American Jews favored the release of Soviet Jewry as a human right. It was in fact a similar regard for human rights that was responsible for the high regard they had for Israel. It possessed the characteristics that liberals cherished, democratic governance characterized everywhere by a working parliament selected through honest elections and an independent judiciary. There were weaknesses, to be sure, especially as concerns the Arab population, but these were correctable in time. On the other hand, Israel's insistence that the Soviet emigrants must settle in Israel, even against their will, flaunted the right of freedom of movement, which could not be denied even if Israel's security was involved.

Such conflicts rooted in the fulfillment of liberal principles could act as a divide between the two communities. Clearly, in terms of ability to sustain itself, liberalism outpaces Zionism and the Holocaust as exercising the strongest, most continuous influence on American Jewry.[16] That sustaining influence emerged again during the contretemps regarding the construction of over a thousand new building units in a disputed neighborhood of Jerusalem in March 2010, when Washington, intent on getting proxy peace talks off the ground, insisted on a halt to construction in the disputed neighborhood. It was interpreted by the Likud leadership as a departure from the previous moderate policy and was probably the beginning of the suspicion of the Obama administration. It was an unaccustomed public spanking for Israel, especially when compared with the unquestioning support that came from the prior Republican administration. Yet from an American Jewish liberal perspective, the Obama administration received the highest marks in fulfilling most other phases of the liberal agenda, from the extension of medical insurance to civil rights and gender issues, from the regulation of Wall Street to advocacy of "green" global warming and conservation policies. The pundits were faced with a dilemma. What would win over the Jewish voter, a strong protective policy for Israel or a more middle-of-the-road approach in the context of a strong domestic liberal program? The answer was not long in coming. By April the polls clearly indicated that not only had Jewish voters not lessened their strong support for the Obama administration, but they also maintained a high level of support when virtually the entire political spectrum had undergone a lessening of enthusiasm for his administration. Liberalism continued to reign supreme among Jews notwithstanding what were believed to be Israel's unmet needs.

The Travail of Race-Based Liberalism

Jewish liberalism not only clashed with "blood and soil" Zionism, but tensions also developed between older New Deal liberals, cooked in the Depression of the thirties, and new postwar liberals steeped in the problem of race in America. What won high rates of approval from Jewish voters in one decade could become problematic in the next. That was surely the case with such issues as affirmative action, which that required abandonment of the cherished principle of appointment by merit determined by examination. Appointment on the bases of race or previous condition of victimization seemed at odds with what many Jews believed was the communal interests of American Jewry. That conflict became more troublesome as the integration question and affirmative action clashed with liberal equal-access principles that enabled Jews to win positions in the municipal civil service in previous decades. The liberalism of the New Deal seemed to be at odds with the race-based liberalism of the sixties and seventies.

The travail of Jewish liberalism's regarding what was first called "integration" and then became affirmative action began years before the successful passage of civil rights laws during the Lyndon Johnson administration. In the immediate postwar years many Jewish families abandoned their ethnic urban enclaves and joined the march to suburbia. Jewish builders like William Levitt and his sons, who had mastered the technology of mass production of houses within the price range of returning veterans, were instrumental in making the suburbanization movement happen. But for various reasons many Jews who remained in their familiar neighborhoods were soon subjected to another population movement of African Americans, whose growth in numbers, caused by internal migration from the South combined with a high birth rate, made the finding of housing a crucial necessity. Formerly, Jewish city neighborhoods became integrated, but not without sometimes serious racial tensions. The movement of populations of different races and cultures posed a serious challenge for Jewish liberalism, especially when it involved the schools, since good public education had become a favorite mobility instrument for Jews. It was assumed the scarce resources available to the school system would have to be expended in bringing these new students up to par.

The control of the schools in such neighborhoods triggered a division between the older New Deal social democrat liberals and the newer civil rights types who surfaced during the Ocean Hill–Brownsville conflict. The New Deal liberals usually followed the lead of Al Shanker, then the president of the overwhelmingly Jewish United Federation of Teachers, whose social democratic political coloration was closely associated with the Jewish Labor Committee. That position rejected public policy for the schools based on racial quotas, affirmative action, and bilingualism, all hallmark liberal issues of advocates of the new race-based liberalism.[17] Believers that the future of liberalism hinged on allowing the race question to become the heart of the liberal persuasion would be disappointed in the difficulties and setbacks they encountered. Fueling the tensions was a conflict between the new principles related to race, which spoke of empowerment, and community control, which tended now to overshadow the older principles of equal access and integration.

Distilled from the election results in 1969 and 1974, there is some evidence in the Jewish neighborhood voting patterns in New York City that suggests the impact of the teacher strikes had little affect on Jewish voting patterns. John Lindsay won the office of mayor in 1965 running on a fusion Republican-Liberal ticket. After Ocean Hill–Brownsville and despite growing racial tension, he beat Mario Procaccino, the Republican "law and order" candidate, with 45 percent of the Jewish vote. In 1974 Abe Beame, the liberal Democratic candidate for the office of mayor, only narrowly beat Herman Badillo, a Hispanic candidate, in the run-off primary.[18] Ocean Hill–Brownsville may have marked a turning point in Jewish liberalism, but the impact, if any, was a long-range one.

Unforeseen was that by the end of the century 30 to 35 percent of Jewish voters would identify themselves as independent but continue to vote selectively along liberal lines usually found on the Democratic ticket. New issues such as the right of "choice" regarding abortion, framed as an issue of woman's rights, witnessed Jewish women making a forceful political debut as leaders of the movement. While the problem of race simmered on a back burner, a series of new issues related to gender, including employment discrimination and sexual harassment, captured the attention of liberals. These waves of liberal reform, which focused seriatim on such issues as age discrimination, the green revolution, and global warming, typically included a disproportionate number of Jewish activists in their leadership and rank and file. It seemed almost as if Jews had become the nation's whistle-blowers.

The new confidence among Jewish liberal activists in assuming a leading role in establishing the reform agenda can be traced at least in part to a younger native born and educated Jewish generation secure in their sense of being fully American. It was not precisely a new phenomenon. There had been among the immigrants a cohort of fast accommodators who demonstrated a strong desire to be American through clothing styles, love of sports, and popular music. In the patois of the street language they were called "alrightniks" by their approving but slower-paced assimilating peers. That desire to become part of urban America was carried into politics. By the sixties and seventies new Jewish voters, many war veterans, no longer lived in the shadow of their immigrant forebearers. Important too was the new feeling of belonging related to the diminution of the open anti-Semitism even during the McCarthy years. At the same time, with the weakening of the Communist Party, the threat to the internal integrity by infiltration of their organizations and agencies had virtually disappeared.

In the conflict between the old and the new liberalism that ensued, the gaining of communal legitimacy was an important asset. Viewed from the outside, distinguishing Jewish liberals from extreme left wingers who seemed intent on realizing the same goals for what was loosely called "social justice" was problematic. But staunch support of Israel, which was prohibited for Jewish Communists sometimes, served as an indication of authenticity and therefore belongingness. Moscow's anti-Israel policy combined with an ill-concealed anti-Semitic rhetoric proved divisive for the party, many of whose Jewish members could not go along with evidence of the Kremlin's animus against a small, vulnerable Jewish state.

From a Jewish perspective the gulf between radical liberals and moderate social democratic types could be wider than the difference between Democrats and Republicans. We have noted that in the ensuing conflict both sides misappropriated or sought reinforcement in religious text, a process one researcher called "religification."[19] That enabled Jewish radicals (not radical Jews) to market themselves as defenders of the Jewish communal interest when in fact ideologically they had distanced themselves from it in the name of universalism. But more important in reshaping Jewish liberalism was the change in the class base of the Jewish masses that began in earnest after World War II. Jewish voters retained their affinity for the Left, but the rise in formal education and rapid professionalization, coupled with the preeminence of race over the class factors in the liberal agenda, affected Jewish political sensibilities. Residing primarily in the nation's largest cities, Jewish voters bore witness to the urban chaos of the sixties. After the storm had settled in the seventies, an opportunity opened for social planning for a deeper settlement of the race problem and a greater focus on the myriad of new movements of empowerment of women in the eighties and of gays thereafter. The disquietude that accompanied urban violence often impinged directly on Jewish neighborhoods, and another felt reality was the declining quality of public education that resulted from housing integration. It was this last factor that more than anything else encouraged Jewish wholesale participation in the "white flight" to the suburbs. Suburbanizing Jews carried their liberalism with them, but like transplantation in a different soil, a liberalism grew that abandoned the notion that people everywhere were after all people. Yet the move was based on a somewhat painful acknowledgment that a change in the composition of the neighborhood affected the quality of life. The sustained Jewish drive for a secure middle-class status would also have a vote in determining the shape of Jewish political culture.

From New Deal to Race-Based Liberalism

Ever in search of new groups that required empowerment, the nation's unresolved race question became the primary civil rights issue by the early sixties. Its push to occupy the center of the liberal agenda was not uncontested. The volatile race issue would become but one of several civil rights issues that would arouse liberal fervor. Included also were women's rights, gay rights, indigenous native people's rights, and usually issues relating to the most recent immigrant arrivals from Central America and the Caribbean.[20] Since some of the last-mentioned groups were illegal, immigration policy, which had always been a major issue in Jewish politics, now joined the civil rights agenda. Supplementing specific groups were a cluster of "green" issues concerning the preservation of the natural environment and global warming, in addition to issues concerned with the decline of the variety of species, which stretched from saving the whales to preserving the rain forest of Brazil. On the economic front liberals continued to be involved with the standard cluster of issues related to the role of government in the economy that is at the very center of the nation's political dialogue. On the ballot such issues are translated into candidates and resolutions calling for restructuring for a more equitable tax to the future of the entitlement programs such as Medicare and Social Security. The political dialogue in the twenty-first century is increasingly involved with budget, who gets what. For liberals, that may turn out to be the most difficult politics of all.

For American Jewry the moderation of the race question in American politics may lead to an entirely new phase in the development of liberalism based on a restructuring of the black-Jewish alliance, which played a significant role during the civil rights era of the fifties and sixties. It would help Jewish voters to devote their energy and resources to what is becoming the primary issue on the national political agenda, the role government should play in society. That would be in keeping with the growing awareness that the race question is part of a larger issue of class in America.

The national polity has gone almost as far as it can in creating a level playing field by legislation. The gulf between the races still exists and in some respects has grown deeper. It awaits the solution of the poverty problem, which is not confined to race. There are programs on the liberal agenda that address the requirement of increased education and training for workers and the growing American underclass. But that would have little affect if the entire economy is near collapse. A strong government role in stimulating, regulating, and assuming responsibility for fiscal operations, including banking and Wall Street, is familiar ground for an older generation of Jewish liberals. It is the historic juncture where the immigrant Jewish voter fully entered American politics. One can be fairly certain that the recent economic crisis would reenergize the basic sense that government has a role to play in the economy, a rationale that grew weaker in the years of buccaneering free-enterprise capitalism that preceded the near meltdown. President Obama's program of strengthening community colleges and other training institutions to elevate the skill level of the workforce has a built-in affinity for Jewish voters who place enormous confidence in education in normal circumstances. The idea of changing the framing of the race question from race to class has an attraction for Jewish voters who have been struggling with the race issue for decades. From the liberal Jewish perspective such an approach could prove beneficial to all Americans at the bottom of the economic ladder that includes a disproportionate number African Americans. Whatever the case, since liberalism is forever seeking out problems in need of attention, we can be fairly certain that in years to come economic issues to stimulate the economy and steps to create a level playing field such as training and retraining the workforce will dominate the liberal agenda. For the Jewish voter who lived through the Great Depression of the thirties it is familiar ground.

Liberalism has become such a catchall classification that to observe that it is the cornerstone of American Jewish political culture carries little analytic weight. The sheer broadness of the liberal agenda leads to infinite class and regional variations, so that to speak of the liberal agenda could in many instances be translated into those voters who are deeply involved in the political process but retain a personalized set of regional or religious or other influences that shape behavior. It is become possible to be a conservative Orthodox Jewish voter favoring "faith-based" government-sponsored programs, yet take a liberal position of the issue of a graduated income tax. It is that reality that is behind the humor of the Jewish college student who announces to her parents that she has become liberal, only to receive the response, "yes, yes . . . of course my child, but what kind are you, Orthodox, Conservative, or Reform?" Today we would have to add that if the family was affiliated with the Reform or Reconstructionist branch of American Judaism the probability that they would be liberal on the entire liberal agenda would be very high. These branches are more likely to draw modern secular Jews who are liberal minded.

Concealed by the broad liberal classification are deep divisions within the Jewish polity that sometimes challenge the usefulness of the term "Jewish liberal." Special historic circumstances, such as a murderous Arab hatred of the "Zionist enemy," were hardly the only reason for departure from normal liberal behavior codes. We have noted that in the thirties the idea of a merit system for civil service appointment that meant the curtailment of the corrupt city machine was the essence of Jewish liberalism. Clearly the merit system served Jewish interest, but it also created an even playing field for municipal employment. We witness

Jews stubbornly holding on to this liberal principle of fairness and equal access. The "pink slips" issued by Rhody McCoy to Jewish teachers, which triggered the Ocean Hill–Brownsville conflict, further split the liberal consensus among Jews between those willing to broaden the liberal program to include a race-based principle embodied in community control and those who insisted on the continued validity of civil service reform based on merit-based appointments.

With all its variations in contemporary Jewish liberalism, there was a special communal interest to come to grips with the nation's abiding racial malaise. The bedrock of concern for the underdog and a support of communal altruism have persisted. An aspect of the struggle to abolish slavery was waged in biblical terms, and Jews as "People of the Book" were requested to produce scriptural justification for abolitionists and anti-abolitionists alike.[21] The race issue resurfaced on the American political stage almost at the same time that American Jewry reached a new high level of political influence and activity during the fifties. The interest in the race issue was not new when it again came to the fore in the post–World War II years, but the willingness of Jews to become fully involved beyond the philanthropic effort was. At the very center of liberal sensibilities during the sixties was the issue of civil rights, which from a historical perspective marked the first major attempt to deal with the unresolved racial question since the Reconstruction period. Jews now became deeply involved in the popular protest techniques designed to raise the race question higher on the nation's political agenda. Liberal Jewish advocates did so despite awareness of the internal communal tensions it often generated. Jewish involvement in the civil rights struggle extended from the founding of the NAACP by Joe Spingarm and Henry Moskowitz in 1915 to include Julius Rosenwald's funding of the National Urban League, Stanley Levison and the Southern Christian Leadership Conference, the role of Marvin Rich and Alan Gartner in funding the Congress of Racial Equality (CORE), and leadership roles played in sustaining black colleges by Jacob Billikopf, who served as chairman of Howard University's board of trustees. It was so extensive that a question arose regarding the term "Christian" in the name of the Christian Leadership Conference. Similar concerns regarding Jewish overrepresentation later developed among upcoming black activists in NAACP and CORE. It is far too early to claim that the election of Barack Obama in 2008 can in some small measure be attributed to a Chicago group of Jewish liberals led by students of communal organization like Saul Orlinsky, and to others like Samuel Levinson of "parchment peace" fame and founder of Chicago's Abraham Lincoln Center (1917). That Chicago, like Philadelphia, maintained its own vigorous center of Jewish liberalism to rival that of New York will surely be part of the story of liberal Jewish leadership and the civil rights struggle, when it comes to the fore again.

There is little agreement among researches on the motives behind the deep Jewish involvement with civil rights, which differed markedly from the pattern of other ethnic voting blocs. The sense of mutual victimization and the linkage of their national identity to the fate of African Americans, echoed in the popular Negro spiritual "let my people go," is often cited as evidence of the sympathy Jews felt for the oppressed American Negro.[22] Jews had experienced slavery in biblical times and persecution in the modern era. But as popular as the spiritual may have been, the affinity with the black crucible based on a mutual historical experience does not make for good history. Orthodox Jews, steeped in Bible learning, were rarely involved in the civil rights movement. Many of the young Jewish freedom riders, including the martyred Michael Schwermer and Andrew Goodman, stemmed from secular Jewish left-wing families. Similarly, the frequently cited idea that Jewish support of the struggle for civil rights for Negroes found its roots in the prophetic aspect of Judaism seems too neat and self-serving. Jewish Communists who took an early lead in the struggle probably were more familiar with Marx and Lenin than with the biblical prophets. Aware that those who claim to be closest to the religious tradition are least likely to be committed to liberalism, researchers like Hasia Diner attribute Jewish support of the African American struggle for civil rights to a strategy contrived to open the possibility of Jewish group interest to be defended under the guise of universal liberalism. Jews were supposedly primarily aware that their security would be enhanced without openly having to expose their own self-interest.[23] They would also support affirmative action for "certified minorities" to raise them to equal status and to create a level playing field, in the parlance of the time, even if it worked against Jewish communal interests, as in Ocean Hill–Brownsville. That rationale seems too convoluted to have been a communal strategy. It is difficult to imagine such a conspiratorial strategy, much less that Jewish communal organization could agree to implement it. More likely is the high correlation between the university liberal arts curriculum, which attracts Jewish students in disproportionate numbers, and liberal proclivities.[24]

There is a less-contrived explanation that offers a clue to the Jewish overrepresentation in the civil rights movement. It stems from a strategy conceived by the leadership of the American Jewish Committee that became concerned about the high level of ethnic and racial tensions that could interfere with national mobilization for the war effort after the Detroit race riots of 1940. Under the leadership of John Slawson and his assistant Selma Hirsch, the AJC developed the idea of marketing racial tolerance as though selling a product through advertising, much the way Berlin marketed anti-Semitism. In the early postwar years Hollywood pitched in with two remarkable films, *Crossfire* and *Gentlemen's Agreement*, that went far to expose the damage wrought by anti-Semitism, a malady unfamiliar to much of the film-going audience. The marketing strategy viewed the struggle for civil rights as being one for the minds of American men and women. It was an effort to alter the consciousness of the nation.

The costly victory in Europe against a racialist enemy made the immediate postwar years peculiarly conducive to start the long effort to reshape American minds on the race question. Thousands of American soldiers had seen the results of Nazi racialism when they came upon the gruesome concentration camps. The press featured a beloved General Eisenhower viewing the skeletonized bodies of victims strewn around a liberated concentration camp. In a sense, there was an understanding that the sacrifices of the war were somehow related to the problem of race and that the nation had chosen the side of tolerance and openness. When the Korean War broke out just six years later, President Truman announced the desegregation of the nation's armed forces. That was among the earliest government initiatives on civil rights. In the years that followed there would be many more.

The Neoconservatives and the New Left

We have noted that during the seventies the political scene was overshadowed by the unending war in Vietnam, which enlisted the energies of activists and momentarily left the liberal agenda unattended. Even as the old Left was leaving the historical stage the war spawned a new kind of activism that came to be known collectively as the New Left. Frequently the disaffected children of old Left progressive parents, these disproportionately Jewish young people, enraged by the costly war in Vietnam for which they might be conscripted, successfully mobilized the emerging youth culture centered on the college campus for a new kind of politics. Both the neoconservatives and the New Left originated in some measure within the Jewish polity, but only the former group emerged out of the bitter strife within the Jewish Left during the twenties and thirties. The New Left was born out of a generational strife between a "progressive" parent generation that had experienced the Depression followed by a cataclysmic war and the "boomer" postwar generation that lived in comparative prosperity. In contrast, the neoconservatives projected their influence by playing the role of "public intellectuals" outside the university and used a series of political journals like *Commentary Magazine* to promote their ideas. The New Left was more a political style or tactic that, aside from ending the war, was largely bereft of ideology.

Having few systemic ideas and taken with values derived from psychotherapy, the New Left welcomed the social psychology of Antonio Gramsci and the Freudian Marxism of the Frankfurt School, which was sometimes on the reading list of their history courses, as were Paul Goodman and C. Wright Mills. They were concerned with mending the system and extracting the country from the morass of Vietnam rather than a revolution from below as foreseen by Karl Marx. The New Left developed an entirely new promotional strategy based on an attention-getting public relations featuring outrageous behavior and confrontation rather than compelling ideas. Led by the Students for a Democratic Society (SDS) and energized by the unending war in Vietnam, its arena was the college campus, where it accessed the burgeoning youth culture to make its political mark. The provost or anyone of the "establishment" rather than the distant capitalist became the enemy. Politically, New Leftists were at opposite ends of the political spectrum, anchored on the Right by the Neocons, and the Vietnam War serving as a kind of axis. Like the Neocons, there was little attempt to organize a formal vote-getting operation. Neocons may have taken their leave from the Jewish liberal norm at least in the foreign affairs arena, but culturally they remained part of the stodgy parent generation that spoke of "struggle" and aspired to build a better, freer world. Members of the SDS were radicals, but the term "red-diaper" babies sometimes applied to them can be misleading. For young SDSers becoming radical may have been an unspoken strategy for breaking out of a confining parental ethnic straight jacket. They were in fact often in full rebellion against the leftism of their parents. Released from the discipline of dogma and party, they aspired to individual fulfillment. The aspiration of building a society based on social justice remained, but had little to do with their struggle against a government that they felt was intent on stealing their youth. Unlike their parents, they knew no other culture than the American and practiced free-enterprise radicalism where everyone did their own thing.

As in the case of the neoconservatives, the founders of the New Left's core organization, SDS, as well as the yuppies and Berkeley's Free Speech movement, were disproportionately of Jewish origin.[25] Yet one seeks in vain for a telltale Jewish trademark such as a concern for the welfare of Israel, nor did affiliated Jews view the activities of the SDS with great group pride. I have elsewhere identified both groups as "Jews by accusation" because of uncertainty about whether they are legitimately classifiable as part of an ongoing Jewish political culture.[26] For a time the realpolitik dimension of neoconservative thinking, especially in the area of foreign policy, became an acceptable part of conservative thinking, but with the end of the cold war and the collapse of the Soviet Union in 1991, there was no place for its strategies for counteracting the Soviet threat to go.

Whether the New Left should be considered part of Jewish liberal political culture presents a problem. Student political activism was well known in European universities, but until the student strikes for peace in the thirties on the City College campus, where student radicals were sometimes called "cafeteria commies," they seldom occurred on the football-loving American campuses.[27] The leadership of the SDS and the Berkeley Free Speech movement, as well as the yuppies, was in its early stages disproportionately composed of Jewish youth.[28] But the causes espoused were not the exclusive domain of Jewish political culture, certainly not the ending of the war in Vietnam, which became a generational passion. At the same time the cause that might identify the SDS as part of Jewish political culture, the support of Israel, was conspicuous by its absence. Whether Jewish or not, the most interesting facet of the SDS is that by attaching itself to a folk-singing, long-haired, raucous, burgeoning youth culture on the college campus, it had developed a new kind of power in the political arena that momentarily allowed it to exercise an inordinate influence on one facet of foreign policy. It can claim credit for hastening the end of the unpopular war in Vietnam. The use of the university campus as a staging ground for a new political demand or program will surely not be forgotten by those anxious to promote political change. But otherwise the New Left appears to have been a political blip that vanished with the end of the Vietnam War in 1975. In a final accounting historians may well conclude that its impact was more cultural than political. Though housed in the same container of Jewish political culture, neoconservatism and the New Left seem only remotely connected to its liberal essence. They are specific to a certain time and place, like lumps in a liberal soup.

Jewish Liberalism in the Final Stages of the Cold War

During the 1970s concern with the security of Israel and with the release of Soviet Jewry from the Kremlin's grip created a quandary for Jewish liberals. Both issues inevitably drew Jewish political interests to the right-wing side of the cold war rivalry. The realpolitik aspect of the rightist sensibility evinced a greater interest in the security question and sought to exploit Soviet human rights trespasses. Moscow's role in reinforcing Arab hostility against Israel and its rejection of the right of emigration for its Jewish population hardened the anti-Soviet animus among Jews. At the same time the end of the war in Vietnam and the signing of the Helsinki accords in August 1975 opened space in international relations for a move to a more moderate centrist posture that held out better hope for peace. Liberals suspected that the Kremlin's conciliatory spirit was temporary. The formulation of the Brezhnev doctrine, by which the Kremlin reserved for itself the right to suppress uprisings in its sphere by armed intervention, and especially the Warsaw Pact's suppression of the Prague Spring in August 1978, presented ample evidence that Moscow continued to be a threatening expansive force. The repression of the Alexander Dubzek regime by military force became a major factor in the disenchantment of the remaining members of the Jewish Left still inclined to give the Kremlin the benefit of the doubt. Former Jewish Communists and progressives who were reluctant to take an anti-Soviet stance now also refashioned themselves as Social Democrats and joined the broad Jewish liberal stream. It was a conversionary pattern that had begun in the thirties. These converts to the liberal Left were not yet ready to totally abandon the progressive elements in the domestic politics that had been the favorite arena of the old Left. They contributed to the new energy in pushing the liberal agenda in emerging issues of the nineties such as environmentalism, gender equality, gay rights, and universal medical care, with the result that civil rights issues were pushed to the margin of concern. By the end of the twentieth century the liberal camp, which claimed perhaps 80 percent of Jewish political allegiance on major issues, seemed secure.

The Jewish vote for the older George Bush declined precipitously from a high of 38 percent in the election of 1988, a high normal rate for a Republican candidate, to 10 percent in 1992. The cause for the decline was believed to be a politically suicidal confrontation with Israel defenders on the security question. Some pundits, including the younger Bush, who ran for the presidency in 2000, credit the Jewish vote for limiting the tenure of the elder Bush to one term. They gave an estimated 80 percent of their vote to Bill Clinton, the Democratic candidate in the election of 1992. Four years later their support was virtually repeated, allowing Clinton to become the first Democratic president to hold the Oval Office for two full consecutive terms since Franklin D. Roosevelt. A clear liberal political trajectory can best be discerned in the way Jews cast their ballots in presidential campaigns between 1988 and 2008, when Jewish voter support for Democratic presidential candidates varied from a low of 64 percent for

Dukakis in the 1988 election to a high of 81 percent for Al Gore in the election of 2000.[29] Several factors including name recognition and liberal credentials may have been involved in Gore's record high.

But the Jewish vote was not awarded merely because the candidate claimed some affinity for the liberal position. Personality and other circumstances could make almost a 20 percent difference in degree of support. Liberalism itself seemed to experience a decline with the election of George W. Bush in 2000. A series of domestic and foreign events, such as the after effects of the impeachment trial of Clinton, led to a loss of Democratic forward momentum, the party in which the liberal program was ensconced. Historians will sort out the conflict over George W. Bush's victory over Al Gore in the election of 2000 by court decision for years to come. The tabulation of the Jewish vote in certain Florida election districts, which became key to determining the presidency, gave the nation an image of the importance of the Jewish vote in certain pivotal states.[30] Despite an election whose validity a good portion of the electorate doubted, the victorious Bush administration mounted an assault on the political Left that marks one of the great turning points in American political history. The Bush program went from a serious plan to privatize the social security system to a willingness to modify the principle of a graduated income tax based on the rationale that the millions restored to the wealthiest Americans would help shore up business, since the wealthy were the "job producing" class.

An event that could not have been predicted, the September 11, 2001, attacks on New York's Twin Towers and the Pentagon, targets chosen by Al Qaeda to yield maximum impact, changed the political map and overshadowed Bush's challenge to liberal gains won decades earlier. Instead the nation confronted a new conflict that featured polarities similar to those associated with the cold war years. Included was a new version of the Jewish question posed by a deeper Islamic threat to the existence of the Jewish state by a militant Iran that was not an Arab state. Again, a Jewish question was pushed to the very center of international politics. Aside from human losses, the 9/11 surprise attack ushered in a period of political stress soon dubbed the "war on terror," which like all wars absorbed the nation's interest and deflected resources from domestic ameliorative programs.

Convinced of the existence of Iraq's nuclear program that threatened the regional power balance, the nation became involved in a war in Iraq that soon developed into a quagmire that impacted American politics for the next seven years. In the election of 2000 Jewish voters had given even greater support to Al Gore, the Democratic candidate, then to Bill Clinton, his predecessor, an indication of the lack of enthusiasm for the war. Gore later criticized the devious manner in which the invasion of Iraq was staged. Despite the charge that American Jewry supported American involvement in a war against one of its bitterest enemies in the region, American military intervention in the region posed serious problems for the Jewish electorate, including the strengthening of the image of American Jewry as a controlling "lobby" that had pushed the nation into war to further an imagined Jewish interest. For the conspiratorial political Right it was but a short hop to imagine that the neoconservatives had manipulated the invasion. In fact the reverse was the case. In the polarization of national politics that deepened as the longest war in American history became more costly in lives and treasure, most liberal American Jews viewed the war as a great error.

Withal, the disturbing impact of the war in Iraq had little noticeable impact on long-range liberal principles that Jews hold dear. Liberal values concerning personal freedom remained a constant in the Jewish liberal mentalité, as did support of the regulator role of government in the economy. In the name of personal freedom, the Jewish voter is more than twice as likely as his fellow American to support personal choice for abortion. Sexual orientation is consigned to the private realm. After several headline business scandals, beginning with Enron in 2001, wracked the economy and awakened an interest in the excesses of white-collar crime, officials like Robert Morgenthau, the district attorney of Manhattan, led the nation in the need for greater regulation. Jewish voters continue to support programs that aim to advance the public health of the nation. They remain overwhelmingly on the liberal side of resolving the nation's outstanding political issue even when there is conflict with other mainstays of their political culture concerning Israel. In a word, in the new political world of the twenty-first century the long-range political profile of American Jewry has remained constant. Ironically, it may be the only element in the dynamic life of American Jewry that has.

There was one new factor that played an important role in the replenishing of the wellsprings of Jewish liberalism in the final decades of the twentieth century. Generally there is a fairly high statistical correlation between educational level attained by voting cohort and the degree of support given to liberal causes. Not surprisingly, the liberal state of mind is incubated in Jewish homes managed by native-born parents boasting the highest formal educational level in the nation. Jewish children have in common their experience of higher education.[31] It has replaced the immigrant experience and the Jewish labor movement as the principal generator of a liberal mentality. But for the Jewish liberal it is not only that the university is an engine that produces liberals, though conservatives have long claimed that that is so. It relates to the admiration and sometimes uncritical acceptance of outward signs of learning, degrees held, plays seen, crossword puzzles completed. A president whose language usage is poor or whose culture is limited to an interest in sports does not easily win the heart of Jewish voters.[32] They seek some sign of intellectual depth and character in candidates for the highest office.

Even so, identifying Jews as overwhelmingly in the liberal fold does not account for the broad cache of issues on which there is no strong liberal position. One can be liberal on one issue, like favoring *Roe v. Wade*, but also support stationing more troops on the southern border with Mexico to achieve securer borders. There are degrees of liberalism and there are Jews who on the scale of politics are extremely conservative, if not precisely for political reasons. Certain sensitive issues can never gain total agreement within the community. Gay rights and sundry movements for gender equality ran up against Jewish law (Halacha), which is one of the mainstays of the Orthodox subculture of the Jewish voting bloc.[33] We have noted that the Jewish voter whose middle-class status was often earned through the merit system was not notably enthusiastic regarding the series of government policies imposed under the name of affirmative action.

A closer study of the statistics yields a more complex picture. The perhaps 750,000 Soviet Jewish refugees admitted to the United States between 1967 and 1991 who are disaffected from anything they believe to be tainted by "socialism," are notably more conservative than most of their fellow Jews. At the other end of the political spectrum is a highly secularized young Jewish bloc of Jewish boomers, many of whom were involved in the anti-Vietnam War movement and in the civil rights struggle, whose ideological passions and degree of dissidence are reminiscent of the former Jewish Communists who were union organizers.[34] All together, about 60 to 80 percent of student radicals were of Jewish origin in the sixties and an astounding 30 to 50 percent of the founding core leadership group of the SDS were Jewish. The same overwhelming predominance was found in related organizations like the yuppies and Berkeley's Free Speech movement, five of whose seven leaders were "of Jewish origin."[35] Nevertheless they represent a small dissident generational cohort that momentarily fell within the militant left-wing stream not typical of the Jewish Left. Also included under the liberal umbrella one could find Jewish voters, sometimes disparagingly labeled "limousine liberals," who only selectively supported the liberal agenda. There were wide disparities on the national security question as it concerned both the United States and Israel. We have already taken note of the widening gap between American Jewish liberalism and the path Israel is taking in relation to the Palestinians. A lessening of Zionist fervor among younger American Jews is imagined to be the result. If true, that would be the strongest indication of the depth of Jewish liberalism. (A full examination of that supposed decline is discussed in chapter 4.) It is difficult to avoid the conclusion that Jewish liberalism is a political cloth of many colors and for that reason is not easily wielded as a political instrument. It is more a sensibility than an ideology.

For the Jewish liberal the Zionism that has become part of Israel's statecraft poses a dilemma. The indefinite continuation of low-level war with the Palestinians contains the seeds of an agonizing choice for American Jews between ethnic loyalties, which include concern for the security of Israel and their commitment to fundamental liberal principles. In their domestic politics they find that the need for American diplomatic and military support for Israel remains imperative, but after the so-called Arab Spring it is more than ever unacceptable to support corrupt dictatorships or "plutocracies" that assure the flow of precious oil while minimally preserving the peace with Israel. It seems too heavy a price to pay for an uncertain security. It is not difficult to foresee that the popular anti-Israel-*cum*-anti-Semitic sentiments extent among the Arab masses could find a release in these newborn societies if they choose to become Islamic republics on the Iranian model. On domestic issues the Jewish liberal dilemma is equally disturbing. It involves confronting the reality that the maintenance of even minimal social welfare nets and building schools in Afghanistan is in budgetary conflict. There are no longer political support and economic resources to have both guns and butter, especially if it is spread on someone else's bread. A choice may have to be made between furthering liberal nation building and policies that assure a level playing field at home.

One of the primary tasks for American Jewish liberalism in the second quarter of the twenty-first century may well be to develop strategies to manage the nation's retreat from its superpower status to shore up its broken political and economic systems. The political ground is shifting to respond to the new reality. The ameliorative social and economic role of government, at the heart of Jewish liberalism, faces a strong political challenge. Continued federal support of the social welfare legislation begun during the New Deal has become the major issue in domestic politics. We witness a kind of historical replay of the situation of the Great Depression of the thirties, including a deepening of class tensions. We have already noted the basic issue of American politics that defines the difference between liberals and conservatives, and the issue that most clearly defines liberal American Jewish political culture concerns the role government should play in the economy and society generally. In the great debate of 2011, the conservative pressure to control a burgeoning deficit is again directed at limiting entitlement programs, all done in the name of libertarians "getting the government off our backs." That entails the end of Keynesian deficit financing of such entitlement programs as the new "Obama Care" at home and the curtailing of government spending abroad, particularly the billions that are given to Pakistan, Egypt, and, of course, Israel. It is on the domestic political scene that the pending change will be most telling for American Jewry. It may well be that like all Americans, what will preoccupy American Jewish voters in the forthcoming decade is not politics at all but the more immediate task of retaining their hard-won middle-class status.

A change in world power arrangements would bring with it a change in the role Israel plays in American Jewish political culture. In a word, the years to come may witness a widening gulf between Israel and the dominant liberal portion of American Jewry. It would deepen the gap between its universalistic liberalism and its still powerful ethnicity. The declining number of Jews who have lived through the years of the Holocaust would find the need to choose between their country and Israel agonizing, their children and grandchildren less so. Thankfully historians are not called on to be prophets, so that even if these projections should contain an element of truth they are a long way from realization. We save the possible development of, or otherwise obtaining, weapons of mass destruction by Iran and perhaps Saudi Arabia for the following chapter, only noting at this juncture that such a development would bring the discussion of the liberal component of Jewish political culture to an entirely new level that concerns the survival of civilization itself.

The general humanitarian principles of Jewish liberalism remain constant, but the way they are applied is in constant flux. The activist impulse witnessed during the civil rights struggle is a comparatively recent phenomenon. At its heart is a concern for human welfare, whatever form that may take at the moment. It remains constant, as does its conviction that the trajectory of societal development is ever upward. The passion for human betterment is Jewish liberalism's driving force. Liberals feel themselves on the side of history. That optimism may be challenged in the years to come when a much-weakened economy undermines the middle-class status of many American families. When all is said and done contemporary liberalism is primarily a middle-class phenomenon. The coming years may test the link between American Jewish liberalism and Israel, Zionism's perpetually endangered offspring.

Changing Terms and Voice of Jewish Liberalism

Hearing voices is considered an early sign of schizophrenia, but those who hear a Jewish liberal voice in national politics are not mentally ill. There is such a voice in American politics, and the opinions it transmits are varied yet constant in their concern for human welfare. The problem is that there is no way of determining whose voice it actually is, since there is no legal communal mandate for any person or agency to speak for American Jewry. With the exception of the nonsectarian neoconservatives, the message delivered, whether it concerns saving the whales or advocating the right of abortion, is recognizably Jewish, especially on matters concerning Israel. But determining who speaks for American Jewry remains as uncertain as ever. Since much depends on access to the media, those who claim to speak for American Jewry do not necessarily reflect the grassroots political consensus. We are left with the nettlesome condition that, with the exception of a nearly unanimous consensus on church-state separation, we hear Jewish voices but not a sole voice that speaks for the Jewish community.

Jews too hear voices. They are the voices of anti-Semitism, and again it is difficult to determine the nature of the threat such voices may pose. A neighbor who finds that Jews are too "pushy" is not listed in the ADL's annual listing of anti-Semitic incidents. Such incidents suggest latency and normal intergroup tensions. Yet they might serve as kindling for a greater conflagration and it is therefore also dangerous to ignore them. It is admittedly problematic to raise the alarm about anti-Semitism when the symptoms of the disease are concealed. American Jews have the nation's near-highest per capita income and rate of professionalization and a high rate of intermarriage, hardly symptoms of exclusion. It is placed on the liberal agenda together with other unresolved group tensions, a transitory phenomenon that can be alleviated with proper education, but in a post-Holocaust world that casualness may belie its seriousness. Anti-Semitism, after all, is a phenomenon that has existed for so many millennia that, like war, it has earned a major place in Western history as a primordial force, nor is it limited to the West.

Something that resembles anti-Semitism has recently emerged in the reiteration of an old charge that Jews exercise too much influence in determining foreign policy. That accusation has been triggered by the reality of a high degree of political engagement that is an intrinsic part of Jewish liberalism. The complaint charges that Jews are too controlling, especially in the area of foreign policy for the Middle East.[36] Its irrationality notwithstanding, the notion that a small ethnic minority not equaling more than 2.1 percent of the nation's population controls America's foreign policy in the Middle East has become a sine qua non of the anti-Semitic imagination. Paradoxically, a vision that sees a Jewish tail wagging the American dog, if true, would reveal more about the weakness and vulnerability of American decision making on the highest level than it does about the exercise of Jewish political power. It is worrisome because the imagination of inordinate Jewish power to be used against the national interest is the most recognizable symptom of that ancient malady.

What lends credibility to fantasies regarding inordinate Jewish power is the reality of the high degree of Jewish engagement in national and local politics. It is not merely things said in the public square by people who happen to be Jewish. There is an identifiable Jewish voice in the American polity made more audible because the voices of other ethnic blocs are rarely heard today. Jewish communal leaders, public intellectuals, pundits, and lobbyists of every variety, joined by a disproportionate number of journalists and sundry experts, project appeals for action, correction of errors in policy, and sometimes just advice on how to proceed to elected representatives. Costly page-long ads are purchased in the nation's leading newspapers to make certain that the voice purporting to speak for American Jewry, or at least some portion of it, is heard. Yet despite Jewish ownership of some of the nation's leading newspapers and electronic media, a Jewish voice was not easily heard during the years of the Holocaust.[37]

While some form of liberalism remains regnant among Jewish voters, the fact that it is a broad sensibility rather than a precise ideology makes it difficult for liberalism to sustain itself as a political movement. The problem of sustaining a Jewish liberal voice was deepened by the postwar decline of membership in Jewish secular mass organizations like the American Jewish Congress and the mass membership Zionist organizations. The umbrella organizations of the Jewish labor movement such as the Jewish Labor Committee (JLC) and the United Hebrew Trades (UHT), which supported liberal programs, are today only organizational shards.[38] Secularization with its inherent detribalization enhances the universalistic liberal mind-set, while at the same time it diminishes the agencies and networks that might promote and implement a liberal program.

There may also have been a decline in a certain type of individual Jewish political personality, recognizable in the immigrant generation, that was an important factor through which the liberal agenda was heard.[39] The decline of liberal organizations was also affected by the fact that after its establishment Israel faced a perennial security problem, hardly an ideal political environment to realize liberal principles. We have noted that not only did Israel's polity focus more on security, which required a high budget for defense, but its Labor Party, which served as the traditional carrier of a liberal program in social democratic form, also declined after the second Intifada. Today it tolls barely 16 percent of the popular vote that determines the apportionment of seats in the Knesset.

While the case is yet unproven, Jewish liberalism in America seems better able to sustain itself in the immediate decades after the establishment of the state. Most Jewish voters were convinced that Jewish survival and development hinged above all on the survival of Israel rather than a particular ideological persuasion. In a peculiar way Israel's special security needs narrowed the breadth of Jewish politics. Maintaining an expensive military required support from the American government, which in turn required American Jewry to learn a sectarian politics based on special interest. Political activism was hardly new for American Jewish leaders, but advocacy for Israel was more overt and tended to narrow its normally broad liberal agenda, especially among intensely committed Zionists and devout Jews. On the grassroots electoral level, what may have been an early sign of a general weakening of the Jewish liberal voice occurred in New York State's gubernatorial election of 1988, when for the first time the Conservative Party drew more votes than the Liberal Party, which then lost its legal status as a party.

It is a paradox that while Jews readily identify themselves as liberal, they sometimes deviate from the liberal position in the give-and-take of local politics. Some have experienced serious second thoughts on such policies as affirmative action and housing integration and have spoken out against liberal policies during campaigns. Local opposition to affirmative action programs and school integration were only part of the story. Sometimes that disaffection took the form of concern about neighborhood violence. Demands for additional neighborhood security ranked especially high in Chassidic enclaves like the Crown Heights section of Brooklyn that borders on Ocean Hill–Brownsville. That communal race-based tensions persisted was reflected in the Jewish voting split on the election of David Dinkins, a liberal African American candidate in the New York City mayoral election of 1989.[40] The overwhelming Jewish support of the nation's first black presidential candidate in 2008 may indicate that the black-Jewish rift in the liberal camp has finally been overcome and that Jewish voters are now fully on board for a race- and class-based liberalism. But in the parlance of politics, the black-Jewish alliance, which is imagined to have existed during the years of the civil rights struggle and before, has not in recent years been active in the political arena.

Given pending demographic and cultural changes within the Jewish community, it would be premature to conclude that the future of the American Jewish relation to liberalism is predictable. The fast-growing ultra Orthodox subcommunity rejects an almost sacred liberal principle of church-state separation and abortion rights. The vote of these closed and commanded communities is also less independent and therefore more deliverable.[41] A second smaller group of about five hundred thousand affiliated Soviet Jewish immigrant voters and their descendants also have a more conservative voting pattern, as do the children of mixed marriages. Both subgroups do not adhere to Jewish political norms and numerically compose only a minor dissidence. But when considered together with Jewish voters who list themselves as independent and others who have become disaffected from liberal altruistic behavior, the still-overriding liberal Jewish majority shows considerable issue-to-issue variation within its preference for the Democratic Party. In recent elections it has gone as high as 90 percent for Lyndon Johnson in 1968 to as low as 45 percent for Jimmy Carter in 1980, a spread of 45 percent. That great variance leads some researchers to view the Jewish vote as a "swing" vote. It sometimes can be that locally, but only on rare occasions in a national election. Nevertheless, given these and other circumstances, some pundits imagine that the weakening of the Jewish voting bloc's abiding loyalty to the liberal wing of the Democrat Party is a possibility.[42] The fact that New York City, once the center of liberalism, has changed to being a center of Jewish conservatism in which Orthodox and Soviet immigrants now help determine its political coloration is submitted as evidence for the possibility of a change in Jewish political allegiance. Yet Jewish liberalism today persists in newly developed population centers on the West Coast and the Southwest.[43] In the early Obama years, despite disappointment in the president's leadership style, there was little sign of a turn to the Right. For many liberal Jewish voters, Barack Obama was not liberal enough and too conciliatory.

Given the analogous events between the economic crisis that began in 2008 and the crisis faced by Franklin Roosevelt in 1933, the recent regulatory reforms and "bailouts" undoubtedly remind older Jewish voters of Roosevelt's "one hundred days" that initiated the New Deal program. It was that heady period when government was doing something that served as a mainstay of the Jewish liberal imagination. But reminiscences do not politics make. More likely is the continued fragmentation of the Jewish vote as the individuations inherent in modernity and the weakening of communal ties have their impact. The effect of loss of cohesiveness on Jewish political influence is predictable since certain conditions must be present in order for the Jewish vote to become a political reality. We have noted previously that to the extent that it does coalesce, the Jewish vote can be crucial in a presidential election because of its location in the five pivotal states that determine 78 percent of the distribution of electoral votes. However, for that weight to develop there must also be unity on a specific binding issue and there must be sufficient geographic concentration. When 25 to 30 percent of Jewish voters were concentrated in the New York metropolitan area, a Jewish impact was predictable. That is less true today.

Balancing this gloomy prognosis for Jewish liberalism, there are factors that augur well for its continued vitality. There seems to be an almost organic connection between general Jewish values and liberalism that are not easily excised. Formal education, the most important of these, is reflected in the high percentage of Jewish university graduates who absorb liberalism as part of their education. In a sense the right-wing rhetoric that sees a liberal college education as the "engine of liberalism" has some merit, especially among Jews who tend to equate intelligence and academic literacy with a liberal political posture. There is, however, little assurance that the university's liberal arts curriculum and the faculty that goes with it will forever remain a citadel of liberalism.

The largest and most political weighty portion of an increasingly fragmented Jewry will in all likelihood continue along the liberal path that has served as the lodestone of Jewish political behavior since the arrival of the Jews of eastern Europe. Yet determining today where the Jewish voter stands on a specific issue can be problematic since the old benchmarks no longer exist and a broad definition of liberalism allows many different views to march under its banner. Formerly, affiliation with a Reform congregation or secular Jewish organization like the American Jewish Congress (AJCong) could serve as a fairly reliable indicator of voting preference. In the decades before World War II members of the AJCong were more liberal or closer to the social democratic immigrant political culture than were members of the American Jewish Committee (AJComm). Thirty-seven percent of contemporary Jewish voters identify themselves as independent and therefore ostensibly less likely to take political cues from rabbis or community leaders. The mobilization threshold has become higher than it was during the campaign to win the release of Soviet Jewry. The liberally inclined Jewish vote is not so much collectively delivered as it is composed of each autonomous voter choosing similar preferences in the voting booth. There are of course Jewish voters who cast their ballots for the conservative, usually Republican, candidate, but they remain a minority of usually less than one-fourth of the Jewish vote. Newspapers read and journals subscribed to added to educational level attained have become better indicators of Jewish voter preferences than membership in a congregation, organization, or income level.

The broad liberal cast of Jewish political culture seems assured for some years to come, but in the free atmosphere of America change is inevitable. It is also true that regional, generational, and cultural variations develop gradually over time within a voting bloc. Changed voting behavior such as the move from the Republican to the Democratic Party that occurred in the twenties required almost a decade to materialize. In a formerly notably anti-Semitic state like Minnesota, nominally Jewish candidates now vie for office using their Jewishness as a political asset.[44] Similarly, on a once central issue like the security of Israel, the concern of the contemporary generation of Jewish voters does not reach the levels of anxiety of the first and second postimmigrant generations. New passions and anxieties carried by a younger generation replace the old. The nation's increasing rate of formal education contains a hidden dividend for Jewish office seekers and voters. It promotes not only a high rate of professionalism among Jews but at the same time generates a more tolerant electorate relatively free of the anti-Semitism of an older, less open-minded generation. It is no accident that since the 1920s the university has replaced small business as the single most important agency giving American Jews access to the promise of America. The nation is full of small businesses developed by first- and second-generation Jewish immigrants that were given up when, aspiring to "higher" things promised by the arts or the professions, the children rejected going into the family business. As noted earlier, the key to Jewish political behavior today may be determined more by the proportion of higher-education degrees than by the attraction of small business of former generations. From its immigrant base in democratic socialism to the liberalism that developed between 1920 and 1970, the aforementioned change in Jewish political culture can be partly attributed to its altered class configuration that saw Jews rise from the immigrant working class to the lower middle and middle class.[45] Unlike the Democratic Socialist proclivities of the immigrant generation, the political liberalism of the second and third generation was anchored in a developing, formally educated middle class, or at least one aspiring to be so.

Barack Obama and the Liberal Dilemma

Barack Obama's inauguration in January 2009 casts a new light on Jewish liberalism. Such a resounding election victory for an African American candidate might simply have been considered a fitting culmination of the civil rights movement, in which Jews were heavily invested. Yet the candidate's credentials as a liberal Democrat did not at first mobilize strong Jewish political and financial support. There was apprehension that the Jewish vote would not come through, especially among older Jewish voters who never fully adjusted to a race-based liberalism and feared that Obama, whose father was Muslim, would pressure Israel to make concessions on the issue of Jerusalem, the settlements, and the refugees. But that apprehension, fueled by a Republican campaign strategy that predicted that Obama would abandon Israel, proved to be misplaced. The overwhelming Jewish vote for the liberal Democratic candidate gives the political analyst a fairly clear picture of American Jewry's political culture as it emerges in the first half of the twenty-first century.

Not since the years of Franklin Roosevelt have liberal-minded Jews felt such a close affinity with a Democratic presidential candidate. The administration's approach to the economic crisis and the protection of existing entitlement programs and their extension seemed to be acting out a political scenario conceived by a liberal Jewish *Sanhedrin*, had there been one.[46] The massive government intervention in the unforeseen economic crisis seemed reminiscent of Roosevelt's experimental approach to the Depression. Advisors like David Axelrod, Obama's chief strategist and media advisor, and Rahm Emanuel, former White House chief of staff, undoubtedly reminded older Jewish voters of the bevy of Jewish advisors in Roosevelt's inner circle who drew the ire of anti-Semites.[47] Moreover, there was the aspiration to extricate American troops from Iraq and the promise of programs like universal medical care, which had been on the liberal agenda for decades but never realized. But there was a departure from the virtual unanimity in the Jewish electorate regarding Franklin

Roosevelt. There now was in play in the community and in the national political arena a militant conservative Jewish group whose voice in the media could not be ignored. The Jewish political voice in the twenty-first century may have far less coherence.

The Obama administration offers an opportunity to observe what Jewish politics, its strengths as well as its foibles, will be like in the twenty-first century. The issues and qualities Jewish voters seek in a candidate have changed over the years, yet certain constants remain. The Jewish electorate of the 1930s would have far less favored Clinton, and one could not imagine that Ronald Reagan could garner the astounding 39 percent of the Jewish vote he did in 1980. The higher level of education and urbanity has diminished the tendency to favor patrician liberals like Wilson and Roosevelt. What is new about Jewish political behavior is its cooler, more operational character that places overweening ideology on a lower level of importance. The contemporary Jewish voter has ideals, but they are not collected in some basic text; neither is there "an end of days" model that allows the world to be viewed in completed form. The liberal world is always a work in progress. Replacing principles with actual programs is the drawing power of legislation like the administration's proposed national healthcare program, which reaches beyond the give-and-take of local politics to attract voters that are politically neutral but favor such a program. There are programmatic liberals who may oppose the right of abortion but favor a massive investment in the improvement of the schools system. Today the number of programs the voter supports that fall under the liberal banner can calibrate Jewish liberalism. The independent, formally educated new voters pick and choose their preferences. The notion of a collective Jewish vote, like the notion of a unified Jewish community casting identical ballots, is less imaginable today. Jewish voters may end up voting for the same candidate and favoring the same positions, but they do so individually and there are many aberrant Jewish voters.

If a specific all-encompassing dogma presenting the basic principles of a liberal belief system seems no longer in the picture, the drawing power of a liberal candidate or issue that articulates most, if not all, of the liberal principle that most Jewish voters support can momentarily sometimes act as unifying factor. Jewish voters were almost unanimous in opposing

George W. Bush's limitation of federal funding for stem-cell research. In practice the candidate the liberal Jewish voter prefers is often the lesser of two evils rather than a staunch supporter of the liberal agenda. So complex and incompatible in their diversity have the choices before the voter become that it is often no longer possible to choose a purely liberal candidate. It becomes a matter of degree.

Given support of a requisite portion of liberal issues, what will win the support of Jewish voters is difficult to predict, since like all moderns they are not all of one sensibility. Jimmy Carter had many of the requisite liberal qualities Jewish voters look for, yet never gained popularity with the Jewish electorate. John Kerry possessed impeccable liberal credentials, yet never achieved the popularity of Bill Clinton, who promptly moved to the political center once in office. Certain nonpolitical personality characteristics seem to play an important role for Jewish voters. What seems to draw the Jewish voter is a certain kind of open political persona, committed to major liberal causes but when necessary able to see beyond them.[48] The intensity of devotion to the big liberal idea of the time does not necessarily assure Jewish voter support. If either Al Sharpton or Jesse Jackson had been the black candidate to run against John McCain in 2008, they would not have gained 78 percent of the Jewish vote, as did Barack Obama.[49] It was as much an estimate of the candidate's intelligence rather than color or a sense of completion of the civil rights struggle that brought an overwhelming Jewish vote for Obama. Of course it didn't hurt that the Jewish voter also sensed a certain grace and balance, flavored with a sometimes self-deprecating Lincolnesque sense of humor.

Yet it is difficult to identify the precise factors that translate into intelligence, which counts so heavily among Jewish voters, nor is it the whole story. General Dwight Eisenhower garnered an amazing 40 percent of the Jewish vote in the 1956 election despite the fact that compared to the eloquent Stevenson he butchered the English language. Beyond the politics of his father, some pundits expressed doubt about Kennedy's liberal bona fides. He abstained from the senate vote condemning McCarthy and demagogically invented a fictional missile gap in the 1960 campaign. Yet with the help of an eloquent speechwriter, and armed with wit and charm and the authorship of a book, he was awarded with 82 percent of the Jewish vote. Jewish voters seem drawn to candidates who display a generosity of spirit combined with a mastery of detail, as noted in policy wonks like Bill Clinton. But a candidate's charisma and general popularity also play a role. It may be that George Bush's managerial style, which transmitted a sense that he had assigned the details and the implementation of policy to underlings and was otherwise disengaged, convinced Jewish voters that the Republicans candidate lacked sufficient depth to run the country.

Attraction to the candidate's persona can outweigh his or her support for the Jewish agenda and of course a well-organized and funded politi-cal campaign also has a great deal to do with who gains office. There is a special twist that relates to the behavior of the Jewish voter. The high level of Jewish support for the candidacy of Ronald Reagan in 1980 and 1984, despite the fact that his views stood at the opposite end of the politi-cal spectrum, and the negative Jewish reaction to the Bittberg incident in 1985, may have been related to his amiability and his strong support of Israel.[50] On the other hand, despite his unprecedented abandonment of the "honest broker" position in support of Israel, George W. Bush failed to capture the hearts of Jewish voters because certain human factors, balance, competence, empathy for the less favored, and class favoritism, especially in the distribution of the tax burden, proved to be far more important. Similarly, despite his religiosity and moral uprightness Jimmy Carter failed to win the heart of the nation's Jewish voters, nor did Rich-ard Nixon, who wanted desperately to win Jewish support. Yet despite his rawness and southern rural quality, Bill Clinton's obvious brightness as reflected in mastery of detail and political smarts did eventually gain the full support of Jewish voters. It was as if the liberal Jewish voter was convinced that anyone aware of the so-called true facts was bound to be a liberal. Jewish political preference for certain candidates is related almost as much to a certain kind of "presence" as it is to the depth of the candi-date's liberalism. Ralph Nader has articulated a reform position that in many cases was eventually adopted by mainstream liberal reformers. Yet he never attracted the normal quotient of votes Jews award to reform-minded third-party candidates.

Clearly Jewish liberal passions are at their zenith when the candidate combines a liberal sensibility with a good political presence. The contents of such a presence relate to a certain personal security combined with a high level of formal education, well-spokenness, a sense of balance, and, if possible, a sense of humor. It seeks out the educated, well-spoken candidate and assumes that a commitment to certain liberal principles will follow since supporters of such issues as stem-cell research or abortion rights are assumed to be more informed and intelligent. When added to other attributes sought by the Jewish voter in candidates for office, the results can be formidable. Barack Obama possessed virtually all the characteristics attracting the Jewish voter: a political persona that reflects a certain amalgam of knowledge on issues, language usage, character, and an even temperament. Yet these attributes might have come to naught had it not been for Obama's race. That gave the liberal Jewish voter an opportunity to perform an act of historic justice that confirmed his liberal goodness. It is as powerful and irrational a political motive as that of a racist voter's desire to keep a black man out of the same Oval Office.

Withal, liberalism in all its shadings persists among American Jews even while considerable generational variety prevails. Studies of the New Left dominated by young Jews shows that they may have been ahead of their parents and their classmates in targeting the new issues, whether it was the war in Vietnam or the environment. "Young Jews have received a liberal tradition from their parents," observes Alan Fisher. "In turn they have been a radicalizing force on their parents."[51] Core issues dealing with race and class are in continuous flux. Parents can be chagrined at the length their children have gone to realize a cherished principle such as racial tolerance. They truly never guessed who was coming to dinner.

The issues on the new liberal agenda, like abortion rights, planetary warming, the impact of secondary smoke, the Darfur genocide, and the Arab Spring, are startlingly different in substance and potential impact than issues that seemed life-and-death matters in the immediate postwar decade. You cannot get more global or universal than the threat embodied in climate change. Generally, Jewish activists are not distinguishable as a distinct subgroup in the liberal camp, though some liberal issues like matters concerning church-state relations and foreign policy issues concerning Israel continue to have a special importance for them. The war on terrorism may appear as a catchall slogan for most liberals, but for Jewish liberals whose attachment to the security of Israel is important it goes beyond sloganeering. Like liberal voters generally, Jewish voters have become part of a largely university-educated cohort concerned about solving problems of collective survival in a complex problem-ridden world.[52] We have noted that Jewish citizens sometimes form a disproportionate segment of the subpolity that brings these problems to public attention. They are, however, too small a minority to control any of these interest groups, nor do they propose a distinct liberal Jewish angle to solving them. They are shaped above all else by their need to become part of a universal humanity. Yet, while in the United States philosemitism may have become as common as anti-Semitism once was, Jews are still compelled to confront the tensions in their communal world; that obligation stems from a special historical circumstance of having directly experienced or indirectly witnessed living in a hostile, sometimes murderous world.

On the day-to-day local issues there is no specific liberal Jewish fingerprint. Jewish voters generally favor more government spending on public education and are less supportive of defense expenditures, but so do many other voters. They are urban and urbane, which translates into greater concern about environmental issues like pollution and global warming and saving threatened species. They are supportive of the central ideological planks of what passes for contemporary liberalism, which goes from universal medical insurance to closing the racial gap in education standards and achievement. Yet on the local level where programs to implement the liberal agenda are at play, on issues such as busing to achieve school integration, or public housing in their vicinity, and even access to public beaches near their beachfront homes, Jews are as likely to be found as opposed as their neighbors.

That sometimes startling contrast between the rhetoric of liberalism and how its advocates behave on certain sensitive issues can best be understood by the lack of uniformity in the degree of liberalism held. While more Jews are likely to be liberal compared with other voters, not all

Jewish voters are liberal and many are only selectively so. Some are supportive of general liberal aspirations, but not in the immediate concrete reality. For example, they may favor drug rehabilitation centers or soup kitchens, but not in their neighborhoods. The core universalism of university-educated Jewish liberals differs from that harbored by working-class low-income Jews, whose preferences regarding issues like school busing and school decentralization are not noticeably different from their gentile neighbors. While Jews score higher on a general measurement of liberalism, they are in fact liberal "in certain selective ways." We have already noted that much depends on whose ox is being gored.[53]

We have mentioned another reason for the sometimes indistinct character of Jewish liberalism on the grassroots level that makes it possible for the Jewish vote to become a swing vote in close local elections. A universally popular conservative candidate like Ronald Reagan exercises considerable pull on the Jewish vote. But in the end, the preference of the formally educated Jewish voter for the more liberal candidate of either party may have as much to do with the candidate's political persona, language usage, depth of knowledge—what passes among Jews as the telltale signs of intelligence—as the depth of his or her liberalism. Some researchers simply attribute Jewish voter preference to an overwhelming preference for competence, effectiveness, and integrity.[54] The list of so-called Rockefeller Republicans touched by a liberal sensibility—like Jacob Javits (New York), Richard S. Schweiker, Hugh Scott, and Arlen Specter (Pennsylvania), Clifford P. Case (New Jersey), Edward Brooke (Massachusetts), and Lowell Weicker Jr. (Connecticut)—favored by Jewish voters is fairly long. Jewish liberalism has been a persistent phenomenon but it is also a malleable one. It has been known to move beyond the confines of the Democratic Party.

Summing Up

The cornerstone of Jewish political culture remains its abiding liberalism, defined in broad terms. It is a liberalism baked in a Jewish historical oven that extends from the Enlightenment to the present. The overriding concern for Israel and the lasting effects of the Holocaust serve to recast it to fit current Jewish sensibilities, but the basic humanness remains despite the challenge of contemporary events, especially the persistence of genocide as public policy.

Despite the fact that traces of their historic anomalous position in organized society can still be found, perhaps because of it, American Jews are one of the nation's most politically active and engaged ethnic groups. That conspicuousness goes beyond the voting volume that brings their toll to 5 percent of the electorate though they are less than 2.1 percent of the population. In virtually every movement for change and reform, from women's liberation to the mobilization against ethnic cleansing in Bosnia and Darfur, from the campaign for a universal healthcare program for all Americans to concern about secondary smoke, Jews have played a leadership role. They are disproportionately, but not exclusively, the funders and the activists that fuel and energize the world of protest in the public square.[55] In a word, Jews continue to make a difference in American politics after other ethnic voting blocs have become subdued or altogether silent. It is difficult to imagine what the American political arena and American liberalism would be like without its Jewish players. Withal, the amplification of the American Jewish voice in the polity does not change the fact that Jews remain a comparatively small minority often lacking coherence and cohesiveness. It is not that they exercise a special political power, but like all groups in the American polity they are empowered. It is in the empowerment of various groups in its polyglot electorate that the secret of America's remarkable political stability is contained.

We have noted that the sources of Jewish liberalism and the activism and engagement that come with it are multiple. A 1969 survey by the American Council of Education shows that political activism among Jewish students begins in high school, so that by age twenty-five they are more than twice as likely to have participated in election campaigns than non-Jews of that age. Yet such engagement is not uniformly characteristic and Jewish student radicalism is confined to a small atypical minority. Orthodox Jews have been less active as individuals in the political arena. They cannot be observed demonstrating for the right of abortion or warning about global warming.[56] Unless brought to the surface by an unpopular war such as Vietnam, the engagement begins in earnest in young adulthood and it goes hand-in-hand with a secular liberal sensibility. Still, Judaism is after all a religion of deeds that maintains that prayer and observance alone is insufficient to "repair the world." One can assume that somewhere in the mix of soil in which Jewish liberalism grows there has survived a Judaic or at least a secularized high sense of moral obligation that resembles religious commitment. That stimulant is abetted when Jewish liberals use religious tenets to support their humanitarianism and the high ethical standard that exists in the Jewish liberal mind-set. However, in the political arena it advocates the building of a "wall of separation" to separate government from religious institutions.

Because Jews remain liberals of a certain ethno-religious stripe, they play a key role as the nation's interpreters of its underlying democratic principles. Still, the idea of a collective political conscience fashioned by a common history and anchored in Jewish peoplehood is increasingly difficult to maintain. The existence of a monolithic American Jewish political culture is belied by the sharp cultural, ideological, and religious differences that exist within the Jewish electorate. Jews only learned to share a common ethnicity in America. Before World War II, regional and thereby cultural European origins were so wide that they became a source of Jewish humor.

When added to class and political differences, the Jewish governing threshold seemed low. Indeed, during the Holocaust when Jews needed to speak to the Roosevelt administration with one voice they were unable to do so. Such deeply held political and regional culture loyalties made the determination of a single Jewish communal interest problematic. The political representative ready to do the bidding of his or her Jewish constituents often hears a cacophony of voices emanating from a riven community seemingly more intent on tearing itself apart then speaking to power holders with one voice. Yet within that proliferation of postures and beliefs one can find certain constants associated with liberal humanism. Generally they are a concern for the underdog and the corrections of what are perceived to be inequities in the American social system to which they now feel they belong. American Jewry is American and shares its values as well as its foibles.

But a Jewish wrinkle in its political persona may in fact be found in the persistence of some form of liberalism that often exerts a more powerful influence on its political culture than wealth, class, or faith. What is strange is that an increasingly unaffiliated affluent Jewry remains as staunch in their support of liberal causes as were their parents and grandparents. Next to African Americans, Jews remain the most liberal voting bloc in the national electorate.[57] It is almost as if these humanistic principles have become a permanent feature of what being Jewish means in America.

Efforts to change that preference by Jewish public intellectuals who argue that liberalism is against American Jewish interest have been fruitless. Jewish voters continue to be the Democratic Party's most loyal ethnic constituency even when the signs of their former ethnicity are hardly visible. If there is a price to pay for such loyalty it may come in an unexpected area. Listening to the bitter conservative rhetoric of the most recent presidential election that spits out the "L" word as if it was a terrible disease, some Jewish citizens may begin to suspect that, if indeed liberalism has become so anathema, can America's Jews who are its principle carriers be far behind.

4

The Liberal Zionist Entanglement

The Historic Roots of Zionism:
Communalism in the Jewish Diaspora

Zionism began as a national movement like others incubated in the nineteenth and twentieth centuries, with one marked difference. Customarily, national movements claimed the right of nationhood for people already living in the land. Zionism proposed to bring Jews living in exile back to reclaim the land and to restore nationhood to a people that for thousands of years had lived outside the land. The hope and spirit of renewal generated by the movement's proposed *yishuv* (return) did not generally convince Jews to uproot themselves. No matter how fervently they prayed for a "next year in Jerusalem" it remained a distant hope that bore little relation to their daily lives. Ingathering was the movement's major weakness before World War II. The dream of rebuilding Zion could not compete with the practical realities of resettlement. When Jews felt the need to emigrate it was the American Zion that beckoned.

The dream of homeland was slow of realization. Before the Holocaust the rapid embourgoisement of American Jewry and those of Western Europe was a far cry from the image of a lamenting people awaiting return to their homeland sung by their poets. It was precisely in their local communities where the evidence of enduring peoplehood could be found. In preindustrial Europe Jewish communalism often came close to possessing near-legal and economic autonomy within the host cultures, which generated a sustained experience in self-governance. As elaborated in chapter 1, it included institutions such as the *Beth Din*, a trusted court system, and sometimes a *Kehillah* that acted as a legislative assembly

167

and treasury.[1] In the seventeenth and early eighteenth century in New Amsterdam, the Jewish community enforced its decrees by exercising its power to eject noncomplying members from the congregation and by denial of burial in the community cemetery. Though by the beginning of the eighteenth century it was possible for Jews to live outside the Jewish community and its law and still maintain a modicum of their ethnic Jewishness, such isolation was difficult to bear in an age where the religious corporation reigned supreme. Later there also developed a Jewish presence at international conferences, where Jewish communities were represented by organizations like Alliance Israelite Universelle (1860), Allianz Israelitische Zu Wien (1873), and Hilfsverein der Deutschen Juden (1901). Though American Jewry was organized on a voluntary basis after the republic was established, it too belatedly joined the club with the founding of the American Jewish Committee (1906), the Joint Distribution Committee (1914), and later the American Jewish Congress (1918) to help manage the affairs of world Jewry.[2] In a word, an international Jewish presence composed of several organizations representing the largest Jewish communities was in place at the Congress of Vienna (1815), Berlin (1870), and Versailles (1918) before the establishment of the Jewish state. A sovereign Israel is a relatively new presence in contemporary international affairs, but the international recognition of an entity representing the Jewish communities is not. American Jewry became linked to the mysterious ties that bind world Jewry well before the Zionist movement came to dominate those ties.

A Troubled Implantation: American Jewry and Zionism

If American Jewish political culture has a fingerprint at all, it lies in its staunch support of a sovereign Jewish state. That support has remained fairly constant even when a majority of American Jews may oppose the expansionist fervor of the regnant Likud Party. Yet viewed historically, American Jewry's passion for Israel is comparatively recent. We have previously noted that its full development was hampered by the inherent tension between nationalism represented by Zionism and the universalistic ingredient in liberalism. The influence of the latter played the major role in shaping American Jewish political culture.

Zionist ideology did not for various reasons easily embed itself in American immigrant culture. The hope and the reality of resettlement in Palestine were focused on European Jewry, especially the impoverished Jews of eastern Europe. There the sense of hopelessness coupled with poverty and the physical threat of pogroms was palpable. That sense of foreboding and threat was not part of the American Jewish experience. The motivation for the Eastern immigration was rooted in the promise of America for personal emancipation, not for the rebuilding of a Jewish homeland. Jewish settlement in America was thus the antithesis of the Zionist vision of Jewish destiny. It is in that sense that history had pitted the two enterprises, American Jewry and Zionism, against each other.

Yet viewed from a religious perspective, the Jewish settlement in America could not be seen as a source of redemption. Almost from the beginning of the Eastern immigration, some would argue even before, Jews seemed particularly receptive to the siren call of secular modernity. The rabbinic sermons were full of warnings that in America Jewish youth would "fall away" from the faith. They pointed to numerous signs, from failure to keep the Sabbath to a startling growth of immorality, that warned that Judaism could not survive in America. But warnings about the allurements of a "tref (unkosher) medina" fell on deaf ears. By the eve of World War II American Jewry had cast off much of the cloak of formal religion, composed of the myriad laws and regulations that shape the behavior of Orthodox Jews, in favor of an amalgam of practices that included a powerful mix of religious, ethno-cultural, and secular ideologies.

It was not until the threat of national socialism, which established itself in Germany after 1933, that American Jews came fully to embrace political Zionism or at least their version of it. Israel would come to play a binding role, much the way concern for eastern European Jewry did before its destruction. But that Zionism's crucial resettlement imperative and the assumptions that once established a Jewish state would supercede Jewish communities in the diaspora or speak for them was not part of that schema. For Jews the settlement in America was homeland. Before the establishment of Israel only a trickle of American Jews, the majority of whom were aged and observant, chose to resettle in Palestine.[3]

The relationship of American Jewry to Zionism and Israel is extremely complex. Considering that Israel is a sovereign nation and American Jewry is one of several voluntarily organized ethnic groups composed of free citizens of a modern pluralistic nation, a comparison of the political behavior of the two polities may be an exercise in futility. The organizational structure of American Jewry was always based on voluntarism, which meant that it was subject to the vagaries caused by contending commitments that exist in a pluralistic culture. Israel, though singular, was never the only claim on American Jewry's loyalties. The Jewish citizen could at once be a fanatic baseball fan, a wine aficionado, and a contributor to Zionist causes. Indeed, as American Jewry's original strong connections to European Jewish politics and culture faded, new elements of cohesion, of which Zionism was one, developed. Israel became a major concern of an American Jewry at the historical juncture when forces of modernity were eroding its tribal bonds. The individuation inherent in secularization would also eventually weaken the peoplehood tie to Israel furnished by the Zionist movement. Yet while Israel and American Jewry are independent entities with entirely different bonds of cohesion, a strong link between them persists and is so recognized in the international arena.

The earliest vision of the Jewish settlement by the founders of modern Zionism often circumvented the nationalism problem by limiting their vision of homeland to the idea of a cultural center and a haven for Jews who needed one. American Jewry did not view itself as part of that victimized group. From the outset the American approach was practical rather than ideological. That became evident during the thirties when the Roosevelt administration's reluctance to receive Jewish refugees convinced American Jews that Jewish survival required a territory where Jews were sovereign. Triggered by news of the depredations, there began an extraordinary effort encouraged by Labor Party leaders like Ben-Gurion to bring a Jewish state into existence. The effort by the now-regnant Zionist movement, which began during the war and reached its zenith in 1948, marks a high point of American Jewry's effort to influence American foreign policy.[4] It was the circumstance of the Holocaust that brought American

Jewry to act as a separate identifiable agency in American politics through the instrument of the American Zionist movement. Some argue that contemporary Jewish political activism is a resonance of that continuing concern regarding the security of Israel and that American Jewish politics is confined to the issue of securing Israel. In fact, it is much more than that.

Pre-State Historical Background: American Jewry and Diaspora

The political hyperactivity related to the founding of the state in 1948 was not American Jewry's first effort to influence American policy in the Middle East. During World War I the nascent Zionist movement had enlisted Louis Brandeis into its fold and helped bring the Wilson administration to support the Balfour Declaration. The well-known legal scholar Felix Frankfurter was called on to convince Henry Morgenthau Sr., the Jewish ambassador to Turkey, to curtail his efforts to detach Turkey from the Central Powers. The breaking of Ottoman rule in Palestine, then the southernmost province of Greater Syria, was requisite for the establishment of the future Jewish state or cultural center. But for American Zionists these early building blocks, the Balfour Declaration and the granting of the mandate to Britain at the San Remo Conference (1921), was the beginning of a decade's long effort to garner the support of the American government to realize their goals.

On the American Jewish political stage the growth of a Zionist movement was not always welcome, since it posed a threat to the crucial communal fundraising effort called "the campaign" and also again raised the troubling dual loyalties question. In the first two decades of the twentieth century political Zionism had made some inroads in the German-Jewish dominated polity, but progress was slow. The vast majority of Jews emigrating from eastern Europe after 1870 had after all chosen American Zion, which offered far greater opportunities for enterprise then the small, beleaguered *Yishuv*. Only after immigration was restricted in 1924 did the possibility of rebuilding Zion in its ancient Jewish homeland begin to take on new life.[5] It was the foreboding events in Europe that set the stage for the full development into the movement for an actual Jewish commonwealth in Palestine. The rise of the Nazi threat, which spoke of extirpation of European Jewry before the Final Solution, gave the small Jewish settlement in Palestine a new aura.

The massive eastern European Jewish immigration to the United States differed sharply in motivation from the small *Aliyot* (ascendants) (waves of immigrants) that chose to settle in Palestine. Yet a sense of people-hood based partly on common language and a distinct ethno-religious culture indigenous to eastern Europe had developed. It is that preexist-ing commonality possessing elements of a common political culture and governance that is frequently overlooked by Middle East experts trying to account for the high priority American Jewry gives to the security of Israel. The Zionist movement could claim that history was on its side, since Jewish diaspora communities, as noted, were often self-governing in all but name. The Minority Rights Treaties advocated by Louis Marshall and approved by the League of Nations had gone as far as mandating the establishment of Jewish schools in reestablished Poland, taught in their own Yiddish language. All that was missing for nationhood was actual repossession of its ancient land, which a special fund had already begun buying back *dunam by dunam*.[6]

Many "uptown leaders" like Jacob Schiff, Henry Morgenthau Sr., and Louis Marshall dismissed the dream of a return after millennia of exile as a dangerous fantasy. True there had always been a trickle of mostly pious older returnees, which was supplemented during the last quarter of the nineteenth century by immigrants energized by a kind of liberal European nationalism associated with the names of Mazzini and Cavour, who successfully unified Italy. These waves of immigration joined the small Jewish settlement that had continued to reside in Palestine since the destruction of the second temple. Though the overwhelming majority of Jews who sought haven in the nineteenth and twentieth century viewed America as their Zion, for political Zionist this small settlement in their ancient homeland was sufficient evidence that a Jewish presence in the Holy Land had never ceased. Without such a claim the Zionist movement might have deteriorated into romantic myth.

An observer peering into the future from 1905 would not have been able to foresee the dominance of Zionism in American Jewish communal politics in the thirties. With the exception of a group of Reform rabbis, many of whom had eastern European backgrounds, the dominant Reform branch of Judaism was unalterably opposed to any form of nationalism, which is how they classified Zionism. Democratic socialism carried forward by the Bund shaped the ideological center of gravity of the masses of immigrants from eastern Europe. Bundists believed that the solution to the "Jewish problem" would come as part of the revolution that would surely happen. Socialist ideology viewed Zionism as a retrogressive movement of bourgeois nationalism that would turn Jews inward and away from the forces of universalism and progress. Already noted was the opposition of the right wing of the Orthodox branch that included some Hasidic courts.

Most important, the diaspora condition itself militated against the idea of a Jewish homeland. Liberalism, which succeeded democratic socialism as American Jewry's regnant political persuasion, was not completely at one with the sectarianism inherent in the Zionist idea. We have already noted that the discomfort was concealed for years by the conviction that Israel was itself a model liberal state. Jewish public intellectuals like Lionel Trilling were convinced that Theodor Herzl's political Zionist idea that advocated a Jewish state was a minor thing compared with the eternality of classical Judaism based on scripture and historical tradition. Others like Judah Magnes and Horace Kallen, following the path of Achad Ha'am (Asher Ginsberg), sought a middle road between nationalism and liberalism. In the twenties a smaller group of socialistically oriented Zionists, who carried in their ideological baggage the idea of reclaiming the land through labor, dreamed of reshaping Jewish diasporic identity, which they believed was somehow unhealthy. The kibbutz movement became the most distinctive feature of Socialist Zionism. More important, the image of the *Chalutz* (pioneer) and the kibbutz gained enormous popularity among American Jews.

But the reconciliation of the nationalistic element in Zionism with the universalistic element in socialism and its successor Jewish liberalism was never fully achieved. As is often the case today, Socialists of the radical eastern European stripe viewed the Zionist idea as retrogressive. The heroic rhetoric replete with the promise of renewal barely concealed the nationalist underpinning of Herzl's Zionism. In the twenty-first century, disaffected left-wing scholars like the late Tony Judt, who had experienced kibbutz life, came to feel that Israeli "blood and soil nationalism" was no less retrogressive than the twentieth-century racist nationalism that plagued Europe, and that the creation of Israel was therefore a historical error.[7] A similar distaste plagued some Western Jewish liberal universalists who were likely to stem from the cosmopolitan urban culture developing in Europe. It was in that urban/urbane culture that Jews, including some of principal leaders of the Zionist movement like Haim Weizmann, Nahum Goldmann, and Rabbi Stephen Wise, seemed to be most at home.[8]

Whatever else Zionism purported to be it was a product of the liberal nationalism of the nineteenth century rather than a modern incarnation of tribalism, the predecessor of the "blood and soil" version of right-wing Zionism today. That polarity inevitably led to a Right-Left split within the Jewish polity. Orthodox conservative Jews ally themselves with Christian fundamentalists to view Israel as the spiritual center of the Jewish people with biblical overtones. Liberal Jews, such as those associated with the Reform movement that came late to Zionism, oppose them. It was the Holocaust that convinced them to follow the lead of the Jewish majority and support the creation of the Jewish state. History, they then argued, had made an exception of the Jews, whose need for a homeland was a matter of life and death. That the Jewish state subsequently assumed a democratic form and demonstrated exemplary concern for social justice made the change in position easier. Today liberal Jews, many of Reform background, remain in the forefront of concern about civil rights for Israel's Arab citizens.[9]

By the twenties two distinct survival strategies, the Zionist aspiration for a Jewish homeland and the idea that Jewish rights in the diaspora could be assured by the legal mechanism of minority rights, were in play. Louis Marshall, one of the leaders of the Jewish delegation at Versailles, did not intend for the world Zionist movement to go out of business as a result of his success in having minority rights adopted by the League of Nations. He did not believe that the two strategies were incompatible. The Jewish settlement in Palestine would be one of several Jewish settlements around the world. The newly created or re-created nations born at Versailles were compelled to incorporate minority rights clauses in their founding charters, but it soon became apparent that Marshall's victory was a pyrrhic one. The idea of separate minority rights, which seemed to open the door for Jews to become a nation within a nation, aroused adamant opposition in insecure states like Poland, which housed many non-Polish minorities.

But the rapid growth of restrictionist sentiment in the United States gave the Jewish question in Europe a new urgency that now consumed much of Marshall's energy. The passage of the Emergency Immigration Law of 1921 followed by the Johnson-Reed Law of 1924, with its national origins formula, signaled that the golden age of mass immigration was drawing to a close. Where would the Jewish "huddled masses" settle now? Predictably, the Zionist voice counseling the need for a Jewish homeland became more insistent. It was reflected in an increase in the number of Zionist fraternal orders and organizations like the American Jewish Congress, as well as a new competitiveness in the all-important fundraising arena.

Newly minted Zionists were less sensitive to the dual loyalties question and more reform-minded concerning communal governance. Undoubtedly that was a reflection of the influence of reformist Progressive movement. Muckraker journalists like Lincoln Steffens and Ida Tarbell were highly appreciated among the Jewish immigrant cognoscenti like Abraham Cahan, editor of the *Forward*. Boiled down to its essentials, the progressive's answer to the problems facing the American democracy as embodied in Bob La Follette's "Wisconsin idea" was "more democracy." Zionism, which embodied the Jewish peoplehood idea in its purist form, became a crucial ingredient in the shaping of American Jewish liberalism and led naturally to the idea that a communal election was necessary to determine how American Jewry would be represented at Versailles. The democracy idea became the seedbed of Rabbi Stephen Wise's Zionist-oriented American Jewish Congress, which became the most liberal of organizations in the Jewish polity.

Political Zionism then was hardly an unknown movement when events in Europe pushed it to the fore in the American Jewish mind-set. By the 1920s the American Zionist movement had become a player in communal politics. That was reflected in the wrenching conflicts over the distribution formula of the proceeds of the annual fundraising campaign. As religious and communal ties based on a common ethno-religious culture weakened, Zionism came to be viewed as a possible building block for Jewish continuity. Based on that rationale, American Jewish leaders like Solomon Schechter, Judah Magnes, Horace Kallen, Stephen Wise, and Mordecai Kaplan advocated for funding the Jewish settlement in Palestine. American Jewry would not be called to send its children to help settle Israel, but their absence would be compensated by its philanthropic effort embodied in a coordinated annual campaign whose yields were rising during the "prosperity decade" of the twenties. Budget politics, who gets what, became the driving force in the communal polity. It shaped its politics and went far to determine its leadership.

A search for the roots of American Zionism leads to a paradox. American Jewry is ensconced in a society that is held together by a centrifugal in-gathering principle, "out of many, one" (e pluribus unum). It is far from a perfect instrument, but perhaps more than other ethnic groups, American Jewry was appreciative even of its incomplete inclusion in the American *pais legal* and the sense of having a place in a pluralistic society. For the immigrant generation that sense of acceptance was a far cry from their experience in eastern Europe. Yet the sense of also belonging to a separate historical stream, of which Zionism is merely the latest manifestation, remained an aspect of the Jewish political identity. Concern for such threatened Jewish communities abroad was a substantial part of Jewish political activity since the nineteenth century when the Damascus blood libel (1840) led Jewish leaders to request diplomatic intercession from the Buchanan administration. By the turn of the century requests for diplomatic intercession in Romania and tsarist Russia had become pro forma. A preexisting outward tilt of concern was concretized with the development of the American Zionist movement. It was an American variation of Zionist ideology, requiring no actual resettlement of American Jewry in a prospective homeland, but with a strong interest in *K'lal Yisrael*, the universal community of Jewry, that took hold in America. It is one of the most recognizable aspects of American Jewish political culture.

Few foresaw that in the post-Holocaust years the Zionist movement would become dominant in community governance as over 80 percent of American Jewry favored strong support of Israel. How it overcame the challenges posed by the seductive pull of America was as much a matter of historical circumstance as organizational energy.

By the late 1930s there were almost 550,000 Jews living in Palestine, while an American Jewry of over 4 million was on its way to becoming the most successfully integrated Jewish community in the diaspora. It replaced German Jewry, which before the Reich embarked on its genocidal policy was considered the most successful and secure in the Jewish diaspora. That the conversion of American Jewry to some form of Zionism occurred simultaneously with its assumption of the leadership of world Jewry was no coincidence. The destruction of European Jewry left a leadership vacuum, while the world Zionist movement offered a ready instrument to replace the indirect governing arrangements of the prewar period. The bitter years of the Holocaust demonstrated that the disunited American Jews were ill prepared to assume leadership of the world Jewish enterprise.

Lest the commitment to their resettlement in America be undermined, the movement was required to purge itself of the ideological mandate that one must settle in Israel in order to be an authentic Zionist. It was Louis Brandeis who solved the problem posed by the fear of dual loyalties. To be a good American," he counseled, "one must be a good Jew and to be a good Jew one must be a Zionist." Brandeis's high status among the new immigrants, matched only by the popularity of Albert Einstein, went far to solve the vexing dual loyalties question, but we have seen that it raised another problem. Should threatened Jewish communities be supported in place by philanthropy and legal instruments like minority rights clauses or should supported immigration to Israel become the primary rescue strategy? The potential immigrants who were often reluctant to undergo the wrenching experience of resettlement alone could make such a decision.[10]

The story of Zionist ascendancy begins in the years after World War I, which promised a settlement of the national question, considered then a basic cause of the conflict. Included in the Fourteen Points, on the bases of which the Allied hoped to end the war, was the right of national self-determination, which included the Jews. The role of other Abrahamic tribes who shared claim to the "Holy Land" would be solved in years to come. One group headed by Horace Kallen, Judah Magnes, and other members of public Jewish intellectuals who leaned towards Zionism favored the actual resettlement of the ancient biblical heartland then known as Palestine and eventually the establishment of a Jewish cultural and political center after a model proposed by the Zionist thinker Achad Ha'am. There was as yet little open talk of a Jewish nation-state. The Zionist claim for a national homeland found little consensus in American leadership associated with the "uptown" American Jewish Committee, whose president, Louis Marshall, we have seen, strongly advocated an alternate legal solution that proposed guaranteeing Jews minority rights in place, as part of the Versailles Treaty assured by the League of Nations. There was much contentiousness in the Jewish delegation at Versailles.

The recruitment of Brandeis, who assumed leadership of the chaotically organized movement, was a Zionist coup marking a great change in Brandeis's reclusive public life. His reputation was based on his legal innovations that opened the gates for a more effective regulation of the trusts through the courts. Brandeis, as noted, was only dimly aware of the Judaic sources of his reform impulse until he was recruited for the movement in 1912. His tenure as president was not an easy one. After his appointment to the Supreme Court in 1914 the accusation of a conflict of interest eventually compelled him to mute his public advocacy and the open leadership of the Zionist movement. It was a portent of the problematic status more militant factions of the Zionist movement would face in America.

During the thirties the developing world economic crises followed by the foreboding events in Germany disrupted American Jewry's preoccupation with its synagogue building and general communal development, compelling more attention to the welfare of Jewish communities overseas.

The ascendant American Zionist movement staked its claim for a bigger role in Jewish communal governance and a greater share of the all-important yearly fundraising campaign. Its appeal for communal democracy helped the Labor Zionist wing of the American Zionist movement to fuel a Jewish American form of liberalism focused on Jewish problems.[11] Its advocacy of ethnic peoplehood did not require religious adherence or congregational affiliation. Zionist leaders like Rabbi Stephen Wise heightened the sense of ethnic Jewishness while at the same time opening a door for the increasing number of unaffiliated Jews to advocate secular reform issues such as the corruption of the city political machine. Wise forged a link between secular Jewishness and the liberal reform agenda that has exercised a profound influence on American Jewish political culture.

In summary, at the close of World War I the American Jewish polity was composed of several factions living in an uneasy relationship with one another. Jewish ballots were predominantly cast for the Republican ticket since the turn of the century. But after World War I the political weight of the vote of the Eastern immigrants, strengthened by Al smith's failure to win the "Brown Derby campaign" in the election of 1928, which touched on the sensitive religious question, was garnered by the Democratic Party, where it as remained ever since.

Jewish communalism during the twenties was a fragile affair. German Jews were not anxious to surrender their leadership, while the more recently arrived Eastern Jews, bedeviled by left-wing radicalism on the one side and religious conservatism on the other, were not able to fully grasp the leadership to which they felt entitled by their growing numbers. In their former homelands Jewish politics was volatile and riven. Now the freeness of the American environment opened the door wider for conflicting factions to find their own way. Superimposed on all was a growing Zionist movement with its own solution to the perennial Jewish survival problem. It would take time to convince an American Jewry preoccupied with making its way to the middle class of the gloomy prognosis for the survival of European Jewry.

During the interwar years it was historical circumstance that helped Zionists make their case. But in the Levantine world of Jewish organizations in which group and personal interests were intertwined, changes came more slowly. The ties between the large national diaspora organizations like the "Joint," the Alliance, and the Hilfsverein, who assigned themselves a governing role, the existing Jewish settlement in Palestine was incorporated into the Palestine mandate providing for a Jewish Agency for Palestine in (1922). But matters did not flow smoothly. For Zionists this first instance of governance since the exile, granting quasi-legal governing authority over the Jewish community in Palestine, was a great cause for celebration. The Jewish Agency would come to play an important role in the international arena. In an effort to become "a permanent address for the Jewish People," it strove to absorb non-Zionists into its leadership and legal councils. Yet even after the establishment of the state the possibility for the Jewish Agency for Israel (JAFI) to govern proved to be limited by the reluctance of communal organizations to share their fundraising capacity with the Agency, limiting its capacity to raise needed funds in the diaspora. One could not govern without a source of revenue, and yet diaspora communities did not easily surrender their prerogatives to Keren Hayesod, the fundraising arm of the World Zionist Organization (WZO). During the twenties the conflicts with the United Palestine Appeal over the proportion of the collection of the joint campaign collection that should be assigned to the *Yishuv* were often bitter until the formula for distribution was agreed on.

Even before the mandate was unanimously ratified by the League of Nations in 1922, the world Zionist movement was at loggerheads with American Jewish leadership. Convinced that the only real solution to the Jewish problem was to ultimately resettle all Jews in Palestine, they opposed Louis Marshall's push for national minority rights clauses. When the "Joint," Alliance Francaise, and Ort established craft schools in postwar Poland, Zionist spokesmen argued that the money would be better spent in the *Yishuv*. The outcry reached a high point with the JDC's financing of the Crimean resettlement project through its subsidiary Agro-Joint in 1924, retaining agricultural experts like Joseph Rosen, who was associated with the despised territorialists.[12]

But wracked by internal strife in the post–World War I decade, the American Zionist movement remained divided. Intent on organizational reform, the newly organized Brandeis group predictably encountered serious opposition from the original leadership group led by Louis Lipsky. The organizational strife that became a fingerprint of American Jewish life seemed to deepen as the threat of destruction of European Jewry loomed. Still, a robust politics may after all also indicate that there was something worth fighting about. It is possible to conceive that the enormous sums collected by Jewish philanthropy may have been a double-edged sword. On the one hand it played a crucial role in building up the Jewish settlement in Palestine and offered needed succor elsewhere. But on the other, it reinforced deeply held ideological and religious differences by imposing a "spoils" element on American Jewish politics. To this day a great deal of energy in domestic communal Jewish politics is expended in determining who gets what.

The Thirties and the Ascendency of American Zionism

Offering an ideology for revitalization, a tie to the world Jewish enterprise, and a credible strategy to best solve the growing refugee crisis of the thirties, the American Zionist movement of the immediate prewar years was ideally situated to convince American Jewry that its time had come. The love of Zion after all was one of Judaism's oldest loves, preceding the Enlightenment, out of which grew liberalism and its promise of emancipation. In any case, the signs that the principles of liberalism embodied in the promise of emancipation were being undermined by the events in Germany were unmistakable. If the citizen's rights before the law could be withdrawn in one fell swoop as they were by the Nuremberg Laws (1935), then the hope of emancipation was illusionary. It made the Zionist argument for the need of an independent sovereign Jewish state all the more compelling.

The new reality was not easy for the immigrant generation to accept. Despite the arrest of many Jewish radicals in the Palmer raid episode and the simmering anti-immigration hearings in Congress, conditions for earning a livelihood were good. The economic crash was still years away and an American Jewish attachment to a distant homeland had not yet been welded into place. Jews were largely still themselves immigrants or the descendents of immigrants who hoped to find their Zion in America.

That preference was based on practical rather than ideological consider-ations. The opportunities for "making it" in America, whatever shape that might take, were far better in the "land of opportunity." The case was far different in contemplating resettlement in Palestine. Such a move required a generous dose of political or religious idealism. The land itself was first in Turkish hands and after the San Remo Conference became a "Class A" British mandate.[13] A small strip of land that, after Jordan had been sepa-rated from it, was no bigger than New Jersey, Palestine never possessed the capacity to absorb the millions of European Jews who would eventu-ally need a haven; neither did American Jewry have the political leverage to convince Britain to revoke its 1939 White Paper limiting immigration and land sales to Jews.

It was as much historical circumstance as organizational energy that brought American Zionism to the fore in the thirties. Contrary to contem-porary popular belief that imagines an indifferent American Jewry, the ominous developments in Europe had an early resonance in the Amer-ican Jewish mind and politics. American Jewry was probably the most interventionist-minded ethnic voting bloc during the thirties. The turn to Zionism was the most direct Jewish response to anti-Semitism that could be imagined. It does not come as a surprise that its growth during the thirties raised some fear that the benevolent full Jewish integration model would be compromised and the well-integrated German Jews would be cast out of the *pais legal,* as was done in Germany through the Nurem-berg Laws. If it could happen in an "advanced" nation like Germany, it could happen anywhere. That was the theme of Upton Sinclair's popular polemic *It Can't Happen Here* (1937), which sought to warn Americans of complacency regarding the fascist menace. The subsequent failure of the beloved Roosevelt administration, the neutrals, the Vatican, and agencies like the International Red Cross to consider a more active rescue policy for the endangered Jews of Europe until it was too late generated a deep trauma in the Jewish communal psyche. It is the basis of our discussion of the relationship of the Holocaust to Jewish political culture in the fol-lowing chapter.

Anti-Semitism was at the heart of national socialism, which saw itself triumphant, the wave of the future. The threat faced by German Jewry was now echoed in almost every nation, including the United States. But while it acted like a growth hormone for the Zionist movement, it also created great dilemmas for Zionism, since both Nazism and Zionism were dissimilationist, that is, they agreed that the answer to the Jewish problem was for Jews to get out of Europe. Zionism was conceived as a movement to finally end millennial anti-Semitism by removing the target, the Jewish people. The statehood aspiration was abetted by the reality that the hope of full emancipation with civil and political rights and security as citizens of other nations was forlorn. The national minority rights clauses that newly formed nations were compelled to include in their founding charters by the League of Nations were everywhere resented, nowhere more so than in the new Polish republic, which held the largest Jewish population in Europe. It was precisely the Weimar constitution (1919), which took the emancipation process to its completion by granting Jews full and equal citizenship rights, that the National Socialists could not abide. Zionism, which argued that Jews need a state of their own to survive as a people, became increasingly acceptable even for the comparatively secure Jews of America.

Those Socialists who continued to hold out the hope that the coming Socialist society would everywhere permit full integration of Jews seemed removed from reality as the world filled with extruded Jewish refugees. That was the despairing atmosphere in which a commonwealth resolution was introduced at the annual Zionist conference convened at the Biltmore Hotel in New York in May 1942. The following year a conference convened by Henry Monsky, president of B'nai B'rith, brought together the largest representative assembly in American Jewish history. A stirring speech by Rabbi Abba Hillel Silver, matched only by the oratorical ability of Rabbi Steven Wise, stampeded the 501 delegates from every state in the union to pass the commonwealth resolution favoring the immediate creation of a Jewish national state. American Jewry had found its leader of the moment. He was a Republican from Ohio and a brilliant organizer who soon moved his aging competitor, Rabbi Stephen Wise, from center stage. Silver became head of the American Zionist Emergency Committee (AZEC) and quickly mastered the art of public relations and mass organization. To his friends he boasted that he could flood Washington with ten thousand telegrams within hours after it was requested. The vigorous lobbying to bring a Jewish state into being began in 1944, the same year that the Jews of Hungary and Slovakia, the surviving remnants of European Jewry, were being deported to Auschwitz.

At the historic juncture when European Jewry was slated for liquidation, American Jewry was poised to reach new heights in professionalization and per capita income. There was evidence in the prosperous twenties and even in the Depression-ridden thirties that America was different. Here the hope of emancipation had not failed, as it had in Europe with horrific consequences. Carried forward by a patrician president who sought out Jewish talent, the liberal principles of inclusion embodied in emancipation were working. That difference in fortune is one of the bitter contrasts on the Jewish historical canvas that later became the source of a troubled reading of the witness role of American Jewry during the Holocaust.

It was, then, the Holocaust that brought American Jewry to the unswerving commitment to Israel for which it became known in the fifties and sixties. That high level of devotion was primarily the provenance of the immigrant generation and their children who bore witness to the Holocaust. In later decades of the century Zionist ideology was more lightly carried by American Jews but remained a crucial element in their political identity.[14]

America and Israel: The Cold War Years

That American Jewry would play a crucial role in the creation of Israel was hardly conceivable as World War II came to an end. Propaganda regarding Jewish controlling political influence in the Roosevelt administration had become a standard theme in anti-Semitic rhetoric in the Reich and at home. But fueled by the grim revelations emanating from newly liberated Europe, which gave the earliest details about the death camps, few foresaw that a heretofore quiescent Jewish leadership, pressured by leaders of the *Yishuv* in Palestine, would successfully push for the recognition of the newly declared Jewish state. That campaign marks the high point of Jewish influence on American foreign policy. Not all of Truman's policy advisers shared American Jewish joy at the birth of the Jewish state. Some were alarmed that a small ethnic constituency with a special interest seemed able to gain control of policy in a strategic oil-rich area.

Well into World War II the Middle East, including the Jewish settlement in Palestine, was considered a British sphere of interest and off limits for American colonial expansion. Within the State Department the sentiment of most "old hands" was anti-Zionist and to some degree anti-Semitic. The passivity of the Roosevelt administration to the Jewish quest for statehood was partly a reflection of the indifference of American public opinion. Political leaders simply viewed the "Holy Land" as the birthplace of Christianity rather than a strategic hot point in the impending cold war. To be sure, discovery of oil in the region in the interwar years awoke a commercial interest that blossomed into a strategic one during World War II. Still, during the interwar years the strategic importance of the Middle East ranked below the Far East, where China was an important field for American missionary work and where a Japanese threat to the Philippines was palpable.

The war changed the nation's power status and with it the focus of the national interest. Before the cold war totally altered the conventional wisdom regarding the national interest in the Middle East, many foreign-policy experts agreed with wartime military leaders like General George Marshall, Roosevelt's military chief of staff, that American national interests would be best served by a close link to the oil-rich Arab rulers. But at the war's end in 1945, with the exception of many American Jews, few Americans envisaged that a Jewish state would come to occupy such a central place in the nation's strategic thinking.

When President Roosevelt met the king of Saudi Arabia on his return from Yalta in February 1945, his primary effort was to safeguard the nation's growing dependence on Middle Eastern oil. He also had some vague idea that the budding Arab-Israeli conflict in Palestine could be resolved by a UN trusteeship, an idea that never gained traction after it ran into Arab opposition. For American Jewry and the Zionist enterprise the salvaging of *Sherit Hapleta* (the saving remnant) survivors of the Holocaust became a primary goal that dominated its political agenda during the postwar decade. The rehabilitation of the survivors, now called Displaced Persons, was demographically and ideologically inextricably bound up with the development of the Jewish state. More than any other factor it was the creation and nurture of the new state and the survivors that compelled American Jewry to learn the art of practical politics, which included the myriad special political skills, organizations, lobbying, fundraising, polling, and public relations that became part of the Jewish political arsenal.

As the full extent of the genocide became known, especially its systemic implementation as part of a modern state's public policy, there developed a Holocaust consciousness among American Jews based on a realization that the intent of the Final Solution was not merely the physical annihilation of the Jewish people but also the very memory of their presence in history. That awareness explains much of the enormous communal effort to retain the memory of the Holocaust, discussed in the following chapter. A confluence of the national interest, represented by the Truman administration, and an American Jewish community ready to assume the mantle of leadership previously ensconced in Europe now existed. The basis of postwar American policy in the Middle East would be rooted in the new power realities stemming from the cold war and a Jewish state that, much to the chagrin of Moscow, clearly supported Western values and interests.

There is little agreement on the reasons for Truman's decision to extend diplomatic recognition to Israel, a move that proved to be one of the most consequential diplomatic steps ever taken in American foreign relations. Some argue that it was a practical political consideration, the need to assure the Jewish vote in an election year.[15] There was also some evidence that the Arab states could not be convinced to accept a Jewish state in their midst. A UN partition plan could not stave off the war that would follow the declaration of statehood. The early granting of diplomatic recognition may have been partly out of sympathy with the barbaric victimization of the Jews of Europe and partly a response to the extreme pressure on Truman. Though cautioned about the possibility of the invasion by neighboring Arab states following a declaration of statehood, Truman seemed not fully aware of what was at stake. As it happened, the invasion of Israel by her Arab neighbors and the unlikely Arab defeat in a David and Goliath scenario gave Truman's precipitous recognition of Israel a visionary character. It was Soviet arms, channeled through its new satellite Czechoslovakia, that allowed the ragtag army of Israel to circumvent the American arms embargo and wring an unlikely victory from its hostile Arab neighbors. But a suspicious Kremlin soon grew aware that its hope to attract the new state to the "Socialist camp" was forlorn. Instead Israel's victory became the first in a series of cold war victories over Soviet interests in the region. The victory did not solve Israel's security problem, which became perennial, but it served as the foundation of an alliance that resembled the kind of bond America developed with Britain after the Anglo-American Alliance of 1902, which had considerable influence on international power arrangements in the first half of the twentieth century. There too, a state with a similar culture and language, but much weakened by two costly wars, retained a special friendship with Washington that kept it afloat during World War II. Truman's recognition of Israel marked the beginning of a special relationship that would go beyond the normal one maintained with a cold war client state.[16]

The actual creation of the Jewish state did not magically bring harmony and tranquility to the much-weakened world Jewish enterprise. Organizational disunity that hampered rescue efforts during the war continued. Nationwide organizations like the American Jewish Committee, JDC, and HIAS did not willingly surrender their role to Israel, which naturally assumed that the leadership of world Jewry would come to the new state. Through JAFI Israel already possessed the governing apparatus to bring the diaspora communities together. We have already noted that, especially for American Jewry, such preemption was not acceptable. Under the Proskauer–Ben-Gurion Agreement, Israel promised not to subvert the existing relationships with such international organizations through unilateral negotiations in the name of the Jewish people.

Thirty years later a kind of division of labor had developed, which usually worked well. There were certain things that a sovereign nation acting in the international arena, such as attending international conferences or making needed protests via the diplomatic pouch, was better equipped to handle. Similarly, American Jewry could become Israel's advocate before the American seat of power. A far-reaching diplomatic coup can be attributed to Nahum Goldmann, president of the World Jewish Congress. Though a prominent member of the Jewish Agency and the World Zionist movement, Goldman, who resided in America, viewed his role as being the first world diplomat of the Jewish people, and as such set up a World Conference of Material Claims and negotiated the crucial reparations agreement with Konrad Adenauer, the Christian Democrat chancellor of West Germany. The need for capital was great, but the question of reparations was too delicate to be handled by Israel alone, since the idea that the Jewish state was the direct heir of the destroyed Jewish community of Europe was not legally established, nor was the idea of reparations to compensate for the lives and property lost uniformly acceptable to Jewish diaspora communities and Israel.

The standard image of a unified conspiratorial world Jewish community belied the contentiousness that persisted between Israel and American Jewry. As late as the seventies and eighties, issue after issue arose that reflected the gulf that divided Israel and American Jewry. Most noteworthy was the three-decade effort to extricate Soviet Jewry, which led to a rift concerning the question of resettlement. Israel insisted that resettlement of refugees carrying Israeli visas was her prerogative, only to confront hundreds of "drop outs" who, like their predecessors after 1870, preferred to settle in the United States.[17] For Israel, demography and security were inseparable. These 3 million Jews considered "lost" behind the iron curtain were viewed by Israel's strategists in both ideological and strategic terms. Israel planners hoped to bring out these Jews who had barely survived the onslaught of the wartime German *Einzatsgruppen*, when they were again subject to a systematic government/party effort to finally destroy the remnants of Russian Jewish religious and secular culture. Faced with long-range demographic crises as a result of the liquidation of the Jews of Europe, whose eastern segment would have provided the population stock for the new state, Israel viewed the surviving 3 million Jews of Russia to fulfill that need. It established a secret bureau on the highest level of government to implement that goal. The cry for "freedom of movement" became a human rights cudgel in the cold war and a crucial instrument in the collapse of the Berlin Wall in 1989. Citizens of East Germany were also anxious to "vote with their feet" for a freer life in the West.

But as a growing number of Jews were released from their Soviet cage it became evident, to Israel's chagrin, that, as at the turn of the twentieth century, it could offer little competition to the seductive pull of America. Soviet Jewry could not be manipulated to serve Israel's demographic need. Thousands would not allow themselves to be resettled in Israel despite the fact that their release was enabled by the possession of an Israeli visa. The often bitter conflict that ensued could serve as the surest evidence that the conception of American Jewry as an instrument in Israel's diplomatic arsenal is far from being a reality.

From the perspective of American Jewish political culture, American Jewry's special connection to Israel holds the highest place, but its weight has not always proved easy to bear. There are elements in the foreign-policy establishment that rue the nation's closeness to Israel and view the mantle of security cast over Israel as manipulated by the "Israel lobby." That charge raises the bugaboo of "dual loyalty," which still threatens a community many generations removed from its mass migration.

Yet the political hyperactivity of American Jewry is far from the only, or even the most important, element Washington considers in fashioning its Middle East policy. The tie is more than appears on the surface. The strength of the American commitment to the security of Israel goes beyond its domestic political resonance. Israel has become an important element in the defense of American interests in the Middle East. Should the conflict between Israel and the Palestinian be magically resolved, the relations between Israel and the United States would still have a greater weight than relations with Ireland or Italy. Today the American nurture of Israel is primarily based on strategic considerations. Since 1950 the degree of Jewish support varies from decade to decade. Israel was only peripherally involved in the seven-year war with Iraq and the subsequent hostilities in Afghanistan. It maintained a studied apartness as old internal power relationships were rearranged in Egypt, Libya, Tunisia, and finally Syria during the Arab Spring. The Jewish voice in Washington sounds unseemingly loud compared with other hyphenate voices seeking to influence policy, like the Italian or Irish American, which have become barely audible. That is so because of the Jewish electorate's generally higher degree of political engagement and because other hyphenate groups do not face an existential problem as does Israel. Yet, fueled by the fanatic religious animus of Shia's Islamism, the mere existence of Israel becomes a source of tension. Armed with nuclear capability, Iran's foreign-policy goal of reclaiming the Middle East for Islam dwarfs the regional instability posed by the Israeli-Palestinian problem.

Washington's close bond with Israel developed over time. In its early years it did not possess the intensity it assumed during the height of the cold war and the encounter with Islamic terrorism. During the Eisenhower years, precisely when American Jewish support for the new state was at a high point, a comparative passivity toward the Jewish state prevailed. An arms embargo compelled Israel to turn to France. Like Britain and France, Israel was compelled to withdraw from the Suez Canal in 1956 at Washington's behest. Israel did not easily fit into the containment strategy of Secretary of State John Foster Dulles, which was based on friendship with the Arab states of the Middle East, especially Saudi Arabia, embodied in the Middle East Treaty Organization (METO) and the Baghdad Pact. Washington was still seeking a secure network of allies to protect its interests. The search generated some surprising changes. The close wartime relation to Britain became subdued and was ultimately replaced by NATO. Eventually Germany, which recovered from the war faster than Britain or France, was welcomed back into the Western club. During those troubled years it was the extraordinary political and financial support of American Jewry that enabled Israel to hang on and wait for better times. So intense was Jewish feeling for Israel that rabbis complained that a new idolatry called "Israelism" threatened to undermine the faith.

The better times arrived with the advent of the Kennedy administration in 1960, when a deeper Soviet penetration of the Middle East threatened. We have noted in another context that the growing threat to

Israel's security gradually deepened American Jewry's focus on Israel and intensified its efforts to influence America's Middle East policy. American Jewry's political resources were enlisted in that effort. But the relationship never came close to the model of control envisaged by Senator Fulbright and others. The deep interest Israel's security aroused in American Jewish citizens is partly rooted in the intractability of the Arab-Israel conflict. Should the threat to Israel's security vanish, it would become possible to imagine a reversion to a "normal" interest in foreign policy, which to the dismay of some would continue to be deeper than that of most citizens of the republic. No other American ethnic group musters such an abiding and broad interest in American foreign policy. It goes beyond the security of Israel to a deep sense that Jewish security the world over is linked to the well being of America.

We have noted that the Israel question also demonstrated a high potential for generating division within the Jewish polity. Those with the deepest commitment to Israel seemed less able to maintain the characteristically broad interest Jewish liberal voters maintained in other domestic and foreign policy issues. That contrast between those secular liberal Jewish voters who held a multiplicity of interests aside from Israel and those who focused exclusively on Israel would become one of several Left-Right divides in the Jewish polity. One can only speculate about how the American Jewish political profile would have developed had a solution to the Middle East problem, rather than the continuous low-level serial warfare, been found. The focus of the Jewish vote on Israel is real, but it is not a determinant of the entire Jewish political agenda. Its primary interest lies with the nation with whom it has chosen to cast its lot, and whose interests it is believed are remarkably consonant with the security of Israel. It is not a total mutuality. American Jewish voters are far less interested in Iraq and Afghanistan than they are in the machinations of Iran, which at the time of this writing may soon develop a weapon of mass destruction. If and when that occurs, the relationship between Jerusalem and Washington will enter a new phase. It is, after all, primarily Israel that faces an existential threat from a nuclear Iran. Washington has found a way to live with nuclear-armed hostile powers like the Soviet Union, China, and most significantly, North Korea.

Israel-Diaspora Relations: The American Jewish Factor

The existence of an American Jewish polity is a not new on the stage of Jewish history. It preceded the establishment of the sovereign Jewish state by almost three centuries. The existence of Israel required adjustments and accommodation by all diaspora communities, but none so much as American Jewry, which alone emerged from the Holocaust stronger and more viable demographically, organizationally, and financially than all other Jewish communities combined. With the destruction of European Jewry, the leadership of world Jewry, ensconced for centuries in Europe, fell to American Jewry. The mantle of leadership did not always rest easily on American Jewish shoulders. Its leadership did not aspire for such a leadership role and was not organizationally equipped to play it. The war had demonstrated that American Jewry was barely able to govern itself. There were other factors as well, which included the new configuration of the Jewish world after the Holocaust, especially the existence of a sovereign Jewish state whose Zionist leaders very much wanted to assume a leadership role.

The establishment of the Jewish state inevitably raised the question of the presence of two distinct political centers exercising two different kinds of power. Israel was a sovereign nation, while diaspora communities that wanted to act above and beyond the philanthropic sphere were compelled to work through their host governments. Activity relating to Jewish communities abroad often raised legal and political problems. Was there such an entity as "world Jewry?" If so, who spoke for it in the international arena? The relationship between American Jewish agencies like the "Joint" and HIAS, armed with their own mission and budgets, continued to play their normal roles. Jewish organizations like the American Jewish Committee maintained special relations with a resurgent Germany. Several American religious and secular agencies entered into discussions with the Vatican regarding such things as anti-Semitic facets of the Catholic liturgy. Others like HIAS sought to help Jewish refugees from the Soviet Union to settle in the United States, to the dismay of the Jewish Agency. These private activities on the international stage, which included everything from the training of rabbis to international Jewish sports activities, raised endless problems for the new state, which sought to offer leadership to communities that Zionist ideology informed them were moribund now that a Jewish state was in existence.

For the ill-defined American Jewish polity, Israel posed yet other problems. How deeply should it be allowed to involve itself in American politics on Jewish matters? Should prominent Israeli leaders endorse candidates or otherwise intervene in American elections? Should American Jewish dollars be used to support campaigns of Israeli politicians? Such matters often involved complex legal questions that were not readily resolvable. Yet they could pose a threat to the well being of American Jewry, especially if they conjured up the vexing dual loyalties question. It was an abiding concern, for that question had traditionally distinguished American Jewry from other ethnic voting blocs. More important, the persistence of such conflicts of authority could weaken the ties that bound the two communities together and thereby weaken the Jewish presence in the face of abiding hostility. Who should negotiate the reparations agreement with a resurgent Germany? Could Israel, which came into existence only after the Holocaust, negotiate with Bonn for reparations? Could it act as an agent for the estate of the murdered Jews of Europe?

The problem of conflicting interests and spheres of activity between diaspora communities, which meant in effect American Jewry, and Israel did not emerge suddenly with the creation of the state in 1948. After much trial and error it had ostensibly been solved by encouraging the representation of diaspora in the first Jewish Agency created by the governing charter of the mandate in 1922 to help administer the Jewish settlement in Palestine.[18] The Jewish Agency for Israel (JAFI) focuses primarily on immigration and resettlement, but also assumes other government functions that depend on financial aid from abroad. But the existence of a body that is also part of the governance of a foreign country and serves as a conduit for philanthropy ran into congressional opposition in 1963, especially by Senator Fulbright (Dem. Arkansas) who chaired the Senate's Foreign Relations Committee. The American section of JAFI was subsequently ordered shut down by the Department of Justice. Today it operates in a reorganized setting and continues to register as an agency of a foreign government. The linkage of Israeli agencies to American communal organizations organized in federations reflects the complexity of that relationship.[19]

In the past, finding a clear division of labor between American organizations involved in activities abroad and the Israeli government agencies like JAFI sometimes proved troublesome, especially in such areas as relations with the Vatican, Holocaust reparations, and protection for threatened Jewish communities. As a sovereign nation Israel is able to enter into treaties and agreements, while American Jewish communal interests in the international arena often require the support of the American government, which, if indeed such a collective position can be determined, is not necessarily forthcoming. Despite complaints about the overweening Jewish influence in the making of foreign policy, in the absence of a clear connection to the national interest there was little assurance Jewish leaders would be able to influence government policy to support what they believe to be the Jewish interests. Roosevelt's rejection of a more active rescue policy during World War II, a failure that had a tragic effect, is a good case in point. Not only did the urgency of the need fail to bridge the communal divisions, but it also proved unable to convince Roosevelt to step up his efforts, until 1944 when it was all but too late. Sometimes, as in the aforementioned case of the resettlement of Soviet Jewish emigrants, the conflicts between the activities of Jewish organizations like HIAS and JDC with JAFI were not easily resolved.

Rather than the image of a unified Jewish community focusing its political advocacy on an agreed-upon issue, the effort to project influence through lobbying and personal contact is often fraught with contention stemming from deep historic divisions, which in the absence of a legal base for communal governance are almost impossible to resolve. Anyone can become involved in Jewish communal politics and anyone does. Not only are political differences deep and abiding, but there is also little agreement on who speaks for American Jewry. The result is that the administration can choose the voice it wants to hear from the several that cry out to be heard. A government change in policy, such as an insistence that housing construction cease in disputed areas of the West Bank, can wreak havoc in the Jewish polity. If, for example, the elusive peace treaty with the Palestinians in which the State Department has been so deeply involved ever materializes, it will likely expose deep-seated conflicts between the expansionist sections of Jewish public opinion and those who favor a two-state solution. Jewish opinion on the attainment of peace in Israel is far from monolithic. A decision in either direction can further divide the American Jewish polity between its liberal secular and communal/observant wings while undermining its relationship with government. It is possible to imagine that the perennial aspiration of the Republican Party to win over the Jewish vote could finally occur if some future Democratic administration insists on concessions that are viewed as deepening Israel's existential threat. While American Middle East policy is conceived and implemented to serve the national interest, when played against the security of Israel, policymakers become aware that the American Jewish voter is also drawn to a preexisting-coexisting Jewish historical stream.

Clearly, there exists a separate politics in the relations between Israel and American Jewry not usually found in the relationship of other immigrant groups to their former mother country. Its most recent manifestation involves conflicts that stem from continuing activities of agencies anchored in diaspora communities dealing with religious, cultural, and diplomatic matters. There exists about twenty-five such multicountry associations that involve everything from sports (Macabe), the World Union of Jewish Students (WUJS), the World Council of Synagogues (WCS), and the World Jewish Congress that conducts these nongovernment relations. Jews are joiners and until recently boasted every kind of organizations human flesh can be heir to, from singles clubs to players of Mah-Jongg.

Yet while Jews display a penchant for forming and joining organizations, they are at the same time plagued by problems stemming from identifying clearly who can claim to be a Jew and which legal agency could possibly adjudicate such questions. Ostensibly, identifying who is Jewish is a simple matter—any child of a Jewish mother. But in practice the question of Jewish identity and conversion, to which it has become linked, has become highly political. It concerns not only a domestic matter involving Soviet and Ethiopian immigrants, but also Israel-diaspora matters involving marriage and conversion. The Conservative, Reform, and Reconstructionist branches of Judaism are not recognized in Israel, where the Orthodox branch reigns supreme. That means they cannot perform basic communal religious functions, such as granting marriage certificates or divorce decrees, in Israel. Conversions performed by Reform or Conservative rabbis in the United States are not recognized by the Israeli rabbinate. While some progress has been made, there is little integration under one religious umbrella. A secularized Jew seeking to have his marriage to a convert recognized in Israel would encounter problems requiring supervision of the conversion process by an Orthodox rabbi. On the grassroots level, in Israel it is the Orthodox rabbinate that is empowered to determine who is a Jew. None of these contretemps would ever have seen the light of day had it been politically feasible to separate church and state at the time of the founding of the state. But history also had a voice, one held by premodern elements that had to be convinced to join in the state-building enterprise. Rather than bridging the religious and cultural differences among Jews, the special arrangements Ben-Gurion was compelled to make with the powerful Orthodox community in Israel when the state was established has exacerbated them. The special position of the Orthodox rabbinate and the place religion has in the public square of Israel has become one of the most important factors weakening the ties between a predominately secular American Jewry that has for years fought for a wall of separation between church and state and the situation that prevails in Israel.

Differences in approach to basic democratic tenets were bound to develop between related people raised in different social and cultural environments. The sense of kinship between American and Israeli Jewry persists, but as such political and cultural differences grow more pronounced, the distance separating them is bound to widen. Clearly the philanthropic and political support given by American Jews is based on something more than the prospect of an enjoyable tourist visit to the Holy Land. A glimpse of that deeper feeling was revealed during the Six Days' War, which triggered a wave of patriotism not only in Israel but also among American Jews who want to see their team win. The June War in 1973, on the other hand, served to remind American Jewry how fragile was Israel's security. Both wars revealed that the sense of interdependence between the two communities lay just beneath the surface. The question facing researchers is whether that closeness can be maintained when confined to the single strand of a common religion, on the observance of whose tenets they do not see eye to eye.

Still, there are balancing developments that strengthen American Jewish ties to Israel. In recent years the growth of anti-Semitism in the Islamic world, which targets Jews anywhere for terror attacks, creates a bond based on common peoplehood. The telltale sign that an anti-Semitic threat makes Jews everywhere targets is found in the 1994 blowing up of the Jewish Mutual Association, the headquarters of the main governing agency of the Jewish community in Buenos Aires, with the loss of eighty-five lives, by a Hezbollah unit trained by an arm of Iranian intelligence. There was nothing anti-Israel about it except that the victims were Jews and therefore fair targets. The incident put American Jewry on notice of a great danger faced by all Jews qua Jews.

Reinforcement of that sense of common threat came from an unexpected source, the Socialist movement of Europe, whose consistent positions against Israel were identified by many as rooted in the familiar specter of anti-Semitism. (How one distinguishes between anti-Semitism and anti-Israelism, and whether indeed there is a distinction is a separate problem.) Heretofore anti-Semitism on the Left was associated with the communism of the Soviet Union. Anti-Semitism emanating from Europe's Democratic Socialist parties came as a surprise.

The increase in anti-Semitism so soon after the Holocaust was a special disappointment for Zionists. The elimination of anti-Semitism by returning Jews to their ancient homeland, where they could become again a "normal" people, was the major aspiration of Zionist thinkers. Some warned of the growth of Judeophobia in the Islamic world, fed partly by a sense of Palestinian displacement. Few foresaw an anti-Jewish animus from the world of European socialism, the ideology that served as the handmaiden of the very Labor Zionism that governed Israel in its early years. Anti-Semitism was sui generis, it seemed to have little to do with what Jews were and whether they lived in their own land or among other nations. Fueled by Arab extremism, represented by Hamas in Gaza and Hezbollah in Lebanon, and also extending to Jewish communities in the diaspora, the new anti-Semitism has generated a genocidal rhetoric, much of it traceable to Nazi wartime propaganda. Ironically, there were some Jews who recognized that the dream of normality sought by Zionist forefathers was not to be. Israel had become the lodestone of anti-Semitism. In a perverse way, the animus faced by Israel became evidence of its Jewishness.

The reappearance of virulent anti-Semitism, laced with threats of genocide and acts of terror, had the effect of strengthening the complex relationship between American Jewry and Israel. It demonstrated that Israel, like European Jewry during the Holocaust, couldn't rely for its security on other nations or agencies like the United Nations. With the distinct exception of the United States and Germany, Israel, like wartime Jewry, was not considered part of the "universe of obligation," which persuades nations to respond to threats of genocide. In October 2011 the Palestine authority, whose predecessor had rejected a UN partition resolution in 1947, won acceptance of a resolution for membership. A few weeks later the Palestinian authority was accepted for membership in UNESCO, one of its best-known agencies. The humiliation of Israel, organized by a nonmember against a member in good standing, demonstrated how low Israel's status had fallen in the family of nations. The attack on the southern tier of Israel by armed groups aroused little reaction in the UN, while Israel's response raised cries of "disproportionality."

In the absence of world outrage against the open use of terror, American Jewry joined other diaspora communities to rally to Israel's defense. The perception that the playing field was again uneven generated in some Jewish voters a sense of distrust and the idea that Jews can only depend on their own power to assure survival. Whatever the gap between the nationalistic defensive stance in Israel and the weakening of Jewish identity among American Jews, a tie based on a growing awareness that both are under attack for their Jewishness strengthens the American Jewish bond with Israel. All of which is to say that there has developed a balance between historic processes that act to weaken the ties between American Jewry and Israel with the persistence of anti-Semitism that strengthens them.

In some measure the political activism of American Jewry emanates from the sustained low-level war that Israel's neighbors have waged against her since the establishment of the state. It has heightened the politicization of American Jewry and made it a factor beyond its numbers in the fashioning of American policy in the Middle East. Next to its abiding liberalism, the sustained conflict between Israel and the Palestinians has had the deepest influence in shaping American Jewish political culture. The very intractability of the conflict combined with the imminent development of weapons of mass destruction by Iran suggests that the Israeli-Palestinian conflict contains the possibility of breaking out of its regional confines. That is not intended as hyperbole. If we compare its sustained volatility to a normal crisis trajectory, then, with the possible exception of the Kashmir dispute, it is the oldest unresolved crisis in the post–World War II era. Like an old active volcano it may erupt at any time.

The proliferation of weapons of mass destruction (WMDs) generates additional volatility. At the insistence of her neighbors in the years to come, Israel will be requested to acknowledge her possession of an arsenal of WMDs, to permit UN inspection of her facilities, and to become a signatory of the Non-Proliferation Treaty, which she will undoubtedly refuse. With the growing possibility of nuclear capability in Iranian hands, the crisis has assumed the ominous possibility of a thermonuclear exchange. Confidence in the peace-building propensity of the Oslo Accords (1994) is spent and a peace based on a two-state solution was seriously undermined when Israel's evacuation of its Gaza settlements was followed not by a softening of the Palestinian position but with an unrelenting Hamas rocket attack on Israel's southern frontier. The nuclear threat is not limited to Iran. Under certain circumstances it can as readily be imagined as emanating from an Israel that has already allowed itself several preemptive strikes to prevent Iraq and Syria from getting the "bomb." Such a precipitous action suggests that Israel's decision makers are in the throes of a "never again" strategy that stems directly from Iranian threats at total annihilation, and beyond that to a keen historical awareness of the circumstances surrounding the radical Jewish losses during the Holocaust. Even paranoids have real enemies, and Jews have, after all, lived a classic paranoiac nightmare; they experienced a world that wanted to murder them and gave them no haven. Awareness of that mentality is crucial to understanding Jewish political behavior.[20] Israel's political leadership already operates as if faced by a murderous intent bent on genocide. That paranoid state of mind is less evident in American Jewish political culture, but it is there among the survivors and witnesses who have not forgotten the genocide experience.

Under normal conditions Israel might indeed have become for American Jewry what Ireland is for the American Irish and Italy for Italian Americans, a beloved but distant place to visit. The binding kinship ties might have weakened over the years. But after sixty-two years of Israel's challenged existence, that normalization could not develop. The most ominous factor in the Israeli-Palestinian conflict is that despite its relatively small scale measured in terms of the number of casualties, and despite innumerable attempts at finding a way out of the conflict, the problem refuses to exit the world stage.

The bellicose Hamas response to Israel's evacuation of its settlements in Gaza may have done more to convince the Jewish voter in Israel and the United States that a peace based on concessions does not work, certainly not when there are Islamic extremists waiting to move into the power vacuum. Projections are problematic, but after the hope invested in the Oslo peace process was shattered by the failure of the Gaza disengagement (2005) and after the success of the separation wall in halting terror attacks, Israel's position has hardened. Its Labor Party, which together with the smaller parties of the Left acted as a container for the various branches of the peace movement, receives only 16 percent of the vote today. Almost no one today speaks of the Olmert-Livni convergence plan (2006) that went further in defining the boundaries of a possible two-state solution than all prior negotiations. Instead there is a hardening trend that may culminate in yet another round of fighting, this time with missiles in the Iran-refurbished arsenal of Hezbollah in Lebanon.

The growing diplomatic isolation of Israel and the European Left's joining in a campaign to delegitimize the Jewish state is already having an impact on American Jewish political culture. It has deepened the rift in the American Jewish polity between the liberal secular center Left and the center Right. The former is concerned with peace in the Middle East as one of several problems, including the domestic problem of economic recovery and regulation of Wall Street that face America and its Jews. The latter focuses primarily on Israel's security problem. For the liberal center Left, the future is uncertain. The promise that each succeeding Jewish generation will achieve at least as much as their parents has become less possible. That promise is important for American Jewry, which remains one of the nation's most upwardly mobile communities. At the time of this writing a new effort at direct peace talks between the Palestinian Authority and Israel is underway, but it is a redundancy and so problematic that there seems little hope that it can come to pass.

With the passing years it is becoming less possible to think of the protracted conflict between Israel and Palestinians as discreet and solvable on its own terms. In its early years Bin Laden's Al Queda focused its hostility on the United States, while its animus against Israel seemed an afterthought useful to retain a connection with the Islamic world. But with the entrance of Iran and a resurgent Taliban in Afghanistan and Pakistan, the Islamic world seems to be tipping toward religious fanaticism, which places Israel at the center of its enemies list. The Islamic Republic of Iran, which leads the campaign to unravel Israel, is not an Arab nation and has little reason other than an Islamic faith held in common to sacrifice its treasure and its sons. It is that vision that makes the existence of Israel appear as the trigger of what the historian Samuel Huntington has described as a "clash of civilizations" between Islam and the West. He views that clash as a dangerous polarization that contains the seeds of driving history back to the dark ages.[21] There has grown a crusading movement stretching from the Philippines to Yemen and from Chechnya to the Islamic provinces of China (Ughur) that threatens to destabilize and threaten the continued economic development of non-Islamic neighbors. Hamas, for example, shows little interest in creating a viable economy for its over 1 million inhabitants, yet it consigns thousands of young armed men to police its beaches and social networks to make certain that people are properly dressed and adhere to Islamic rules of moral behavior. The Taliban in its crusade against the education of women is busily destroying hundreds of schools for girls. The nation in the center of the storm is Israel, which is aware that the Jihadist movement in Islam contains a genocidal threat to its existence. It is that overriding conflict, in which the low-level war between Palestinians and

Israel is a comparatively minor part, that will dominate American Jewish concerns in the decades to come.

The concern of Jews of all stripes for the security and welfare of Israel goes beyond the normal concern of other immigrant groups for their former homelands. To be sure, Jewish immigrants from eastern Europe felt some nostalgia for the "old home," especially in matters of cuisine, which they altered to comply with the laws of kashrut. There are still lilting Yiddish melodies about the beauty of "Slutz," where the youthful years were spent. Their writers like the composers of Negro spirituals, sang lovingly of the Jordan, but Jews and African Americans alike had never seen the river that was conjured from the biblical image. The tie to the Holy Land was based on a religious memory rather than a felt historic reality. Jews are largely the descendants of this massive Eastern immigration that occurred when Israel did not yet exist. The economic and political circumstances that forced the Jews of eastern Europe to uproot themselves do not lend themselves to building loving memories of their former homeland. During the pre–World War II decades and in the years after the war, few visited the Jewish settlement in Palestine and fewer still chose to resettle there. There was even less desire to visit their former blood-soaked homes in Europe. Unlike the experience of other immigrant groups, the Jewish immigrant's first experience of really feeling at home occurred here.

If that is the historical reality, then one needs to inquire about the roots of the strong ties to Israel that form part of our triad of American Jewish political culture. How did a rapidly Americanizing and secularizing community build a common sense of belongingness, which Zionists call Jewish peoplehood? We have already taken note that the sense of belonging and even governance was rooted in diaspora communities well before the creation of the state.[22] It was undoubtedly strengthened by the American Zionist movement, many of whose leaders saw in Zionism a source of attachment that would reinforce Jewish peoplehood as religious and cultural bonds weakened. Members of Zionist organizations from Hadassah to the Labor Zionist Alliance built organizations that lived and taught the culture through schools and summer camps. Some, like *Habonim-Dror*, even organized youth groups to prepare Jewish youth for the kibbutz movement. In one recent study, the extension of these Zionist-oriented secular organizations may have outnumbered, and for a time projected a stronger influence than, the better-known religiously organized institutions.[23] The Zionist-advocated sense of peoplehood might have been contrived and imposed from on high, but in the interwar period it found fertile soil in the immigrant and postimmigrant generation. A later further strengthening of ties to a Jewish homeland stems from the memory of the Holocaust, which is discussed in a following chapter.

5

Israel's Resonance
in American Jewish Politics

There is a lack of certainty regarding the degree to which the Israel issue determines Jewish voting preferences. On the one hand, there is evidence that a mere rumor that an office seeker is less supportive of Israel than his or her opponent is believed to be sufficient to turn the Jewish vote.[1] On the other hand, the disposition of the Jewish vote, which is believed by some pundits to be related to a candidate's position on Israel, is a normal feature of all major elections and many local ones, and is often raised for strategic reasons. In a recent example, during the campaign of 2008 a top adviser to Barack Obama's campaign discovered that the Jewish community was "sensitive and anxious" and needed constant reassurance concerning their candidate's support of Israel.[2] Israel and the Jewish vote was again a perennial question among the punditry during the campaign of 2012. Yet, as we have noted, the importance of Israel in mobilizing the Jewish vote is not as predictable as some pundits have assumed, especially when it concerns such controversial matters as the West Bank settlements and the two-state solution.[3] We have noted the existence of a veritable political arsenal composed of activists, fundraisers, and lobbyists that can be made available to Jewish candidates ready to play a supportive role for Israel. There are several ways these political instruments can be deployed in relation to candidates and legislation to do with Israel. There can be "punishment" of politicians who take up the cudgels against Israel by withholding monetary support during campaigns or extending support to his or her opponent. Such direct action is rare and somewhat circumscribed by the McCain-Feingold campaign funding laws. More typical would be the candidate who mutes his anti-Israel position in order to accommodate his pro-Israel constituency. Since such supporters do not necessarily hold the same position, the candidate is sometimes compelled to make a choice. The ballots of liberal Jewish voters whose support of Israel is based as much on the fact that Israel is a liberal democracy, albeit and imperfect one, may entail opposition to the extension of West Bank settlements. In certain election district the reverse position may be necessary. The most recent evidence indicates that overwhelming support for Israel, as was the case during the George W. Bush administration, is not a guarantee for winning the Jewish vote, nor is moderation an assurance of loosing it, as in the case of the Obama administration. Given the character of the Jewish voter and the complex nature of Jewish political culture, the wielding or promise of delivery of a Jewish vote is a dubious proposition.

Withal, in recent years some specialists have come to believe that the ties that bind American Jewry to Israel are overshadowed by the continued Jewish support of a wide range of positions that fall into the liberal camp. In the election of 2003, when liberal principles such as stem-cell research were rejected by the Bush administration, even an unprecedented strong platform plank committing it to the security of Israel did not produce the promised increased Jewish vote for the Republican ticket.[4] Yet Nixon's puzzling comeback in 1972 after a dismal showing of Jewish support in 1968 may have been related to his firm support of Israel. The escalation was temporary. Despite Nixon's personal intercession during the Yom Kippur War with crucial military hardware, Jewish support of his impeachment after Watergate reached 81 percent compared with 59 percent for the general population.

The attraction of an unprecedented 39 percent of the Jewish vote for the election of Ronald Reagan in November 1979 again raised Republican hopes that his overriding interest in the security of Israel would increase Jewish support for the Republican ticket. Republican campaigners were disappointed with the results of the election of 1984 when Reagan ran against Mondale, who was considered a liberal's liberal; the normal Jewish preference reasserted itself. The Jewish vote for Reagan declined by 8 percentage points. Reagan swept forty-nine states in a Republican landslide, but received less than one out of three Jewish votes.[5] George Bush (the elder) won only 11 percent of the Jewish vote in the succeeding elections of 1992, down 23 percent from 1988. Some attribute the precipitous decline of Jewish support to his appeal for support against unnamed "powerful political forces," a euphemistic reference to the "Israel lobby" made at a press conference on September 12, 1991.

We learn that the much-feared "Israel lobby" may influence American policy, but when a particular piece of legislation conflicts with a dearly held liberal principle there is little assurance that the position favored by AIPAC will convince Jewish voters to change their minds. From the perspective of Jewish political culture, some form of liberal ideology seems omnipresent, as if determined by a genetic code. In the 2008 campaign, McCain's rejection of choice regarding abortion rights, almost unanimously supported by Jewish voters, acted in some degree to nullify his strong stance on Israel's security. Not even McCain's reputation as an appreciator of Israel's military strength, which he saw in strategic terms as an enhancer of American influence, could win over the support of the Jewish voter. Some liberal issues were so sacred that they could not be abandoned. His position on stem-cell research and his antiabortion stance, combined with his support of oil drilling on the northern slope, repelled liberal Jewish voters. In the end only 22 percent of the Jewish vote went to McCain, 3 percent below that earned by Bush in 2004.

Determining the degree of support the Jewish voter will give to an issue or candidate often depends on the candidate's ability to find a balance between Jewish voters' inherent liberal proclivities and their desire to safeguard Israel. That balance is difficult to strike when it conflicts with issues high on the liberal agenda such as equality of treatment by government for Palestinian citizens of Israel. Protecting Social Security has a high priority among Jewish voters, who form one of the oldest voting blocs in the nation. Issues concerning Social Security or abortion rights arouse strong feelings, but they are also subject to the whims of communal subcultures, such as the ultra-Orthodox community or the deeply conservative Soviet Jews, that are driven by different needs and experiences. In the case of the ultra-religious Jews, the notion of "chosenness" or "election" at the center of Judaism is in conflict with the liberal proclivity for pluralism and universality. The urban/urbane Jewish liberal may speak highly of Jewish communalism, but he abhors Jewish tribalism. Sometimes the fissures within the voting bloc seem incomprehensible to the outside observer. Orthodox Jewry, for example, consistently draws high marks for its strong support of Israel. But within the religious bloc there are Chasidic courts and elements within the Agudath movement that oppose Zionism and the existence of Israel in its present form. The Jewish vote has a liberal center of gravity, but it is not monolithic. Like all sovereign nations, American Jewry notwithstanding, Israel is compelled to face decisions concerning its very survival alone. Given an issue that might trigger a thermonuclear holocaust, such as destroying Iran's A-bomb facilities and delivery vehicles, there is no certainty that even those elements that consistently support Israel would go along. American Jewish leaders were not consulted regarding the invasion of Gaza in 2008 and do not expect to have a veto on whether to eliminate Iran's effort to produce an atomic bomb. There is undoubtedly continuous consultation, but Israel's highest decision makers make the final decision alone, especially when survival itself is felt to be directly at stake.

How a group organizes itself for political activity and casts its ballots can serve as a fingerprint to its political culture. But caution is required, since to interpret it correctly the image also requires a familiarity with the American Jewish historical context. For example, the almost unanimous support given by Jewish voters for Roosevelt's New Deal program can best be understood in the context of the social democratic proclivities of the immigrant generation. Similarly, Jewish voter support of Israel is incomprehensible without some understanding of the impact of anti-Semitism and the Holocaust, which makes events in the Middle East an area of Jewish concern beyond that of the general American voter. It is in that context that the hyperactivity of Jewish lobbies and pressure groups can best be understood. The Jewish citizen is not merely another average American voter when hearing of a suicide bomber in Tel Aviv or missiles landing in Sderot. Israel is a state founded with the help of American Jews after an enormous catastrophe that claimed one out of every three Jewish lives. There are Jewish voters alive who are convinced that the failure to find haven, and the actual denial of a haven in Palestine in the teeth of the crisis, makes the witnessing nations complicit in the slaughter of their kin. Yet while Israel is a preeminent interest, we have noted that the Jewish voter is far from forming a single-issue voting bloc. The telltale sign of all liberally inclined citizens is the plurality of issues with which they are concerned and the frequency that such issues can be in conflict with one another. The liberal Jewish voter is compelled to choose, or better to prioritize, when the Israel issue is in conflict with others on the political agenda. Is retaining the unity of Jerusalem under Israel's rule as important as achieving peace in the area? The response varies with the background of the Jewish voter. A member of Peace Now who may feel less of the passion that faith infuses usually sees such matters differently than a member of a religious group like Young Israel. Strangely, it is that plurality of sometimes conflicting interests that compels the liberal Jewish voter to prioritize, which is then interpreted by single-issue advocates as weakness rooted in Hamlet-like indecision.

Beyond that, the charge that Jews exercise undue influence on the making of foreign policy for the Middle East has become the sign of a certain kind of political mind-set that is inclined to view the normal legal exercise of political influence exercised by an empowered minority as un-American.[6] Utter certainty regarding Middle East policy based solely on a single conception of the Jewish interest not only runs the risk of overstepping the bounds of ethnic power on the national stage, but it also brings in its wake a complex problem that up to this historical juncture has been beyond resolution by the American political process. If, for example, American policy favors setting part of eastern Jerusalem aside to become the capital of the contemplated Palestinian state, it would inevitably confront those thousands of Jewish voters who could not abide a division of a now-united Jerusalem. But the problems such a step poses on the domestic political scene is only the beginning. The fate of Jerusalem is, after all, a religious as well as a political issue. The Jewish traditional view regarding the status of Jerusalem is based on the assumption that it is a holy city for the three Abrahamic religions and should not be claimed by one, even with assurances of complete free access to the holy sites. The claim that Jerusalem belongs exclusively to Israel and the Jewish people remains problematic, even if it has served as Israel's capital since 1967. Jerusalem is not an ordinary piece of real estate. There are Christians and Moslems who inevitably view Jerusalem as a center of their religion and Israel's co-option as an act of supreme Zionist arrogance. The Jerusalem question contains the possibility of awakening powerful latent interests of American church groups who have a separate political interest of their own. The Evangelic Christian community that strongly supports Israel is but one of several branches of American Protestantism that has an abiding interest in the Holy Land. There are missionary enterprises, whose institutions and universities still function, that are far closer to the world of Islam than to Judaism. Despite their beleaguered status, Christian Arabs are historically counted as the strongest nationalists in the region.

A greater danger is posed by the fact that not far beneath the current conflict between Israel and the Palestinians lurks a religious passion rarely spoken about openly. A hint of its existence can be heard in a terminology that speaks of the ancient Christian crusaders as if they are a current enemy and uses an anti-Semitic invective reminiscent of that current during the Holocaust. A united Jerusalem under Israel's control has the potential to fuel the still latent three-way religious conflict between the Abrahamic faiths. The region itself is aflame with renewed religious fanaticism already well on the way to compounding what was basically a regional political conflict with an incendiary religious component. It was Israel's Prime Minister Ariel Sharon's untimely visit to the Dome of the Rock that triggered the second Intifada in 1982. The outward signs of religious fanaticism are already visible in Gaza, which, under Hamas tutelage, calls itself an Islamic republic and polices its beaches to assure proper dress for women. Christian sects in Lebanon are more beleaguered then ever under the watchful eyes of a Shi'a Hezbollah. It was not Jerusalem but the Twin Towers that was bombed on September 11, with the loss of thousands of innocent lives. The primary target is the United States, and within that target is American Jewry, which many in the Islamic world are fully convinced controls American policy. Paradoxically, the disposition of Jerusalem, which is one of three issues that needs agreement for peace between Palestinians and Israelis, has the potential of generating a deep division among Jews. The passion for Jerusalem as a "holy city" is stronger by far among religious Jews of all stripes than it is among secular liberal Jews, who often view it as simply an example of sacred real estate whose worship is a form of idolatry.

In summary, the American Jewish connection to Israel remains supportive beyond other hyphenates to their "mother" country, though there is a widening gap on issues like the settlements and on what the nature of that support should be. The sources of the strength and endurance of these ties are manifold. An important factor slowing normalization of ties has been the protracted Arab-Israeli conflict, which serves as one of several factors that accounts for American Jewish hyperactivity, especially in the area of Middle East policy. The obligations of that freely entered-into relationship for American Jewry go beyond the financial. They generate a countercurrent to the ongoing acculturation process and occasionally provoke charges of Jewish control of foreign policy in the Middle East. If such charges were credible, they would have stronger negative implications for our foreign policymaking process than the imaginings of the working of a demonic Jewish power, which is a mainstay of the anti-Semitic imagination.

Jewish Liberalism and Israel: A Waning Passion?

The decade of the 1950s witnessed the blossoming of the American Zionist movement, which contained the idea of ethnic peoplehood in its most pristine modern form. Former non-Zionists could now support it as a survival instrument. The newly established Jewish state would be more than simply another beleaguered Jewish community that had a claim on Jewish philanthropic largess. The post-Holocaust survival of world Jewry was uncertain. Germany may have lost the war, but the victory came too late for European Jewry. The radical losses experienced by European Jewry coupled with the destruction of their religious and cultural centers added up to a possible death blow for the Jewish enterprise.[7] The Jewish state would open a new page in Jewish history by becoming a center of Jewish civilization to replace the center in Poland lost in the Holocaust. It would assure Jewish continuity. There was cause for hope.

But that buoyant spirit did not survive the fifties, sometimes called "the golden decade" in the American Jewish experience. The pursuit of a higher living standard offered much to distract American Jews, who turned inward to secure a firm place in the American middle class. The postwar enthusiasm for the Jewish state contrasted with the moderate support in the early decades of the twentieth century when the immigrants were focused on establishing their lives. Jewish cultural leadership remained based in Europe. There was a generous willingness to assign a larger portion of the growing philanthropic dollar so that Israel might build itself up economically, and the survivors, many in need of special care, might live out their remaining years in a supportive environment. With European Jewry in ashes, Israel became a timely substitute for the lost Jewish communities of Poland and Western Europe.

Yet, while challenging Israel's desire to act as spokesman for world Jewry, the mantle of leadership did not lie easily on the shoulders of American Jewry. As the full extent of losses extending beyond the millions of lost lives to cultural institutions, schools, Talmudic academies, libraries, and above all the spirit that kept them alive became known, there developed a sense that by itself American Jewry did not possess the cultural energy and the independent organizational structure to assure continuity. The fulfillment of Zionist aspirations for a homeland was predicated on the Jews of eastern Europe becoming its basic population stock. That stock no longer existed, and a central problem was how to compensate for the biological deficit after the Holocaust. There were farsighted Jews who foresaw the possibility that the 3 million "lost Jews" of the Soviet Union could be liberated and partly compensate for the demographic deficit left in the wake of the Holocaust. The assumption, which proved to be unfounded, was that they would all choose to settle in Israel rather than the choice of the United States favored by their grandparents.

By the late 1990s the demographic shortfall was on the road to partial solution with the successful release of Soviet Jews, over a million of whom ultimately settled in Israel. Victory in the '67 war gave Israel and American Jewry an enormous emotional lift, but the hoped-for light of peace at the end of the tunnel did not appear. Unresolved was the sustained low-level war waged by the Palestinians, which had successfully enlisted the support of the entire Islamic world and a good part of Europe's Socialist movement. Overshadowed by these life-threatening problems, the signs of decline of the American Zionist movement, which had been totally devoted to the development of Israel, was hardly noticed. By the 1970s its mass organizational base, once the pride of the community, was becoming a shadow of its former self. Hadassah, Pioneer Women (Na'amat), and the American Jewish Congress first experienced an ageing followed inevitably by a decline in membership. The summer-camp programs vanished from the organizational map, the lecture programs were unattended, the countless journals lay unread. Some organizations displayed a momentary glow of life by becoming virtual tourist agencies for Israel. But the spirit of building, of coming to be, was gone.[8]

We can speculate endlessly about the reasons for the decline. Such a transition is best viewed as part of the natural life cycle of modernizing communities. Few were concerned with the communal loss of social capital indicated by the decline of fraternal organizations. Social networks were no longer necessary for the college-educated postimmigrant generations. They now did for themselves what the myriad of fraternal organizations used to do. The welfare state with its pensions and Medicare did the rest. But few were aware that the weakening of ties of faith and ethnicity generated a cooler secular mind-set that the ever-popular sentimentalization of the Yiddish-speaking culture of their parents could not conceal.

There were compensations for the loss. During the early days of statehood few were able to foresee that Jewish American liberalism, which had deeply penetrated Jewish political culture with the New Deal, could furnish an additional link to the newly established Jewish homeland. There had always been a sense that Jews deserved their own state, for much the same reason that Poles and Czechs and dozens of national cultures were granted statehood by the League of Nations. It was natural and right, and in the Jewish case especially imperative after the Holocaust. When the state developed along the lines of Western parliamentary democracies, the liberal Jewish voter found yet an additional reason to support Israel. It complemented the prevailing liberal persuasion, that democracy was after all best for all, that dominated Jewish political culture. Zionism in effect seamlessly fit into Jewish political culture, whose highest expression was democracy. No problems were encountered in supporting a liberal domestic program and Israel at the same time. But with the election of Menahim Begin and the wielding of a "blood and soil" nationalism in May 1977, that tie between liberalism and Zionism too began showing signs of wear.

Some believe that the roots of American Jewish liberalism and the Likud disjuncture could be found in Israel's endless security problem. Liberals customarily view the overriding concern with the needs of national security, which requires budgeting for arms at the expense of butter, to be a difficult choice. Israel's Labor Party did not deny the need for security, but was sensitive to the enormous burden carried by the citizenry. Its position on issues like the West Bank settlements and the civil and political rights of the indigenous Palestinians was more influenced by secular norms than by the Likud. Aware of Israel's long-range need for peace, Israel's Labor Party and smaller associated parties of the Left were more willing to consider a compromise position not unlike that reached by American Jewish liberals to realize that end. There are few signs that a matching reasonableness would emanate from the Arab world, whose case against the existence of Israel was far simpler. The Arab world saw no reason why Islam should pay the price for the barbarism of the Christian world that sought to liquidate European Jewry. So argued Moslem spokespeople before international tribunals like the United Nations.[9] For some on the political Left the national self-determination principles of liberalism deployed to argue the justice of establishing Israel now seemed equally appropriate for establishing a Palestinian state. Some went further to state that the creation of Israel was a historical error.[10] American Jewry's concern for Israel remained undiminished, especially when there was ample evidence that governance in Israel was confluent with cherished liberal ideals. Still, the idea that there were two moral rights at play in the Israel-Palestine conflict, an observation submitted originally by Ben-Gurion, became increasingly the reality among some Jewish liberals. Many were sensitive to the fact that the creation of the state entailed an injustice to its Arab inhabitants. It was the two-state proposal, a solution implied in the 1947 partition plan then rejected by the Arab world, that became one of the foundation stones of the continuous peace negotiations. It is strongly favored by American Jewry and every American administration that has had to come to grips with the problem.

Liberal Jewish supporters touted Israel's independent judiciary even while they remained sensitive to the excesses of the occupation and the need for a Palestinian state, which they assumed would be equally democratic. Albeit imperfect, Israel has achieved a caring welfare state close to the model of American Jewish political culture. Its 1995 National Health Insurance Law offers a standardized basket of medical services including hospitalization. Like the kibbutz, Israel's welfare services appealed to the deeply held liberalism embedded in American Jewish political culture. Similar liberal proclivities were at the heart of proposed solutions for such issues as the Palestine refugee problem and the disposition of the West Bank settlements, both of which impinge on the long-range security of the state. The difficulty in finding a peaceful solution to these problems involves the very existence of Israel. There are no precedents for a nation voluntarily embarking on a slippery slope by surrendering almost one-third of land it claims against the wishes of a majority of its citizens. At the same time there are few signs that even a second and third generation of dispossessed Palestinians who identify their exodus in 1948 as "the catastrophe" is ready to move forward toward a permanent solution.

By 1970 American Jewry had a split-screen view of the situation in the Middle East. If "blood and soil" Zionism was anathema to the liberal Zionism that flourished in America, there were facets of the Zionist experiment that warmed the hearts of citizens of all sections of the political spectrum, especially the flourishing economy based on a developed "high tech" sector. If a division between Israel and American Jewry is indeed deepening, as some pundits maintain, it is rooted in the disparate political solutions envisaged for creating a stable peace in the region. That issue serves as the axis of Jewish politics in both communities. The division is not geographic. Israel's parties of the Left come close to liberal Jewish positions in America, and at times it seems that the staunchest proponents of the Likud position, especially regarding the West Bank settlements, are right-wing American Jews. On the surface it concerns such immediate issues as the future of Jerusalem, the "right of return" for Palestinian refugees, and the disposition of the West Bank, which would include the borders of the Palestinian state and therefore cannot be separated from the question of the Jewish settlements. After five failed negotiations both sides know what concessions they have to make to finally attain the elusive peace, but the yawning gulf between the two sides remains. In the public mind such consistent failure indicates that there may be greater historical forces at play involving regional ambitions of Iran and unbridled religious passions loose within Israel and the Palestinians in the area.

Liberalism versus Zionism

Israel's uncertain future is found in the ironic fact that her victories in war seemed to compound her existential problem. The fruits of the June War that led to Israel's occupation of the West Bank turned out to be toxic. The victory awakened the "blood and soil" religious nationalism that made the territories formerly governed by Jordan a burden beyond the ability of its fragile polity to absorb. The Israel polity was deeply divided between a fiercely determined religious minority who claimed the entire biblical land of Israel as their right and those who felt that the need to integrate over 1 million West Bank Arabs would undermine the Jewish character of the state. By the 1970s the disposition of what the "All Israel" movement identified as ancient biblical Judea and Samaria was becoming problematic. The settlements that had been developed by the messianic *Gush Emunim* (bloc of the faithful), mostly younger members of the National Religious Party, were growing with the help of indirect government budgeting. With the election of Menahim Begin in 1977, the settlement movement gained momentum and the rift between the Likud-dominated government and the liberal factions of American Jewry deepened.[11] For older American Jewish Zionists the change in the Israel polity and Zionism was a radical one. When they were young the militancy and pioneering spirit of Zionism reflected in the kibbutz movement and *Histadrut*, Israel's all-powerful labor federation, came from the Left. Now the expansionist zeal came from the religious Right, who insisted that they were carrying out God's will and that the Left, motivated by godless socialism, had in fact paradoxically acted as God's agent by preparing the way for the Messiah's coming. It was a difficult adjustment that some American Zionists were unable to make. Rather than opening a path to peaceful coexistence with the Palestinians, the victory of Israeli arms in 1967 exacerbated the situation so that six decades after the establishment of the state the Palestinian claim that it had been wronged seemed more alive than ever. Concealed beneath the hopeful UJA "We Are One" fundraising slogan, a gulf between the political Right and Left, which matched the rift between the Jews in Israel and American Jewry, had developed. Divisions between Left and Right were not new in either polity, but this one seemed unbridgeable.

Contrary to what many Jews imagined, the Palestinians were in the process of becoming a nation, using the very fact that they had been wronged as a building block. The staying power of the Palestinian resistance also had an impact on Israel's lively community of academic historians. A proposed change in the historic narrative questioned the official story regarding the origins of the Arab refugee problem in 1948 reinforced the feeling among some Jewish liberals that the Palestinian claims to the land had some validity after all and had to be accommodated.[12] The establishment and survival of the Jewish state was traditionally linked to the liberal preference for history's victims, to which Jews had a special claim. But for many liberal Jewish voters the sense that Israel warranted special care, that it was David bravely facing the Arab Goliath, was difficult to maintain, especially after the June War. Unburdened by the responsibilities that come with actually exercising sovereign power, the long-range answer to the Palestinian problem for American Jews was a two-state solution that held sway in the early stages of the crisis. Ben-Gurion had openly proclaimed that the land was large enough to accommodate both Palestinians and Jews, and Judah Magnes, the former American-born chancellor of the Hebrew University in Jerusalem, had shaped much of his public life on insisting on the rights of the Palestinian population. Before the creation of the state the left-wing Hashomer Hatzair faction of Mapam advocated a binational state.[13] Now the issue was drawn. By 2010 the question was whether the settlement movement could be halted and rolled back without tearing apart Israel's social and political fabric. Prior attempts to evacuate settlements by government use of its police power did not bode well for the success of such an enterprise.

We have seen that both liberalism and Zionism supported the idea of a Jewish state. But Zionism, which is basically a nationalistic movement, posed an inherent conflict with the universalistic thrust of liberalism, especially among younger Jewish voters who did not experience the Holocaust. Predictably, the concessions for peace that liberal American Jews are ready to make, willingness to consider evacuating Jewish settlements outside the security block on the West Bank, sharing Jerusalem with Palestinians for the capital of their state, and a solution to the refugee problem based on mutual compensation—goes beyond those most security-minded Israelis are willing to make. The pervasive liberalism of the younger American Jewish generation requires an abandonment of "blood and soil" Zionism and a readiness to take greater risks for peace. A seeming unbridgeable gulf developed between the Zionism of liberal American young people and the majority of Israelis. Those in Israel affiliated with the Labor Party, and other parties of the Left who share the "softer" peace strategy, have been pushed into a minority position. Many have become convinced that the former strong ties to Israel are waning among the upcoming younger generation of American Jews.

The disaffection that occurs when Jewish liberals are faced with a choice between their values and issues like the expansion of West Bank settlements does not bode well for the continued influence of the Zionist idea among American Jews, even when the settlements are defended as a requirement of national security. When American Jews are forced to confront that choice, it is clearly liberal universalistic principles that win out over nationalistic or religious ones. "Members of the less ardent Jewish streams will increasingly choose their liberalism over their Zionism," predicts one pundit, who points out that only 54 percent of non-Orthodox Jews below the age of thirty-five remain fully comfortable with the idea of an exclusive Jewish state.[14] Even if that figure is exaggerated, the greater reality is a growing generational dissent. The indifference to Israel and to things Jewish generally is part of a lack of concern for politics and a narrowing of focus on self. A good percentage of Jewish college youth has not entered the public square, and there is some skepticism if they ever will. There are no statistics available, but a general observation of the young people involved in the "Occupy Wall Street" movement does not yield the customary involvement of a disproportion number of Jewish activists one expects to find. The indifference to Israel, if indeed there is a specific indifference to Israel, may have little to do with liberalism and much to do with a general malaise regarding the direction the country is taking. It is too early to tell what Jewish youth is thinking about regarding Israel or if they are thinking about it at all at the time of this writing.

But among committed Zionists the absence of agreement is reflected in an emerging new organizational configuration that now shows conflict between two Zionist lobbying organizations. AIPAC (American Israel Political Action Committee), the older agency, generally follows the line laid down by Israel's Likud-dominated government. The newly organized J Street, named after the address of its modest offices in the nation's capital, joins Israel Forum and other agencies in strongly favoring a two-state solution and other concessions to pave the way for an end of the "occupation." Behind the widening breech is a near consensus in Israel's polity that Israel's existential problem requires strong security measures rather than the approach of a liberal-minded American Jewry that favors concessions to set the stage for two states living side-by-side in a benevolent relationship modeled on Canada and the United States.

But what of the sundry observations that American Jewish youth is turning away from Israel? Liberal Jewish families ostensibly raise liberal Jewish children. But the nurture and development of the highly secularized Jewish youth cohort, who composed a disproportionate share of the activists during the civil rights and antiwar movements that helped bring Lyndon Johnson down, went beyond their liberal family background to challenge the prevailing liberal culture that spawned them. They represent a less well-known aspect of liberal Jewish upbringing that assumes that reaching full maturity requires breaking away from communal and family authority in the name of autonomy and independence. One observer concludes, "Well before Jews achieve voting age, the majority have already staked their personal claim of independence from family authority."[15] In a word, denying the role of religious or governmental and even familial authority serves as one of the seedbeds of Jewish activism. The activists of the sixties and seventies developed along different lines than did young Jews who simply grow away from family and community and are self-involved and generally less politically concerned than their parents. The youth cohort of the Jewish New Left did not so much break away from communal authority as they challenged its leadership. That is what the strikes and picketing against the Jewish federations in various cities during these years signified. But when the Vietnam War ended, matters returned to normal and probably had only an oblique relation to American Jewish political culture. It was a kind of youthful rebellion triggered by the special conditions of the time.

It is not only that young Jews are becoming less Zionist-oriented than their parents and more liberal, but as observed by Peter Beinart and others, the younger generation of American Jews also seem more than ever to be busy getting their lives together and have placed concern for Israel on a low-flame back burner.[16] But even if the statistics deployed are reliable, they do not tell the entire story. Recent studies find that over the last quarter century, American Jewry's relation to Israel has been generally stable, and such decline of devotion in the younger Jewish generation as may have been discovered in other studies are more attributable to different life-cycle stages rather than generational turnover.[17] It is that they are younger and more concerned about their own future, one that is far less envisageable for the younger Jewish generation than it had been for the older generation. Will there be suitable employment as professionals? Will they be able to collect Social Security upon retirement? Will they be able to afford beautiful homes like their parents? After Iraq, Afghanistan, a critical economic downturn, and a deterioration of the nation's political process caused partly by the abandonment of the right wing of the Republican Party to retain the requisite standards of a "loyal opposition," it may be that America's Jews can no longer assume, as they have in the past, that a strong America will be there for them and for Israel.

Today, Jewish students on college campuses are less affiliated with Jewish communal life, especially its Zionist/Israel linkage. That disaffiliation was revealed by the research of the demographer Steven Cohen in 2007. The study has become the source of a tempestuous discussion concerning the tension between American Jewry's liberalism and its concern about Israel, which, in the face of the existential problem posed by the Jihadist phase of Moslem extremism, has veered politically to the Right. For some observers the tension is imaged in peculiar terms. Supposedly, American Jewish liberals leave their Zionism at the door when it comes to the question of abandoning the West Bank settlements, while more committed Zionists leave their liberal principles behind when it comes to matters of security like the arming of Hamas or Hezbollah. Unforeseen by either side is that political positions are also affirmed or denied by the flow of events on the ground. Arafat's 1982 Intifada and the more recent withdrawal from Gaza changed many liberal minds regarding the possibility of peace.

That seems to be what happened in Israel. The cost of subsidized housing in the settlements and securing them and the roads leading to them, added to the myriad of hidden costs, have limited budgeting for needed social welfare programs in Israel proper. The result has been a dire shortage of housing, a deterioration of medical care and the education system, and a general lowering of the living standards in the lower tiers of Israeli society. Maintaining a middle-class living standard has become impossible for many. The difficulty of life in Israel is not a new revelation. It may well be that the flow of emigration (*Yerida*) is fueled by the difficulty those starting out have in negotiating Israel's economic system.[18] There has also been an inordinate concentration of wealth, so that Israel has among the highest gaps between rich and poor among developed nations. The result has been an Israeli popular version of the "Arab Spring," a series of protests and street actions involving many thousands of young people. It is a new voice in Israel politics on which the weakened Left will surely capitalize by insisting that resources be focused on problems at home. Few pundits predicted such a development and fewer still comprehended its meaning.

Undoubtedly there has been some leveling of the passion for Israel, especially among the more liberal younger generation of American Jewry; but rather than being a response to the international outcry regarding the imagined injustice done to the Palestinians, it is also rooted in the fact that liberal American Jewry has never been a single-issue constituency. There are issues like the war in Cuba, Vietnam, Iraq, and Afghanistan that require the expenditure of American treasure and lives, and that arouse deep concern in the Jewish electorate. We have noted that the general engagement of American Jews in the issues of the day is high compared to the general voting public. That involvement is as an American Jew, not simply as a Jew. The fate of Israel is a primary issue, but it is not the only issue that concerns the American Jewish citizen. American public support for Israel has never been higher and may be part of the Islamophobic response to the destruction of the Twin Towers and the wars in Iraq and Afghanistan that followed. It is also possible that Israel may be witnessing a kind of "normalization" from the high levels of enthusiasm that prevailed during the years immediately following the establishment of the state and again after the '67 war.

That normalization or leveling of high ideological commitment may also be hastened in both communities by a fatigue factor. Except for the peace with Egypt, which turned out to be a cold peace, there seemed little hope that peace in the area would prevail. That uncertainty became clear after the war in 1973 and the Intifadas thereafter. The building of a wall to "lock out" suicide bombers seeking to infiltrate was fairly effective, but it merely led to a new tactic in an unending campaign to keep the Palestinian cause in the headlines. The Palestinians, aware that a direct military confrontation with Israel would lead to certain defeat, developed a form of low-level warfare that pitted a modern nation-state against an organized resistance that operated outside the state system and laws of warfare.[19] That tactic was behind the missile attack launched by Hezbollah in July 2006, an Iranian armed faction within Lebanon but not answerable to the Lebanese government. Compelled to respond, Israel launched a deadly land-based counterattack that caused many civilian casualties and massive damage to Lebanon's infrastructure. Operation "cast lead" in July 2009 against Hamas in Gaza had similar origins and results. Such low-level warfare does not pose an existential threat but disrupts normal life. When the effect of such attacks accumulates over a period of years, the resultant lack of regional security itself has a negative effect on economic activity and development. The sheer length of the Arab-Israeli conflict, with relatively little progress toward peace, is a sobering factor that created a conviction among many American Jews that there was little hope of a solution to the problem. The land of Israel that has occupied such a central place in the political imagination of American Jewry seemed destined to remain a beleaguered homeland compelled to exist in a hostile neighborhood. The crisis has been so long on the world stage and the attempts to resolve it so forlorn that, like an overdone marketing campaign, the Jewish and general public have been saturated and to some degree tuned out. The Zionist dream of normality, which since 1948 applied equally to the Jews of America, seemed more like a dream denied.

American Jews could not remain insensitive to the sometimes real but frequently contrived trespasses endlessly trumpeted against Israel by Palestinian propaganda. During the years of the cold war anti-Israel propaganda was not confined to the Soviet sphere, but was commonly circulated among the parties of the non-Communist Socialist Left as well. A knee-jerk anti-Americanism based on the conviction that Washington was the leading advocate of colonialism and Israel was its instrument became the conventional wisdom of the European Socialist Left. In its support of Israel, the "old Left" was now viewed as a failure. "We are all Hezbollah now," cried European Socialists desperate to display their revolutionary bona fides. Israel was detested not only in its own right but also for being bound to American imperial interest. Not far beneath was an anti-Semitism that did not hesitate to borrow wartime Streicher images to buttress its own.[20] When the right-wing Likud Party assumed power under Menahim Begin in 1977, the stage was set for a more divisive politics in Israel.[21] A favorite target for attack was the much-touted kibbutz movement, whose members were at the ideological heart of Israel's establishment and an important element in the American Jewish early "adoration" of Israel. Many older kibbutzim, which were not part of the nation's security perimeter, had never shown a profit and negotiated their indebtedness through special arrangements with the national treasury, as if they were exempt from having to balance their books. The charge from the Likud right wing that the Socialist-minded kibbutz movement had never really paid its way was not long in coming. The kibbutz had become a citadel of privilege rather than the symbol of renewal and rebuilding it once was. One by one the buttressing images of Israeli society were minimized so that the heroic images prevalent in the early years gave way to something less valiant. The diminishing of the icon of the *Chalutz*, plow in one hand and rifle in the other, and the kibbutz to which he belonged, had a negative impact among American Jews who, like other Americans, held pioneers in special favor. The *Chalutz* who devoted his life to the service of the Jewish nation was hardly the "cool" hero celebrated by the younger generation. Israel remained close to the hearts of American Jews, but they now were able to see Israel in less idealized terms. It was a nation like others with corruptions and vulnerabilities. Zionists had always spoken of making Jews a normal people, but few were prepared for this kind of normalization.

The loss or diminution of heroic icons undoubtedly contributed to normalizing the vision of Israel among young people. Aside from emotional exhaustion, there was something in the liberal mind-set of succeeding generations of American Jews that encourages a less proprietary approach to Israel. Aside from a universalistic worldview, liberalism, unlike its Socialist predecessor, had not developed a compelling "end of days" vision. We have mentioned previously that in many ways it was more a sensibility than an ideology. But Zionism was formed as part of the nineteenth-century ideology of liberal nationalism and focused on how to fulfill the destiny of one specific people rather than all of mankind. Just as the Poles would have their Poland, the Italians their Italy, the Jews would have their Israel. It was to be a Jewish state, not merely a state for the Jews. After the Holocaust the need for such a state seemed imperative.

Zionist nationalism, especially its religious component, demanded all kinds of contortions for liberals who were concerned about the universe, not merely a tribe within it. Israel's need for diplomatic, political, and financial support compelled American Jewry to narrow its broad interests. The need to master the practical arts of politics in order to mobilize support for Israel's security narrowed its natural universalistic thrust. To be sure, Israel had developed all the desirable attributes that capture the hearts of liberals, including a robust parliamentary democracy with an independent judiciary and a free press, which gave voice to an often raucous political dialogue. Its failures concerning the Arab population were not concealed. Its Arab population, composing over 15 percent of the general population, theoretically possessed the full legal rights of "citizens," but that concealed the reality that a kind of subcitizenship status had developed in which Arab communities got far less allocations from the government for infrastructure, schools, and roads. Israelis countered that neither do the Arabs pay their fair share of taxes.

In practice the concept of a Jewish state could not easily be accommodated to secular liberal principles like separation of church and state. Israel's dominant Orthodox branch jealously guards its monopoly on many family-related matters. It refuses to recognize the legality of conversions, marriages and divorces granted by the Conservative and Reform branches that prevail in America. The wall of church-state separation so central to the liberal sensibility hardly exists in Israel. It is perhaps the absence of that particular protection for a secular lifestyle that has become a serious source of tension between the two Jewries. By not permitting American-ordained non-Orthodox rabbis the right to practice their calling, an important group of opinion leaders is alienated. So fierce are Israel's religious wars that some secular Jews have given up hope that Israel can ever become a modern secular society where men and women are equal and the burden of citizenship, which is especially heavy in Israel, can be equally borne. The religious exemption granted by Ben-Gurion at the time of the founding of the state creates internal divisions within Israel and deepens the gulf that separates Israel from secular liberal American Jewry. The religious secular tensions are played out in a different arena in the United States. The various subcommunities of Orthodoxy in America have recorded demographic growth, but unlike the situation in Israel, Orthodox law does not establish dominance. Jewish secularism can hold its own in America, and while there are no precise statistics on attrition in the Orthodox community, the challenge of raising an Orthodox generation in a highly seductive host society must be a constant concern.

These areas where Israel's practices come into conflict with liberal principles are periodically reinforced by steps Israel feels compelled to take ostensibly for security reasons, but which in fact are often rooted in the political dynamics of Israeli society. They range from prohibiting public transportation service in most cities on the Sabbath to gender separation at the Wailing Wall (*Kotel*). The most significant of all, the settlements in the West Bank, grew out of a religious rationale and is primarily, but no longer entirely, an Orthodox phenomenon.

We have earlier noted that the narrowing the breadth of American Jewish political culture cannot be understood without taking into account the effects of the continuing security threat to the Jewish state.[22] At the same time, it is also true that for American Jewish liberals the security of Israel has become one of many issues, and not always the most important one, that moves Jewish politics on a given path. There is an abiding inner tension in American Jewish political culture. As long as Islamic fundamentalist factions like Hamas and Hezbollah remain irreconcilable to Israel's very existence and possess the ability to threaten Israel's security, the center of gravity of Jewish politics will shift to the right and the "softer" stance of liberalism, held by a majority of American Jews, will languish. The security of the state is given priority over everything else. But the unforeseen is always possible. In the case of a particular grievous attack on Israel, American Jewish political opinion can shift sharply to the Right. The weight of the Israel/Zionist element in American Jewish culture is to some degree determined by the way the historical cookie crumbles in the region. Should the ritually repeated Iranian threat to wipe Israel off the map become supported by atomic weapons and the ability to deliver them, there will be little talk of peace and reconciliation in either Israel or in the American Jewish establishment.

The omnipresent tension between liberal principles and threatening facts on the ground produces a sectarian flavor in American Jewish political culture. It is not a new phenomenon. Until the Holocaust, for Jewish thinkers like Hannah Arendt, Martin Buber, and Judah Magnes, the very idea of lessening the universalistic character in favor of establishing the state seemed retrogressive.[23] As in Socialist ideology and the original American form of liberalism, the power of the state was considered a threat to the freedom of the citizen, and those with a Socialist-Marxist tinge aspired for Israel to leap frog over the "retrogressive" bourgeois national stage of development. As long as the trespasses regarding the treatment of Palestinian citizens did not deepen, Israel's otherwise robust democratic processes continued to serve as a Jewish liberal bridge to Israel. The Israel labor Left, which has a close resemblance to Jewish liberalism, is aware of the weaknesses that have appeared. They are on an agenda of things yet to be achieved.

Finally, an important element shaping the Israel/Zionist aspect of Jewish political culture is how the Jewish voter receives and processes information about Israel. As Jewish citizens increasingly identify themselves as "just Jewish" but not affiliated, they are more exposed to opinion-shaping American media that view the Middle East problem as merely one of several facing the nation. The special ethnic focus such as former generations of Jewish readers may have gleaned from the Yiddish or Anglo-Jewish press barely exists today and is not part of the opinion-shaping force that informs younger secularized Jewish voters. Most news and opinions concerning the Middle East and other areas where news is being made to which formally educated, politically conscious American Jews are exposed comes from the national media rather than the Yiddish or Anglo-Jewish press on which their parents and grandparents were largely dependent. Today the view of Jewish issues received from the general media addresses a broad American readership and is necessarily more detached when covering stories of Jewish interest.[24]

To be sure, Jewish public intellectuals still play an influential role, especially among the disproportionately high number of Jews who are involved in intellectual pursuits in academia, publishing, and think tanks. These intellectuals and the courts that form around them act as sounding boards and amplify the view of the favorite "guru" of the moment who plays the role of opinion leader. Whether they are academicians, writers, journalists, or sundry essayists, what public intellectuals have to say is given extraordinary weight in a community that has a high regard for the written and spoken word and intellectualism generally. While the Jewish representation among the intellectual opinion leaders is disproportionately high, they do not transmit an exclusively Jewish message. Public intellectuals value their autonomy and consider themselves apart from Jewish advocacy. They seek to address a national audience. When

Jewish intellectual scholars like the late Tony Judt spoke of matters close to Jewish concern, their voice had a special resonance among Jews, but it is important to be aware that these scholars do not speak only to Jews.[25] On the other hand, Allan Dershowitz, the well-known Harvard Law School professor whose passionate defense of Israel is a constant feature of the Jewish media, has a lower credibility among the highly secularized Jewish intellectual class.

From the late Walter Lippmann to Norman Podhoretz, from Republicans like David Brooks to liberals like Thomas Friedman, public intellectuals influence the thinking of the political class who either by profession or inclination involve themselves directly in the political process. Jews are far from being alone in their deep involvement in the nation's political dialogue, but they are disproportionately represented in the opinion-making elite, which perforce sees the world through American eyes. Newspapers like *The New York Times* or *The Washington Post*, and perhaps a half-dozen highly regarded journals whose focus is sociopolitical high culture, such as *Harper's*, *The New York Review of Books*, *The New Republic*, and *Commentary*, project a distinct political voice, amplified today by certain TV anchormen like "Charlie" Rose as well as the bloggers whose comments fill cyberspace. These voices have all but replaced the Anglo-Jewish press in shaping Jewish public opinion. Public intellectuals who write in these outlets may share a vaguely Jewish sensibility, but they are not voices of the Jewish community nor are they necessarily supporters of Israel and Zionism. In a word, the voices that influence Jewish public opinion today are a far cry from those that once were read in the *Forward* or the syndicated coverage of the Jewish Telegraph Agency. When one adds to that readers who identify themselves as "just Jewish," the result is a Jewish citizen less involved in Jewish politics as it concerns Israel and related issues. It is not only the fact that the media that shape Jewish public opinion are less Jewish; it is that the Jewish reader is too.

The national media cover the Jewish story as part of the general news. Their coverage of the Arab-Israeli conflict can support or reject the Jewish position, if indeed such a position can be found. Jewish readers anxiously awaited Tony Judt's articles in *The New York Review of Books*, since he had Jewish credentials and in addition composed beautiful narratives. The work of John J. Mearsheimer and Stephen M. Walt that first appeared in *The London Review of Books* appeared subsequently in several "think tank" publications and was finally published in book form in 2007, *The Israel Lobby and U.S. Foreign Policy* by Farrar, Strauss and Giraux, was in a sense more limited to the "Jewish lobby" than the far-ranging comments of Tony Judt. The aforementioned contention of Peter Beinart that American Zionism has clashed with the liberalism of American Jewry and emerged the worst for wear are as much part of the American political dilemma concerning the excess influence of lobbying as they are exclusively Jewish. The Anglo-Jewish press, the monthly journals still published by some Jewish organization and agencies, no longer attract a significant Jewish readership. Broadly based media outlets whose primary interest is the omnipresent American debate on how the American national interest is best served shape American Jewish public opinion. In that narrative the Jewish interest, when it plays a role, is secondary and often incidental. The result is that the contemporary American Jewish voter comes into the arena armed with a cooler, more detached view conceived from the vantage of the American national interest. That may be close to the Jewish interest, but not necessarily identical with it. American public opinion media, which remains overwhelmingly pro-Israel, shapes the voter's position. Increasingly the voter views the Israel-Palestine conflict from an American rather than a purely Jewish angle. The support of Israel becomes less a passion and more a favored intellectual defensive position often argued in terms of how the national interest is best served. Once the shaping forces affecting the Jewish voter are understood, then the simplistic notion that young American Jews are abandoning Zionism in favor of liberalism can be viewed in context. What else can American Jewish opinion regarding Israel be but American?

Summing Up

Of the three factors here considered as decisively shaping the political culture of American Jewry, those related to the development of the American Zionist movement and Israel are most difficult to evaluate. The political support that Israel requires from Washington remains in many ways the primary focus of organized Jewish political activity. Yet while the passion for Israel has normalized since the heady days of the state's founding and the elaborate Zionist organizational structure has contracted, normalization would be quickly reversed should yet a new Iran-sponsored war against Israel become imminent. While the Jewish state has given American Jewry a homeland, because Israel remains threatened it can never play the role of a beloved but separate country as Ireland now plays for the American Irish, or as Italy plays for opera-loving Italian Americans, at least not while the normality promised by Zionism remains unrealized.

The triad on which American Jewish political culture rests—liberalism in its various forms; Zionism and commitment to Israel, its offspring; and the Holocaust—are intertwined but are notably different in how they fit into the amalgam that composes political culture. Each emits a different kind of signal that projects the sense that Jewish political culture does not emanate from one organically whole people. On the one hand, there is the Jewish state that has yet to gain acceptance and is therefore compelled to focus on its security. It is that circumstance that drives Israel's polity culture to the Right. To some extent that is true of the American Jewish polity as well. On the other hand, there is an element in both communities that is liberal, which locates itself slightly to the Left of center on the political axis. There may be little agreement among Jewish citizens on how best to sustain Israel, but few will take issue with the fact that both sides are devoted to doing so. Paradoxically, the genocidal rhetoric aimed at Israel that fills the airwaves weakens the liberal underpinning of Jewish political culture. Only two generations removed from the Holocaust, the liberal Jewish voter is bound to wonder if the nations that compose the "universe of obligation" that would assure the security of Israel can be relied on.

Jewish politics in the United States and Israel serves as an arena for the conflict between the universalistic element in Jewish liberalism and the nationalistic element in Zionism. The split within the Jewish polity between secular modernists, willing to find some accommodation for the sake of peace, and believers who view such accommodation as a betrayal of the faith, is also a symptom of Judaism's incomplete passage to modernity. There are Jews on both sides of the divide who are convinced that precisely that persistence of the tradition is where the secret of Jewish survival lies. Resisting modernity does not mean that the instruments of modern transactional politics remain unknown to the ultra observant. Orthodox conservative Jews have little compunction in forming alliances with Christian fundamentalists, who also have a special place in their theology for the Jewish return to Zion. Liberal Jews, including the secularized and those associated with liberal Reform and the Reconstructionist movements, do not view such support as a misalliance. They cherish Israel as a liberal democracy whose religiosity is acceptable in the same way that England's Anglicanism is. Western democracies are characterized by a willingness to depart from orthodoxies like church-state separation to find some form of accommodation.

The space for such accommodations seems to be growing smaller in Israel. The special "priest-like" status of the Haredi fundamentalists is increasingly challenged. The thrust of Israel's Right, whether it concerns judgments by military courts in the West Bank or racialist resolutions proposed in the Knesset, are signs that the security situation has taken a toll. Israel's political architecture, which so warms the hearts of Jewish liberals—a functioning party system, an independent judiciary, the rule of law—seems less immune from erosion. The wonder is that despite all, Israel retains a reasonably functioning parliamentary democracy, though she has experienced only a momentary truce in the sixty years of her existence. In its unending struggle for place in the region, Israel feels compelled to seek support in those sections of the political spectrum where it can be found, among the Neocons, Evangelicals, and those elements already at war with Islam who are inherently illiberal and prone to use raw power. The strategic dilemma of Jewish liberalism is that Israel's geopolitical situation compels it to fortify the state built on liberal values with corporeal military power that includes weapons of mass destruction. It is forced to forsake the most central principle of the liberal sensibility, that it be a free secular state composed of "citoyens" equal before the law, rather than a merely a Jewish one. While insisting that Israel stay true to its secular liberal principles, it witnesses its neighbors, Hamas in Gaza and Hezbollah in Lebanon, increasingly attracted to the Islamic republic form of government that abhors the secular democracy of the West.

At the heart of the problem of having a liberal secular state that can negotiate an acceptable peace is the unresolved issue of the role of religion. For the largely secularized Jews of America, religion is viewed as a cultural phenomenon rather than an agency that delivers a "diktat" to the state. We have noted that it was primarily the dire threat to Jewish survival posed by the Holocaust that convinced non- and anti-Zionists to support the creation of the Jewish state. They were able to reason that history had made an exception of the Jews, whose need for a homeland was a matter of life and death. Subsequently the fact that the Jewish state assumed a democratic form and demonstrated exemplary concern for social justice made the exception granted easier to negotiate.[26] In recent years, however, the idea that peace must be negotiated with a state that designates itself Jewish has become a stumbling block for Palestinian negotiators who speak of the need for secular democracy but at the same time must deal with people on their side who cannot accept an "infidel" state in the Islamic *Ummah*.[27] In a word, there is little in the current situation of deepening religious passion on both sides that encourages the hope that a way can finally be found to build a solid lasting peace. We can expect that the Israel issue will fuel and shape a good part of American Jewish political culture for many years to come.

If kinship, a common faith, and history bound American Jewry to Israel in the first half century of its existence, then one might justifiably wonder what will bind it in the second half when these three bonds have grown weaker. Still, the American Jewish tie to Israel is not an ordinary one. The investment made in assuring its survival is extraordinary, as if both communities are aware that they are all that is left of a once-thriving civilization. We have noted that American Jewry has always tilted outward to fulfill its obligation to *K'lal Yisrael*, and the continued challenge to Israel's very existence makes it the prime candidate for American Jewish attention.[28] That is a defining part of American Jewish history. Even in the unlikely case that over the passing years latent historic forces develop that act to loosen American Jewish ties to Israel, it could not easily manage to do so. Islam's hostility toward Israel has gone far beyond a political conflict over the same land. It target is Jews qua Jews, anywhere they reside. That extension helps actualize the bond between diaspora and homeland. That is, after all, what Zionism and the state to which it gave birth aspired to but could never fully realize. It has made Israel and the worldwide community of Jews one. In the torrents of anti-Semitic images projected by Arab propaganda, both are imaged as one and Islamic extremists target both. The attacks on Jewish communities outside Israel, in Buenos Aires or Paris or London or Portland, Oregon, indicate that Islamic terrorists make no such distinction. In the case of the blowing up of the Jewish community center in Buenos Aires, a non-Arabic Islamic terror squad was able to enlist the support of the local police. The current Iranian regime in Teheran considers itself at war with Jews everywhere.

These realities overshadow the recent speculation regarding the weakening of American Jewish ties to Israel. No one predicted at the outset of this unending conflict that Islamic hostility to world Jewry would provide reinforcement for American Jewish support of Israel. It is a particularly strong tie for American Jews who have witnessed the bloody suicidal attack on September 11, 2002, in Buenos Aires and the several attacks thereafter. American Jewry's commitment to Israel is only remotely connected to the organizational world of American Zionism, which is imagined to project an unhealthy influence on the nation's foreign policy. It is generated by ties of kinship and beyond that by a mysterious sense of being bound by history and a common destiny. It is beyond politics and ideology.

These people-to-people bonds will undoubtedly continue to link these two separate communities after the once-extensive organizational world of American Zionism has disappeared from the historical stage. From a historical perspective, the Zionist movement has after all achieved its objective with the establishment of the state. It now clutters the stage and competes with Israel's government. Today the priority given to Israel by the American Jewish voter is only remotely related to Zionist organizations like the Zionist Organization of America and Hadassah, which belong to an earlier generation. The American Jewish Congress, once the largest liberal Zionist-oriented secular organization, has closed its doors, while the still-surviving Zionist organizations are so riven that no consensus about a future course can emerge. Yet the perennial enemy is at the gate; at least many Jews still imagine their situation in those terms. There are blood-curling threats and physical attacks and terror that are viewed as an attack on Jews everywhere. Threats and terror attacks may seem an unworthy phenomenon on which to hang the survival of an ancient people. But in a strange twist they also serve as evidence that there are foes that view Jews as a special people worthy of attack even when some Jews have their doubts.

Strangely, contentiousness between America Jewry and Israel has its positive aspects. The mere fact that there is something to argue about is an affirmation of vitality. The contenders are alive and feisty. That became evident during the tensions during the Soviet immigration issue when Israel and American Jewry sometimes found themselves at loggerheads about the Soviet "drop outs" who insisted on resettlement in the United States rather than Israel, the "homeland" designated on their exit visas. Sometimes the conflict explodes into the open. That occurred when in May 1976 B'reira, a progressive Jewish organization that attracted young left-wing Jews, published a letter in *Interchange* under the title "The Time Has Come to Say No to Gush Emunim." B'reira was soon pictured as threatening Israel's security, and when certain members met with Palestinian counterparts, the Council of Presidents of Major American Jewish Organizations (CPMAJO) roundly condemned them. Clearly the perpetual crisis has narrowed the boundaries of what is permissible and changed the balance of power within the community. The Left emerged from the war in Lebanon in total disarray, while the once-premier centrist Zionist Organization of America (ZOA) has moved to the Right.

Not only has the world of organizational Zionism shrunk, but also the Left liberal position is diminished in the United States and in Israel. We have noted that the Israel issue shares the American Jewish agenda with several others issues, including how to recover from the deep recession and the weariness over sixty-year crises that seems irresolvable. Withal, for the foreseeable future candidates for local office or the

Oval Office risk the loss of Jewish support if they allow themselves to be labeled as anti-Israel.

We have seen that it was the creation of the Jewish state in 1948 that gave American Jewry an uncommon political focus on the welfare of the newborn state, especially in the years immediately following the founding. The most visible though far from exclusive manifestation of Jewish political culture is its focus on the security of Israel. That does not mean that there is always agreement on how it is best served. The primacy of Israel remains important to the Jewish voter, but with the development of Israel's economy and the ability to defend itself that interest shared attention with other issues of concern to the liberal mind-set such as the wars in Vietnam, Iraq, and Afghanistan, atomic proliferation, and global warming. Jewish leaders have gone to great length to assure American support for Israel and it has been that which more than anything else has generated accusations that Jews exercise an unhealthy influence on American foreign policy in the Middle East. For those preoccupied with concern about inordinate Jewish power, the unanswered question concerns finding actual evidence of the projection of such influence. Does American Jewish power account for what has become a virtual alliance between Israel and the United States, or did Israel, as a strategic asset, attract the American foreign policy establishment? In some respects it is a chicken and egg problem. For the Jewish voter, the paradox may be that the natural confluence of interest between the United States and Israel in the Middle East and other areas has inherent in it the possibility that it feeds the myth, central in the anti-Semitic imagination that Jews possess inordinate political power. The bitter irony is that the Holocaust has not put such mythical thinking regarding Jewish power to rest.

That the Arab world would be unable to reconcile itself to the existence of a thriving Jewish state in its midst was not acknowledged by most Jewish and many Allied leaders in 1948. Ineffective in almost every endeavor at modern governance, Israel's Arab neighbors found a measure of cohesiveness in their collective opposition to Israel. The ensuing conflict was waged by low-level warfare and an almost total blocking action on the diplomatic front designed to delegitimize Israel. Paradoxically, Jewish apprehension is sustained by the perceived Arab threat to Israel's security and fuels American Jewish hyperactivity in the foreign-policy area, especially the Middle East. That apprehensiveness contributed in some measure to making what was essentially a local conflict between Palestinians and Jews into a larger and potentially bloodier world conflict of a religious and cultural nature between Islam and the Western world. At the time of this writing the conflict seems more intractable than ever, which assures that events in the Middle East will remain a primary shaping influence of American Jewish political culture.

The mass popular rallies organized during in the early years of the state and the organizational structure to carry the Zionist message forward is no longer an important part of the American Jewish political scene. Political lobbies like AIPAC and J Street have replaced them, and the diplomatic delegation of Israel, guided by its separate mandate, transacts Israel's business directly with Washington.[29] Aside from political support of an important section of the American electorate, there is little in the way of philanthropy that Israel requires for its very existence from American Jewry. In the over six decades of Israel's existence, the terms of the relationship with American Jewry have changed. Israel undoubtedly welcomes American Jewish political support, but there is little agreement on what best constitutes such support and there is less need today for Israel to come "hat in hand" soliciting it. Israel has strategic importance in its own right that would earn Washington's attention even were there no Jews in America. That does not mean that the crucial Israel/Zionism plank will soon disappear from the political culture of American Jewry or from the party platforms during election years. Each party will outdo the other in the effusiveness of its Israel plank designed to attract Jewish political support. In the end, the welfare of Israel is, after all, a political question as well as a strategic one. But for the American Jewish citizen it is something beyond that. It serves as evidence that Jewry has survived a horrendous attempt to eliminate it from history. How that has impacted its political culture is the subject of the following chapter.

6

Holocaust Consciousness, Liberal Hope

If liberalism in its various manifestations represents the soul of American Jewish political culture, and Zionism and its offspring Israel represent its central focus, then the Holocaust is its obsession. The experience of genocide has been absorbed into Jewish communal memory now extended onto the third generation. It has become a major theme in its scholarly and popular journals. Memorials to the victims are omnipresent in its communal meeting places. Special prayers have been incorporated into its religious rituals. Drenched in the Holocaust experience, Jewish political culture contains a paranoiac streak whose threads are everywhere. Defense agencies like the Anti-Defamation League of B'nai B'rith are charged with ferreting out every sign of hostility.[1] The idea of having a haven in Israel that must accept all Jews by its "law of return" did not seem strange in the eyes of the wartime and immediate postwar generation who experienced the Holocaust either directly or indirectly. How could it be otherwise? Our task here is to discover how that trauma impacted the American Jewish political psyche.

Impact of the Holocaust Experience

It was a foregone conclusion that the Holocaust would challenge the optimism regarding mankind's potential for good so characteristic of liberal Jewish political culture. Many liberal-minded Jews became convinced that the primary assumption that there exists a caring world, or at least a world that can be convinced to care, did not apply for Jews. Yet the mentalité that

237

a concerned "civilized" world could be awakened to cruelty and injustice and would act, as it did not for European Jewry during the Holocaust, persisted. We have noted that Jewish liberalism, which is rooted in that optimism, is made of sturdier stuff that takes it beyond political ideology. Today it takes the form of sounding the alarms when genocide threatens. That accounts for the disproportionate Jewish membership in organizations that alert the world to genocidal threats in Bosnia or Darfur. The survival of Jewish civilization was insufficient: "Mere existence for Jews, *even in the wake of Hitler*," observes Bill Novak, a voice of the countercul-ture of the seventies, "is simply not enough."[2] The activism previously noted in Jewish political behavior finds its roots partly in that kind of rationale. When joined later to opposition to the war in Vietnam, activism, especially among the young, attained an uncommonly high resonance in Jewish politics.

Yet the presence of the Holocaust in Jewish political culture is differ-ent from its liberalism and Zionism. There are no lobbyists in the halls of Congress tirelessly promoting the Holocaust. In the sad note it plays regarding humankind, we see that the Holocaust is positively contrapun-tal to the liberalism and Zionism that share a place with it in Jewish politi-cal culture. It is the response to a historical catastrophe that came close to ending the Jewish presence in history, rather than a shaping political idea or cultural persuasion. Predictably, the Holocaust is far more rooted in communalism than in liberalism and Zionism. It is virtually impossible to find a Jewish congregation or fraternal order that is not programmatically involved with the memory of the Holocaust. Its communal journals, its museums, its scholarly conferences, its impact on religious ritual far out-weigh the resources devoted to the promotion of liberalism and Zionism.[3]

Still, politically the trauma of the Holocaust seemed to have little impact on the liberal core of Jewish political culture. Despite Roosevelt's resistance to the inclusion of the rescue of European Jewry in Amer-ican war aims until it was too late, the older generation of Jewish vot-ers remained committed to New Deal liberalism. In a sense the Jewish activism of the immigrant generation that focused on improving work-ing conditions was reborn when thousands of Jews living in America's urban centers gathered in massive protest rallies during the refugee crisis between 1938 and 1941 to appeal for admission of Jewish refugees to Palestine and the United States. In 1940 German Jewish children stranded in France by the outbreak of war became a special source of concern. But as previously noted, Roosevelt rejected the Wagner Rogers Act, which would have given them haven outside the quota, as was done for non-Jewish British children, "victims of the Blitz." Mass protest rallies with thousands of participants resumed in the immediate postwar period to agitate for the recognition of Israel and for the admission of Jewish DP's after the Harrison Report revealed that in many cases they were being housed in barracks together with their wartime tormentors. The liberalism still within striking distance of the social democracy of the immigrant generation believed that demonstrations and street action were the proper response to crises.

During the Holocaust years dissenting voices began to be heard regarding the hushed Jewish response to the Holocaust. In the case of Peter Bergson, whose group began with an effort to recruit a Jewish army and reached its peak in 1943 with the introduction of a congressional rescue resolution, the accusations against Rabbi Stephen Wise were sharp and telling. Yet they emanated from outside the community. Bergson and his group were Palestinian Jews, members of the Irgun, a militant right-wing group alien to the overwhelmingly social democratic qua liberal orientation of American Jews. Some blame the administration's inaction on the passivity of influential Jews around Roosevelt, members of the so-called "Jew Deal," Sam Rosenman, Isador Lubin, Ben Cohen, Herbert Lehman. Once the pride of the community, now they were roundly criticized for not having used their influence in the cause of rescue. In the search for someone to blame for their wartime failure, they did not exempt themselves. The exception was Henry Morgenthau Jr., a marginal Jew close to Roosevelt, whose remarkable rediscovery of a Judaism his family no longer practiced is discussed later. But Morgenthau was not a communal leader and before he became active in the rescue cause in 1944 he had few contacts with Jewish community leaders.

Rooted in a feeling of guilt about not having done all that might have been done, the self-blame continued for decades. In 1970 at Columbia University the Radical Jewish Union interrupted religious services to demand that Temple Emanu El, the flagship congregation of the liberal Reform movement, declare its opposition to the war in Vietnam. The protesters were arrested, but not before they accused the rabbi and his staff of being part of the *Judenrat*, a reference to the leadership that ostensibly betrayed Jews in the ghettoes of occupied Europe.[4] In truth Roosevelt's listless response to the crises went far beyond the failure of leading Jews in his inner circle to act. The possibility of including the rescue of European Jewry in the nation's war aims was beyond the political influence of American Jewry to achieve. By the time the light of victory could be seen at the end of the tunnel in 1944, most of Europe's Jews were already in ashes. But the sense of failure remained and is today deeply ingrained in Jewish memory.

The Holocaust experience too seems hardly to have moved the psychic furniture of the Jewish liberal mind that was by definition optimistic about the possibility of making mankind better, more moral, more caring. There was no campaign to purge Jewish political culture of what might, in a post-Holocaust world, be considered misleading and dangers beliefs. American Jews seem as inclined to do the "right" thing as ever.

The task of constructing the Holocaust narrative naturally fell to the numerous writers, researchers, artists, and spiritual leaders who sensed in their innermost hearts that their world had been shaken. Some used their new consciousness to warn about the shortcomings of American culture and society or to analogize psychic distortions that occur because of the experience of torture. Others saw the anonymous mass dying in the death camps or in the bombing of Hiroshima or Dresden as the extension of modern science to its lethal logical conclusion, reached when society's moral laws are broken.

Some note that the slight shift to the Right on the political spectrum may indicate such a loss of faith.[5] But aside from the Jewish voter's tilt to the center, that might as easily be attributed to the aging of the Jewish voting population; there is barely a change in Jewish voting behavior since the thirties and forties. Jews were liberal before the Holocaust and by and large remained so afterward. Yet the deep communal concern about

the Holocaust that is reflected in American Jewish life generally is manifest. Writers like Betty Friedan, Bruno Bettelheim, Robert Lifton, Stanley
Elkins, and others who are overwhelmingly secular and liberal and usually marginally Jewish extrapolated meaning from the Holocaust to help
explain a particular malaise in general society that was not necessarily
Jewish.[6] That could involve anything from prevailing racism or gender
discrimination to the decision to drop the bomb on Hiroshima on August
6, 1945. Betty Friedan, for example, compared the sterility of suburban
life for the captive mother as a form of concentration camp incarcera-
tion, albeit a physically comfortable one. Bruno Bettelheim and Stanley
Elkins viewed the experience of total powerlessness, as in concentration
camps or the slave experience, as leading to regression and infantiliza-
tion. Underlying Robert Lifton's writing is a perceived analogy between
the mass anonymous dying by fire in Hiroshima and the death camps.
The horrendousness of the Holocaust experience was used to buttress the
liberal critique of society, or at least their version of it, but the assumption that there is a one-to-one relationship between the Holocaust and the
lever a Jewish voter pulls down cannot be easily made.

A possible explanation for the constancy of left-of-center Jewish political culture stems from the Holocaust itself. The idea of a "solution" by
genocide of an imagined social problem stemmed from the Right of the
German political spectrum. In the United States, too, anti-Semitic incidents such as the lynching of Leo Frank or the ranting of Fritz Kuhn
and Father Coughlin inevitably came from the Right. The idea that anti-
Semitism could just as easily be incubated in the "Stalinoidal" Left did
not take hold fully until the infamous Doctor's Plot in 1953, though there
was ample evidence during the purge trials of the thirties that Soviet Jews
were distrusted. Add to that the moral complicity involved in the unwillingness of the witnessing nations and agencies to recognize that the Western world itself was burning in the ovens of Auschwitz, and you have a
case that indifference stemmed from the Right while the primary hope
that something might be done to save those that might be saved came
from the Left. There was a special disappointment when it became clear
that the Roosevelt administration, in which Jews had invested so much,
and the Vatican, which represented the moral spirit of Christianity, and

the International Red Cross, which stood for a similar caring spirit on the ground, did little to stay the hand of a state that implemented genocide as public policy. Even today Jewish citizens have difficulty fathoming the overwhelming power of the Axis and the fact that until victory could be seen at the end of the tunnel after the Nazi defeat in the Battle of Stalingrad in February 1943, Allied leaders did not feel they had the power to stay the hand of the executioners, at least not between 1940 and 1944, when most of the killing occurred.[7] In the mind of many Jews it was a murderous Nazi intent linked to Allied inaction that sealed the fate of European Jewry. But the degree of criminality of witness and perpetrator, as any good trial lawyer will attest, produce qualitatively different orders of guilt. The former is a moral failure not embodied in a code of law and therefore without sanction. Those most prone to accuse the witness of failure to act wield a liberal cudgel concerning moral behavior, one highly recognizable among Jews.

The Holocaust's most profound affect on the political culture of American Jews lies in the development of a catastrophe perspective that surfaced at the end of the war when the full extent of the Final Solution became known. Today threats to push the Jews into the sea, whether uttered by an Iranian foreign minister or a Saudi Jihadist, are taken as a serious threat to the survival of the Jewish people. A lesson has been learned. During the thirties few could imagine a government-administered plan to liquidate a segment of the population. Hitler's threats as explicitly written in *Mein Kampf* and later openly stated before the Reichstag were, to be sure, fearsome, but few took them as warning. A pervasive silence of witnessing nations could already be observed during the thirties when the depredations against German Jewish communities occurred. Imagining genocide was also difficult for its intended Jewish victims. It was especially hard for Jews to imagine that Germany would be its wielder. Before it embarked on its genocidal spree, American Jews considered Germany among the most advanced Western nations. After a late start Germany had gone far along the road to Jewish emancipation. Conceived and written by Hugo Preuss, a well-known Jewish legal scholar, the Weimar constitution (1919) became a high point in the emancipation process. In some cases it went beyond the rights of citizenship provided for Jews in other nations of the Atlantic community.

The Weimar Republic did not prevail and instead became the target of Nazi wrath. It was with the fall of the Reich and the opening of the gates of the camps that dotted the landscape of formerly occupied Europe that a sense of despair about the human condition took hold. Among Jewish survivors it was compounded by a catastrophe perspective that became embedded in its political culture, which amplified minor anti-Semitic incidents into portents of a coming genocide. In the case of the massacre of returning Jews in Kielce, Poland, the pogrom wasn't so minor.[8] As a rule surviving Jews were not welcome back, especially among the local people who had occupied their homes. The earliest postwar manifestation could be felt in the early fifties during the McCarthy period when many American Jews imagined that the espionage trial of the Rosenbergs (1951), coupled with the Slansky trial in Czechoslovakia (1952), was sufficient evidence that the murderous hatred of Jews behind the Holocaust had not magically disappeared but merely assumed another form. Strangely it had become as easy to imagine an anti-Semitic conspiracy in the Socialist camp as on the political Right, where McCarthy ranted about Communist infiltration of the State Department. The department had over the years earned a reputation of being unfriendly to Jews.[9]

The Holocaust Experience and Communal Politics

Perhaps the most crucial factor in determining how American Jewry processed the Holocaust experience is the role played by the survivors resettled in the United States after the war. Despite the fact that survivors had been granted the opportunity to share in American Jewish prosperity, a certain ambivalence concerning American Jewry's witness role during the war years sometimes prevailed. It may have been triggered by a historical, cruel comparison. The same war that brought death to millions of their European kin opened the way for American Jewry to accelerate their economic and social ascendancy. The question of the adequacy of the American Jewish response to the Holocaust might have arisen in any case, but the presence of the survivors who were beginning to play an important role in communal politics raised it with a special ferocity. Did American Jewry do enough?

At its heart lies the unanswered and perhaps unanswerable question of Jewish power. How much power did American Jews, who were not winning medals for popularity in the thirties, possess? Could Jews have done more to affect the basic foreign policy of a nation reluctant to enter the war, certainly not a war to save the Jews of Europe? Without some resolution of the power question the Jewish wartime and postwar communal response to the Holocaust cannot be resolved.[10]

The power question was complicated because the notion that Jews possessed enormous power was also at the heart of the anti-Semitic imagination. It was not simply a question of determining how much power American Jewry possessed, but also of determining the extent to which the inability of American Jewry to speak to Roosevelt with one voice diminished that power. The cohesiveness of Jewish communalism required to produce a coherent voice was weakened by the passion Jews invested in support of conflicting ideologies. During the war years it often seemed that there were several separate communities vying for dominance. Aside from the insufficiency of power to achieve the goal of rescue, it was also the absence of a single voice to speak to power that diminished its ability to make itself heard. The twin issues of Jewish disunity and Jewish power are central to determining the relationship between Jewish political culture and the Holocaust.

The Holocaust, which called on American Jewry to fully assume the mantle of leadership that for centuries was exercised by European Jewry, produced little agreement on what strategy to follow to save Jewish lives. Given Berlin's determination to see the final solution through to the bitter end, rescue options were limited and totally dependent on the actions of the American government. There were no independent rescue instruments in Jewish hands during the war years. American Jewish leadership was relatively inexperienced in international politics. Its debut on the Jewish world political stage did not fully occur until the negotiations at Versailles at the end of World War I, when Louis Marshall succeeded in getting minority rights clauses into the newly formed and reconstituted nation created by the League of Nations. Newly organized and plagued by fear of charges of dual loyalty, the American Zionist movement encountered resistance to the idea of a Jewish state. During the war years Zionist leaders still encountered difficulties introducing a commonwealth resolution calling for a Jewish state. Much of the Reform movement could not muster great enthusiasm for resettlement in Palestine and continued to oppose the idea of a Jewish state even after news of the deportations. We have seen that it required a special effort, engineered by Rabbi Abba Hillel Silver, to get the Commonwealth Resolution passed at the American Jewish Conference in August 1943.

When the crises developed there were admittedly few opportunities for a community that lacked sovereign power to act. The customary instruments of philanthropy were inadequate when deportations followed by ghetto concentration were involved and the war itself prevented such aid from reaching the targeted Jewish communities. When an ad hoc Jewish organization successfully negotiated a "Statement of Agreement" with Berlin that would have permitted the phased immigration of most German Jews over a three- to five-year period, it became clear that, even had such resettlement havens been available, such an endeavor was far beyond the financial and political power of private Jewish philanthropic agencies.[11]

We have seen that the Holocaust deepened the divisions within the Jewish polity, weakening its advocacy in the Oval Office. The president, who followed the example of Al Smith in drawing on Jewish talent, once wished that the Jews would have a pope, like "normal" ethnic advocates. Yet had Jews been able to speak to Roosevelt with one voice, there is little certainty that his administration's distancing itself from news of the death camps would have changed. Roosevelt was convinced that allowing German propaganda to picture the war as one to save the Jews would have interfered with mobilization. Better to inform Jewish emissaries that visited the Oval Office to plead the rescue cause that the fastest way to save the Jews of Europe was to win the war as quickly as possible. That was the strategy until 1944 when, possibly anxious about his hope for a fourth term and after conferring with Henry Morgenthau Jr., Roosevelt agreed that a War Refugee Board (WRB) should be established. The establishing of the board was the high point of the American rescue effort, but it was not established until January 1944 when much of European Jewry already lay in ashes.

Jews wanted Roosevelt to do more. But there was then no established legal mechanism for determining how communal interests and values might be transmitted to power holders. Since no legal instrument existed to determine who should speak for the community, all factions spoke for their clients at the same time. During the bitter years of the Holocaust, Hillel Kook (alias Peter Bergson), not an American citizen and representing a foreign organization, to the dismay of mainline Zionists, also claimed a leadership role and even opened an "embassy" in Washington to advocate a much stronger approach than did Rabbi Stephen Wise, who had occasional access to the Oval Office.

The crises revealed that despite its formidable organizational structure and philanthropic network, American Jewry had not yet succeeded in welding itself into a unified community. The resulting contretemps was not unlike the one encountered years earlier by Louis Marshall's reliance on legal strategy to try to wring an apology from Henry Ford and for the attacks against Jews to cease in Ford's *Dearborn Independent*. The idea of a public apology was anathema to the more militant "downtown" Jews, who favored direct action such as boycotts. Often leaders representing different factions of the same party assumed conflicting positions. Louis Brandeis could not agree with Louis Lipsky, head of the majority faction of the general Zionist organization, regarding fiscal and general management operations and eventually left the organization. Things had not changed much during the following Depression decade. Conflicts between the major national organizations and between communal leaders did not magically heal with news of the catastrophic events in Europe. The Zionism Rabbis Wise and Silver jointly professed did not bring them together. Jewish life was so fractious that a serious argument could be made challenging the assumption that there was a single unified American Jewish community during the years of the Holocaust. Subject to often bitter, unresolved internal tensions, Jewish leaders never succeeded in speaking to Roosevelt with one voice, even during a life-and-death crisis like the Holocaust. The unenthusiastic response of the Roosevelt administration to the Final Solution went beyond indifference. Many in

Washington only heard a cacophony of voices from the Jewish factions who claimed to speak for the community.

The communal strife proved exasperating for those national leaders who sought to unify the community in the face of the crisis. Since there was no communal political instrument that could yield an agreed-upon agenda, an "outside" organization like the Bergson group, convinced that the establishment was not doing enough, was determined to act as the gadfly. What decision makers saw during the years of the Holocaust was a riven people who sometimes seemed more intent on tearing one another apart than on accessing power. Though the political environment is much cooler today, communal fissures remain deep. In the absence of any fiat to govern, well-organized interest groups from the extreme Left and Right sometimes preempt the communal voice. The openness of American Jewish political culture, which encourages all legitimate interests and ideologies to contend for attention, means in effect that no one can speak for the entire community. The communal leader that finds his way to the center of national power represents only one of several contending factions. The Jewish voice that seeks to speak in the corridors of power therefore often seems confused and indecisive.

These factors hardly exhaust the reasons behind the failure of Jewish voices to be heard in Washington during the Holocaust. The structure of ethnic power, as compared to a sovereign power like Israel, is not wielded directly. In order to play a role on the world stage, special interest groups must enlist the American government to intercede diplomatically where their interests abroad are involved. That endeavor is problematic if the ethnic interest cannot be projected as concomitant with the national interest. In the case of immigration policy during the thirties, the absence of a confluence of Jewish communal with the national interests was apparent. As was previously noted, national public opinion strongly favored restriction of immigration during the Depression. From the outset, the possibility of getting the Roosevelt administration to offer haven for those fortunate enough to avoid the clutches of Nazi authorities was problematic. Not until 1945, when victory was certain, was the immigration law circumvented to permit a symbolic group of refugees to settle temporarily in Oswego, New York.

Moreover, Jewish communal leaders had not yet learned how to generate political pressure to shape public opinion and public policy. It takes years to affect public opinion, and on certain key issues like immigration, public relations cannot by itself realize the desired change. To this day the prospect of liberalization of immigration policy musters considerable popular opposition. The hyperactive communal advocacy of Jewish activists noted in the postwar years was first developed during the prewar refugee crisis. The effort was largely unsuccessful. Roosevelt was particularly adamant on immigration policy. By 1942 the issue had broadened to concern actual rescue. Here too there were difficulties. In the context of the national war effort, the projection of a special Jewish need seemed to many political leaders as unseemly special-interest pleading. State Department officials like Assistant Secretary of State Breckinridge Long stated continually that the law he was charged to administer clearly prohibited the admission of refugees. The failure to soften the administration of that law goes back to 1924, when the restrictive Johnson-Reed Act became law. Jewish leaders testified against the law during congressional hearings, to no avail. The possibility of changing the immigration law after the initial failure was almost nil. No amount of protest or activism could have changed that crucial fact. Such a response is especially rare when it concerns immigration policy during a depression.

The consequence of that failure was that the charge of Jewish indifference has become common currency in certain circles in the Jewish community. But in truth it was a case of democracy at work. There is no assurance that the democratic process will always yield a humanitarian response. Some researchers writing about the refugee crisis in recent years are so appalled at the hardness of the response in both London and Washington that their work reads more like a lament rather than a historical narrative. That is also generally true of the Bergson and Jarvik indictment of American Jewry and its leadership.[12]

Yet Jewish effectiveness in projecting influence on foreign policy was effectively exercised after the Holocaust to win Harry Truman's diplomatic recognition of the newly established state of Israel. The decision for recognition was made in the empathetic context following confirmation of news of the horrific working of the Final Solution. But the moment of communal harmony and joy that followed U.S. recognition was brief. Deep ideological and religious communal strains did not magically vanish. Dissent regarding the role the new state should play in international relations concerning the Jewish question soon surfaced among classical Reform leaders and other still powerful "uptown" agencies such as the American Jewish Committee. Yet there was some reason for hope. There was no group on the Jewish political spectrum that advocated return to the prewar condition. Thenceforth the Jewish communal dialogue was characterized not by a debate on whether a Jewish state should be in existence, but rather how the security of Israel could be best served.[13] That change reflects the new communal power arrangements after the Holocaust, which convinced the overwhelming majority of American Jews that the Zionist rationale for establishing the Jewish state was borne out by history.

That consensus was a far cry from the situation during the thirties and war years when agreement on how to respond to the refugee/rescue crises was nigh impossible to achieve. The Jews of Germany had to get out, but the *Yishuv* could not absorb all and resettlement elsewhere ultimately became the administration's priority solution, much to the chagrin of Zionists.[14] The establishment of Israel quenched the last embers of a heated conflict, but history does not allow us to forget the communal role of the American Zionist movement during the interwar years and the refugee crisis of the thirties. The contemporary split in the American Jewish polity between Right and Left, between AIPAC and J Street, is its contemporary resonance. The wartime division went beyond the customary tensions concerning budgetary sharing of the philanthropic dollar. It concerned such things as convincing Zionists to lend their talents and organization to alternate resettlement schemes when it became apparent that Britain would not abandon its restrictive immigration policy for Palestine, embodied in its White Paper of 1939, which limited entrance visas and land sales.

Then as today, immigration was a life-and-death issue for the Zionist movement. The anti-Zionist argued that despite the Holocaust it was still possible for Jews to find security and cultural fulfillment in the diaspora. Zionists did not need to argue at all. They merely pointed to what was happening in Germany, the most advanced of Western nations, to buttress their position that survival required an independent Jewish sovereign state. The argument, much toned down to be sure, continues to this day. But in the prewar years the practical rescue effort concerned widening the doors of America to offer haven to thousands, perhaps millions, of Jewish refugees between 1938 and 1941. Placating Arab sentiment was a cardinal plank in London's war strategy, which they were determined to uphold. The *Yishuv* was the only community prepared to help these hapless Jewish refugees, but like American Jewry it lacked the power to change basic British foreign policy. Sadly, had the Zionist effort to compel Britain to revoke the White Paper been successful, the Jewish settlement in Palestine would still not have been able to absorb the millions that required a haven in the unlikely case that the Reich would allow them to leave.

Should the Zionist movement have given greater support to the movement to resettle European Jews elsewhere, as in British Guiana and the Dominican Republic, when it became apparent that few established nations were willing to offer havens? Dozens of such small-scale possibilities were received by the Roosevelt administration. But Zionists like Rabbi Stephen Wise could not wholeheartedly support the resettlement of Jews elsewhere for the duration. That would deflect the needed funds to develop the Jewish settlement in Palestine. Resettlement elsewhere threatened what they believed was the best opportunity for Jewish survival. In years to come historians of the Holocaust will have to deal with the question of whether resettlement did indeed offer a viable opportunity for rescue and, if so, should the Zionist movement be held to account for missing a rescue opportunity.

The unresolved resettlement issue leaves in its wake the question of whether the Zionist movement made a strategic error in not abandoning its hopeless campaign to lift the White Paper and commit its resources, especially in pioneering, to the resettlement movement. The Bergson group was alone among the Zionist organizations that counseled the separation of the homeland from the rescue goal as offering the best opportunity for rescue. These conflicts were not resolved during the crises and continue to this day to be debated in the historiography of the American Jewish response.[15]

It was also the resettlement question that, together with the commonwealth issue, stood in the way of a single communal voice reaching the Oval Office. Paradoxically, the failure to come together during those critical years also undermines the classic anti-Semitic notion that there exists Jewish political power and coherence able to pull the nation's foreign policy out of its self-interest grooves toward the Jewish interest. Even if such a possibility existed, American Jewry would probably not be able to agree in which direction to pull.

In the desperate years of the Holocaust the rescue measures called for seem unrealistic today. The term "genocide" had not yet been invented, but it was clear that the Reich was intent on liquidating European Jewry and had already invested resources to achieve that high-priority goal. The militant Zionist Revisionist Bergson group mounted an often effective campaign to break the curtain of silence that had descended on the Final Solution, yet even its voice was drowned out by the news of the war itself.

Today it is difficult to imagine that political, class, regional, and religious divisions resulted in the lack of coherence in the Jewish voice projected at the Oval Office and Congress. By the time the war came in 1939, the descendants of the eastern Jewish immigration formed the demographic core of American Jewry. They supported Roosevelt not because of his foreign policy, which they felt was too timid in opposing Hitler. They loved him, we noted, for his willingness to use government power in a Keynesian countercyclical program to fight the Depression. There would be relief, and then recovery, followed by reform of the system. For the eastern European Jewish immigrants and their children, the economic intrusion of the New Deal into the economy reinforced their social democratic proclivities. It also brought the Jewish electorate fully into the political system and enabled them to vote for a patrician Episcopalian, which they did in overwhelming numbers.

The New Deal not only built a bridge to allow the Jewish voter to cross into the American polity but it also imposed some coherence on a widely diverse community. Unfortunately that unity was confined to two major issues. Jewish voters were virtually unanimous in their support of a regulatory role of government in the economy and they strongly favored intervention to counter German expansionism in Europe. But on issues like the role of faith and secularism and how best to organize society, they divided on the basis of class, region of origin, and cultural values, even on diet. Superimposed on a culturally and ideologically fragmented community was a tripartite division of the religious enterprise, which often had a negative spin-off effect on communal cohesiveness. In its moment of great need the Jewish electorate found little common ground within itself and with the national community of which it had become part. The political reality was that the Roosevelt revolution was virtually the only thing Jews agreed on. In all else their communal politics was strife-ridden. The president did not have to speak to Jews at all or could speak only to those Jews he preferred. The four attempts to bring the major organizations under a single umbrella to represent American Jewry to the Oval Office failed. Instead American Jewry, which had developed an extensive organizational infrastructure, remained divided. Few imagined that the proliferation of organizations was in fact a symptom not of communal health, but of fragmentation.

Still diversity of interests is often a sign of democracy at work. A clearer, more coherent voice might have been achieved had some modicum of unity prevailed. Yet even then there can be little assurance that sufficient political leverage could have been mustered to compel a reluctant Roosevelt to address the travail of European Jewry. American ethnic politics was based on the assumption that a common Americanism would in time displace the group consciousness of the immigrant voting blocs. In the throes of such a displacement, American Jews were in the process of developing into a voluntary voting constituency less bound by ethnicity and less deliverable at the polls. There existed no legal political mechanism to formalize the leadership process within the ethnic communities, so that it was not possible to determine who spoke for American Jewry. We have previously noted that in practice anyone so inclined could make such a claim and sometimes did. When in January 1944 the president modified his "hands-off" strategy on Jewish matters to form the War Refugee Board, it was done at the behest of his Jewish secretary of the treasury, Henry Morgenthau Jr., whose affiliation with the organized Jewish community was strengthened as a result of his awareness, as a government insider, of the actual operation of the massive German genocide operation.

We leave for last the most pervasive condition of all, the centuries-old process of becoming modern, which leads inexorably to the loss of tribal wholeness. Jewry, especially the Jews who risked immigration and transplantation, by pre-selection were more open to the modern. That may partly account for the speed with which they changed from a collective tribe of six million to six million tribes of one. That process has released enormous new energy but also meant the loss of a single communal voice. It is as futile to condemn American Jewry for disunity during the years of the Holocaust as it is in assigning them a single pervasive political persona today. Variation is the hallmark of modernity. For contemporary Jewry the bitterest irony may well be that the memory of the Holocaust serves today as one of the unifying threads in the community. The memorialization of the Holocaust is a linchpin of Jewish communal cohesiveness that could not be developed during those years. Instead its memory has become a lesson on the price of disunity.

Politics is about power, how to get it and keep it. Through law it civilizes man's Hobbesian struggle for personal power. After all is said and done regarding the Holocaust, it is the power question that was the grand determinant of policy. American Jewish disunity during the Holocaust is important because in theory it affected its communal power, its ability to speak to the Roosevelt administration with one voice. To make a judgment on what decisions were and were not made by the Roosevelt administration, we need to know how much power American Jews possessed to shape public policy as well as how much power Roosevelt had to discharge the responsibilities that come with power. We have noted elsewhere how problematic the power calculus is in a society where much of it is exercised in the private realm. There are also countervailing power holders to oppose the Jewish interest. Immigration restrictionists in Congress were a formidable power in the thirties. Political power in America is in constant flux. The Roosevelt of the "one hundred days" was not the Roosevelt of the ill-fated court-packing scheme and the renewed economic crises that began in 1937. Indeed, we need to know something about possibilities. In the absence of sovereignty how much actual power did American Jewry have to fulfill the role it assigned to itself? Could they have met these self-assigned responsibilities as an ethnic group seeking to enlist the help of the federal government?

The question of the American Jewish response to the plight of European Jewry during the Holocaust has become a major determinant of how American Jewry views itself. That in turn contributes to the shaping of its political culture, whether it is inclined to overuse or underuse the influence available to it. It also requires an understanding of where men like Henry Morgenthau Jr. and the Jews Roosevelt chose to bring into his inner circle of advisers belong in the decision-making process. Trying to influence American wartime priorities to include rescue was far less possible than projecting Jewish support for domestic policy or purely political issues such as Roosevelt's quest for a fourth term.

There is little agreement on what political power actually consists of. At its source is the ability to garner votes, but power it is also corporeal, composed of tanks and guns and bombs and also ideas, values, and assumptions about how life is best lived. American Jewry's witness role during the Holocaust was limited to acting through the American government, where even the amplification of its influence beyond 3.5 percent of the population did not give it nearly sufficient power to change wartime priorities. Anti-Semitic rhetoric notwithstanding, even a fully empowered Jewry skillful in using public relations to amplify its power did not come close to controlling the nation's wartime priorities. To imagine that it was otherwise, as many do, is evidence of the continued prevalence of mythic thinking. But Jews were empowered during the New Deal as were many other subcultures in the broad New Deal coalition. Especially noteworthy was the number of Jews in Roosevelt's inner circle. The role of one such is our next focus.

A Holocaust "If Only":
Mobilizing Prominent Jews Near Roosevelt

For American Jews who advocated the rescue of their brethren during the war the charge of indifference is especially painful.[16] Already noted is the skepticism one should maintain in the ability of a comparatively small ethnic minority to change wartime aims. That may account for the Holocaust narrative being full of "if onlies," desperate thoughts on how European Jewry might have been saved. One of the most popular relates to the bombing of Auschwitz and the rail lines leading to the death camp.[17]

The idea of rescue through direct intervention in the killing process through bombing began in earnest in 1943 after the Fifteenth American Air Force occupied air bases in northern Italy, which brought Auschwitz within range. That gave rise to one of several "if onlies" that trouble not only researchers but also all who were effected by the genocide. The bombing of the camps became the most popular "if only" among survivors who actually saw Allied aircraft flying over the camp on their way to bomb the nearby Bunau works. It became for them the "silver bullet" by which rescue could be achieved in time to save lives. But it was never done and instead it became a source of endless controversy.[18] Much of that controversy involves the discussion of possibilities that, as in the case of liberalizing American immigration policy in the thirties, are again related to political power. The American people did not want to admit refugees during the Depression, as they don't want to admit refugees from Mexico and Central America today. The bombing of Auschwitz would have garnered some symbolic importance, but achieved at enormous cost of Jewish lives and the danger of Allied collusion in the Holocaust. Even if such power could have been mobilized, it is doubtful that the Roosevelt administration would have been receptive to an act that could then be imaged to make World War II a war to save the Jews. From a historical point of view, the problem with historians who muster evidence that bombing Auschwitz was possible do not include the political context in which such a decision had to be made. For our purpose here, it is important to recognize that beneath the memorialization process, which reflects the important place the Holocaust has in American Jewish consciousness, political and otherwise, there is a tangled web of conflicting opinions on what the experience means and how best to transmit the memory of what was lost.

Another concerns the missed opportunity to mobilize the Jews in Roosevelt's inner circle of advisers. We note that most of these rescue opportunities were not realizable and grow out of a certain desperation, but the idea of recruiting Roosevelt's Jewish advisers in the rescue effort has the aura of possibility because the recruitment of Henry Morgenthau Jr. in the rescue effort did contribute to the rescue of nearly half of Hungarian Jewry. He is likely to go down in history as the most powerful political leader to emerge from American Jewry and perhaps from world Jewry. It was the high point of an otherwise listless American rescue effort.[19]

Morgenthau Jr. was called on to fulfill a Jewish need because he happened to be in the inner Roosevelt circle as a result of geographic proximity, the Morgenthaus were part of the Democratic machine in Roosevelt's Dutchess County. Morgenthau became the only Jew who was part of Roosevelt's inner circle of advisers whose family was also drawn into the president's social circle. He became one of the most influential cabinet members in the administration.[20] The family owned a farm in Fishkill, not far from Hyde Park, so that it was natural for political ties to be supplemented by social ones, especially when the Morgenthaus had been generous in their financial support and had a son who could serve as a "gofer." Morgenthau's role during the Holocaust offers researchers a prism to observe how Jewish group interest during the Holocaust years ultimately came down to finding a personal conduit to the Oval Office.

Unlike communal leaders like Jacob Schiff or Louis Marshall, Henry Morgenthau Jr. was a marginal Jews who until 1946 had never attended a Passover Seder, the most often-mentioned instance of Jewish observance. He became active in Jewish organizational life only after he resigned from the Treasury Department after the death of his mentor in April 1945. The family contributed to Jewish philanthropy and Morgenthau Sr. helped establish the Free Synagogue ("no dues, no pews"), but preferred a Christmas tree during the "season," not a Chanukiot.[21] For most of his twelve-year public service Morgenthau was reluctant to endanger his ties to the president, who was his mentor and close friend, by raising matters of specific Jewish interest like the refugee crises of the thirties. But as bits and pieces of inside information about the actual operation of the Final Solution crossed his desk and he was made aware of the concealment policy of the State Department, he finally mustered the courage to approach Roosevelt. Strangely, it was Morgenthau's three non-Jewish assistants who in January 1944 furnished him with the data on the State Department's blocking role and impressed upon him the urgency of doing something. That led to the creation of the War Refugee Board and the eventual rescue of half of Hungarian Jewry. Other Jews in the Roosevelt entourage, such as Felix Frankfurter, Sam Rosenman, or Bernard Baruch, rejected such a role. Morgenthau not only fulfilled it but also went on to invent his Jewish affiliation through it. He came to Jewishness via the role his high position in the administration allowed him to play in the rescue drama.

Morgenthau went from being an unaffiliated Jew largely unaware of his religious identity to becoming passionately concerned with the welfare of Israel. The conception and promotion of a plan for the treatment of postwar Germany occupied much of his remaining time in office. Morgenthau emphasized the need to deprive Germany of the industrial capacity to pose a future threat to world peace rather than retribution for the genocide. Germany's industrial plants, especially the concentrations in the Ruhr and Saar, would be pastoralized. The initial positive reception of the plan by Roosevelt and Churchill at the Quebec conference in October 1943 was gradually muted. In August 1944 his position paper *Germany Is Our Problem*, which argued for a Carthaginian peace for the about-to-be defeated Reich, was made public. For a while the Morgenthau Plan gained the agreement of Roosevelt and Churchill, but as the war approached its end and tensions with the Soviet Union began to build, the Morgenthau plan was all but abandoned. Germany would become a prospective ally in the cold war. Morgenthau's influence with Roosevelt on Holocaust matters and postwar treatment of Germany did not survive Roosevelt's death in April 1945. James Byrnes, who became Harry Truman's secretary of state, adamantly opposed Morgenthau's intention to attend the Potsdam conference, where he could advocate his plan for the defeated Reich.

Morgenthau's conversion to activism was probably not an uncommon one in the postwar years. The realization that complete assimilation did not offer protection from a massive anti-Semitic onslaught such as the

Holocaust undoubtedly drew some Jews to reexamine their heritage. His enlistment in the rescue cause suggests that mobilization of Jews in Roosevelt's inner circle offered a realizable opportunity for rescue, especially in 1944 after the tide of war turned in favor of the Allies. He leaves us with an "if only" that might have had an effect had more Jews close to the Roosevelt administration allowed themselves to speak out.

The other "if only" that comes close to realization and might have saved many lives during the refugee phase was the possibility of resettlement, which we have already probed in some detail. The possibility of tucking European Jewry away in some tropical rain forest had an allure in Berlin, where for a moment Madagascar drew attention, as well as in London, which offered British Guiana as a kind of substitute for Palestine. Roosevelt, who fancied himself a nautical person, was also much taken with using Europe's unwanted Jews to pioneer new nation-building enterprises in Africa. It had the advantage of allowing the president to maneuver around the vexing White Paper issue. The White House sponsored dozens of such prospects, but when Alaska and the Virgin Islands were suggested the administration turned a deaf ear. Thousands of entrepreneurial Jews sponsored by the Joint Distribution Committee might have helped the development of a virtually empty Alaska and solved its security problem at the same time.[22] But it was not to be. The State Department did help establish a colony of about eight hundred Jews in Sosua, in the Puerto Plata region of the Dominican Republic, but it was a singular case.[23]

Generally the prospects for successful resettlement were not good because the demographic profile, a highly urbanized, ageing European Jewish population, was not suitable for the kind of agricultural pioneering that was called for. It also required retraining, which was costly. We have already noted that the Zionist movement, which alone in the Jewish world had resettlement experience, was opposed to subsidizing Jewish refugees to settle elsewhere.

The most agonizing "if only" was the possibility that Britain could be convinced to abandon its inhumanly political policy of limiting Jewish immigration to Palestine in the teeth of Berlin's extrusion policy. Had the Zionist aspiration to undo the White Paper been realized in time, many more lives might have been saved. The earlier establishment of a Jewish national home in Palestine armed with sovereign power would have allowed Jews to at least defend themselves. In a perverse way the Holocaust buttressed the Zionist rationale that a return to the ancient Jewish homeland was the only solution that could save lives. The universalistic solution proposed by Bundists, that Jews could thrive as "citoyens" of the "Jewish persuasion" in a secular state, was dangerously misleading and based on a misreading of history. The establishment of the state in 1948 and the defeat of Arab armies that tried to prevent it, followed by the absorption of thousands of survivors from the charnel house of Europe and the ghettoes of the Mahgreb, served as additional evidence that, given support of a sovereign power, resettlement might have saved the Jews of Europe had there been a will to do so.

The proliferation of "if onlies" is not limited to the world of scholarship, but rather may indicate an early inability of Jews to come to terms with the fact of the Holocaust and the radical losses of life it left in its wake. For American Jewish political culture, that difficulty has a particular resonance. A kind of "normalization" is underway through memorialization. But those who foresaw a faster accommodation seem destined to be disappointed. Communal activity related to the Holocaust shows little signs of diminishing. It may be that specific threats of genocide against Jews and continued acts of genocide allow the memory of radical losses to remain fairly immediate in the Jewish political consciousness.

A Variety of Copings with Catastrophe

The Jewish response to the catastrophe of the Holocaust is not cut from a single cloth. The Zionist response was simple in its directness. If there is murder in the heart of the Christian world then a Jewish state should remove the Jews from the killing grounds. But for American Jews whose Zionism was nominal, the response problem was not so easily resolved. The Holocaust reinforced a Zionist rationale while at the same time it challenged the liberal assumption of basic human goodness. Liberals might reason that man's better nature had been momentarily overshadowed by the war and could be reestablished. Indeed, the return of Europe to prosperity and a caring humanistic culture was evidence of that happening.

Most impressive for Jewish liberals was Germany's economic miracle that enabled her to try to compensate for some of the damage done by reparations to individual survivors and to Israel. Some European nations criminalized the denial of the Holocaust. Not all Jews accepted the idea of reparations, but for most, the belated recognition of the travail of European Jewry during the war was welcome.

It paved the way for a kind of reversion to liberal normality touched on in the previous chapter. Jews were in the forefront for alerting the world about the myriad dangers facing humankind, from the threat of an atomic arms race with the Soviet Union to the telltale sign of the possibility of new genocidal bloodletting in Africa and Bosnia. They were again disproportionately involved in the peace movements and programs to feed the starving masses of Africa and Asia and halt impending genocides, as in Darfur. The disproportionate Jewish representation in these activities and movements is all about restoring their faith in mankind and, the Holocaust notwithstanding, their optimism that the trajectory of history to ever greater progress has been restored. The response of Jewish liberalism to the Holocaust was in effect that they would do for the world what should have been done for European Jewry during the Jewish crucible. It is a kind of exercise in restoring the Jewish liberal soul, which had been seriously undermined by the Holocaust.

In the memorialization of the Holocaust there is a division between those who refuse to speak about it and those who speak about nothing else. The last mentioned include professional Holocaust promoters who earn psychic and sometimes real income from speaking about the event, either as witnesses or victims. There is also a growing number who have become so saturated with Holocaust films and books that they have become inured. That inurnment is a far cry from the imagined indifference during the Holocaust of which American Jewry has been accused. That charge has become a major issue in the communal dialogue and in the historiography of the American Jewish aspect of the Holocaust. It was a divisive factor in the early postwar years and subsequently spilled over into its political culture and is reflected in the writing of its history, particularly regarding the memorialization process that has become central in Jewish communal life.

The telltale signs that the inclusion of the Holocaust in the world historic narrative would be problematic stemmed from two sources. The denial of the Holocaust had become a standard element in the anti-Semitic mind-set, which was amplified when it was adopted by some of the Islamic media to make points regarding the existence of Israel. We have noted that Islamic leaders argued that their world was being forced to pay the price for a genocide with which it had nothing to do. Other victimized groups felt that their story also deserved telling. At the United States Holocaust museum, which is partially tax supported, a serious conflict developed regarding a decision to include the Turkish genocide committed against the Armenians in the museum's programs. Passionate opposition to the idea, particularly among survivors, developed. Some felt that there was no parallel between the two events and that the particularity of the Jewish experience would be diminished. A similar reaction occurred when the memorialization of the Roma, who were also targeted for genocide, was proposed. Those opposed to the inclusion of other victimized groups believed that such analogous events would subsume the Holocaust beneath the general category of man's inhumanity to man, and that by their nature, memorialization, whether in the form of museums or monuments, ought as far as possible to be group specific and personalized. Some researchers observed that the Soviet Gulag took more lives than the death camps of the Holocaust. The Soviet killing was not confined to Jews or the implementation of some social Darwinist race-purification theory. It was more likely to target a class or subclass such as Kulaks (land-owning peasants) or simply people who ran afoul of the security apparatus. The government-implemented famine in Ukraine, which took the lives of millions, was also seen as a genocidal program, though Soviet policy did not aim at elimination of Ukrainian people and lacked the systemic characteristic of the death camps; no piles of human hair were carefully salvaged, no gold fillings were collected, no thousands of pairs of shoes and clothing were saved to be reintegrated into the Reich's wartime economy. The surfacing of these other mass killing operations indicated that Berlin's Final Solution was simply a particularly heinous example of a policy of government-sponsored mass murder associated with totalitarian regimes.

But as research progressed it became apparent that while the model of a modern industrial process to produce so many units of death gave the Holocaust a depth and organization that differentiated it from other mass murder events, not only was genocide not historically uncommon but the practice also continued in our own time. So went the counterargument used against those who believed that something radically different concerning primarily the Jewish people had occurred in the death camps. For the Jewish voter the very notion that it was just another mass murder common in history was not acceptable. In the end the Final Solution was a public policy implemented by a modern nation-state that specifically intended to liquidate the Jewish people and also any trace of its history.

On the one hand, there were some who were convinced that the casual grouping together with other wartime atrocities demeaned the Jewish victims. More important, by concealing how the Holocaust was different it acted to conceal the portent of danger represented by the massive social cannibalism of the Final Solution. It was a case of man consuming his own kind by a systemic killing process. There was nothing like it to be found in human history. But there were also those on the other side who, appalled at "shoah business," believed that the Holocaust experience was being used to gain "an income of victimization" both in the political and economic realm.[24] It was that struggle against the anonymity of the dead through mass killing that began the massive effort to identify the victims and sacrilize the killing grounds. The passion to do so may have stemmed from the feeling that the intent of the Final Solution went beyond the taking of Jewish lives. It was also aimed at depriving the Jewish people of their history.

Today not a day passes without some Holocaust story in the media, some news of a new curriculum or museum exhibit, a new movie or play or memoir—the stream is endless and shows no sign of exhaustion. Many survivor memoirs, often privately published, are written as a kind of bibliotherapy that might purge them of the demons that plague those who have experienced indescribable human torture. If there is such a thing as a collective Jewish communal voice, then the endless rhetoric about the Holocaust is saying that we are here. Survivors sound the alarm that genocide remains possible and perhaps even imminent. The witness is obliged to tell about his or her experience as testimony for the affirmation of life. Holocaust memorialization has become a communal ritual that goes beyond the obligation to remember. It is the most powerful affirmation in Jewish political culture of the existence of a self-conscious community.

Strangely, there is also an involuntary element in the propagation of the Holocaust story. It is as if the story feeds on itself. The flow of Holocaust literature, films, and plays, many written and staged by non-Jews, is fueled by the incomparable pathos of the event. Each episode of the terrible happenings that compose the Holocaust story, every family deportation, each dramatic rescue, serves the searching artist with a theme or plot to weave his or her tale. The omnipresence of the Holocaust in American and world culture goes beyond the notion of yet another wartime atrocity to be healed by the passage of time. It speaks to the historical weight of the event.

The very act of projecting a Holocaust message to the world is bound to universalize it. The term "genocide" as conceived by Raphael Lemkin had specific characteristics and was designed originally to describe the destruction of European Jewry. But it soon became common usage for many historical slaughters, from the destruction of the American Indian to the massacres in Kosovo. Once universalized it could be politicized. Such indescribable evil, in which the millions who died represent only the final step in an agonizing journey, could only happen when the state monopolizes power, as in Germany or the Soviet Union.[25] Genocide has political implications. Some hard-back conservative might even go as far as pointing to the parallel between the New Deal, so beloved by Jews, and the *étatisme* of the Nazi Reich and Italy's corporate state. Did not the growth of federal power parallel a similar growth in Europe's fascist regimes? Were not the regulations and codes of fair competition of Roosevelt's National Industrial Recovery Act mimicry of similar programs in German and Italy? If one discounts a distressing penchant for genocide, national socialism, it was argued, was after all not that different than the welfare state, and Roosevelt and Hitler were cut from the same charismatic cloth. Such observations in the postwar decade echoed those made by the anti-New Deal Right in the thirties. It made the Italy where the trains ran on time and the Germany of the celebratory *Partei Tag* seem, if not benevolent, then at least efficient, a strength regarded by many Americans with admiration.

The Jewish "Adoration" of Roosevelt and a War to Save the Jews

During the war the greatest dilemma faced by rescue advocates was somehow to reconcile the administration's information strategy of not allowing the war to be imaged as one to save the Jews with the Jewish electorates' adoration of Roosevelt.[26] For most Jewish voters Roosevelt could do no wrong. That tension increased as news of the actual workings of the Final Solution leaked out of Europe with little reaction from the administration. The curtain of silence was finally partially lifted in 1944 with the establishment of the WRB and the United Nations War Crimes Commission. The full exposure awaited the Nuremberg trials, which marked the earliest instance of Jews having to fully confront directly the German Reich's fanatic determination to destroy the Jews of Europe.

The Jewish voter found many reasons to support the New Deal, but we have noted that in the end Jewish political support was based primarily on Roosevelt's domestic program rather than his foreign policy. Before the war the Roosevelt administration only reluctantly tangled with the deep-seated isolationism of the American people, and thereafter it engaged not at all with the restrictionist congressional opposition regarding immigration. Some imagined that had Roosevelt acted more quickly on the interventionist program favored by Jews and others, Berlin might have reconsidered its war plans and delayed the implementation of the Final Solution, which required some certainty that Germany would emerge victorious. After the attack on Pearl Harbor, care was taken not to allow the war to appear as one to save the Jews, lest it interfere with the rapid mobilization of the nation. The several international conferences held to plan war and postwar policy never had the death camps on their agendas. The government agencies involved with the fate of the Jews used euphemism like "political refugees" in their titles, though they dealt primarily with Jews.[27] Berlin spoke endlessly of Jews. The Allies seldom did.

The interaction of liberalism and the Holocaust is one of the keys to explaining the initial muted Jewish response to the early news of the deportations. For liberal Jews the news was difficult to believe. Like many Americans they were aware of the gruel propaganda that preceded America's entrance into World War I. The hope was that the terrible stories emerging from Europe were exaggerated. It was easy to discredit them since the basic premise of the liberal mentalité—that there exists a caring humanity that includes Jews in its concern—continued to prevail in the Jewish sensibility.

In the immediate postwar years, having emerged victorious over a brutal fascist enemy, liberal sentiment seemed stronger than ever. With an inherent message about the price of racialism, the Holocaust generated strong support for the civil rights struggle, which went on to become the new centerpiece of liberalism we have called "race-based liberalism." The fight against racism was partly rooted in the rationale that democracy required pluralism, which also contained a measure of security against targeting Jews for "special treatment." In supporting access of African Americans to the promise of America, Jews were in some indirect way also assuring the continuance of their rapid postwar climb to the middle class. Racial tolerance served a Jewish communal interest. Yet that kind of strategizing was not without its problems, as noted earlier. When Jewish communal interest such as the merit system of appointment to teaching positions was involved, their liberal principles often gave way to group interest. Tenure of Jewish teachers in Ocean Hill–Brownsville schools was one thing. The march of Rabbi Heschell with Dr. Martin Luther King was another.[28]

Debating the Holocaust: A Communal Exercise

We come next to a discussion of the internalization of the Holocaust experience into American Jewry's communal memory. That internalization would willy-nilly be reflected in Jewish political culture, but from the outset it was a process beset with problems. A bleeding stump of a people that could not be certain that it had not received a deathblow, at least in a demographic and cultural sense, was called upon to celebrate its survival and memorialize its losses. History had given Judaism ample occasion to establish a religious memorialization ritual. A secular component would now make its appearance in the form of an endless stream of memoirs and personal accounts. There is an increasing number of professional histories that indicate that writing the historical narrative is underway. One might even argue that the memorialization process that ensued after the *Shoah* was in itself a community-building activity that went beyond the immense human losses involved in what was basically an attempt to destroy an ancient civilization that had somehow defied the normal life cycle. Such an aim required an attack on the Jewish person and beyond that on the Jewish community, its history its values, the way it lived life. Given the scale of the catastrophe it was a foregone conclusion that some form of formal memorialization would develop. Few imagined that it would reach the enormous scale that it ultimately did. Judaism's communal and personal mourning rituals are rich in stress amelioration. Its religious calendar contains days devoted to former tragedies, such as the destruction of the temple observed on the ninth day of the Hebrew month of Av. Some nevertheless maintain that a culture based on victimization, which is seen as emerging among some Jews, is not a suitable atmosphere for raising children. On the assumption that excessive mourning undermines the notion of a supreme and just God, it is forbidden in Jewish religious law that mandates quick burial and a process of memorialization extended over time. Others take note of the danger that excessive mourning poses to mental and spiritual health. Yet given the scale of the catastrophe, the massive memorialization process that has taken hold seems unavoidable. There are still American Jews alive today who have lost some kin during the war. The counterargument is made that it is not the memorialization that contains the seeds of communal depression and paranoia, but rather twentieth-century Jewish history, from which there is no escaping.

According to one writer, the legacy of the Holocaust on Jewish political culture is in the "hypervigilance of the haunted," resonated in the fear of again becoming the victims of history.[29] It is not pathological because it lacks a major ingredient of paranoia, a departure from reality. Moreover, the hyperactivity of the American Jewish citizen in the political arena is hardly resonant of a depressed paranoiac spirit. The unending conflict with the Palestinians, coupled with their unwillingness to accept Israel's legitimacy, encourage many Jews to imagine that their world continues to be threatened.

Whether fraudulent or authentic or an amalgamation of both, barely a day passes without some mention of the Holocaust in the media. It has become part of the nation's storehouse of popular knowledge that the average citizen can identify together with the winner of the World Series or National Football League playoffs. The name of Anne Frank has become as well known as Joe DiMaggio. In the Jewish community where this touting of the Holocaust first became rooted, we have already noted that the process of bringing it to public attention has become a source of controversy. The volume of cultural and openly promotional material in the public realm that relates to the Holocaust raises questions of the authenticity of the remembrance process. The term frequently heard is "trivialization," which refers not only to the proliferation of shoddy sentimental material on every level but also the regret that noise rather than silence, surely a more fitting way to mourn, has won the day.[30]

It is argued that Holocaust memorialization became a minor industry called "shoah business" because of supposed instances where it has been misused for fundraising and political purposes. The argument of misuse or overuse is one of the major themes of the controversial study by Peter Novick.[31] The author wants to know why the promotion of Holocaust consciousness has reached its high point so many years after the event. Why now and why in America, which was, after all, distant from the killing grounds of Europe?

The first query regarding the time lapse has now been answered in a massively researched study that shows beyond a doubt that the premise that there was a time lapse of almost two decades before American Jewry gained awareness of what had happened and developed its memorialization process is simply not borne out by the evidence. A Jewish population already immersed in thousands of personal survivor accounts and a fairly uniform memorialization ritual welcomed the Eichmann trial in 1962, which was conceived by Ben-Gurion to make certain that the Holocaust would not be forgotten by a new post-Holocaust generation. The cataloguing of new organizations established, books written, programs initiated, and legislators petitioned is so massive that clearly it is nigh impossible to make sense of American Jewish political culture without understanding the underlying role of the Holocaust.[32]

But Novick's second point—why here and why the development of a culture of memorialization that at its worst is commercial, corrupt, politicized, so that it almost demeans Jewish losses, is not so easily put to rest. One can acknowledge that there developed a pattern on the grass-roots level that went from self-promotion to false claims about victimization and heroism. There developed "a psychic income of victimization" indulged in by witnesses and survivors, which some came to call "shoah business." The problem with Novick's model is that the Holocaust story today is no longer an exclusive preoccupation of Jews or survivors who experienced it. It is in the public realm, which means everyone, writers, artists, and plumbers, Jews and non-Jews, imbibe it as experience and distill meaning from it. The proliferation of fraudulent or simply trashy promotional accounts, while a sad resonance of the low estate of popular culture, is a far cry from Novick's primary suggestion that a Zionist-oriented American Jewish leadership was exploiting the Holocaust to make a case for Israel.

That observation has inherent a conspiratorial element that deserves special attention if only because the conspiracy charge echoes classical anti-Semitic propaganda, which can be heard today in the Islamic press and among Holocaust deniers. The charge that there exists a strategy to use the Holocaust for political or commercial ends, a conscious organized effort to misuse the memory of the Holocaust, requires more than the stories gleaned from the Anglo-Jewish press to gain veracity. Where there is conspiracy there are conspirators who have names, who write memos with dates, whose agencies hold meetings where minutes are taken. Such a serious charge requires a "smoking gun." I do not mean some public-relations professional composing a brochure that reminds readers that there are still Holocaust victims who require aid—"please send money." When all is said and done, Novick's charge needs better evidence than the massive amount of journalistic evidence he has collected. For such a strategy based on exploiting the Holocaust to develop and be implemented, a clear leadership decision of major organizations that govern American Jewry, or think they do, has to exist. Since there is no Sanhedrin that could have made such a collective communal decision, it would probably be sought and occasionally found in the files of nationwide Jewish organizations or groupings of organizations. The history of the Jewish organizational world during the years of the Holocaust and today shows that it is incapable of unified action either for good or bad. That is in fact the reason why much Jewish political action remains in the realm of organizational *ukazi* and *pronuncimientos*. American Jewry rarely has one agreed-on position, which leads to the difficulty of determining "who speaks for the Jews?"

It may well be that the flood of stories written by survivors who have for years maintained their silence has a more innocent source. Released from a personal trauma, they finally feel free to speak and do so. Whatever the source, stories of the Holocaust flood our airwaves and film screens perhaps more than any other single World War II event. There does not seem to be an artist, writer, or musician who has not tested his creative energy to distill some meaning from it. Finding a meaning for such a horrendously irrational act has been elusive. The numbers that have been successful can be counted on the fingers of one hand. Great care needs to be taken because there is great potential for slander in the indictment that is emerging about the misuse of the memory of the Holocaust. It is not merely a quest for a meaningful story that draws artists and writers and survivors to this event. It contains a searing truth about our time in history. These accounts, often written in extremis, are usually not great literature, but the best are revealing and tell us much about what humans are all about. The Holocaust acts like a magnet to draw creative artists of all sorts, innocent or corrupt, seekers of raw emotion as well as seekers of attention.

The astounding growth of Holocaust consciousness goes far beyond a promotional conspiracy. It is difficult to conceive of Jewish citizens who have not imagined in their innermost hearts what might have happened to them had they lived in Europe during World War II. Many of their ancestors had that misfortune, and today the countless accounts of what they experienced feed the trauma. Is there a Jewish child who hasn't imagined his victimization the way Anne Frank imagined it or the boy with his hands up emerging from the smoking ruins of the Warsaw ghetto? That deep emotion aroused by Anne Frank's story is not confined to Jewish children. The knowledge that there can be murderous intent armed with state power that removes all security somehow taps the deepest wellspring of human anxiety. It is almost impossible not to confront it when trying to come to terms with our time in history. More than anything else it is the valence of the event, to borrow a term from chemistry, which accounts for its prominence in the arts and media. That the victims were overwhelmingly Jews naturally makes it especially relevant to Jews, but it is more than a Jewish story. The ripping away of a loved one and the deprivation that followed, the loss of freedom for an unknown crime, the thousands of human dramas that resulted from a societal upheaval, are, after all, the rich stuff that the human drama is made of. That too accounts for the public prominence of the Holocaust story. What better source does a budding dramatist or writer need to test his or her mettle?

This discussion concerns the impact that a modern, powerful nation-state's decision to mass murder a seemingly well-integrated community of its citizens had on the political culture of a related group in America. Productive citizens are, after all, the lifeblood of a society, and all the indications were that German Jewry was culturally and economically unusually productive. Seven decades later it still seems incredible even to contemplate the implementation of such a policy and the fact that a citizenry could be mobilized to directly or indirectly become involved in it.[33] It is that horrendous datum, that it happened not in a rainforest or jungle but in the most advanced societies in the world, that places it at the crucial center of the American Jewish political stage. It shook the confidence in modernity that was at the heart of the liberalism that defined their political culture.

Most contemporary American Jews know the world of the Holocaust largely through the survivors that live among them, yet it's impact is no less powerful for being vicarious. In that narrative the joyful, affirmative pre-Holocaust aspects of Jewish life in Western and Eastern Europe is overshadowed by the events of its denouement. The narrative of victimization is not imposed from on high down to the masses of Jewish citizens. Rather it flows upward from survivors and the myriad congregations, fraternal orders, and family circles that generate the political and cultural persona of the community. It has deepened the consciousness of American Jewry already unusually concerned with history's victims.

Holocaust Consciousness in American Life

There is a gap between historians who write the history of the American Holocaust witness as it might and should have happened and those who try to explain why events occurred as they did.[34] The former group views the Roosevelt's listless rescue effort and the imagined indifference of American Jewry as a story of failure. It is based on the assumption that there is a mandate for moral action in the Judeo-Christian tradition that was not adhered to. It is the former group joined with the survivor community in America who bring to the social and political arena what one historian has identified as a bill for pain suffered. There is no need to solve a complex question with theological overtones here. We have noted that the phenomenon of action taken at great risk is inevitably involved with the question of the possession of political power that is required to fulfill an assigned moral responsibility. It is central to any examination of political culture. Politics after all essentially deals with the process by which communities civilize power relations. We have previously noted that when dealing with Jews, the power question inevitably becomes tangled in the mythic notion at the core of the anti-Semitic imagination that sees Jews as possessing inordinate power. Yet without some estimate of how much power and what kind of power Roosevelt and American Jewry actually possessed, and some knowledge of Berlin's determination even after Stalingrad (March 1943) to win the war that might still be won against the Jews, the historical narrative is in danger of becoming a lament about human indifference.

The American government has acknowledged its failing witness role during the Holocaust in various steps it has taken. The U.S. Holocaust Museum, strategically placed on the Capital Mall and partly government financed, features among its exhibits a full exposure of the nation's failure to act during the war. It is a remarkable reaffirmation of where democratic governments stand and serves as a model now for several other governments. That a lesson has been learned regarding the role of the Holocaust witness is found in the case of the Clinton administration offering temporary shelter to Bosnian Moslems in Ft. Dix, New Jersey, to shield them from Serbian genocidal intent. Former President Clinton publicly regretted his failure to confront the genocide in Rwanda. President Obama imposed a "no fly zone" in Libya and announced that he will not stand idly by while a cruel dictator slaughters the citizens of Benghazi. Descendants of the refugees of the thirties fortunate enough to find haven here have occupied the highest policymaking positions in the nation.[35] These steps go beyond merely regretting failure. They transmit that a moral lesson has been learned. Many states have added the study of the Holocaust to their curricula in elementary and high school. Yet signs of how difficult it is for the nation-state to fill the role of moral agent abound. While aiding the insurgency against a tyrannical Quidaffa regime in Libya, the Obama administration rejected the idea of intervening militarily in the Libyan uprising. The recent case of Syria's war against its citizens of a different branch of Islam, in which thousands were killed, found Washington again unwilling to intercede directly.

Undoubtedly American Jewry has helped awaken the nation's consciousness of the Holocaust not only by means of its public relations and teacher education programs. There is also a spillover effect from the intense Holocaust dialogue that is omnipresent in the Jewish community. When it is clear and focused, the Jewish voice, which is not unfamiliar in public arenas, especially in the quests for moral elevation, carries considerable weight. There is an ongoing debate on whether a moral posture has a place in the making of foreign policy. The debate on whether the bomb should have been used to obliterate Hiroshima and Nagasaki grows evermore shrill, as does the debate between historians on whether Wilson's fourteen points and Roosevelt's Atlantic Charter, two more recent examples of the insertion of a moral note into policy, really serve the national interest.

Yet in a democracy the nation's moral stance has earned some political weight. Public sensitivity to massive atrocities like genocide may be related to the nation's rising education level, which may also contribute to the high Jewish interest in this question. Nor is that quest limited to the United States. Interest in the Holocaust and concern about contemporary potential genocides has become transnational. From the bloodbath in Tiananmen Square to the celebration of democracy in Tahrir Square in Cairo, the United States is believed to represent a more morally progressive vision of the future. It is expected to point the way forward. The quest for high moral purpose lives side-by-side with earthier motivations, so that assigning moral mission to foreign policy rests on fragile ground, especially when it is argued that such a charged policy does not directly serve the national interest.

The ongoing debate on the morality issue is rooted in the uncertainty about where the moral high ground lies and its relationship to the national interest, about which there is a greater uncertainty still. The current apprehension in Arizona regarding an inflow of undocumented immigrants from Mexico is reminiscent of the attitude toward Jewish refugees trying to reach America's sheltering shores in the thirties. Yet eight years later the United States was among the first witnessing nations to develop a strong Holocaust consciousness.[36] It has taken the lead in alerting the United Nations where the threat of genocide is imminent and has intervened directly in Bosnia. It may well be that consciousness of the Holocaust could serve as a measure of the depth of democracy. It is surely no coincidence that countries where Holocaust denial is an acceptable part of the political dialogue, as in the Arab world, are also those that rate lowest on the scale that measures the depth of commitment to civil rights and democratic procedures.

Holocaust Consciousness and Anti-Semitism

We cannot leave an examination of Holocaust consciousness in Jewish political culture without touching on anti-Semitism, which fueled the depredations. There is the contention that in its racialism the Holocaust is dissimilar from the normative anti-Semitism that historically prevailed in Europe. In that sense Hitler gave anti-Semitism a bad name. Nazi anti-Semitism was of a particularly virulent kind that required genocide to fulfill its goal of racial purification. It was political and pseudoscientific and enforced by the state as public policy. To shelter a Jew in occupied Europe was to break the law. That fact alone sometimes triggered the intervention of witnessing governments like the United States on several occasions when American Jewish citizens were caught in the Nazi racial net. It was that virulence and collective impact that may have caused its victims to long for the old normative anti-Semitism, which at least did not culminate in death camps. After the distinction between normative anti-Semitism, believed to lie latent in all European societies, and Nazi genocidal anti-Semitism became clear in the thirties, American Jewry became aware that something new and lethal had developed within a familiar ancient plague. Governments like France, in the throes of the older anti-Semitism, readily took to the new and willingly deported their Jews, often before they were ordered to do so. In the East, local populations often needed no reminder to initiate the earliest bloody pogroms, which in some cases continued after the Nazi yoke had been broken.

For American Jews the question of whether America could succumb to Nazi-type racial anti-Semitism is always in the background. Its elements could be found in the immigration laws of 1921 and 1924, whose underlying concept of Nordic supremacy, on which the quota system was based, was similar to the Nazi racial principle of Aryanism. As mentioned in chapter 1, exclusion of Jews followed by extrusion caused enormous apprehension among Jews.[37] The linkage became clear during the refuge crises of the thirties when extruded Jews were denied refuge for much the same reason as they were being deported from the Reich. They had the misfortune of being in an undesirable racial category. The relationship was not entirely surprising. The emergency immigration law of 1921 and its permanent successor in 1924 were both triggered by rumors that Polish Jewry was poised to flood America, ostensibly to plant the seeds of communism. The State Department, which then administered part of the immigration law through its consulates and visa procedure, found such rumors credible because it was immersed in an organizational culture of antiforeignism and particularly anti-Semitism. Jewish applicants had found places in the nation's premier law and medical colleges, but almost none could be found in the Department's Foreign Service. It was a genteel anti-Semitism, but anti-Semitism nevertheless. Jewish mothers knew not to allow their sons and daughters to prepare for the Department's Foreign Service examination, but few understood that it was but the tip of the iceberg until war became imminent in 1938. During the *Anschluss* in March

1938, photos of the physical beating of Jews could be viewed in the press. On the night of November 9, the now-infamous *Kristallnacht* (night of the broken glass) nationwide pogrom, which witnessed the burning of hundreds of synagogues and breaking of windows in Jewish-owned shops, it became clear that the Jewish question had gained the highest position in the Reich's politics. Far from spontaneous, the pogrom had all the earmarks of being organized by government authority. It was a portent of things to come.

But in the United States things remained tranquil. Hans Dieckhoff, the German ambassador, complained that the "new" Germany lost much American approval because of the pogrom. Apparently Americans did not think it was sportsmanlike to beat up on a white disarmed minority. But the administration of the immigration law told another story. The increasing strictness of enforcing the "Likely to Become a Public Charge" (LPC) provision of the law during the Herbert Hover administration resulted in few Jewish refugees gaining admission. Only in 1939 were the relevant quotas filled.[38] The final blow came in 1938 when the deportation of *stattenloss* (stateless) *Ost Juden* began.[39] Aware that they were facing a catastrophe, many Jewish families sent their children to neighboring France where things were still fairly secure. When the war broke out in September 1939, thousands of these German Jewish children were stranded without parents or family.[40] Some were able to make their way to Vichy or unoccupied France after the armistice in June 1940. That crisis serves as the background for the aforementioned desperate congressional attempt to save these children made by Senator Robert Wagner (Dem. New York) and Representative Will Rogers Jr. (Dem. California). Lacking Roosevelt's support the bill died in committee. It took four crucial years to circumvent the strict administration of the immigration law. In 1945, when the war was all but over, Roosevelt signed an executive order granting 983 mostly Jewish refugees temporary shelter in Fort Ontario near Oswego, New York.[41]

It was America's response to the refugee crisis of the thirties that amplified the apprehension of American Jewry. It also fueled a massive flow to the banners of the American Zionist movement. An American version of political Zionism became one of the three pillars of its political culture. That conversion of non-Zionists to the fold was rarely based on familiarity with the esoteric Zionist theorists of Zionist ideology. American Jews simply saw that in an uncaring, threatening world Jewish survival required some piece of real estate where they could be sovereign. Today few would have denied that basic folk truth. Had they had possession of their own state, Jewish loss of life would not have occurred or at least been lessened. It was that compelling truth, which became clear during the refugee crises, that set the stage for Zionism becoming a basic plank of American Jewish political culture. For many Jews the only answer to resolve their vulnerability and the rampant anti-Semitism released by Germany abroad and in the United States was in Zionism.[42]

A great tension within the Jewish political soul developed during the Holocaust years. The war allowed full reign to their powerful universalistic sensibility, which was embodied in the Atlantic Charter and information films on "Why We Fight." It was as if the entire Allied world was coming to believe what Jews always understood instinctively. But the liberal credo under which the war was fought could not hide the fact that the Jews of Europe were being slaughtered and nothing could or would be done to rescue them.

Viewed through the prism of the triad that serves as the basis of our discussion, the Holocaust experience challenges the universalism of Jewish liberalism. At the same time, having seen the abyss, much of Jewish political activism is focused on sounding the alarm to warn that a politics based on genocide is in the air, especially in the Middle East. They warn the same world that did not come to their aid in their moment of extreme need that it could happen again, as in Darfur or Bosnia or Rwanda. Their assumption remains that there is a world out there that cares and would respond. One imagines that especially Jews should know better. Yet hope continues to live side-by-side with fear in the Jewish political soul.

The Holocaust as a Major Factor in Jewish Political Culture

We come finally to the remarkable staying power of the Holocaust as an issue in Jewish politics and culture. It colors the history of the second half of the twentieth century and does not seem to have been damned behind the barriers of the twenty-first. The sustained memorialization under-taken by American Jewry and in Israel may be partly explained by the sheer scale of the slaughter. They were kin. But how to account for the seeming endless stream of Holocaust museums, films, books, newspaper stories, and even cartoon characters projected as mice, which seems to have spilled over into the political culture of the entire world. The Holo-caust has become a reference point in international culture as well as diplomacy. That stands in sharp contrast to the wartime silence concern-ing the fate of the Jews of Europe.

Whatever its breadth and depth, and impact, the Holocaust unhappily belongs to Jewish history, where it is classified as an episode in the mil-lennial history of anti-Semitism. The social psychologists have presented numerous theories to explain the mystery of the persistence of anti-Semitism. But the continued growth of Holocaust consciousness, more than seven decades after the event, eludes full explanation. The increase in Holocaust denial indicates that the impact itself has become part of the litany of anti-Semitism. We have noted that some researchers question whether the Holocaust itself can be explained solely by its relationship to normative anti-Semitism. They see it as part of an attempt to rearrange the ethnic/racial composition of Europe based on eugenics derived from social Darwinist thinking, a major element in Nazi ideology. Historically, the dispersion sometimes followed by massacre of Jewish communities is not a new phenomenon. Exilic Jewry itself came into existence as a result of such coerced dispersions. It is also maintained that by dint of its scale and the use of the industrial processes at the heart of modern life, the Holocaust is a historical novum. There are no other historical instances of a massive state-organized social cannibalism.[43] If it is indeed an example of how a modern industrial society can loose control of the ethical and moral guide posts that regulate human behavior, with consequences that reach beyond the victims to shake the pillars on which modern civiliza-tion is based. The precedent threatens all. If in former times the sword, or whatever the weapon of choice may have been, was used to achieve mass killing, there should be no surprise that modern industrial techniques became the preferred instrument in later times. In that sense, the Holo-caust is linked to our modern world. In fact much of the dying during the

Holocaust was not done exclusively in the five death camps, but rather by shooting and other means by special police units (*Einzatsgruppen*), and many died when denied the normal necessities needed to sustain life. In some measure it was neither scientific nor efficient. A decision to slaughter millions of productive human beings and expend resources in doing so is not modern, despite the piles of hair and the piles of clothing that could be collected from the victims for reintegration into the Reich's wartime economy. The genocidal impulse is ancient, the implementation is modern.

Berlin's decision to rid the world of Jews concerned a people who held citizenship in every nation in Europe occupied by Germany. That fact should have automatically made it a political issue. But Jewish communities located in neutral nations were virtually alone in calling attention to the slaughter of innocents. In the case of the largest of these communities, American Jewry, the Holocaust issue went on to become an integral part of the atmosphere that shaped its political culture. Historically, massacre by government fiat and programs for the extirpation of the tribal enemy that fell short of genocide were probably more the rule than the exception. The Final Solution was a government program, part of the Reich's public policy, not unlike a government program to build highways, and therefore part of the politics of the Reich. Once the government bureaucracy was programmed for genocide it did its work much the same way it performed any other duty such as tax collection or snow removal. It was not until the war ended and a full realization of the intent of the death camps developed that Auschwitz became a new term in the lexicon of international and domestic politics. American Jewry and Israel had much to do with awakening the post-war world to the new deeper threat in human relations brought to the fore by the Holocaust.

Our emphasis on the technical and racialist aspects of the Holocaust tends to overshadow the fact that it was implemented by state agencies armed with government fiat. We should not be surprised that our current interest continues to have a political dimension. When today we ponder what to do about a rogue nation that has embarked on ethnic cleansing, as in the case of Serbia, the alternatives we consider are basically in the political realm. Things would have been different if a group of armed pirates went on a murderous rampage. That is the action of a criminal mob. The Holocaust was a legal program undertaken by a sovereign state. It was state policy.

Whether Jews stemmed from Greece or the German-occupied British Channel isles, from France or the Mahgreb, they were earmarked for deportation and death. Berlin focused on Jews as one people. In a sense, a unity was imposed on them that they were unable to impose on themselves. In the camps Jews did not magically come together to face their common fate, and in the United States, where the achievement of such unity might have been possible, the several attempts at speaking to the Roosevelt administration with one voice proved futile. The Jewish political voice needed cohesiveness and coherence to be understood. It possessed neither. Only in the memorialization process did such a voice ring out. In some sense, the warning contained in the fact of the Holocaust became a building block for Jewish unity. Its high point was the virtual consensus reached for the creation of a Jewish state. The political culture of American Jewry might have been far more amorphous and difficult to identify had the Holocaust never happened.

In the end one wonders if it was possible to avoid worldwide Holocaust consciousness, at least in the political class. Is there a thinking person alive who has not contemplated what might have been the fate of mankind had Germany won the war? The introduction of a race-based policy of rearranging the map of Europe may seem outrageous today, but enforced by a powerful state such a policy has inherent in it the power to become a central political issue of our time. That too may account for the persistence of the Holocaust story in the United States, where evidence of state laws based on racial eugenics have come to the surface. Had it taken hold in the world's most heterogeneous society as it did in Germany, it contained the possibility of liquidating a sizeable proportion of the American population in the name of improving the breed.[44] When considered together with Hiroshima and Nagasaki, which also entailed the use of science and technology to impose mass anonymous dying by fire, Auschwitz may in years to come be considered part of a radical new condition that man entered during a period of total war. That may be the most penetrating response that can be offered to those who see the deep and abiding interest in the Holocaust as the effect of a promotional campaign.

Withal, while memorialization is a permanent feature in Judaic religious culture, there is no certainty that the current configuration of secular Holocaust remembrance will remain part of American Jewish political culture. The need for each aspiring writer to test his or her mettle on the Holocaust theme will surely diminish as new man-made catastrophes occur. We have already noted that the liberalism and Zionism of the immigrant generation has undergone changes over time. Living cultures ultimately find a way to maneuver around even the deepest trauma to allow life to go forward. The surprising thing is that after seven decades there are still more museums on the drawing board, more books being written and plays staged, and more religious rituals being developed. Seventy years after the fact, a suit is brought against the French railway system for facilitating the one-way journey of the deportees. The provenance of stolen paintings is challenged in the courts and the art object is returned to the survivor's family. Holocaust awareness seems "hotter" than ever. Its staying power may serve as a measure of the historical weight of the event. But ultimately the act itself will regress into a dim memory ready to be marked in the Jewish religious calendar and to be ensconced in ritual and observed once every year, as is the destruction of the temple on the ninth of the Hebrew month of Av. Even that does not assure permanence since it is a secular mind-set that today draws Jews more than the Decalogue. Like all modern people American Jewry is basically temporal, it lives in the present. The second and third generation is no longer able to feel the Holocaust's immediacy as did the generation of survivors. The millions spent on such programs as "The March of the Living" only delays the journey into oblivion. The hundreds of mass graves recently disinterred in Belarus and Ukraine barely make a dent. There is no way of halting the forward momentum of communal life, no matter how traumatic the past. Man also needs to forget in order to go forward.

If, like all historical events, the Holocaust is destined eventually to be integrated into tribal and individual memory, then why consider it as a pillar of American Jewish political culture as we do here? Here, too, the answer may be that the Holocaust's resonance in American Jewish political culture does not stem solely or even primarily from memorialization or books and plays written about that tragic happening. Unlike the liberalism that is a constant in Jewish political culture, the Holocaust acts like a catalytic agent. It tests the validity of the cherished assumptions that prop up liberalism, the existence of a caring humanity, at its very heart. Given the animus of its regional neighbors, even the survival of a parliamentary democracy like Israel cannot be taken for granted. For Jews, the depth of evil of the perpetrators and the indifference of the witnesses is always there. There is the memory of their kin to contend with.

Yet liberal Jewish voices persist in calling on the world to be better than it wants to be, or perhaps can be. Jewish hope persists, but it is not unscathed. The Jewish world cannot live without such hope and so it calls on the world to warn of the abyss Jews have experienced. Zionism and Israel, its offspring, have become key facets of its political culture, partly as a reward for foreseeing the failure of emancipation. For American Jewry, who assumed the role of midwife to the birth of Israel, the goal of Zionism awaited the Holocaust. Israel did restore a measure of well being and created, at least for the moment, the feeling of security. But it is not possible to proclaim that the Jewish problem has finally been solved with the creation of the Jewish state. Zionism and the state it gave birth to had as its primary purpose the ending of the perennial anti-Semitism that exists in Jewish history like a vicious, biting dog. For Jews, the most agonizing truth of all may be that the one thing the state has been unable to do is to fulfill its promise to normalize the Jewish condition and bring an end to anti-Semitism. Instead, Israel has become its lodestar.

The Holocaust has subjected the elevated assumptions Jews, especially secular liberal Jews, hold about humankind to a reality test, and found them wanting. There are those who believe that such an injection of skepticism about the world and its humanity is an asset for the Jewish political persona. It would help Jewry transform its mind-set from its tendency to idealize the human condition to a deeper understanding of the limits of humankind. It would forestall its forlorn quest for a just world in which Jews could be a normal people. Unfortunately such skepticism runs the risk of extinguishing the flame of hope, which is the fuel of American Jewish political dynamism. To develop such a normal muscular

Jew was the dream of Zionist founders like Theodor Herzl. For a historic moment it seemed that that was happening in America. Despite numerous anti-Semitic incidents, especially during the twenties and thirties, it seemed that Jews were on the way to coming into their own as Americans. The Jewish voter evinced almost a proprietary interest in Roosevelt's New Deal. America held out the hope of normality for the Jewish citizen. But then, despite its vicariousness, the Holocaust, an event happening to related Jewries in Europe, profoundly affected its political psyche. The political culture of American Jewry became rooted as much in what had happened to its brethren in Europe as in the hopeful things it was experiencing in America. At the time of this writing it appears that the Jewish quest for normality is not yet realizable, not in America and not in Israel, but there is some hope that the anxiety generated by the Holocaust on the American Jewish psyche may eventually be diminished.

Epilogue

The Jews of America are prosperous and secure, but the price of full acceptance in the most benevolent host culture in their long history is a progressive weakening of communal bonds. Modernity has sundered the Jewish tribal tent. The political culture produced by a free people is so varied that it raises questions of whether indeed there is such an entity as a single Jewish political persona. The political principles to which Jews commit themselves are an integral part of a shared web of visions and values incubated in urban places where modern Jews choose to live. Historically, Jews may have tasted the free air of the city earlier and more deeply than others. That urbanity poses a problem for the researcher since such an electorate cannot easily be differentiated into Jewish and non-Jewish voters. Secularized voters who have a high level of formal education, like Jews, tend to pull down the same voting levers. When pollsters tabulate the Jewish vote they tell only part of the story. There is little in the statistics that tells us why they vote the way they do and why there is sometimes great variance in their preferences. This study is based on the assumption that beyond locating the Jewish vote slightly left of center in the Democratic Party, there exists a deep liberal sensibility rooted in its history, which shapes its political behavior.

We have noted that Jewish voter reaction to a liberal candidate is far from Pavlovian; certain well-known names like Dwight Eisenhower do not necessarily elicit a negative response in the voting booth. But there are markers that help identify the Jewish voter: special concern about the security of Israel, issues concerning the Holocaust, opposition to capital punishment, favoring *Roe v. Wade* and most green issues like saving the whales. There is in fact a liberal position on virtually every issue on the domestic political agenda, and the Jewish voter favors most, but not with equal fervor. There was considerable opposition to affirmative-action legislation. That ambivalence is less true of foreign policy issues, and it does not of course mean that all Jewish liberals will vote the liberal position on every issue. We have noted that dissidence too is part of the Jewish liberal persona.

But a Jewish liberal political voice there is. For every one Jewish voter who identifies himself as conservative there are two who proclaim themselves liberal, precisely the reverse of the general electorate. Read the endless speculating about the Jewish vote in the next election. Hear the charges against the "Jewish lobby" controlling the nation's Middle East policy. Note the disproportionate number of Jewish pollsters, campaign managers, and pundits. Surely this disparate assemblage does contribute a disproportionate number to what the political scientists identify as the "political class," those who by dint of officeholding, profession, or passion are totally engaged in the political process. On certain issues they form a "voting bloc" and spawn a "special interest group," which some pundits consider an important and others a dangerous factor in American politics. The liberalism that some see as the Jewish voter's identifying sign turns out, on closer examination, to be a persuasion rather than a prescriptive ideology, and therefore subject to broad changes over time. It has taken American Jews from the social democracy carried by their immigrant forebearers from eastern Europe to the liberalism of America, and if the dynamism of the engaged Jewish citizen is sustained it may yet become many other things.

Viewing American Jewish political culture through three distinct lenses, liberalism, Zionism/Israel, and Holocaust consciousness, as this book does, also poses special problems. Like a braid composed of unequal strands, the three interrelated narrative streams are of unequal historical weight. Liberalism acts as the *kochlefel* of American Jewish political culture.[1] It stirs the pot, adds new issues when required, and has much to say regarding the content of the two strands that interact with it. None propose a hardened dogma on how life should be lived, only that the citizen should, within reason, be free to live it. That is the libertarian aspect of Jewish liberalism, but it is the liberalism of egalitarianism enhanced by government programs that winds its way through the sections of this book. That the citizen needs to be free and also secure is requisite in Jewish liberalism.

Special concern about Israel is a telltale sign of ethnicity in Jewish political culture. Yet modern Zionism is in fact an issue of relatively recent vintage in American Jewish political history. Most American Jews had after all voted with their feet to seek their Zion in America, and their political thinkers were more drawn to the Achad Ha'am vision of a Jewish cultural center in Palestine rather than a sovereign political state. Such a formulation of Zionism avoided the bugaboo of dual loyalties an accusation, which haunted early immigrants. A Jewish commonwealth, as if to suggest membership in the British Commonwealth, really came into its own in the immediate years before the Holocaust and then quickly developed because of it. There was an American Jewish Zionist movement with philanthropic overtones since the second decade of the twentieth century, but it was the Holocaust that welded statehood into Jewish political culture, and there it has remained ever since.

The American Jewish commitment to Israel remains strong, but a gap has developed regarding the steps that are required on the crucial security question to assure Israel's continued viability. In years ahead the American Jewish commitment to the welfare of Israel may shift away from the biblical "blood and soil" defense of the Jewish state to a liberal rationale, which defends Israel as a liberal democracy proffering a two-state solution to the conflict with the Palestinians. That possibility of realization depends on the prospect for regional peace. There is hope that the Arab Spring, which began by sounding familiar principles of Western democratic values of inclusiveness, transparency, rule of law, and gender equality, may turn Arab energies inward to national development and away from hatred of Israel as its binding instrument. But viewed from a contemporary perspective, it may be a long time before that vision becomes a reality. It may never do so.

That does not mean, as some have suggested, that there is diminishing support for Israel among American liberal, younger Jewish voters. The measure of the depth of American Jewish commitment is best seen in its response should Hezbollah and Hamas decide to use their huge arsenal of missiles against Israel. Such an attack, frequently threatened by Hassan Nazrallah, leader of Hezbollah, would also be a moment of truth for American Jewry, which beneath all else is aware that the possible unraveling of Israel may deliver a mortal blow to American Jewish communal survival as well.

Withal, several factors on the political horizon may deepen the gap between the two polities and alter the role of Israel in American political culture within which American Jewry plays its role. A change in international power arrangements, which sees a retraction of America's reach as a world power with a subsequent diminution of its protective role of Israel, is not so far-fetched. History teaches that the life cycle of great powers is finite. It is probably premature to shout about such a possibility from the rooftops, but after three costly wars and a searing near meltdown of the economy, the reversion of an exhausted America to seek "domestic tranquility" within its borders is conceivable. While not now imminent, we may witness a shift in the tectonic plates on which the world power calculus is based. Some would see it as the final episode of the cold-war era, in which the surviving contenders gradually withdraw from the international arena to make way for new aspirants for world power. There is no assurance that the American seat of power will remain strong and committed to its alliance with Israel, and make no mistake, it is an alliance. More important, there is no certainty that American Jewish communalism, which has been on a downward trajectory for decades, will forever be able to muster the cohesiveness and the political coherence to project a clear voice in the corridors of American governmental power.

For our purposes here it is sufficient to note that the Zionist/Israel pole of the triad concerns the American Jewish "adoration" of a related yet legally foreign nation on which much of its political activism and resources are expended. I again use the term "adoration" to remind the reader that during the fifties and sixties and after the 1967 war there were complaints by some rabbis about American Jewish "Israelism," considered a forbidden idolatry, so strong was the drawing power of the Jewish state. That sense of special concern still exists just beneath the surface. Yet increasingly, Israel's destiny lies fully in the hands of its citizens. American Jewry can only play a supportive witnessing role as advocate before the seat of American power. Despite the accusation that in determining Middle East policy the Jewish tail wags the American dog, that role has always been a limited one. Just as one can sense Holocaust memorialization becoming normalized, so one can also foresee that should the turmoil in the region diminish, Israel, as the primary issue in American Jewish politics, will also normalize. There are two caveats that need to be added. At the time of this writing the end of Middle East regional turmoil is not in sight, and that "normalization" does not mean that the American Jewish relationship with Israel will be similar to that of a former immigrant group to its homeland. The relationship is not the same as the American Irish with Ireland or Italian Americans with Italy. For Jews, Israel is beyond politics and beyond nostalgia for homeland.

Seven decades after the founding of the Jewish state, the Zionist idea has a less powerful hold on the Jewish political imagination. The refugees that roam the world today are not Jewish and the crucial need for territorial space has passed. Thousands of Soviet Jews preferred their Zion in America rather than Israel. Confident that Israel can fend for itself, many American Jews take Israel's physical survival for granted. Despite turmoil in the Middle East and threats of pushing Israel into the sea, her security situation has actually grown less dependent on outside agents. Organized in both historic time in the diaspora and in their ancient space in Israel, Jews generally can feel more certain about their ability to survive. Yet on a deeper level their insecurity persists as if a perennial in Jewish life. There is uncertainty whether historic memory is sufficient to withstand the siren call of a seductive, secular consumer-oriented culture. At the same time Israel, which exists in "Jewish space," wonders whether it can survive in an age of weapons of mass destruction. It feels compelled to respond to a felt threat to its survival, which in turn raises concerns about Israel's ability to continue to generate sufficient energy and resources to maintain a modern, achieving democratic society. Almost seven decades after the end of the Holocaust, the existence of the Jewish state seems unable to allay the paranoiac streak that lay latent in the American Jewish political soul.

Noted in the foregoing pages is that the almost successful effort to erase the Jewish presence from the pages of history was a terrible reality, not a paranoiac fantasy for Jews. It was hoped that the establishment of Israel in 1948 would mitigate that apprehensiveness and sense of threat, which is embedded in Jewish political culture. Indeed, there are those who argue that the Jewish enterprise has never been more secure now that Jews are organized in time, as are American Jews, and in space, as in Israel. Yet the sense of threat persists. The low-level war waged by Islam, urged on by displaced Palestinians, some now in the third generation, is determined to undo one of the few success stories among states established after World War II. It has steered the Zionism that might have had at one time a liberal aspiration to become "a light among the nations" to morph instead into viewing itself as a buttress against an Islamic anti-Semitism reminiscent of the very Christian European variety for which it was intended as a solution.[2]

Some have noted a parallel between the Jewish and Palestinian path to nationhood; an exiled people seeking return to its homeland. That analogy may or may not contain some truth, but their mutual stubbornness in rejecting history's verdict seems mysteriously to resemble the political character of the two related Semitic people. For American Jewry and the Jews of Israel, there is in the protracted Arab-Israeli conflict an existential problem. It is not only embodied in a military threat. It stems also from awareness that to have lost European Jewry and to then witness the possibility that Israel, after decades of relentless pressure, could be in danger of unraveling, may finally signal the end of a Jewish presence in history.

Finally, the problems posed by the continued impact of the Holocaust consciousness in Jewish political culture, especially its relationship to its regnant liberalism, warrant attention. Having seen the abyss, much of Jewish political activism is focused on sounding the alarm to warn that a politics based on genocide is in the air, especially in the Middle East. Though the Holocaust experience challenges the universalism that exists at the heart of Jewish liberalism, Jews warn the same world that did not come to their aid in their moment of extreme need that it could happen again, as in Darfur or Bosnia or Rwanda. Their assumption remains that there is a witnessing world that cares and would respond. One imagines that especially Jews should know better. Yet hope rooted in its liberalism continues to live side-by-side with existential angst in the Jewish political psyche.

Holocaust remembrance and alarm that sometimes assumes the character of a minor industry may eventually be moderated. The passing of the survivors in the coming years may mellow the desire for undoing the anonymity of the deaths that in some measure fuel Holocaust memorialization. That already seems to be happening and it may be accelerated by events few can foresee. The Holocaust has not inhibited acts of genocide. We may in years to come be beset by natural and man-made disasters that dwarf the loss of life during the Holocaust. An earthquake with accompanying tsunami as occurred recently in Japan, a severe draught or flood, or a fanatic Jihadi successfully poisoning the water supply of a major metropolis, can take millions of lives. The nightmare vision of a nuclear exchange accompanied by enormous loss of life haunts contemporary man. The impact of future massive bloodlettings may alter the inner balance of our triad by compromising the fueling hope inherent in liberalism.

At the apex of the triad on which American Jewish political culture has developed is some form of liberalism whose primary political expression is that a government role as regulator, caretaker of the physical environment, and stimulator of the economy is imperative for national well being. Zionism and Holocaust consciousness are more reactions to historical events whose intrusion into the polity remains in the realm of ideas and passions. We have noted that liberalism goes beyond political ideology to a more visceral feeling. For Jews it is a form of historical consciousness impinging on their secular identity, a state of mind. Even while it allows a broad range of positions it exercises a powerful influence on the shape and content of Jewish political culture. It is that long-range sustained effect that accounts for the special place it assumes in this study.

Jewish liberalism has been related to the nation's political culture since the creation of the republic. A new dimension was added with the arrival after 1870 of the eastern European immigrants who carried in their cultural baggage a broad social democratic sensibility, to which we can trace its statist character. Whatever else social democracy meant, government had a role to play in human affairs. Reliance on the state also developed out of Jewish communal needs as guests in the land of others. Its liberalism is an amalgam of the two. Today for local issues such as school budgets and related property taxes or water usage, with the possible exception of church–state issues, Jewish liberalism differs little from its general American cohabiter. There is little that distinguishes the Jewish liberal on issues like gay marriage, conservation measures, gun-control laws, abortion rights, local education, healthcare, and tax policies. Yet on other issues concerning affirmative action and foreign affairs, there can be some deviation from the national liberal standard. One size fits all, except on issues that have a special significance for Jewish voters. Jews are more supportive of military aid for Israel while at the same time preferring higher government spending for education and research in the sciences, such as cancer or stem-cell research. They are generally less enthusiastic about massive military spending. Jews favor government gun-control regulations and keep fewer guns in the home. In a strange way membership in gun clubs, which is disproportionately low among Jews, may serve as confirmation of Jewish liberalism.

The differences with ordinary liberals are not so much in issues supported or opposed but in levels of engagement. We have already noted that Jews are more likely to be politically engaged. They communicate with their legislative representatives and send letters to the editors of newspapers. They are deeply involved in local politics played out on school boards and civil organizations.[3] The difference between native-born and Jewish liberalisms was especially noteworthy during the pre–World War II years when Jews were far more supportive of an interventionist policy compared with the isolationism that prevailed in the heartland. There was little Jewish opposition to Roosevelt's Destroyer Bases Deal or to lend-lease, even when it was extended to the Soviet Union after June 1941.[4] There was also a barely discernable difference, in tone if not in substance, during the early years of the cold war. Having experienced firsthand the tactics of the extreme Left in their communal politics, Jews generally were early to recognize the danger to world peace posed by the Kremlin.

At the same time the early unforeseen Soviet development of an atomic bomb in 1949 followed by the invasion of South Korea in 1950 were disheartening, in the sense that occurred so close to the end of World War II that it seemed that perpetual war rather than the liberal dream of peace and international comity had become the default condition of international life. The Jewish voter did not muster great enthusiasm for the war in Vietnam. Draft-prone Jewish youth were disproportionately involved in protesting the Vietnam War and in their role as Freedom Riders during the civil rights movement in the South. The case is revealing because few young people from ethnic voting blocs were similarly involved in such proportion. In those rare instances when we can sense a Jewish consensus, much depends on whose ox is being gored. Lyndon Johnson was wont to point to the inconsistency of Jewish opposition to military intervention in Vietnam while at the same time advocating ever more military aid for Israel against threatening Soviet client states like Syria and Egypt.

On most issues there is little to differentiation Jewish from general liberals. During the Bay of Pigs disaster and the Cuban missile crisis that followed, Jewish voters shared the general perception that the world was teetering on the edge of disaster. On the other hand, events like the slaughter of civilians in Syria or a murderous rampage in Mexico arouse only a normal level of interest among Jewish voters. The latest and ultimately successful communal effort to influence American foreign policy was the campaign to win the right of emigration for Soviet Jewry, which, strongly influenced by the Holocaust analogy to "save" Soviet Jewry, became heated during the Nixon administration in the seventies.

Yet there is no "official" voice that speaks for American Jewry on domestic or foreign-policy issues. In recent years leading Jewish legislators like Senators Carl Levin (Dem. Michigan), then chairman of the Committee on Armed Services, and Charles Schumer (Dem. New York), member of the Senate Finance Subcommittee on Social Security, Pensions, and Family Policy, have favored "bringing the boys home" from Iraq and Afghanistan as soon as possible. These are prominent Jewish lawmakers who voice their personal positions, which customarily are not far removed from the consensus in the Jewish community, though the positions taken by Jewish lawmakers like the former Senator Joseph

Lieberman and House Speaker Eric Cantor indicate that there is a wide spectrum of political positions held by leading Jewish politicians.

Instances when Jewish political positions are out of step with majority liberal opinion are infrequent. In cases when they can be found and tabulated at all, they are usually matters of degree. Jews were more engaged in the civil rights issue than other ethnic voting blocs. In several cases such as the Korean or the more recent war in Iraq and Afghanistan, which are more distant from direct communal interest as in the case of Israel, determining the Jewish position is problematic since there exists no instrument that can state with certainty who speaks for the community. That voice can and has been preempted, as in the case of Middle East policy. More recently, citing some Jewish neoconservatives as evidence, the Jewish position on the invasion of Iraq has been misstated. The charge is then "mainstreamed" by other pundits, who are similarly convinced the "Jewish lobby" controls Middle East policy, to become a "truth" amplified by the media that American Jewry had gotten us into the war in Iraq.[5]

The issue that draws our special attention because it clarifies the ideological divides between Jewish liberalism and the general American electorate, which is part of the dialogue between Democrats and Republicans, concerns the role of government in the lives of the citizenry. The question of how much power government should have is the major axis around which the American political dialogue is organized. "That government governs best which governs least" is a Jeffersonian maxim at the heart of Republican sentiment that expresses the fear that government power poses a threat to liberty. There is much in the unhappy history of the twentieth century that reinforces that fear, but, viewing government as an instrument to "repair the world," the majority of Jewish voters consistently departs from the national conservative consensus that fears government power and seeks to limit it. But there are exceptions to the inclination to favor government regulation. Jews favor abortion rights and gay marriages despite the fact that under normal circumstance such issues are close to being considered private family matters that many Jewish voters feel should be immune from government interference. In some cases, finding the line between the two can pose a problem. On a practical operational level, it is the role assigned to government that partly defines

Jewish liberalism. More egalitarian then libertarian, the Jewish voter supports public policy, especially when it helps bridge the gap between economic classes.

In a much-simplified form we can view the conflict over the role of government embodied in the slogan of the French Revolution, "Liberty, Equality, Fraternity." The conservative Right tends toward libertarianism, while the Left is devoted to egalitarianism enhanced through government regulation and agencies. There is conflict inherent in that division since by previous condition and genetic endowment we are not equal. If men and women are free to develop their unequal talents, then liberty and equality are forever in conflict. Jewish liberalism, which we have noted is in some measure an American version of social democracy, is consistent in throwing its weight on the egalitarian side. It views most government entitlement programs as helping to create an even playing field. The *étatisme* characteristic of American Jewish political culture can be traced back to its roots in eastern Europe, where it was deeply embedded in Jewish communalism. The dilemma for Jewish liberals becomes apparent in their resistance to community control of schools in Bedford Stuyvesant. Many Jews fought hard to protect their gains in winning access to the municipal civil service through the merit system. It was a libertarian position. In the 1920s and early thirties, liberals fought for reform of the Tammany machine in New York by advocating examinations to hire the fittest teacher.

Yet such unwillingness to change principle is not characteristic of Jewish liberalism, which has undergone several basic changes over the years. Such changes are inherent in its political role as change agent. It is the role the Left has traditionally played in parliamentary democracies. It seeks out new issues to place on the political agenda. In a sense the liberal Left proposes while the conservative Right seeks to dispose. The workings of that somewhat oversimplified model can be seen in the contemporary issue of same-sex marriage and the related issue of "don't ask, don't tell" in the armed services. Several liberal groups propose the acceptance of same-sex marriage in the name of "equal rights." It becomes part of the political dialogue featured daily in the media and sounded in the nation's legislative assemblies, where it will ultimately be decided. How the balance is struck depends on the balance of power between the two forces, liberalism and conservatism. When the two forces are in balance the resolution waits a tilting of the political dialogue and consensus in one direction or the other. In the case of same-sex marriage, the process may go on for many years with some "red" states never agreeing.

Conservative Americans tend to reject the idea that empowerment of all groups is part of the logic of democracy and also the key to political stability. Once empowered, such groups seek to realize their interests. In addition to its change seeking, the apprehensiveness generated by Jewish liberalism is related to its political hyperactivism, which in turn is rooted in its need to seek government intercession to insure the safety of threatened Jewish communities abroad. That quest became more pronounced after the establishment of the Jewish state in 1948, but in fact there has been a Jewish presence in Washington since before the Damascus blood libel in 1840. Historically, beleaguered Jewish communities requiring diplomatic intercession seem always to be present on the world stage. It is Jewish persistence in projecting influence in Washington that serves as the sharpest differentiation from other ethnic voting blocs with whom it is compared. Beleaguered Jewish communities abroad compel American Jewish leaders to make the trip to the Oval Office and the halls of Congress more often than do "normal" ethnics. What appears to some to be Jewish hyperactivism in politics is in fact a resonance of its continued insecure position in the world and is largely confined to the arena of foreign affairs. American Jewry tilts outward to hear better the pleas of its brethren. There is of course no law that restricts the participation of a special interest group in the political process. Some in fact would hold up the engagement of Jewish citizens in the political process as a model of civic virtue. Yet from a Jewish perspective, power wrought by proxy and exercised indirectly through diplomacy has proven to be insufficient.[6] Unlike Israel, American Jewry lacks the hard power of a sovereign nation to place military forces in the field; it relies on its ability to influence the American government to project protective power in its stead.

In practical American politics, Jewish liberalism is linked to the liberal wing of the Democratic Party and is additionally strengthened by the growing number of Jewish voters who list "independent" rather than a party affiliation. Nonaffiliated independent Jewish voters are likely to vote liberal on domestic issues though their vote may be less deliverable as part of a Jewish voting bloc on foreign policy issues. The classification "liberal" encompasses a broad preference of candidates that sometimes includes support of Republicans who are dubbed as liberals. Supporters of the late Nelson Rockefeller, Jacob Javits, and Abraham Ribbicof come to mind. Although no Republican candidate for the presidency has ever won the majority of the Jewish vote since the election of Theodore Roosevelt in 1904, some Republican candidates have been more preferable than others.[7] Richard Nixon won only 17 percent of the Jewish vote when he ran in 1968 against Hubert Humphrey, a classically liberal candidate. Yet Ronald Reagan won a remarkable 39 percent of the Jewish vote against Jimmy Carter's 45 percent in the election of 1976. It was the highest percentage of Jewish voting support for a Republican candidate since Eisenhower won 40 percent of the Jewish vote over Adlai Stevenson in the election of 1956. Dwight Eisenhower's victory over Adlai Stevenson is all the more noteworthy since Stevenson possessed most of the character traits that the Jewish voter favored. He was well spoken, favored liberal causes, and had a high level of formal education and a patrician background.[8] On the grassroots level where the ballots are cast, liberals support the liberal candidate, but when a particularly popular Republican candidate like Eisenhower or Reagan is involved, Jewish voters are not immune to their charm.

There is a persistent misunderstanding of Jewish liberalism among newly minted conservative Jewish public intellectuals like Norman Podhoretz, who is convinced that neither from a communal self-interest nor from a pocketbook vantage does the liberalism of the contemporary Jewish voter make sense.[9] Yet the political behavior of post-emancipation German, French, and English Jewry is, after all, not that different from that of American Jewry. It may not be going too far to suggest that for Jews, liberalism clearly goes beyond being merely a point slightly left of center on the political spectrum. It is a persuasion embedded deeply in their exilic experience. It reaches beyond the left wing of the Democratic Party affiliation to a collective persuasion. Yet we can note that deeply rooted historical consciousness does not mean that on the temporal level the Jewish voter is exempt from the impact of untoward incidents like a physical attack on Israel. Such incidents have overnight turned the Jewish vote into total support of a "conservative" or even a right-wing position.[10] We have noted how quickly Jewish behavior at the polls can change during the Ocean Hill–Brownsville conflict and the riots in the Crown Heights section of Brooklyn. But whether the conversion to voting the Republican ticket was permanent was questionable. The Crown Heights riots involved an Orthodox Hassidic community normally not in the Jewish liberal fold. The Hassidic voter was concerned with "law and order" before the incident in Crown Heights. Senator Alphonse D. Amato's reputation of a staunch antiliberal Republican candidate gained him considerable support among Jewish voters in Brooklyn and Queens. Yet, in the election of 1998, when his reputation was stained by charges of corruption, his share of the Jewish vote fell from 40 to 27 percent. Similarly, Frank Rizzo, the "law and order" candidate for mayor in Philadelphia in 1973, lost 40 percent of his Jewish support when he sought to change the third-term charter limitation. Mayor Bloomberg ran into similar trouble when he sought charter change for a third term as mayor of New York. In fact the conservative trend among Jewish voters in New Jersey and Pennsylvania declined in 2002 when liberal candidates like Ed Rendell regained the governorship of Pennsylvania with strong Jewish support and Frank Lautenberg won the New Jersey Senate seat. Those pundits who see a shift to a conservative or popular candidate like Ronald Reagan as a realization of the hope that the Jewish voters are finally abandoning their liberalism are often disappointed by a reversion to the liberal candidate in subsequent elections. In a standard predictable local political situation, the Jewish vote remains slightly left of center in comparison with other ethnic voters.

Voting behavior alone does not reveal the depth of Jewish liberalism since the character of the Jewish vote cannot be fathomed in a single election. There are in fact several levels of liberal commitment among Jewish voters. Moderate Liberal Jewish voters sometimes turn out to be not so liberal, just as conservative candidates often turn out to be not so conservative once faced with the realities of governing.[11] A liberal Jewish voting constituency in Connecticut did much to develop the political career of Senator Joseph Lieberman, who subsequently not only felt compelled to give up his affiliation with the Democratic Party but also crossed liberal red lines by supporting faith-based federal welfare programs and running against the liberal trend that increasingly viewed the war in Iraq as a catastrophic Bush error.

An incident such as the bombing of the Twin Towers, which brought the reality of terrorism home to the American voter, caused a precipitous abandonment of cherished liberal principles regarding privacy. Seventy percent of Jewish voters now abandoned their opposition to a national identity card system and 66 percent now supported expanded camera surveillance on streets and public places. Abstract Jewish liberal principles regarding privacy remain in place rhetorically, but liberalism is not a voting *diktat* imposed by a party apparatus. It is anchored in a state of mind that proves to be remarkably plastic.

That is so because there are factors other than the depth of a candidate's liberalism that influence Jewish voter preference. These factors account for the wide variation in enthusiasm for liberal and conservative candidates. How candidates present themselves personally can play a decisive role for the Jewish voter. That includes such things as language usage and the impression of some intellectual depth. Most important is the talent to transmit a sense of self that, though difficult to define, has some relation to transmitting what was once identified as character and personal integrity. These personal factors can outweigh such ideological liberal factors as passion for the underdog, and even an assurance of patriotism and love of country, which are standard declamations on the campaign speaking stump. To win the Jewish vote it also helps to possess a good formal education or its equivalent in business achievement. Oddly enough, with all their concern for the underprivileged, Jews are drawn to patrician candidates like Franklin and Theodore Roosevelt over populist candidates like Andrew Jackson or more recently John Edwards. Except for Dwight Eisenhower, the Jewish voter does not seem to be impressed with military credentials. In a word, the favorite Jewish candidate tends to look much like what the Jewish voter aspires to be, intelligent, progressive, and engaged. Could it have been otherwise?

We have noted that to limit the identification of Jewish liberalism to a specific point on the political spectrum does not do it justice. Theodore

Roosevelt's penchant for empire building, today anathema to the liberal imagination, was acceptable in another time and political context. His love of conservation and devotion to preservation of the nation's natural treasures would gain considerable traction among contemporary liberals if he were not also know as an enthusiastic hunter and sportsman. Such judgments are difficult because liberal standards are themselves ever-changing. Liberals responds to the world as it is and only then conceive of the world as it should be.

Which of liberalism's broad array of principles and values come into play depends very much on the context of the time. It would be interesting, for example, to learn what the long-range impact of the recession, which began with the economic meltdown of 2008–2009, might have on liberal thinking. It is safe to assume that American liberals, including its Jewish component, will turn their attention to economic issues such as unemployment; a reminiscent yet not quite the same focus as prevailed during the New Deal decade. One can already hear the great debate regarding Keynesian deficit financing. The New Deal spoke of the "forgotten man," while the Obama administration speaks of restoring the middle class. The issue of inclusion and civil rights submitted by liberals in the sixties and seventies would now be amalgamated with the uneven effects the economic downturn, caused by high unemployment and foreclosure rates, has on low-income families. The outline of the debate is already clear: resentment regarding the financial bailout of the banks that were "too big" to be allowed to fail, chronic unemployment and underemployment, a gradual abandonment of the graduated income tax, an unprecedented concentration of wealth in fewer and fewer hands, a declining middle class, and above all a lowered living standard for the next generation. These are the budding issues that will stoke the political dialogue proffered by liberals. It is safe to predict that despite all the signs that the Jewish electorate is growing more conservative, it will be in the forefront of the call that the nation must do better for its "have nots."[12] The coloration liberalism assumes is determined by the condition of the nation at a particular moment in history. By its very nature the national political dialogue, which Jewish liberalism helps shape, grows out of contemporary condition of the American people. Like farmers, liberals harvest their crop of issues and market them for the national political dialogue.

Given the maverick character of Jewish voters, predicting their preferences in years to come is a foolhardy venture. In the past Jewish voters have shown a penchant to form their own third party in New York State, but also to disproportionately veer off to third-party candidates, particularly when they are on the left side of the political spectrum.[13] On the one hand, we are dealing with an ethnic voting bloc whose loyalty to the Democratic Party is unmatched. On the other, it is also a voting bloc of some volatility that prefers a broad range of alternatives within its liberalism. In a sense the Jewish vote is at once noted for its constancy to the Democratic Party and yet, over certain issues and candidates, comes close to being a swing vote.

American Jewry's comparatively high level of commercial success began early and, with the arrival of the eastern European migration, was followed by high levels of formal education and professionalization. That cumulative higher level of education may by itself be sufficient to account for the deeper Jewish political engagement, especially an abiding interest in the making of public policy. Today that high level of engagement in the public square is readily identifiable. Jewish citizens play a disproportionate role as the nation's opinion leaders. Scholars and journalists of Jewish background are prominent in explaining American culture and history to America in the media, the professoriate, and as public intellectuals. There is little in their various messages that are of discernable Jewish interest, nor do secular liberal Jewish voters confine themselves to matters of specific Jewish interest. There is a paradox in this. The individuation that accompanies embourgoisement and achievement broadens the vision of the individual Jewish citizen and leads to a diminishing of the collective Jewish political voice in a kind of trade off, the higher the class status and estate, the lower the affiliation. Most American Jews identify themselves as secular, which means that they are usually less affiliated religiously and communally. In a sense American Jews are becoming 5.5 million tribes of one rather than a collectivity. It may be that only after leaving the voting booth does the autonomous detribalized Jewish voter discover that his or her equally autonomous Jewish neighbor has pulled down the same voting levers. Yet pollsters show no hesitation in identifying a "Jewish vote" as long as it is a Jewish voter who, for whatever reason, is puling down the voting lever.

There is a fractiousness entailed in the loss of communal cohesion. The most likely reason for a future change in Jewish voting patterns is that the Jewish voter may become less Jewish, less influenced by communal behavior modes. The inability of Jews to speak to political power holders with one voice was already apparent during the Holocaust. Clearly the political acculturation of American Jewry has been somewhat slower than the immigrant groups with whom they arrived. But the process is ongoing and Jewish survivalists are haunted by a vision that American Jewry will experience a similar decline. Beyond the vision of the "melting pot" in which that fear is rooted is a process equally threatening to continuity and the ability to generate a political voice. It is the individuation that defines modernity. That process means that the communal roots of Jewish liberalism are leaving the historic stage. Its continued vitality stems more directly from secular modernity than the religious culture it no longer knows.

The assumption here is that the Jewish electorate will continue to develop as a highly individuated yet politically and culturally engaged voting bloc as in the past. That engagement, which in some areas borders on hyperactivity, assumes that American power will continue to play a leading if somewhat diminished role in the world. We have noted that the condition that historically most concerns the Jewish voter has been the vulnerability and insecurity of Jewish communities in the diaspora. With the establishment of the Jewish state, that concern was transferred to Israel. In a sense American Jewry is more politically active and engaged in the corridors of power because of world Jewry's historic vulnerability. Today that feeling of threat is focused on the Islamic world and is based on their sense that there ought not to be a Jewish state with its own claims and power flourishing in its *Umma*, the lands for which Islam has a theocratic claim. Strangely, it is led by Iran, an Islamic but non-Arab state. In the mind-set of Jews who continue to somehow feel themselves belonging to a certain people, that feeling of vulnerability stems from an awareness that to have lost European Jewry, and then to witness the sustained threat to its successor Israel, places the quest for communal survival as a Jewish presence in history at the very heart of American Jewish political culture.

In the end most things on the Jewish political agenda are related directly and indirectly to the quest for survival. That is true of the myriad issues gleaned from the foregoing pages, from the struggle for a liberal immigration policy to placing the rescue of European Jewry on the wartime agenda, from agitation for the recognition of Israel in 1948 and its diplomatic and military support thereafter to the campaign for the release of Soviet Jewry. Many of the issues Jewish leaders brought to the American government involved some aspect of immigration policy. In the twentieth century extrication of threatened Jewish communities became a centerpiece of the strategy for physical survival as a people. It continued to be a concern after the establishment of Israel and serves as evidence, if any is needed, of American Jewry's attachment to Jews the world over as well as its confidence in the promise of America. Strategies for rescue and survival by liberalizing immigration policy drew upon the liberal agenda and had almost unanimous support among Jews. But there are few examples that can be cited where Jewish liberal interests single-handedly were able to have their way with government policy. Jewish influence and votes, even when buttressed by the general electorate, was usually insufficient to deflect the national consensus that came to oppose immigration. To open the gates even partially for Jewish Displaced Persons after World War II required skillful public-relations campaigns, lobbying, and political activism. The campaign to gain admission for Soviet Jewry that generated the Jackson-Vanik amendment was more successful. The amendment is one of the most remarkable examples of special interest influence in American diplomatic history. Remnants of the law remain on the books to this day.

The communal interests of American Jewry were sought primarily through the liberal wing of the Democratic Party, which was accessible to Jewish advocates. Only after such intra-party considerations was it possible to reach the next step, deliberation by legislative bodies and political leaders in adequately high positions. Short-circuiting this formal lawmaking process is rare. The most important role Jewish liberalism contributed to the liberal agenda is witnessed not in the projection of influence for specific Jewish interest such as the security of Israel. It is rather in the use of its influence in helping to place general welfare issues that extend from abortion rights to healthcare to the regulation of the sale of guns on the national agenda. The assumption is that an improvement of the general conditions and standards of life will improve the Jewish condition as well. The welfare of the Jewish citizen is not seen as apart from the national welfare. That remains true in the advocacy for the security of Israel, which the Jewish liberal views as consonant with the national interest.

If until 1991 immigration policy was a continuous concern for American Jewry, then some form of liberalism serves as its driving force. We have noted that liberalism has meant many different things at different times. Its crucial element is a broad, multifaceted sensibility that goes beyond temporal political interest to the notion that America holds a special place as guardian of liberty and haven for the oppressed. The Jewish liberal sensibility is only partly manifested in voting behavior. Jewish liberals are among the most engaged political activists in the political arena. Behind them are thousands of voters whose liberalism resembles more a form of consciousness than a political ideology. With all its inconsistencies it is difficult to avoid the conclusion that some form of liberalism lies at the heart of American Jewry's political soul. It lends a liberal coloration to the two other strands of the triad, Israelism and Holocaust consciousness. The Holocaust may have been incubated in a European crucible, but as reshaped by liberalism it becomes a warning to the nations that the veneer of civilization is thin indeed. Eli Wiesel, spokesperson for the survivors, often sounds that warning. Similarly, liberals increasingly defend Israel on the basis of it being a democracy entitled to exist like all nations rather than part of a biblical real-estate deal promised to the Jewish people. We remain without a specific definition of Jewish liberalism, which may be as much an asset as a liability. To see it as a state of political consciousness allows for a plasticity that can be an advantage in the crisis-ridden present. Unfortunately, it also reinforces the conservative image that finds liberalism amorphous and uncertain.

When Jewish liberalism is distilled to its essence, it comes to the simple truth heard from an elderly Florida snowbird first encountered in the preface, who, when queried about her political beliefs, responded simply that "government ought to do the right thing for its citizens." But that is the beginning of a political dialogue, not an end. The national political debate prevails precisely to determine what is "right" for the nation. We have noted that for the American Jewish voter, "doing the right thing" requires that more weight be given to the egalitarian aspect of public policy. Yet in achieving their high economic status, no ethnic group has more successfully exploited the libertarian dimension also embedded in American political culture. There is perennial hope among Republicans that Jewish voters will finally come to their senses and vote their interests. By all rights, Jewish voters ought to be pulling down the Republican lever when they are in the voting booth. But no great change in Jewish political sentiments and behavior is on the horizon. The majority of Jewish voters remain attached to a political culture whose primary principle is that government should be an agency for the improvement of the human condition. They present a long list of what that entails.

Finally, these ruminations are intended more as an explanation of, rather than a history of, Jewish liberalism and the central role it plays in Jewish political culture. That permits us entry into the normally forbidden spheres of prophecy offered here as musings about where we are going. It is not a task without peril. In the foregoing pages what we classify as "liberal" is in fact a broad constellation of values that have in common openness to ideas of improvement of the human condition. Unfortunately, that sensibility cannot by itself give the Jewish survivalist much comfort. The Holocaust, which is deeply embedded in Jewish consciousness, cautions that there is little that can stay the hand of those intent on harming them except their own sovereign power. For Holocaust survivors, personal experience substantiated the existence of a savage Hobbesian world. In a sense, Jewish liberalism is a quest for a social order to replace that world. Its unresolved problem is not, as its critics maintain, that it runs against Jewish self-interest. A liberal world in which nations strive for a higher level of human interaction would permit a crisis-weary people to restore its energies and fully exercise its talents. The quest for such a world is in the interest of a people that have been historically insecure. But thus far the evidence accumulates that the political architecture that could enable the realization of the liberal quest for a higher level of human interaction remains beyond what domestic and international politics is able to develop. The world teeters from crises to crises and the domestic political system seems to be dysfunctional. Yet, however they are castigated by conservative opponents who hurl the "L" word into the political arena as if liberalism was a disease, they optimistically develop yet a new entitlement program that they imagine will improve the lot of the less fortunate. Of that we can be certain, but where that impulse comes from is less certain. Unlike their social democratic predecessors, Jewish liberals are no longer armed with a vision of a perfect world to come, nor are they bound by a religious imperative. They have embarked on a mission to improve their world, program by program, from which they do not feel "free to desist." It is how they invent themselves.[14]

Notes

Select Bibliography

Index

Notes

1. Jewish Political Culture: The American Wrinkle

1. There is a lively interest among Jewish researchers concerning the nature of Jewish political culture and power. David Vital, for example, confines his definition of general Jewish political culture to such things as self-regulation by means of communal judicial mechanism enforced by communal authority without recourse to government. David Vital, *A People Apart: The Jews in Europe, 1789–1939* (Oxford: Oxford University Press, 1998), i–ii. See also Alan Dowty, "Jewish Political Culture and Zionist Foreign Policy," in David Vital, Abraham Ben–Zvi, and Aaron S. Klieman, *Global Essays in Honor of David Vital* (New York: Routledge, 2001), 311. For general discussion see Henry L. Feingold, *Jewish Power in America: Myth and Reality* (New Brunswick, NJ: Transaction, 2008); Michael Waltzer, ed., *Law, Politics, and Morality in Judaism* (Princeton: Princeton University Press, 2006); Daniel Elazar, *Community and Polity: The Organizational Dynamics of American Jewry* (Philadelphia: Jewish Publication Society, 1976); David Biale, *Power and Powerlessness in Jewish History* (New York: Schoken, 1986); Jonathan Woocher, *Sacred Survival: The Civil Religion of American Jews* (Bloomington: Indiana University Press, 1986); David Novak, *Covenantal Rights: A Study in Jewish Political Theory* (Princeton: Princeton University Press, 2000); and J. J. Goldberg, *Jewish Power: Inside the American Jewish Establishment* (New York: Addison-Wesley, 1996).

2. Hedrick Smith, *The Russians* (New York: Ballantine Books, 1977). The distinction is interesting because it implies that the use of coercive police force is required to govern the Russian citizenry, which would otherwise become lawless. The overwhelming popularity of Putin is based on his restoration of order.

3. The Japanese surprise attack on Pearl Harbor, which brought the United States into World War II in 1941, was precedented by its preemptive strike on Sunday against the Russian fleet anchored in the Straights of Shimonoseki, which triggered the Russo-Japanese War in 1905.

4. A similar idea is developed in the epilogue of William Pencock, *Jews and Gentiles in Early America, 1654–1800* (Ann Arbor: University of Michigan Press, 2008).

5. The trade based on the need of the New England textile industry for raw cotton and the need of the South for certain machine-made goods and medicines as well as gold bullion, was widespread, and included many Union army officers.

6. Cyrus Adler and Aaron Margolies, *With Firmness in the Right: American Diplomatic Action affecting Jews, 1840–1945* (New York: Arno Press, 1977).

7. The name is taken from the liberal failed revolution of 1848 that brought many German proponents to American shores.

8. Lee Sigelman, "'If You Prick Us, Do We Not Bleed? If You Tickle Us, Do We Not Laugh?': Jews and Pocketbook Voting," *Journal of Politics* 53, no. 4 (1991): 977–92.

9. See Uriah Dye, *Uriah P. Levy, Reformer of the Antebellum Navy* (Gainesville: University of Florida Press, n.d.).

10. The holder of the highest political post in the nineteenth century was Judah P. Benjamin, who served as secretary of the treasury and in the State Department for the Confederacy during the Civil War.

11. The political aspect of his varied career is examined by Jonathan Sarna, *Jacksonian Jew: The Two Worlds of Mordecai Noah* (New York: Holmes and Meier, 1981).

12. In 1819 W. D. Robinson proposed that bringing Jews to establish towns along the Mississippi and Missouri rivers would enhance the development of the West. It was one of several proto-Zionist proposals that preceded actual establishment of Jewish agricultural colonies by eastern European Jews later in the century.

13. There were ranking Jews in virtually every administration in the twentieth century. But with the exception of Jacob Schiff and Henry Morgenthau Jr., Roosevelt's secretary of the treasury, none openly braved the advocacy of a specific Jewish interest. While the Jews belonging to Roosevelt's inner circle, the so-called Jew Deal, did not deny their Jewishness, they were not fully committed Jews. That awaited the appearance of elected Jews rather than those appointed to high office. Then Jews, some observant and Orthodox like Senator Joseph Lieberman of Connecticut, who touted their support of Israel and specific Jewish causes such as the release of Soviet Jewry as well as their membership in a religious congregation, became more common. The election of House Speaker Eric Cantor, who is the sole Republican of the Jewish congressional delegation and its highest-ranking member, may be a portent of things to come.

14. The rising percentage of Jewish voting may also be attributed to rising level of education. By the 1920s the Jewish voter also displayed a maverick character in his preference of third-party candidates.

15. We will note later that the play of Jewish power in the 1970s and 1980s to win the right of emigration for Soviet Jewry, embodied in the Jackson-Vanik amendment, bore remarkable resemblance to Louis Marshall's and Jacob Schiff's earlier efforts to ameliorate the condition of Russian Jewry.

16. It was one of the factors that led to mobilization against the republic by the National Socialists, who dubbed it the "Judenrepublik." The full rights granted were withdrawn with the passage of exclusionary laws after 1933, culminating in the Nuremberg laws of 1935, which withdrew citizenship from German Jews.

17. In 1918 the first and only election within an American ethnic community was held. Over a quarter-million votes were tallied, and a fragile basis for the Jewish delegation to Versailles was established.

18. Arthur Goren, *New York Jews and the Quest for Community: The Kehillah Experiment, 1908–1922* (New York: Columbia University Press, 1970). The Kehillah sought to administer all functions, from monitoring moral behavior to education and health, under one organizational umbrella. It was fully active for only four years and never was able to convince the political social democratic organizations, including the Jewish labor movement and the religious branches, to become involved.

19. Sephardic Jews stem from the Spanish-speaking realm of Europe and Turkey. Galitzianer Jews stem from the easternmost province of the Austro-Hungarian Empire later incorporated into Poland. Litwaks are Jews born in the Lithuanian sphere that was once larger than the related Polish sphere.

20. See Daniel Soyer, *Jewish Immigration Associations and American Identity in New York, 1880–1939* (Detroit: Wayne State University Press, 2001).

21. For the most part the agreement to take care of their own was kept until the Great Depression, when Jewish philanthropy could no longer cope with the great need compelling impoverished Jews to request public welfare.

22. By the time the Nazis came to power in Berlin, the community had been taken over by the new arrivals. It was used by the German foreign office, but ultimately the German-American Bund was broken up, and its leader Fritz Kuhn was jailed in 1940, partly owing to the untiring efforts of a Jewish congressman, Samuel Dickstein. In fact the National Socialist Party did not muster much confidence of faith in the German-American Bund and invested little in it.

23. *Yishuv* is a Hebrew term meaning return and is used as the informal name for the Jewish community in Palestine before Israel was established.

24. *Goldeneh medinah*, the golden land or society, was a popular appellative for America among Jewish immigrants.

25. Resettlement in British Guiana was one of the ideas proposed by Henry Morgenthau Jr., Roosevelt's Jewish secretary of the treasury, in exchange for forgiveness of the British World War I debt. Observing that it would take the settlers fifty years to overcome "the fever," Roosevelt rejected the notion.

26. A term used by Breckinridge Long, the State Department's assistant secretary responsible for refugee matters, in a memorandum advising how Jewish refugees could be curtailed at the consular level. The blocking activities of the State Department went beyond its visa policy and the use of euphemistic vocabulary to conceal the overwhelming Jewish character of the refugee stream. A later report emanating from the Treasury Department was originally titled "The Acquiescence of the American Government in the Murder of the Jews of Europe." Secretary of the Treasury Morgenthau Jr., fearing that

taking up such an ethnic plea could endanger his position in the administration, toned down the title to read "A Personal Report to the President" before presenting it to the Oval Office on January 16, 1944.

27. The postwar admission of Holocaust survivors was a slow-starting affair. After the Displaced Persons Law of 1948, coupled with the Harrison Report (1946) concerning the mistreatment of Jewish DPs, the immigration of Jews became more possible. Between 1945 and 1952, it is estimated that about 137,450 Jews entered the United States; about 100,000 were DPs. Additional thousands filtered in after 1952. Beginning in the 1970s and accelerated by the collapse of the Soviet Union 1n 1991, it is estimated an additional 750,000 Soviet Jews came to the United States. Altogether, postwar immigration (1945–1991) supplemented the existing Jewish population by less than a million immigrants.

28. Amsterdam itself was not liberated until May 5, 1945, but sections of southern Netherlands were liberated months earlier.

29. "Jews in the Mind of America," *Fortune Magazine*, February 1936, 79.

30. Henry L. Feingold, "'It Can Happen Here': Antisemitism, American Jewry, and the Reaction to the European Crisis, 1933–1940," *Moreshet, Journal for the Study of the Holocaust and Antisemitism* 7 (Winter 2009): 187–206.

31. Statistics recently published about the remittances to the home country by immigrants indicates that they are high enough to play a critical role in their economies. That can be most clearly noted in immigrant remittances from Latin America and the Caribbean, the largest group in the United States. In 2003 it was estimated to amount to $30 billion. Eighteen percent of all adults in Mexico received remittances from immigrants in the United States, 28 percent in El Salvador, 14 percent in Ecuador. See "PEW Hispanic Center Research Topics: Remittances," http://pewhispanic.org/reports.

32. See Feingold, *Jewish Power in America*, 136–37.

33. The communal activity of the Catholic Church at the level of the diocese and parish is excluded since it is hierarchical and service is Catholic, in the sense that it is not confined to a single ethnic community. The Church's Council of Bishops wields considerable influence and is in a class by itself outside the ethnic communal power dealt with here.

34. For the political context of successful congressional breakthrough for Soviet Jewish immigration, see Henry L. Feingold, *"Silent No More": Saving the Jews of Russia* (Syracuse: Syracuse University Press, 2007).

35. Of the forty-four Jewish legislators in the 111th Congress there were only two Republicans (Arlen Specter and Eric Cantor), and they were not on the same political wavelength.

36. In June 2011, after several Latin American countries showed signs of favoring the Palestinian side and later voted to recognize the Palestine Authority as a voting member of the UN General Assembly, a Latino-Jewish Congressional Caucus was established. In past sessions there have been several informal Jewish caucuses. Since membership changes, the congressional caucus is virtually reformed with every Congress.

37. The percentage of Jews earning over $100,000 per annum (46 percent) is over twice as high as any Christian denomination. Only Hindu Americans (43 percent) come close. See PEW Forum on Religious and Public Life, Religious Landscape Survey, http://religions .pewforum.org/portraits.

38. I prefer the more general term "ethnic vote" to the immigrant or hyphenate vote. Ethnicity is a more sustained influence than the one-generation immigrant phenomenon.

39. An occasional Jewish appointment to cabinet or ambassadorial positions did occur in the nineteenth and early twentieth century. It was Al Smith as governor of New York who made full use of Jews in his inner circle. Included were Sam Rosenman, Joseph Proskauer, Henry and Belle Moskowitz, and Robert Moses.

40. The highly professionalized campaigns that had developed by the 1970s feature a year-round formal organization to garner the Jewish vote. The Democrats have as part of their permanent party organization the National Jewish Democratic Council (NJDC). The Republican equivalent is The Republican Jewish Convention (RJC). Both are administered by leading affiliated Jewish party members.

41. Theodore Roosevelt had Jacob Schiff and Oscar Strauss. Franklin Roosevelt had a bevy of Jews in his inner circle. But it was Henry Morgenthau Jr., his secretary of the treasury, who ultimately presented the Jewish interest during the Holocaust. Nixon had Leonard Garment and Max Fisher.

42. The occasional exceptions were the Greek American organization to restore Cyprus to Greek rule after the Turkish invasion in July 1974 and the Cuban American effort to continue its anti-Castro resistance from American shores. American Jewry is an exception to the exception, in that its need to influence Middle Eastern policy after its grand effort to establish Israel in 1948 has been ongoing.

43. See Fernando Santos, "Upheaval among New York's Voting Bloc," *New York Times*, July 13, 2008, 1, http://www.nytimes.com/2008/07/13voters.html.

44. See Robert Wistrich, *Terms of Survival: The Jewish World since 1945* (New York: Routledge, 1995), 231–32. The Jewish vote in national elections normally ranges from 65 to 85 percent Democratic.

45. Will Maslow, "Jewish Political Power: An Assessment," *American Jewish Historical Quarterly* 66, no. 2 (1976): 353. Most Jewish defense organizations fall under the Tax Revenue Code Section (501)(C) (3), which grants tax exemption providing they do not "participate" or "intervene" in political campaigns.

46. See James Traub, "In Search of the Liberal Jewish Vote," *The New Yorker*, October 4, 1993; and Peter Beinart, "The End of the 'Jewish Vote,'" *The Washington Post*, October 27, 2004, A25.

47. Biale, *Power and Powerlessness in Jewish History*, 6.

48. See Feingold, *Jewish Power in America*, 3–6.

49. There are a few examples of governance, as in Costa Rica and American Samoa, where corporeal power embodied in armed agencies does not exist or has been minimized.

Such governments are stable but require certain economic and social factors to be in place, often including the security mantle of a state that acts as a protector.

50. While anti-British rhetoric was occasionally heard from individual political leaders, the Anglo-American alliance (1902) continued to be the basic building block of American foreign policy until the post–World War II period.

51. Formally introduced by the Russian-born Jewish ophthalmologist Laconic L. Zamenhof in 1887, its early practitioners hoped it would become a universal second language to foster international peace and understanding. It became particularly popular among Jews, but never realized the aspirations of its founders. The National Socialists viewed Esperanto as part of the international Jewish conspiracy and hounded its practitioners.

52. The peace movements of the twenties were a high point in American idealism. Levinson believed that removing the sanction of legality from war would help maintain the peace. He was instrumental in the Senate's nearly unanimous passage of the Briand-Kellogg Pact (August 1928), which outlawed war as an "instrument of national policy." The term "parchment peace," a response to the Washington Arms Conference (1921–22) by realists, was again used to describe the Pact of Paris in 1928.

53. Jennifer Siegel, "As NYC Mayor, Bloomberg Has Redefined Role as 'Jewish Pol.,'" *Jewish Daily Forward*, June 27, 2007.

54. Michael N. Dobkowski, who has gathered the most complete catalogue of these organizations, cites Daniel Elazar's five major functional categories: religious-congregational, educational-cultural, community relations, communal welfare, Israel-overseas. See *Jewish American Voluntary Organizations* (Westport, CT: Greenwood Press, 1986). That barely touches on newly developing organizations relating to the Holocaust and ad hoc organization like the National Conference for Soviet Jewry that grow out of the crisis of the moment. There are ad hoc organizations that are established to handle a temporary problem like the emigration of Soviet Jewry. There are even umbrella organizations for organizations of related purpose. And there are Zionist organizations that coalesce on the basis of an interest in the security of Israel, though they rarely agree on how that can be best achieved. Every ideology, even a shadow of an ideology, has its organizational expression and voice.

55. In 1999 the United Jewish Appeal (UJA) and the Council of Jewish Federations (CJF) merged to form the United Jewish Communities (UJC). It maintains the federated structure of Jewish governance, but also serves as the final building block in communal governance.

56. For a full description, see Dowty, "Jewish Political Culture," 309–10. See also Biale, *Power and Powerlessness in Jewish History*, 6.

57. Henry L. Feingold, "Was There Communal Failure among American Jews?" in Feingold, *Bearing Witness: How America and Its Jews Responded to the Holocaust* (Syracuse: Syracuse University Press, 1995), 216.

58. There were several efforts to create such unity. The Congress movement was the most important of these. On the local level, most noteworthy was the aforementioned creation of

the New York Kehillah, 1919–1922. It was confined to the local New York level. In the post-Holocaust period the National Jewish Community Relations Advisory Council (NJCRAC) was established in 1944, an initiative taken by the CJF to fulfill the missing role of a central policy advisory council where basic decisions would be hammered out. It is composed of 14 major national Jewish organizations, 114 local federations and community-relations councils, representatives of the major religious branches, and, recently, Jewish women's organizations. But turf battles, especially with the President's Conference and budgetary problems, blocked the fulfilling of its unifying aspiration to become the representative voice of the organized Jewish community. It speaks out on both domestic and foreign affairs issues.

59. The resettlement of Soviet Jewry and the "drop out" problem is probed again in chapter 3 in the context of tensions within the American Zionist movement. See also Feingold, *Silent No More*, 298–302.

60. See Henry L. Feingold, "'Courage First and Intelligence Second': The American Jewish Secular Elite, Roosevelt, and the Failure to Rescue," *American Jewish History* 72, no. 4 (1983): 423–60. There have been great speakers like Rabbis Stephen Wise and Abba Hillel Silver, but a single charismatic leader such as Dr. Martin Luther King Jr. has yet to find a place in the highly fractious communal life of American Jewry.

61. Albert Einstein achieved enormous popularity in the first half of the twenties, but rejected any leadership role such as the presidency of the newly established Hebrew University and later the presidency of Israel.

62. If the highest level of postgraduate education claimed by Hindus is disregarded since a disproportionate number are here studying for higher degrees, then Jews have the highest percentage claiming postgraduate education—35 percent. Hindus toll 48 percent, while the national total is 11 percent. See *Pew Forum on Religious and Public Life*, http://religions.pewforum.org/portraits.

63. "Election Reference Information: Jewish Voting Record, 1916–2012," Jewish Virtual Library, www.Jewishvirtuallibrary.org/jsource/US-Israel/jewvote.html.

64. See Dominique Strapper and Sylvia Strudel, *Ethnicity and the Jewish Vote: The French Case* (New Brunswick, NJ: Transaction, 2008).

65. The party switch can also be noted on the congressional level. The Sixty-sixth Congress (1919–1921) had six Jewish members, of whom five were Republicans. The Seventy-fifth Congress (1937–1939) had ten Jewish Representatives, only one of whom was Republican. Some observe that by the "roaring" twenties it was the Republican Party rather than the Jewish voter that changed.

66. That exasperation at the unwillingness of the Jewish voter to abandon the assumption that political progress stems from the political Left rather than the Right is the theme of Norman Podhoretz, who was among the earliest Jewish intellectuals to support neoconservatism. See *Why Are Jews Liberals?* (New York: Doubleday, 2009).

67. An ethnic vote can still be awakened by specific issues. Cuban American voters are split on the embargo of Cuba. Greek Americans have never forgiven the Turkish invasion

of Cyprus. Polish Americans can still be aroused by the fear of Russian domination and German irredentism. Mexican Americans oppose the rigid enforcement of the new state immigration control laws. But the issues involved are not high priority on the American political agenda.

2. American Jewish Liberalism: How Deep the Roots?

1. Seventy-three percent of Jewish voters identify themselves as moderate or liberal and 23 percent as conservative. Thirty-four percent of Catholics and 42 percent of Protestants see themselves as conservative. Steven Windmueller, "Are American Jews Becoming Republicans: Insights into Jewish Political Behavior," Jerusalem Center For Public Affairs, *Jerusalem View Points*, no. 509 (December 15, 2003). These statistics are in contrast to a 1988 survey conducted by the *Los Angeles Times* that found that 41 percent of Jewish voters identified themselves as liberal and 17 percent as conservative. In contrast, the general voter showed only 18 percent liberal and 30 percent conservative. It is estimated that the distribution of Jewish voting is 15 to 25 percentage points to the left of the American political center and 9 to 15 percentage points more liberal than other white ethno-religious groups "after other sociodemographic characteristics are controlled." Geoffrey B. Levy, *Toward a Theory of Disproportionate American Jewish Liberalism* (New York: Oxford University Press, 1995), 3, 65–66.

2. See, for example, "Why People Are Liberal? Examining Political Liberalism using a Motivated Social Cognition Perspective," www.allacademie.com//meta/p_mla_apa.

3. Both are easily classified as middle class in that they are more educated, 49 percent are college graduates, and more affluent, their annual income is $75,000 or above. They are more likely to live in cities, more likely to vote the Democratic ticket, and 33 percent never marry.

4. Marc Dollinger, "Exceptionalism and Jewish Liberalism," *American Jewish History* 90, no. 2 (2002): 161–64.

5. Malcolm Stern estimates that the intermarriage rate in colonial America was higher than 10 percent. For their greater assimilability, see Malcolm Stern, "Americans of Jewish Descent," *National Genealogical Society Quarterly* 46, no. 2 (1978).

6. Ben Halpern, "Roots of American Jewish Liberalism," *American Jewish History Quarterly* 66, no. 2 (1976): 205.

7. Jewish reformers did not share the assumption of original sin as did Social Gospelers. The Protestant theologian that comes closest to the Jewish approach to reform, that the citizen and the state were obligated to work for justice and righteousness under all circumstances, was Reinhold Niebuhr. But unlike Jewish reformers, Niebuhr was far less optimistic about the possibility of improving the human condition. The problem with Judaism, he was convinced, is that it lacked a concept of original sin.

8. In 1917 Morris Hillquit running as a Socialist won a seat in the New York State Assembly. That year Socialists won ten Assembly seats and seven positions on the Board of Aldermen and one municipal judgeship.

9. Though New York had the largest Jewish community in the nation and perhaps the world, it did not elect a Jewish mayor until the election of Abe Beame, who served from 1974 to 1977. See also Henry L. Feingold, *A Time for Searching: Entering the Mainstream, 1920–1945* (Baltimore: Johns Hopkins University Press, 1992); and Stephen D. Isaacs, *Jews and American Politics* (Garden City, NJ: Doubleday, 1974).

10. This derivative European brand of liberalism that grew out of the Enlightenment is called "Philistine" liberalism by Ben Halpern. The French Enlightenment carried forward by Descartes, Rousseau, Voltaire, and Condorcet emphasized the rule of reason inherent in liberated man's capacity to bring change, while the Scottish Enlightenment, pressed forward by thinkers like David Hume, Adam Smith, and Edmund Burke placed far less trust in reason. It remained for thinkers like John Locke and Montesquieu, who conceived of the idea of dividing government power into its separate functions—legislative, judicial, and executive—to establish the balanced government of separation of powers we witness in the North Atlantic powers.

11. See Halpern, "Roots of American Jewish Liberalism," 195.

12. See Werner Cahn, "The Sources of American Jewish Liberalism," in *The Jews: Social Patterns of An American Group*, ed. Marshall Skare (Glencoe, IL: The Free Press, 1958)

13. Charles Lieberman, *The Ambivalent American Jew* (Philadelphia: Jewish Publication Society, 1973).

14. Steven Windmueller, "Revisiting the 2008 Presidential Election: Reflections on the Jewish Vote," *Jerusalem Center for Public Affairs*, no. 44, May 15, 2009, 1. When Jewish independents finally cast their ballots in a close election they still are more likely to come down for the liberal candidate.

15. For American sources of Jewish liberalism, see Michael Kammen, *Spheres of Liberty: Changing Perceptions of Liberty in American Culture* (Madison: University of Wisconsin Press, 1986); and Louis Hartz, *The Liberal Tradition in America* (New York: Harcourt Brace, 1964).

16. It was founded in New York State with the help of William Buckley and in 1974 outpolled the Liberal Party, also indigenous to that state.

17. That was the silent transaction made during the colonial period. See William Pencak, *Jews and Gentiles in Early America, 1654–1800* (Ann Arbor: University of Michigan Press, 2005), 262–63.

18. Henry L. Feingold, *Zion in America: The Jewish Experience From Colonial Times to the Present* (Mineola, NY: Dover, 2002), 47–48. During the colonial and national periods Jews generally maintained a low political profile. Leaders like Benjamin Nones or the Sheftalls of Georgia, who openly proclaimed their liberal position, were the exception. While Judah P. Benjamin supported the cause of slavery as secretary of the treasury in the Confederacy while representative of a certain kind of "Magnolia" Jew, he was an exception to the rule. When the Confederacy faced a recruitment crisis Benjamin advocated the conscription of slaves into the Confederate army in return for emancipation.

19. Melvin Urofsky and David W. Levy, eds., *Letters of Louis D. Brandeis*, vol. 3, *1913–1915: Progressive and Zionist* (Albany: State University of New York Press, 1973). The family had Frankist roots; a dissident sect had severed its link with Judaism. The Ethical Culture movement in the United States, founded by Felix Adler, a defector from the Reform movement, in its quintessential liberal spirit bears some resemblance to the Frankists.

20. For a full description of this development, see Henry L. Feingold, "The Changing Liberalism of American Jewry," in Feingold, *Lest Memory Cease: Finding Meaning in the American Jewish Past* (Syracuse: Syracuse University Press, 1996), 117–38.

21. The Populist reform period of the 1890s culminated in the Spanish-American War, the Progressive period with World War I, and the New Deal reform period with World War II. Whether the linkage between reform and war in American history is more than fortuitous is open to debate.

22. See "The Jewish Vision of American Liberalism," in Feingold, *Lest Memory Cease*, 135–36.

23. A radical Jew is one who seeks liberation or roots (that's what radical means) through his Jewishness. He may be a Zionist or even a religious Jew. The well-known labor Zionist spokesman Haym Greenberg or Rabbi Joshua Heschel are good examples. A Jewish radical is one who happens to be Jewish by the accident of birth. He seeks liberation for all mankind through a universalist ideology. Among their ranks could be found Emma Goldman, Leon Trotsky, and a host of others who preferred the larger world stage rather than the tribal one.

24. See Jonathan Frankel, "The Jewish Socialists and the American Jewish Congress Movement," *YIVO Annual of Jewish Social Science* (New York, 1976), 203.

25. For a full study of the role of the labor Zionists in the United States, see Mark Raider, *The Emergence of American Zionism* (New York: New York University Press, 1998).

26. Charitable giving is one of the 613 commandments, or *mitzvoth*, that order the life of the observant. It is not only customary to give or to care but it is also the law, of which observant Jews are reminded in the final prayer of all services, the *Aleinu*, which restates the aspiration to "perfect the world under the sovereignty of God." Concern for the welfare of dependent members has been a millennial communal practice that even the smallest Jewish community is hardwired to do by the imperative of *tsedakah* (charity, righteousness) embodied in *Halacha*. Catholic communities also develop an extensive network communal charity, but it is implemented through the hierarchy of the church and given out of Christian love (*caritas*) rather than command of law. Jewish communalism and its inherent welfare role is internalized individually.

27. There are seven thousand Jewish family foundations of various degrees of wealth whose combined assets total between $10 and $15 billion. Evan Mendelson, "The History of Jewish Giving in America," Jewish Virtual Library, www.Jewishvirtuallibrary.org/jsource /Judaism/philanthropy.html. Under the new McCain-Feingold Law, which regulates the contribution of "soft" money, Jewish big giving will be affected. The trend is for more giving

electronically (by Internet solicitation) of small sums. Here Jews are not that different from other givers; 0.27 percent give two hundred dollars or slightly more, and only 0.01 percent give two thousand dollars or more. See Goldberg, *Jewish Power,* chap. 1.

28. With the exception of giving to Israel, Jewish philanthropy today is as much influenced by civil (American) motivation, the Protestant model, as it is by the tenets of Judaism. But the remarkable communal social service anchored in the local federations was in place before government assumed responsibility for the poor during the New Deal. In a word, when the handful of colonial Jewish settlers promised Peter Stuyvesant that they would never become dependent on public charity, they were simply describing what was the norm in Jewish communities.

29. Aside from the conventional statement, which observes that more than 60 percent of campaign money for the Democrats and 20 to 35 percent of Republican funds originates from Jewish sources, there is little precise data on the extent of Jewish giving to political parties, candidates, or campaigns. While Jewish PACS contribute to the campaign of congressmen from both parties, there is a distinction to be made between campaigns funds for pro-Israel candidates and pro-liberal-issues candidates. Senator Joseph Lieberman (Dem. Connecticut) is purported to have received less from Jewish liberal sources in his last campaign than did his opponents.

30. See Lawrence Fuchs, *The Political Behavior of American Jews.* "Religification" is not without its problems. Observant Jews claim that the Reform use of principles like *tikkun olam* is a misappropriation of religious principles for political ends. See Michael Staub, *Torn at the Roots: The Crisis of Jewish Liberalism in Post-War America* (New York: Columbia University Press, 2002), 8.

31. Not all nations manage the total separation at the very heart of modernity. In the United States the major faiths have over time worked out the boundaries between the nation's political and religious life. The legal processes of defining those boundaries were endless and varied. The George W. Bush administration, for example, encouraged tax dollars to support "faith-based" charities. Islam, the third of the Abrahamic religions, never established such boundaries, so that there is a natural tendency in all Islamic countries toward theocratic amalgam such as has become typical of Islamic republics.

32. The IWW (Wobblies) is generally considered the most successful militant left-wing organization in pre–World War I America. During the twenties its ranks were penetrated by Communist activists and converted to a "front" organization of the party.

33. The native American labor movement seemed to follow along classic Marxist lines, which after the bloody strike at Ludlow in 1914 and the Russian Revolution created great apprehension. Using the espionage law of 1917, Wilson jailed thousands of dissidents who opposed the war. The "Red scare" that followed in 1919 led to the deportation of thousands by Attorney General A. Mitchell Palmer, whose home was destroyed by a bomb in June 1919. Jewish radicals remained generally uninvolved in the industrial violence, but were very supportive of the anarchists Sacco and Vanzetti during their trial.

34. See Jack Jacobs, *Bundist Counterculture in Interwar Poland* (Syracuse: Syracuse University Press, 2009). Despite the resistance of the Communists, the Bund in Poland may actually have been growing in strength in the immediate prewar years. Its education movement was premised on the existence of a Jewish national culture with its own language (Yiddish) and literature. In the United States it was the Workman's Circle, the largest of the fraternal orders, that was the clearest resonance of the Bund.

35. Arthur Liebman, "The Ties That Bind: The Jewish Support of the Left in the United States," *American Jewish Historical Quarterly* 66, no. 2 (1976): 285–321. See also Tony Michels, *A Fire in Their Hearts: Yiddish Socialists in New York* (Cambridge: Harvard University Press, 2005).

36. The Orthodox rabbis who brought Rabbi Jacob Josef to the United States in 1902, to be paid by a tax on kosher meat, were under the illusion that they continued to have such authority, an assumption that no longer was the reality.

37. In the pre–World War I years, the Jewish Socialist Federation had about 14,000 members. That number was increased by the thousand of sympathizers in the Jewish labor movement concentrated in the needle trades (the Amalgamated Clothing Workers of America, ACWA; and the International Ladies Garment Workers Union, ILGWU). Add to this the 7,500 members of the Yiddish Language Organization, who entered the party almost wholesale.

38. But the "children's crusade" for Wallace proved in a sense to be the "last hurrah" for the extreme Jewish Left. The Students for a Democratic Society (SDS), the largely Jewish-led campus movement of the late sixties and early seventies that also sought to become embedded in a youth culture, was far more individuated and libertarian in its notion of freedom and use of public relations, and more raucous in its contempt for the "establishment" and the slavish adherence of their parent generation to the paternalism of the party.

39. Robert Cohen, *When the Old Left Was Young: Student Radicals and America's First Mass Student Movement, 1919–1921* (New York: Oxford University Press, 1993). We shall note later that the SDS, which led the campus revolt in the late sixties, rejected the notion of party discipline to which some of their parents had adhered. The college experience served as a background for the New Left abandoning the principle of democratic centralism, which signaled party members to end opposition once a leadership decision had been made.

40. There were five Jewish Republicans and one Democrat in the Sixty-sixth Congress (1919–1921). In the Seventy-fifth Congress (1937–1939) there was one Jewish Republican and nine Democrats.

3. The New Deal Jewish Liberal Amalgam

1. "Jew Deal" became the anti-Semitic label to suggest that Roosevelt was flooding Washington with Jewish appointments. In fact the proportion of Jewish appointments ranked below that of the Hoover administration. Of the ninety-two appointments to the federal judiciary, seven were Jews and fifty-two were Italian Americans; the remainder stemmed from the Protestant community at large. But Jewish appointments to government

agencies were frequently to those most in the public eye, like the unpopular wartime Office of Price Administration or the Security Exchange Commission.

2. Oddly, there was one exception to opposition to a government role in the economy and it occurred in the very industry that government largess helped create. During World War I government in effect took over the railroad system via the Plum plan. The situation changed during the Roosevelt era with government-planned regional development like the Tennessee Valley Authority. During World War II American industrial production was enhanced via government loans. The Manhattan project to produce the atomic bomb was a completely government-run operation. During the Eisenhower administration there began the government-sponsored Federal Highway Program. The movement toward a Scandinavian-type mixed economy was fully in evidence in the government-sponsored space program (NASA). Government seemed to enter where private capital feared to tread. The government role prescribed by Maynard Keynes was a far cry from socialism, but the new Jewish voter was able to support it.

3. If a precise year is required for the moderation of the New Deal aspect of Jewish political culture, it would be 1972, when Richard Nixon soundly defeated the liberal Democratic candidate George McGovern despite a comparative high percentage of Jewish votes.

4. The "four freedoms," as first presented by Franklin Roosevelt in his State of the Union address on January 6, 1941, spoke of freedom of speech, religion, and freedom from want and fear. The Senate never formally ratified them, but like Wilson's "fourteen points," it became the closest the United States and Britain came to stating their common war aims. All nations bound to the Allied cause, including the Soviet Union, expressed support for the "eight points" that came out of the meeting in Newfoundland that produced the Atlantic Charter. Popular acceptance of the "four-freedom" idea was partly attributable to Norman Rockwell's "Four Freedom" posters that appeared in the *Saturday Evening Post* in 1943.

5. These themes, considered in the context of the role the Holocaust continues to play in the Jewish liberal position, are examined in Tony Kushner, *The Holocaust and the Liberal Imagination: A Social and Cultural History* (Cambridge: Blackwell, 1994).

6. Included were the Civil Rights Act of 1964, the Voting Rights Act, the Elementary and Secondary Education Act of 1965, and the Fair Housing Act of 1968.

7. The best description of Nixon's hope to turn the Jewish vote is contained in Peter Golden, *Quiet Diplomat: A Biography of Max M. Fisher* (New York: Cornwall, 1992).

8. Jews have the highest percentage of voters that identify themselves as liberal (48 percent). They are followed by African Americans (32.6 percent). The lowest percentage of voters who identify themselves as Liberal are German Americans (22.1 percent). Tom W. Smith, *Jewish Distinctiveness in America: A Statistical Portrait* (New York: American Jewish Committee, 2005), Table 31.D, 158. The distinction of "most liberal" belongs to the African American voting bloc. During the New Deal era Jews gave anywhere from 88 to 90 percent of their votes to Democratic candidates. By the 1990s it had leveled off at 79 to 82 percent for the Democratic ticket. There were exceptions, however, in the election of 1980, when

Reagan received 38 percent of the Jewish vote. Since the election of 1952, African Americans voted for the more liberal candidate in higher percentages than Jews. The two exceptions were the election of 1956 (Jews, 60 percent Stevenson; African Americans, 59 percent) and the election of 1960 (Jews, 82 percent Kennedy; African American (nonwhites), 68 percent). About two-thirds continue to be registered as Democrats and 16 percent as Republicans.

9. Nixon's anti-Semitic rantings were not reflected in his practical political relationships and appointments. Henry Kissinger, his principal adviser, was given a virtual free hand, and Jews were appointed to chairman of the Federal Reserve Board and other high government posts during his administration. From a Republican perspective the doubling of the Jewish vote for Nixon in the election of 1972 (35 percent) from its low in the election of 1968 (17 percent) marked a sharp rise from the 1969 low point. Nixon finally attained the normal Jewish support for a Republican candidate. McGovern seemed the ideal candidate for the liberal Jewish voter. In a sense, one could consider that "normal" vote for Nixon a minor Jewish defection from liberalism.

10. It included the Civil Rights Act of 1964 and the Voting Rights Act of 1965, which reshaped national politics; Medicare and Medicaid; and new education and immigration bills, consumer protection laws, antipoverty programs like the Food Stamps Act of 1964 and Head Start, environmental laws, and new federal departments of transportation and housing and urban development.

11. The combined votes for the Republican and George Wallace's States Rights ticket was 57 percent, symbolic of a well-defined reversal of prior political alignments. The "solid South" could no longer be claimed as solidly Democratic.

12. Carter won a comparative high percentage of the Jewish vote when he ran against Gerald Ford in 1976 (71 percent), but suffered a precipitous decline in the election of 1980 when he only received 45 percent of the Jewish vote against Ronald Reagan, a decline of 26 percent.

13. See G. Calvin Mackenzie and Robert Weisbrot, *The Liberal Hour: Washington and the Politics of Change in the 1960s* (New York: Penguin Press, 2008).

14. Tom Waldman analyzes the disastrous defeat of McGovern in 1972 and its impact on liberalism, in *Not Much Left: The Fate of Liberalism in America* (Berkeley and Los Angeles: University of California Press, 2008).

15. "Drop outs" was the name attached to Soviet Jews who emigrated on the basis of an Israeli visa, but once out of the reach of Soviet authority and safely settled in Vienna or Rome, rejected (i.e., "dropped out" of) the refugee stream headed for Israel. See Feingold, *"Silent No More,"* 149–60.

16. There exists "a silent liberal Jewish majority," not fully reflected in Jewish organizations and media, that generates an indirect influence on the Jewish political voice. See Paul Vitello, "On Israel, U.S. Jews Show Divergent Views, Often Parting from Leaders," *New York Times*, May 6, 2010, A15, 18.

17. The more recent incarnation of Jewish liberalism is best traced to the Ocean Hill–Brownsville conflict, in which Rhody McCoy, the newly appointed district superintendent, sought to replace a largely Jewish teaching faculty appointed through the merit system with an all-black one appointed by the community and beholden to it. The head of the United Federation of Teachers, Shanker, called three strikes against the district. He was deeply involved in the struggle for civil rights and strongly supported other facets of the liberal agenda. Jewish liberal activists were themselves split on the issue of community control. See Richard D. Kahlenberg, *Tough Liberal: Albert Shanker and the Battle over Schools, Unions, Race, and Democracy* (New York: Columbia University Press, 2007).

18. Yet Mario Biaggi, the supreme "law and order" candidate who had served as U.S. Representative for a Bronx district from 1969 to 1988, before his indictment for corruption, received a surprising 10 percent of the Jewish vote in his campaign to win the Democratic nomination for Mayor in 1973.

19. Staub, *Torn at the Roots*, 5.

20. In cases where the injustice or right concerned individuals, the term "empowerment," frequently used by new liberals, took its place in the liberal lexicon beside older terms such as "access." It suggested that power itself was the most effective instrument for liberation. Its roots may be found in the Marxism of the Socialist Left and also in certain styles of psychotherapy.

21. Dr. Moses Mielziner of the University of Giessen became a leading proponent of the antislavery position of the Bible, while Rabbi Morris Jacob Raphall of New York's B'nai Jeshurun Congregation concluded that there was slavery, albeit of a different kind, among the ancient Israelites. He was denounced as an Israelite with Egyptian principles, as were many others. But Raphall pointed out that Jewish slaves were not "animated tools"; ancient slavery was so surrounded by the regulation of Jewish law, including emancipation in the Sabbatical year, that the saying "a Jew who owned a slave had a slave for a master" was commonly used in rabbinic sermons.

22. For how the biblical "my people" was transformed into the African American people, see Dollinger, "Exceptionalism and Jewish Liberalism," 161–64; and Marc Dollinger, *Quest for Inclusion: Jews and Liberalism in Modern America* (Princeton: Princeton University Press, 2001).

23. Hasia Diner, *A Time for Gathering, 1820–1880: The Second Migration* (Baltimore: Johns Hopkins University Press, 1992), xiv, xii. See also Halpern, "Roots of American Jewish Liberalism," 191.

24. Professors rate highest in identifying themselves as liberal (43 percent), law enforcement officials and building managers rate lowest (10 percent to 11 percent). Patricia Cohen, "Professor Is a Label That Leans to the Left," *New York Times*, January 18, 2010, C1, 8.

25. In the sixties, the general estimate of the composition of campus radicalism was that 60 to 80 percent stemmed from Jewish homes. Similarly, even after the SDS had passed its peak in 1969 and became attractive to the general student population, an astounding 30 to 50 percent were of Jewish origin.

26. See Feingold, *Jewish Power in America*, 107.

27. The interesting exception was the antiwar and military presence on campus demonstrations that occurred at CCNY and other urban campuses where there where Jewish students in sizeable numbers in the years preceding World War II. See Cohen, *When the Old Left Was Young*, 22–41.

28. It is estimated that about 60 to 80 percent of student radicals and 30 to 50 percent of the SDS were "of Jewish origin." The disproportionate Jewish presence in the leadership strata of the SDS, the Yuppies, and Berkeley's Free Speech movement was also apparent. Feingold, *Jewish Power In America*, 125.

29. Elections: 1988, Dukakis 64 percent; 1992, Clinton 80 percent; 1996, Clinton 78 percent; 2000, Gore 81 percent; 2004, Kerry 75 percent; 2008, Obama 78 percent.

30. Over 70 percent of ballots cast by Jewish voters stem from California, New York, New Jersey, and Pennsylvania. If one adds Florida, the Jewish vote plays a crucial role in the states that determine over 78 percent of the electoral vote to win the presidency.

31. Jewish parents send the highest percentage of their children to college (75 to 80 percent), where surveys show that they are far more likely to identify themselves as anti-status quo or far Left (27 percent) as compared with their non-Jewish classmates, who identified themselves as far Left at a far lower rate; 4 percent for Protestants and 2 percent for Catholic students. The political view of the parent generations is less extreme but still quite different from the non-Jewish generation. Seventy-three percent of Jewish voters see themselves as moderate or liberal, and 23 percent as conservative. Catholic and Protestant voters identify themselves as 34 percent liberal and 42 percent conservative.

32. On the Jewish love affair with language, see Amos Oz and Fania Oz, *Jews and Words* (New Haven: Yale University Press, 2012).

33. There is some room for accommodation on the gender question within the Orthodox fold but almost none on gay rights.

34. See Harvey Kler, *Communist Cadre: The Social Background of the American Communist Party Elite* (Stanford: Hoover Institution Press, 1978).

35. It is estimated that 20 to 30 percent of the Freedom Riders were young people of "Jewish origin." Especially noteworthy for the light it cast on the role of young Jews in the life-threatening integration effort in the South was the murder of Andrew Goodman and Michael Schwermer, together with James Earl Chaney.

36. John Mearsheimer and Stephen Walt, *The Israel Lobby and U.S. Foreign Policy* (New York: Farrar, Strauss and Giroux, 2007).

37. See Deborah Lipstadt, *Beyond Belief: America's Press and the Coming of the Holocaust, 1933–1945* (New York: Free Press, 1986); and Robert Shapiro, ed., *Why Didn't the Press Shout? America and International Journalism during the Holocaust* (New York: Yeshiva University Press, 2003).

38. The Jewish labor movement, composed of a triad, the *Daily Forward*, United Hebrew Trades, and Workmen's Circle, was the powerful supporter of liberal causes before World

War II. But a shifting class structure that brought most Jews to the middle class makes it a former shadow of itself. The JLC and the UHT still maintain offices, but the "rank and file" that once composed large Jewish unions such as the ILGWU and the ACW are no longer Jewish.

39. Such characters were known as *ibergegeben*, a Yiddish term to describe a certain Jewish political type passionately devoted (given over) to the cause that they are convinced is one of selfless idealism. The decline of such types may have been a generational factor. The American political climate was cooler and more reserved than the eastern Europe one from which they stemmed. See Tony Michels, *A Fire in Their Hearts*; and Feingold, "Changing Liberalism of American Jewry," 133.

40. Dinkins drew almost half the Jewish vote in Manhattan, but the more conservative Jews residing in the outer boroughs gave Rudolph Giuliani, who ran on a Liberal/Republican ticket, 70 percent of their vote. There was a fragmentation of the Jewish vote along income and educational lines. Dinkins won by a very narrow majority of 2.4 percent, very untypical of New York Jewish voting patterns. For some Jewish voters it was a question of competence, reinforced by Dinkins's later low-key response to Jewish fears regarding the rioting in Crown Heights. See Edward Shapiro, *Blacks, Jews, and the 1991 Brooklyn Riot* (Waltham: University Press of New England, 2006); and James Traub, "In Search of the Liberal Jewish Vote," *The New Yorker*, October 4, 1993.

41. Of the nation's almost 5.3 million Jews, about a half million adhere to Orthodox rhythms, but the Orthodox birthrate is nearly double that of secular Jews. When that is considered jointly with the high attrition rate among the unaffiliated, the Orthodox voting bloc becomes something to be reckoned with in weighing the dominance of the liberal persuasion among Jewish voters.

42. Windmueller, "Are American Jews Becoming Republicans?"

43. Steven Windmueller, "New York as America's Capital City," *Jewish Philanthropy*, February 11, 2010. The judgment is probably premature, since Jewish liberalism also stemmed from the intellectual pundits and public intellectuals centered in New York and Washington, DC. Hollywood remains a liberal center, but the lesser influence of universities like Stanford and Berkeley compared with Ivy League schools and the University of Chicago gives California a more muted liberal voice.

44. In the election of 1990, Rudy Boshowitz (Dem. Minnesota) ran against Paul Wellstone. Both candidates could claim to be Jewish and staunch supporters of Israel. Boshowitz, in a negative campaign, accused the more liberal and more marginally Jewish Wellstone of being "a disturbing element in American politics" and being less connected with the Jewish community, that is, his wife and children were not Jewish. The pandering for the Jewish vote backfired and led to the loss of Jewish votes and partly figured in Boshowitz's defeat. He was the only incumbent senator defeated in the 1990 election. Jewish liberalism proved a stronger force than Jewish tribalism. An equally competitive campaign in 2008 between Al Franken (Dem.) and Norm Coleman (Rep.), two Jewish candidates for the Senate, did not

repeat the fallout but raises the puzzling question of how a state known for the virulence of its organized anti-Semitism in the thirties and a very small Jewish population could nevertheless generate a "Jewish" election issue.

45. See Feingold, "Changing Liberalism of American Jewry," 124.

46. The highest governing judicial and ecclesiastical council in biblical Israel before the destruction of the Temple in 70 AD.

47. The comparison is faulty since only Samuel Rosenman, Roosevelt's speechwriter, could today be classified as a practitioner of the profession of politics. David Axelrod was at once a strategist, a campaign organizer, a media expert, an avid contractor, an interpreter of public opinion polls, and a general adviser who marketed his talents to many candidates including Hilary Clinton, John Edwards, and Christopher Dodd. Similarly, Rahm Emanuel, who began by representing the Fifth Congressional District of Illinois between 2003 and 2009 and aspired to become Speaker. Instead, drawn into the Clinton camp, he allowed himself to be sidetracked to organizational politics primarily as a fundraiser and strategist. That talent was evident on the national party level in the 2008 campaign, where his knowledge of Jewish givers gave him an extra edge. Obama's "Jew Deal" was drawn from a fairly recent profession of politics that specialized in getting clients into office. Few of Roosevelt's Jewish advisers were involved in elective office.

48. The atypically high Jewish vote cast for Reagan, a Republican conservative, in the election of 1980 (39 percent), indicates that the Jewish vote is highly correlated with generally popular candidates who are not necessarily liberal. But two additional variables may have played a role in this election: the unpopularity of a "born again" Jimmy Carter and the traditional drawing power of a third-party candidate among maverick Jewish voters. John Anderson received the customary 14 percent Jewish voters give to most third-party candidates.

49. That was not as overwhelming a percentage as believed. F. D. Roosevelt received around 90 percent of the Jewish vote in the elections of 1936, 1940, and 1944; John Kennedy won 82 percent in 1960; Lyndon Johnson got 90 percent in 1964; Hubert Humphrey earned 81 percent in 1968 (and lost to Nixon); Bill Clinton earned 80 percent in 1992; and Al Gore won 79 percent in 2000, an election in which the Jewish vote, especially in Florida, was decisive.

50. He received 39 percent of the Jewish vote in 1980 and 31 percent in 1984. Strangely, his strong support of the security of Israel did not carry over into support for the release of Soviet Jewry. Reagan's interest in the rescue case was only fully aroused regarding the Evangelics who found shelter in the American Embassy in Moscow in 1977.

51. Alan Fisher, "Continuity and Erosion of Jewish Liberalism," *American Jewish Historical Quarterly* 66, no. 2 (1976): 345

52. From a Jewish perspective, the role of the university in creating political consciousness or of being an "engine of liberalism" is a "chicken-and-egg problem." Similarly inclined professors did not indoctrinate Jewish campus radicals. Many were already fixed in their liberal political beliefs before enrollment. Some would argue that such students actually "liberalized" the colleges during the Vietnam War.

53. In fact middle-class Jews were somewhat faster to flee neighborhoods that were tipping then were their fellow ethnics like Italian Americans; and on abstract issues such as their support of permissiveness in the classroom rather than a more authoritarian approach. Jews are customarily in favor of "progressive" educational methods.

54. See Steven Windmueller, "Revisiting the 2008 Presidential Election: Reflections on the Jewish Vote," *Jerusalem Center for Public Affairs*, April 21, 2009.

55. Today, with the possible exception of Eric Cantor, the Republican Party leader in the House, all Jewish senators and representatives in Congress are Democrats, some more liberal than others. Former Senator Joseph Lieberman (Dem. Connecticut), who had taken a position in favor of the Iraq War, remained liberal on other domestic programs and continues to count as part of the Democratic majority in the Senate.

56. There are some exceptions. The Student Struggle for Soviet Jewry, which was active during the seventies, was composed largely of modern Orthodox youth. The Jewish Defense League (JDL) had few radical leftists. In the eighties one could find on campus small radical youth organizations composed of members of Habonim and Hashomer Hatzair (youth organizations), who maintained both a commitment to cross-racial causes and a strong Jewish identity, expressed largely in ethnic terms such as Klezmer music and Yiddish folk songs. The Jewish communal movement (Havurot) was incubated within the counterculture of the seventies, and activist secular groups like Jews for Urban Justice (JUJ) and other groups were prone to borrow Halachic terminology such as the moral imperative of performing Mitzvot or Tzedakah to "repair the world" (Tikkun Olam).

57. In the election of 1988, for example, Jews gave a higher percentage of their votes (70 percent) to the more liberal candidate, Michael Dukakis of Greek American ancestry, than did Dukakis's own Greek American constituency, who favored the Republican candidate George W. Bush.

4. The Liberal Zionist Entanglement

1. There are examples of a pattern of governance supplementing and sometimes replacing rabbinic authority in the self-governing Jewish community of Amsterdam and the several regional organizations and courts in central Europe and the Kahal system of Ottoman Jewry. The classic example of such governance is the parliament-like Council of the Four Lands that presided over Polish Jewry between 1580 and 1764.

2. B'nai B'rith, established in 1841, was the first of the American Jewish fraternal orders to become active in Europe. The AJ Cong. reformed in 1921 after dissolving itself *sine die* to conform with the agreement regarding American Jewish representation at Versailles.

3. Mass immigration has yet to develop from the United States. In 2009, approximately 3,324 immigrated to Israel from North America. The figure fluctuates from year to year depending on events on the world stage. "Why American Jews Are Making Aliyah," *United With Israel*, February 3, 2011. These figures do not account for the growing number

of Jews, especially from France and Latin America, who hold dual citizenship and own homes in Israel.

4. For a description of this complex process, see Aaron Berman, *Nazism, the Jews, and American Zionism, 1933–1948* (Detroit: Wayne State University Press, 1990).

5. There were Jewish and Christian alternatives that envisaged America as Zion. The Jewish example belongs to the Tammany Sachem Mordecai Noah, who proposed a haven for Jews called Ararat near Buffalo. The American examples of Christian Zionism are evident throughout the colonial and early national period. From Salem to Babylon, American place names sound like a biblical atlas.

6. Part of the oft-repeated public-relations slogan of the Jewish National Fund (Keren Kayemet L'Yisrael) founded in 1907. Its first director was a German Zionist, Max Bodenheimer, who began the process of purchasing land for resettlement.

7. For a full discussion, see Edward Alexander, *Classical Liberalism and the Jewish Tradition* (New Brunswick, NJ: Transaction, 2002), 38.

8. Judah Magnes, who became head of the newly formed Hebrew University, was an exception. His transplantation and acculturation was incomplete. He always considered himself an American Jew living in Palestine. Weizmann, Goldmann, and Wise never resettled in Israel.

9. For development of this division, see Herbert Weisberg, "Social Justice and Self-Interest: Explaining Liberalism among American Jews," paper presented at the meeting of the American Political Science Association, Philadelphia, November 10, 2008, http://convention3.allacademic.com/meta/p_mla_apa_reseaarch_citation/06 PDF.

10. For the well-established Jews of Germany, the decision was especially agonizing and deepened by a demographic factor. It is estimated that most German Jews in the late thirties were "seniors," almost 40 percent over the age of sixty-five.

11. For the original development of this theme, see Raider, *Emergence of American Zionism*, chap. 2.

12. The territorialists who attracted such notables as Israel Zangwill at the turn of the century called for Jewish settlement in Uganda, thus taking the "Zion out of Zionism," according to the Zionists. Josef Rosen, an agronomist, was a major figure in the Agro-Joint resettlement project in the Crimea. To the chagrin of Zionists he appeared again during the Holocaust as a principle organizer of the Sosua resettlement venture in the Dominican Republic.

13. The League divided the mandates into three categories, A, B, and C. The "A" category, composed of territories formerly held by the Ottoman Empire, was the most advanced and held out the promise embodied in Article 22 of the Covenant of the League of Nations that after sufficient "administrative advice and assistance" enabling the former colonies to "stand on their own feet" the mandatory power would withdraw. There were three such mandates; Mesopotamia and Palestine, which included Jordan, were mandated to Britain,

and Syria to France. Most important, Class A mandates were ostensibly being prepared for statehood of some kind.

14. It is estimated that about 17 percent of American Jews were foreign born at the outset of the thirties. Descendants of the "new" immigration probably formed well over 60 percent of the American Jewish electorate.

15. See John G. Snetsinger, *Truman, the Jewish Vote, and the Creation of Israel* (Stanford: Hoover Institute Press, 1974).

16. The analogy of the U.S. "special relationship" with Israel during our wartime alliance with Britain was actually made by John Kennedy in a conversation with Golda Meier, Israel's foreign minister, in December 1962. See "Memorandum of Conversation, Palm Beach, December 27, 1962," in *Foreign Relations of the United States (FRUS)*, vol. 18, *Near East, 1961–1963* (Washington: U.S. Government Printing Office, 1994), 276–83.

17. See Feingold, *"Silent No More,"* 149–86.

18. The prewar Jewish Agency (HaSochnut) was created by article 4 of the mandate to help Britain administer the mandate. Its existence was formalized by the Sixteenth Zionist Conference in 1929 and provided for the inclusion of non-Zionists on the principle of parity. American Zionists were allotted 44 of the 112 seats.

19. The Jewish Agency as currently known was created in 1948 out of the units of the preexisting agency. It is composed of two parts, the World Zionist Organization and the Jewish Agency, and governed by a 120-member Board of Governors, 50 percent of whom represent the WZO, 30 percent the Jewish Federations of North America (JFNA), and 20 percent from Keren Hayesod, the philanthropic arm of other-than-American organizations. An election to determine the distribution of seats and votes in a world Zionist conference is held every four years among the several American Zionist organizations. The number of seats and votes among the organizations is determined by the number of "shekel" purchasers each organization can muster.

20. Its clearest articulation came from Abba Kovner, the renowned resistance leader and poet, who advocated that Israel develop the bomb in order to caution Israel's enemies that "those who survived Auschwitz could destroy the world. Let them know that! That if it ever happens again, the world would be destroyed." Quoted by reviewer Edward Alexander of Dina Porat, *The Fall of a Sparrow: The Life and Times of Abba Kovner* (Stanford: Stanford University Press, 2009), in SPME (Scholars For Peace in the Middle East), *Faculty Forum*, July 7, 2010.

21. Samuel Huntington, "The Clash of Civilizations?" *Foreign Affairs* 72, no. 3 (1993): 22–49.

22. Jewish immigrants did develop a full panoply of *landsmanschaftn* fraternal organizations based on common regional and town origins. There were few such social networks based on locality among non-Jewish immigrants with common roots in Poland or Ukraine, but there are national organizations, many with church affiliations.

23. See Fradle Freidenreich, *Passionate Pioneers: The Story of Yiddish Secular Education in North America, 1910–1960* (Teaneck, NJ: Holmes & Meier, 2010).

5. Israel's Resonance in American Jewish Politics

1. The election of 1868, when Grant faced charges of anti-Semitism, was the earliest reported concern regarding a Jewish vote. Thereafter, concern about its weight has been unfailing among political pundits in national elections. For example, the Jewish vote is said to have played a crucial role in the much-touted Democratic victory in the election of 1948. George W. Bush received only 19 percent of the Jewish vote in the election of 2000, a comparatively low percentage compared with other Republican candidates for office. But after it became clear that he would be the strongest-yet presidential supporter of Israel, the percentage rose by 5 points to 24 percent in the election of 2004. But that support of Israel is not the end all and be all of Jewish political preference is reflected in his consistently low level of Jewish political support at the polls after the war in Iraq went sour. The Jewish vote is also a factor in many local elections where a sizeable Jewish population resides.

2. The claim was made by Rep. Robert Wexler (Dem. Florida), a top adviser. Rev. Wright's support for Hamas in February 2008 threatened Obama's gaining the democratic nomination. Neela Banerjee, "Obama Walks a Difficult Path as He Courts Jewish Voters," *The New York Times*, March 1, 2008, 1, 12.

3. One researcher postulates that its power rests not merely in numbers at the polls but also in the fact that it remains a "uniquely swingable bloc" despite looser Jewish organizational affiliation. It plays a crucial role in Florida, Pennsylvania, and California. Jeffrey S. Helmreich, "The Israel Swing Factor: How the American Jewish Vote Influences U.S. Elections," *Jerusalem Letter/Viewpoints*, no. 446, January 15, 2001. Helmreich believes that it is the fact that 30 to 35 percent of the Jewish vote is swingable on the Israel issue that gives Jews an extra measure of political leverage.

4. See Steven T. Rosenthal, *Irreconcilable Differences: The Waning of the Jewish Love Affair with Israel* (Hanover: Brandeis University Press, 2001). The most recent case of that waning influence came in the election of 2004 when Republican strategists became convinced that Bush's extraordinary strong support of Israel would realign the Jewish voting preference. But the Jews gave a whopping 77 percent of their vote to John Kerry, leading one observer to state that "Bush hasn't realigned the Jewish vote. He has ended it." See Beinart, "End of the Jewish Vote," A25. The older Bush received only 19 percent of the Jewish vote in the election of 2000, a comparatively low percentage compared with other Republican candidates for office. But after it became clear that he would be the strongest yet presidential supporter of Israel, the percentage rose by five points to 24 percent in the election of 2004. The strong position on the security of Israel did not affect the continued low level of support for George W. Bush. The problem for prognosticators of the Jewish vote is that they assume a collective persona. But Orthodox Jews who feel "very close" to Israel (74 percent), as compared

with Jews generally who simply acknowledge its importance (37 percent), are more likely to be drawn to a single issue like Israel. In 2004 Bush attracted these Jews and the newly arrived Soviet Jews who compose less than 10 percent of the Jewish vote, and repelled the great majority of Jewish voters who remain liberal. But many pundits agree with Jeffrey S. Helmreich that the Israel factor continues to be critical in Jewish voting behavior.

5. In the results of the election of 1988 (Bush vs. Dukakis) and 1992 (Bush, Clinton, Perot), the Jewish vote had snapped back to its pre-Reagan distribution. Dukakis received 64 percent in 1988, and in 1992 Clinton received 80 percent of the Jewish vote. Perot, the third-party candidate, received only 9 percent, breaking the precedent that a third-party candidate receives no less than 14 percent of the Jewish vote (www.Jewishvirtuallibrary .org/jsource/US-Israel/jewvote.html).

6. For a full development of how the charge of inordinate power in the hands of a Jewish lobby was being wielded against the national interest, see Feingold, *Jewish Power in America*. The political as well as anti-Semitic aspects of the charge are developed in chapters 1 and 2.

7. The figure of 6 million dead was not reached until the early fifties and is in fact still disputed today. The Final Solution brought the death of two out of every three European Jews, so that the projection of the existence of a European Jewry that might continue to generate that culture was forlorn. Berlin's Final Solution had in fact eliminated the principle pillar of world Jewish culture. Until the creation of the Jewish state in 1948, it was American Jewry that was the most viable inheritor of the cultural legacy of European Jewry.

8. That Hadassah and the AJCongress were deeply taken in by the Madoff Ponzi fraud is a reflection of their desperate financial condition, which serves as an epitaph for once-powerful organizations.

9. That contention was not entirely true. A fanatic anti-Semite and an avid proponent of the Final Solution was the Grand Mufti of Jerusalem, Mohammad Amin al-Husseini, who counseled Hitler to expand the operation of the Final Solution to the Middle East. Husseini played a role in blocking Jewish refugees from Bulgaria, Hungary, and Romania from entering Palestine. Islamic troops that were incorporated into the *Wehrmacht* included a Waffen SS unit from Aizerbaijan and a Moslem Bosnian unit, and finally the *Arabischer Freiheitkorps* of 37,000 men incorporated directly into the German army with the help of Husseini's office in wartime Berlin. Arab historiography underplays his connection with the Holocaust and the German war effort, viewing him merely as a Palestinian nationalist. Generally Jewish historians dispute the Islamic narrative of benevolence to Jews, especially during the golden age of Spain.

10. The late Professor Tony Judt, to whom the statement is attributed, did not quite go that far. His primary objection was that Israel viewed itself as a Jewish state. He would have preferred a "state of the Jews," the way the United States is a pluralistic state of the Americans.

11. Founded in 1974 after the Yom Kippur War, *Gush* was a slow-starting affair. Initially the World Zionist Organization also supported some settlement on the Palestinian side of the "green line." American Olim were well represented among the settlers. An

American settler, Daniel Weiss, served as the first secretary general of the Council of Settlements (Yesha). After the Likud victory in 1977, military, monetary, and logistic support for construction and road building came from the government.

12. The challenge to the official position regarding the origins of the refugee problem in 1948 was initiated by Benny Morris, *The Birth of the Palestinian Refugee Problem, 1947–1949* (Cambridge: Cambridge University Press, 1988). The contention of the new historians were subsequently found wanting, and Morris himself changed his position after the rejection of the peace offer made at the Camp David negotiations in 2000. He came to feel that the threat of genocide might have been mitigated had Ben-Gurion pushed for total expulsion of the Palestinian in 1948.

13. There existed an awareness of the need to find a basis for Jewish Arab reconciliation in the political world of the Yishuv. It gave rise to Brit Shalom (covenant of peace), formed in the twenties by German Jewish intellectuals who had settled in the Rehavia district of Jerusalem, and to Ihud (Union), established in the summer of 1942. Magnes was affiliated with Brit Shalom and headed Ihud. These minority factions saw the solution to the impending conflict with the Arab population in some form of binationalism. See Daniel P. Kotzin, *Judah L. Magnes: An American Jewish Nonconformist* (Syracuse: Syracuse University Press, 2010), 277–301.

14. See Peter Beinart, "The Failure of the American Jewish Establishment," *New York Review of Books*, vol. 57, June 10, 2010, 16–20. In a study completed in 2007, the sociologist Steven Cohen found that younger Jews of the boomer generation who experienced neither the Holocaust nor Israel's beleagueredness during the fifties do not display the close ties to Israel of their parents and are far less able to come to terms with the national security argument to rationalize West Bank settlements. See Brett Cohen, "Liberal Slide Away from Israel Will Continue," *The Jewish Week*, May 18, 2010. See also Irving Louis Horowitz, "'Distancing' from Israel in Jewish American Life" (Berlin: Springer Science+Business Media, 2010).

15. Geoffrey B. Levey, *Toward a Theory of Disproportionate American Jewish Liberalism* (New York: Oxford University Press, 1995), 73–77.

16. The notion expressed by Peter Beinart is that younger secularized American Jews drop their Zionism as they extend their liberalism, while affiliated observant American Jews drop their liberalism as they strengthen their Zionism.

17. The notion that an actual change in attitude has occurred is challenged by Gil Troy, "How Liberalism, Zionism Reinforce Each Other," *The Jewish Week*, July 8, 2010. With the exception of music, students generally seem less affiliated with all other causes as well.

18. The problem of *Yerida*, those who descend or emigrate from Israel, is not well publicized in Jewish Agency statistics. Little hard facts are known regarding those who choose to become *Yordim* and their reasons for doing so.

19. Keeping world interest alive for six decades in what is a comparatively minor problem, judged by the numbers involved, indicates that Palestinian leadership have become masters of wielding "soft" power, that is, power whose long-range effects and tactics are aimed at effecting public opinion rather than holding territory.

20. Julius Streicher (1885–1946) was moderately prominent in the prewar Nazi hierarchy by means of controlling an important position in promoting anti-Semitic propaganda through his newspaper *Der Sturmer*. He was sentenced to death at Nuremberg.

21. The Labor Party had little experience in playing the role of the loyal opposition and Likud had little experience in governance. Except for the formation of national unity government in 1967, the Likud had never been in power, nor had the Labor Party been out of power.

22. A subtheme in Kushner, *Holocaust and the Liberal Imagination*.

23. See Edward Alexander, "Liberalism and Zionism," *Commentary*, February 1986. Hannah Arendt, for example, acknowledged the need for a Jewish politics and became active in Youth Aliyah, but continued to oppose the authoritarianism of the existing Zionist hierarchy.

24. Also taken into account is that the new generation of American Jews is far less addicted to the print media as compared with their parents and grandparents. Graduates of American universities read *The New York Times* the way their ancestors read Talmud, but receive a more detached account of the Jewish story. At the same time, American TV news programs generally have less interpretive news analysis and less coverage of the foreign scene.

25. The late Tony Judt, a well-known historian with impeccable Labor Zionist credentials, echoed the European Socialist Left by noting that Israel's insistence on being a Jewish state is historically out of step with the secular modern nation-state and thereby endangers Jewish survival. Professor Tony Judt, "Israel: The Alternative," *New York Review of Books*, October 23, 2003.

26. For development of this division, see Weisberg, "Social Justice and Self-Interest," note 9, chap. 4.

27. The term *Ummah* is a pan-Arab reference to the collective notion of Islam popular among devout Arab leaders who speak of the unity of the community of believers in the Muslim world and the restoration of the caliphate.

28. Refers to the universal community of Israel, which includes all Jewish communities.

29. The largest and perhaps the last mass rally in recent American Jewish history was convened in December 1987 for the rescue of Soviet Jewry. Such mass rallies were a major instrument in the public-relations campaign during the thirties, when they focused on revoking the British White Paper and the refugee crises, and in the postwar pre-state years when the recognition of Israel was paramount.

6. Holocaust Consciousness, Liberal Hope

1. The Anti-Defamation League (ADL) was founded in 1913 as part of B'nai B'rith, but is today a virtually independent agency that by dint of its defense mission has come to overshadow B'nai B'rith, whose mission was cultural and fraternal.

2. Quoted by Staub, *Torn at the Roots*, 16.

3. The names of hundreds of Holocaust centers and organizations is annually published in a directory by the Association of Holocaust Organizations, edited by Dr. William Shulman and published by the Holocaust Museum in Houston, Texas. There are 293 national and international institutes registered, and 16 major Holocaust museums. See "Are There Too Many Holocaust Museums?" *Jewish Philanthropy*, March 23, 1911. There are, in addition, numerous individually sponsored efforts such as Steven Spielberg's massive videotaping of survivor testimony and the annual "March of the Living" activity. The best work on how the memorialization develops on the grassroots level is Hasia Diner, *We Remember with Reverence and Love: American Jews and the Myth of Silence after the Holocaust, 1945–1962* (New York: New York University Press, 2009). An attempt to develop a philosophical base for the memorialization processes can be found in James E. Young, *The Texture of Memory: Holocaust Memorials and Meaning* (New Haven: Yale University Press, 1993).

4. The charge of betrayal remained part of the political rhetoric of the Jewish New Left long after the publication of Isaiah Trunk's research revealed that such an accusation was clearly an oversimplification of the complex role played by a powerless Jewish leadership during the war. Isaiah Trunk, *Judenrat: The Jewish Councils in Eastern Europe under Nazi Occupation* (New York: Macmillan, 1972).

5. The shift to the Right has been more pronounced in Israel, where the Labor Party, once the leading party of the Left, now garners only 16 percent of the vote

6. Kirstan Fermaglich, *American Dreams and Nazi Nightmares: Early Holocaust Consciousness and Liberal America, 1957–1965* (Lebanon: Brandeis University Press, 2006). The Holocaust theme is probably one of the most frequently used in fiction and film and drama.

7. See Feingold, *Jewish Power in America*, 25–43.

8. In July 1946, aroused by a rumor of ritual murder of Christian children, about forty-two Jews were murdered in Kielce. The pogrom triggered the flight of thousands of Jews to Czechoslovakia.

9. McCarthy's investigatory staff had Jews on it, Roy M. Cohn and G. David Schine, and some staff like Bob Kennedy, who later became associated with liberal politics. The Communist sphere saw Stalin's Doctor's Plot in 1953, which culminated five years of anti-Semitic restrictions later identified as the "black years" of Soviet Jewry. The indictment of two genuine Jewish spies, Rudolf Abel and Judith Coplan, confused the picture further.

10. See Feingold, *Jewish Power In America*, the first effort I know of to bring some order to this question by confronting the power question directly.

11. See Henry L. Feingold, *The Politics of Rescue: The Roosevelt Administration and the Holocaust, 1938–1945* (New Brunswick: Rutgers University Press, 1970), 45–68.

12. The earliest slashing attack appeared in the film "Who Shall Live and Who Shall Die?" produced and directed by Leonard Jarvik. The Bergson line is closely followed and elaborated in David Wyman, *The Abandonment of the Jews: America and the Holocaust, 1941–1945* (New York: Pantheon Books, 1984), which has become the most popular study of this subject.

13. While the American Israel Political Action Committee (AIPAC) continues to be the larger and better-financed lobbying group largely in tune with the Likud government of Israel, there are several smaller lobbying groups, including J Street, which are in dissent.

14. The full and as yet untold story of the resettlement alternative is told in "Could Mass Resettlement Have Saved European Jewry?" in Feingold, *Bearing Witness*, 94–140. Resettlement was also used by Berlin as a code word for the Final Solution.

15. Most researchers agree that more might have been done, but differ on the specifics. On the side of a broad view of what might have been done is Wyman, *Abandonment of the Jews*. Henry L. Feingold brings the power factor to bear and comes to a less accusative conclusion of the Roosevelt administration in "Saving the Jews of Europe: The Failure of the Jew Deal," in *Jewish Power in America*, 25–43.

16. The Jewish witness role is told in Feingold, *Bearing Witness*.

17. Other "if onlies" include: if only the invasion of Europe had occurred a year earlier; if only there had been an attempt to assassinate Hitler; a stronger effort to get London to revoke the White Paper; a more generous policy to admit refugees in 1938; a more strenuous effort to influence American public opinion in 1943; a greater threat of retribution in Allied propaganda, including announcing that the bombing of German cities was retributory. There exists a study of the bombing alternative in which most researchers challenge David Wyman's assumption of its possibility and efficacy. See Michael J. Neufeld and Michael Birenbaum, eds. *The Bombing of Auschwitz: Should the Allies Have Attempted It?* (New York: St. Martin's Press, 2000).

18. See Neufeld and Birenbaum, *Bombing of Auschwitz*, especially my article "Bombing Auschwitz and the Politics of the Jewish Question during World War II," 193–203.

19. I mean by that not an assigned emissary to advocate a Jewish interest but someone who willy-nilly was called on to represent a Jewish interest and did so. Jews of equivalent rank like Henry Kissinger or Walter Rathenau in Germany never crossed that line, nor were they close to the most powerful leader in the world. Morgenthau was at first reluctant to broach Roosevelt on a strictly Jewish issue and had to be convinced by his three non-Jewish assistants that it had to be done. During the refugee crisis Morgenthau was reluctant to become involved. When Roosevelt asked him for a list of wealthy Jews who might fund a resettlement enterprise outside of Europe, Morgenthau reminded the president that to raise money on the scale required you first had to have a plan. See Peter Lowenberg, "Walter Rathenau and Henry Kissinger: The Jews as Modern Statesman in Two Political Cultures," *Leo Baeck Memorial Lecture, No. 24* (New York: Leo Baeck Institute), 1980.

20. The other two "close" advisers were Harry Hopkins, who actually slept in the White House, and Louis Howe, the king maker behind Roosevelt's ascendancy. Technically Judah P. Benjamin, who became secretary of the treasury for the Confederacy during the Civil War, was no longer part of the American government. Aside from Morgenthau, it was probably Sam Rosenman, his speechwriter, who originally was involved with Al Smith,

who was the Jewish adviser most frequently consulted by Roosevelt on domestic political matters. Both Morgenthau and Rosenman had reservations about presenting purely Jewish concerns in the Oval Office. But Morgenthau ultimately did cross the red line.

21. The Chanukiot is a candelabra used by Jews to observe the "festival of Lights" (Chanukah), which customarily falls during the Christmas season. It rates as the most popular of Jewish religious holidays perhaps because like Christmas it also features a gift-giving aspect.

22. The mention of security refers to Attu and Kiska, two islands in the Aleutians off Alaska occupied by Japanese forces in June 1942. The occupation posed a security threat because they lay astride the Pacific Great Circle route needed to supply the Pacific theater. It required more than a year to remove the Japanese troops.

23. Trujillo, the dictator of Dominica, was alone in making an offer of haven for Jewish refugees at the Evian Conference in 1938. After initial hesitation the State Department agreed and helped found The Dominican Resettlement Association (DORSA). For refugee advocates, the Trujillo offer contained a bitter irony. Jews were desired by a race-minded dictator to "lighten" Dominica even while a similar racialist dictator in Berlin was intent on extruding Jewish refugees for reasons of racial blood. See Allen Wells, *Tropical Zion: General Trujillo, FDR, and the Jews of Sosua* (Durham: Duke University Press, 2009).

24. See, for example, Peter Novick, *The Holocaust In American Life* (New York: Houghton Mifflin, 1999). The idea that the Holocaust was being exploited by Zionists and others to gain political leverage was not limited to Jewish researchers. It was common currency in the Arab political class.

25. The total number of World War II casualties, estimated at anywhere from 25 to 32 million, dwarfs the 6 million figure usually approximated for the Holocaust. Most do not realize that total size, the European Jewry was approximately 13 million, which meant that one out of two European Jews did not survive the Holocaust, and in eastern Europe, where the slaughter was greater, only one in four Jews survived.

26. I use the term "adoration" to emphasize the fact that for many Jewish voters the relation to Roosevelt had almost a religious connotation.

27. The agency that grew out of the Evian Conference was The Intergovernmental Committee on Political Refugees (IGC), Roosevelt's quasi-governmental committee to search out resettlement havens was the Presidential Advisory Committee on Political Refugees (PACPR), and the special rescue committee established in January 1944 was the War Refugee Board (WRB).

28. Peter Novick attributes American Jewry's postwar turn to the Right to the American Jewish obsession with the Holocaust that undermined the strong universalistic integrationist element in its political culture. But that is not reflected in their voting patterns, which I have noted continued largely along New Deal liberal lines. See Novick, *Holocaust in American Life*, 10.

29. Dowty, "Jewish Political Culture," 311.

30. That does not mean that all activities relating to the Holocaust are trivial. Some of the museums are in fact world class, as is some fiction. But some popular material is problematic. Gerald Green's celebrated docudrama "Holocaust" applied a well-known Hollywood romantic "kitsch" formula to the story. The result was that the film gained a wide audience and is credited with awakening an interest in the event in Germany and much of Europe.

31. Novick, *Holocaust in American Life.*

32. See Diner, *We Remember with Reverence and Love.* The Eichmann trial did in fact do much to bring the Holocaust to the fore and stands in sharp conflict to those who argue that the depth of the attention paid to it in the United States is mostly a public-relations phenomenon.

33. Since the publication of Daniel J. Goldhagen, *Hitler's Willing Executioners: Ordinary Germans and the Holocaust* (New York: Vantage Books, 1997), the extent of the collusion of the German people has become a controversial issue in Holocaust historiography.

34. The earliest indictment of Roosevelt came from Arthur Morse, *While Six Million Died* (New York: Random House, 1968). It was followed by the far less accusatory Feingold, *Politics of Rescue.* There is general agreement that more could have been done, especially during the refugee phase (1938–1941). The first group is today led by David Wyman and includes Rafael Medoff, who has established an institute bearing Wyman's name. Historians who question the Wyman reading begin with Lucy Dawidowicz and include Henry L. Feingold and Frank Brecher. See Frank Brecher, "David Wyman and the Historiography of America's Response to the Holocaust: Counter Considerations," *Holocaust and Genocide Studies* 5 (1990): 423–46.

35. Henry Kissinger, national security adviser and secretary of state in the Nixon and Ford administrations; Madeline Albright, secretary of state in the Clinton administration; Zbigniew Brzezinski, national security adviser in the Carter administration; Michael Blumenthal, secretary of the treasury in the Carter administration, 1977–1979.

36. Germany has gone further and has embodied the consciousness in laws that monetarily compensate survivors where possible and make it illegal to deny the Holocaust. But Germany is not classified as a witness. It is a nation trying to heal a national identity scarred by its wartime role as perpetrator.

37. See Feingold, "'It Can Happen Here,'" 187–206.

38. Herbert Hoover had heightened the LPC requirements in 1930 in an effort to decrease immigration during the Depression. In 1930 a delegation headed by Wilbur J. Carr visited all the consulates in Europe with a strong recommendation that only 10 percent of the relevant quotas be filled.

39. A condition of having citizenship in no country, a situation similar to undocumented aliens in the United States.

40. The problem of stranded Jewish children was agonizing for rescue advocates, who gave it special attention. The first was the Zionist-sponsored Youth Aliyah, which brought German Jewish children to Palestine, and the second was the now-renowned *Kindertransport*, which brought ten thousand Jewish children to Britain.

41. For the full story, see Sharon R. Lowenstein, *Token Refuge: The Story of the Jewish Refugee Center at Oswego* (Bloomington: Indiana University Press, 1986).

42. For an elaboration of the ascendancy of Zionism during the late thirties, see Ofer Shiff, "Survival through Integration: American Jewish Response to Antisemitism and Zionism during the Holocaust," PhD diss., Brandeis University, 1982.

43. Cannibalism in the sense that the residuum of the slaughter, gold teeth, hair, shoes and clothing, were collected, sorted, and reabsorbed into Germany's wartime economy.

44. There are many who argue that "positive eugenics," and the sterilization programs in several southern states based on it, deserve a "made in America" label.

Epilogue

1. The deep spoonlike cooking instrument used to stir the contents of the cooking pot. Also describes a hyperactive personality.

2. The current anti-Semitism in the Arab world may be a resonance of the special wartime effort of Nazi propaganda to spread its anti-Semitic line to that world. See Jeffrey Her, *The Jewish Enemy: Nazi Propaganda during World War II and the Holocaust* (Cambridge: Harvard University Press, 2006).

3. The difference in degree of engagement is especially apparent in the foreign-policy area, especially as it concerns Israel. Generally political activism is a characteristic of Jewish political culture that is best seen as highly correlated with higher levels of formal education.

4. Taking such a position was not without its perils, as illustrated by Charles Lindbergh's Des Moines speech in September 1941, in which he warned Jews and Anglophiles of the dangers of trying to bring the nation into a war against Germany. The risk was greater for the Destroyer Bases Deal, done by executive order in September 1940, than for Lend-Lease, which came in February 1941 by an act of Congress. By that time isolationism was on the decline.

5. See Jordan M. Smith, "The Media Consensus on Israel Is Collapsing," *The Nation*, January 24, 2012.

6. The failure to get administration intercession during the Holocaust is a classic example. Such intercessions were requested for the Damascus blood libel case, the Mortara kidnapping, the Russian and Romanian persecutions at the turn of the century, the Wilson administration effort to support the Balfour Declaration, and the appeal to Roosevelt during the Holocaust. The most recent example is the request for gaining the right of emigration for Soviet Jewry. The support of Israel falls into a different category since it

does not include armed intervention. See Cyrus Adler and Aaron Margolies, *With Firmness in the Right: American Diplomatic Action Affecting Jews, 1840—1945* (New York: Arno Press, 1977).

7. The immigrant generation supposedly voted for Theodore Roosevelt because his name appeared on their citizenship papers. The reform thrust was then also centered in the Republican-Progressive alliance. Finding the exact year when the immigrant Jewish voter switched allegiance to the Democrats is problematic because in the election of 1912 the Republican ticket was split between Taft and Roosevelt and in the election of 1920 a sizable minority of the Jewish vote went to the third-party Socialist candidate Eugene V. Debs (38 percent).

8. A special reason for Eisenhower's popularity with the Jewish voter is that the defeat of Nazi Germany is ascribed to his leadership. Usually there is some correlation between the national and Jewish preference. The Jewish vote resonates the general popularity of the candidate. But in the election of 1992 George Bush Sr. received only 11 percent of the Jewish vote, about 25 percent lower than average, compared with Clinton's 80 percent. The low percentage was supposedly based on a general impression of being "cool" on Israel. But George W. Bush, who was strongly supportive of Israel, received only 19 percent of the Jewish vote in 2000, and raised it by five points in the election of 2004.

9. Norman Podhoretz, *Why Are Jews Liberal?* (New York: Vintage Press, 2010).

10. After a four-day rampage and the murder of a young Hasidic scholar in 1991, the impact was sustained. In the subsequent two mayoral races by David Dinkins (Dem./Lib.) in New York City in 1990 and 1994, Rudolph Giuliani, the "law and order" Republican candidate, won 75 percent of the Jewish vote when he ran against a classic liberal Jewish candidate, Ruth Messenger, in 1994. Jewish voters were convinced that Dinkins response to the riot and murder was too weak. A similar turn to "law and order" candidates among Jewish voters occurred in Philadelphia and Los Angeles. Republican candidates who stressed the "law and order" issue, like George Pataki (New York), Jeb Bush (Florida), Christine Todd Whitman (New Jersey), won strong Jewish backing.

11. George Pataki supported the Gay Rights Bill in 2002, as did Rudolph Giuliani. George W. Bush campaigned on the slogan of "compassionate conservatism," and his strong support of Israel posed a dilemma for liberal Jewish voters who gave him considerable support in his second campaign. Similarly the liberal Republican Michael Bloomberg, the Jewish mayor of New York, raised property taxes to shore up an endangered city budget process yet retained a high percentage of the Jewish vote. See Murray Friedman, "The Changing Jewish Political Profile," in *American Jewish History* 91, nos. 2–3 (2003): 423–38.

12. Some question if that normal Jewish response will be in evidence in the years to come. They foresee a turn to conservatism. *The New Jersey Jewish News* cites exit polls of Jewish voters for the 2000 presidential election that indicate that younger Jewish voters are more likely to prefer Republican candidates for office (52 percent) than older Jewish voters (6 to 30 percent). Friedman, "Changing Jewish Political Profile," 435.

13. Election of 1920—Debs (Socialist) 38 percent; 1924—La Follette (Progressive) 22 percent; 1948—Wallace (Progressive) 15 percent; 1976—McCarthy, 2 percent; 1980—Anderson, 14 percent; 1992—Perot, 9 percent; 1996—Perot, 3 percent; 2000—Nader, 1 percent; 2004—Nader, 1 percent.

14. Pirkei Avot (Sayings of the Fathers).

The day is short and the work is great . . .

It is not thy duty to complete the work

but neither art thou free to desist from it.

Select Bibliography

Adler, Cyrus, and Aaron Margolies. *With Firmness in the Right: American Diplomatic Action Affecting Jews, 1840–1945.* Reprint ed. New York: Arno Press, 1977.

Berman, Aaron. *Nazism, the Jews, and American Zionism, 1933–1948.* Detroit: Wayne State University Press, 1990.

Biale, David. *Power and Powerlessness in Jewish History.* New York: Schoken Books, 1986.

Cohen, Robert. *When the Old Left Was Young: Student Radicals and America's First Mass Student Movement, 1919–1921.* New York: Oxford University Press, 1993.

Cohen, Steven, and Charles S. Liebman. *American Jewish Liberalism: Unraveling the Strands.* New York: Oxford University Press, 1997.

Dollinger, Mark. *Quest for Inclusion: Jews and Liberalism in Modern America.* Princeton: Princeton University Press, 2001.

Elazar, Daniel. *Community and Polity: The Organizational Dynamics of American Jewry.* Philadelphia: Jewish Publication Society, 1976.

Feingold, Henry L. *Bearing Witness: How America and Its Jews Responded to the Holocaust.* Syracuse: Syracuse University Press, 1995.

———. "The Changing Liberalism of American Jewry." In Feingold, *Lest Memory Cease: Finding Meaning in the American Jewish Past,* 117–34. Syracuse: Syracuse University Press, 1996.

———. *Jewish Power in America: Myth and Reality.* New Brunswick, NJ: Transaction, 2008.

Fermaglich, Kirstan. *American Dreams and Nazi Nightmares: Early Holocaust Consciousness and Liberal America, 1957–1965.* Lebanon: Brandeis University Press, 2006.

Fuchs, Lawrence. *The Political Behavior of American Jews.* Glencoe, IL: The Free Press, 1956.

Goldberg, J. J. *Jewish Power: Inside the American Jewish Establishment.* New York: Addison-Wesley, 1996.

Hartz, Louis. *The Liberal Tradition in America: An Interpretation of American Political Thought since the Revolution.* New York: Harcourt Brace, 1955.

Isaacs, Stephen D. *Jews and American Politics.* Garden City, NJ: Doubleday, 1974.

Jacobs, Jack. *Bundist Counterculture in Interwar Poland.* Syracuse: Syracuse University Press, 2009.

Kahlenberg, Richard. *Tough Liberal: Albert Shanker and the Battle Over Schools, Unions, Race, and Democracy.* New York: Columbia University Press, 2007.

Kammen, Michael. *Spheres of Liberty: Changing Perceptions of Liberty in American Culture.* Madison: University of Wisconsin Press, 1986.

Kushner, Tony. *The Holocaust and the Liberal Imagination: A Social and Cultural History.* Cambridge: Blackwell, 1994.

Kushner, Tony, and Alisa Solomon, eds. *Wrestling with Zion: Progressive Jewish American Responses to the Israeli-Palestinian Conflict.* New York: Grove Press, 2003.

Levey, Geoffrey B. *Toward a Theory of Disproportionate American Jewish Liberalism.* New York: Oxford University Press, 1995.

Mackenzie, G. Calvin, and Robert Weisbrot. *The Liberal Hour: Washington and the Politics of Change in the 1960s.* New York: Penguin Press, 2008.

Michels, Tony. *A Fire in Their Hearts: Yiddish Socialists in New York.* Cambridge: Harvard University Press, 2005.

Novick, Peter. *The Holocaust in American Life.* New York: Houghton Mifflin, 1999.

Oz, Amos, and Fania Oz. *Jews and Words.* New Haven: Yale University Press, 2012.

Podhoretz, Norman. *Why Are Jews Liberals?* New York: Doubleday, 2009.

Raider, Mark. *The Emergence of American Zionism.* New York: New York University Press, 1998.

Rosenthal, Steven T. *Irreconcilable Differences: The Waning of the Jewish Love Affair with Israel.* Hanover: Brandeis University Press, 2001.

Sorin, Gerald. *The Prophetic Minority: American Jewish Immigrant Radicals, 1880–1920.* Bloomington: Indiana University Press, 1985.

Staub, Michael E. *Torn at the Roots: The Crisis of Jewish Liberalism in Postwar America.* New York: Columbia University Press, 2002.

Wistrich, Robert. *Terms of Survival: The Jewish World since 1945.* New York: Routledge, 1995.

Wyman, David. *The Abandonment of the Jews: America and the Holocaust, 1941–1945.* New York: Pantheon Books, 1984.

Young, James E. *The Texture of Memory: Holocaust Memorials and Meaning.* New Haven: Yale University Press, 1993.

Index of Names, Places, Events, and Laws